Hands-On Illustrator 7

for Macintosh and Windows

Clay Andres

MIS: PRESS

A Division of
Henry Holt and Company
New York

MIS:Press
A Subsidiary of Henry Holt and Company, Inc.
115 West 18th Street
New York, New York 10011
http://www.mispress.com

Copyright © 1997 by MIS:Press

Printed in the United States of America

All rights reserved. No part of this book may be reproduced or transmitted in any form or by any means, electronic or mechanical, including photocopying, recording, or by any information storage and retrieval system, without prior written permission from the Publisher. Contact the Publisher for information on foreign rights.

Limits of Liability and Disclaimer of Warranty

The Author and Publisher of this book have used their best efforts in preparing the book and the programs contained in it. These efforts include the development, research, and testing of the theories and programs to determine their effectiveness.

The Author and Publisher make no warranty of any kind, expressed or implied, with regard to these programs or the documentation contained in this book. The Author and Publisher shall not be liable in any event for incidental or consequential damages in connection with, or arising out of, the furnishing, performance, or use of these programs.

All products, names and services are trademarks or registered trademarks of their respective companies.

First Edition—1997

Library of Congress Cataloging-in-Publication Data

Andres, Clay
   Hands-on illustrator 7 for Macintosh and Windows / by Clay Andres
     p.   cm.
   ISBN 1-55828-571-7
     1. Computer Graphics. 2. Adobe Illustrator (Computer file)
   3. Macintosh (Computer)--Programming. I. Title.
   T385.A5125   1997
   006.6'869--dc21   97-28069
                                                                                                                    CIP

MIS:Press and M&T Books are available at special discounts for bulk purchases for sales promotions, premiums, and fundraising. Special editions or book excerpts can also be created to specification.

For details contact: Special Sales Director
                            MIS:Press and M&T Books
                            Subsidiaries of Henry Holt and Company, Inc.
                            115 West 18th Street
                            New York, New York 10011

10 9 8 7 6 5 4 3 2 1

                            Associate Publisher: *Paul Farrell*

Managing Editor: *Shari Chappell*   **Production Editor:** *Gay Nichols*
Editor: *Rebekah Young*   **Technical Editor:** *Antoinette LaFarge*
Copy Edit Manager: *Karen Tongish*   **Copy Editor:** *Sara Black*

Acknowledgments

A book doesn't just happen; it doesn't spring forth full-blown from the head of its author. There are the usual corporate suspects, MIS:Press and Adobe Systems, Inc., as well as the companies who supplied demo software for the CD. But it is the people who have helped push this book along that I would like to thank. My editor, Rebekah Young, foremost, along with technical editor Antoinette LaFarge were always helpful in the extreme, good-natured, and patient. Patrick Ames of Adobe helped resolve my questions when none of the usual channels yielded answers. Congratulations to Brian Gill, of the Studio B agency, who managed to finish the book contract before leaving town to get married.

I'd also like to acknowledge the artists who sent me illustrations to use as examples in the book, Betsy Arvelo, Rob Day, Lance Hidy, Gary Newman, Nancy Stahl, Charles Shields, and Michael Wollner. I wish I could have included more of your works.

And it would all be totally unthinkable without Katharine, the be-all and end-all.

Thank you, all.

To Kenny Grief, advisor, neighbor, and loyal friend, in good health.

Contents in Brief

Section 1: First Looking into Adobe's Illustrator xix
Chapter 1—What It Means To Be a PostScript Drawing Program 1
Chapter 2—New Interface, New Features 15

Section II: Looking Inside the Toolbox 31
Chapter 3—Object Creation: Drawing and Text Tools 35
Chapter 4—Selection and Manipulation 65
Chapter 5—Transformation Tools........................... 81
Chapter 6—Attributes: Applying Strokes and Fills 99
Chapter 7—View Tools................................... 119
Chapter 8—Blending, Tracing, and Graphing 137

Section III: Afloat with Palettes 179
Chapter 9—Shape and Position 185
Chapter 10—Appearance 199
Chapter 11—Layers...................................... 235

Section IV: Menu-Based Tools 255
Chapter 12—Edit and Object Commands 257
Chapter 13—Type Commands and Palettes 293
Chapter 14—Filter Menu and Submenus 339
Chapter 15—View and Window Menus 373

Section V: Illustrator Environment 385
Chapter 16—Files and File Commands..................... 387
Chapter 17—Printing 399
Chapter 18—The Web and Multimedia 409
Chapter 19—Performance, Preferences, and Help 429

Contents

Section 1: First Looking into Adobe's Illustrator xix

Chapter 1—What It Means To Be a PostScript Drawing Program 1
    Vector vs. Bitmap Graphics 3
    Illustrator Vocabulary 4
    Getting Help 5
        To Use Context-Sensitive Help Menus 6
        To View Pop-Up Help 6
Lesson: Basic Drawing Vocabulary at Work 8

Chapter 2—New Interface, New Features 15
    Document Window 16
    Floating Windows 17
    Toolbox Window 18
    Menus 19
Lesson: Kicking Illustrator's Tires 21

Section II: Looking Inside the Toolbox 31

    Section Introduction: The Toolbox in General 32
    To Reposition the Toolbox 32
    To Show/Hide the Toolbox 32
    To Select Tools in the Toolbox 33
    To Select a Hidden Tool 33
    To Select Tool Options 34

Contents

Chapter 3—Object Creation: Drawing and Text Tools 35
Regular Shapes—Rectangles and Ellipses 36
- To Create a Rectangle or Ellipse 36
- To Create a Centered Rectangle or Ellipse 37
- To Specify the Dimensions of a Rectangle or Ellipse 38
- To Create Rounded Rectangles 38
- To Create Squares and Circles 38

Specialty Shapes—Polygons, Stars, and Spirals 39
- To Draw Specialty Shapes by Dragging 39
- To Specify Specialty Shape Options 39

Making Paths—Pen, Pencil and Paintbrush 41
- To Make Straight Path Segments 41
- To End a Path 42
- The Vocabulary of Curves 43
- To Make Smooth Curved Path Segments 43
- To Make Angled Curved Path Segments 44
- Mixing Straight and Curved Path Segments 45
- To Draw Freehand Paths—Pencil Tool 45
- To Draw Closed Paths with a Single Stroke— Paintbrush Tool   46
- To Set Paintbrush Options 47

Editing Paths—Scissors, Knife, and Hidden Pen Tools 48
- To Add or Delete Anchor Points 48
- To Convert Anchor Points Between Smooth and Corner 49
- About the Pen Cursors 50
- To Make One Path Two 51
- To Divide Paths with the Knife 51

Text—The Naked Type Tool 51
- To Enter Type 52
- To Edit Type 53
- Confusion Over Type Selection 54

Lesson: Alphabet Paths 55
- Alphabet Lesson: Part 1 55
- Alphabet Lesson, Part 2 58

Chapter 4—Selection and Manipulation 65
Selection—General, Direct, and Group 66
- To Make a Selection Using the Selection Tool 67
- To Select Single Segments or Anchor Points. 68
- To Select Objects within a Group 68

Contents

- Manipulation—Move, Copy, Delete 69
  - To Move a Path, Object, or Group Using Selection Tools 69
  - To Copy a Path, Object, or Group Using Selection Tools 70
  - To Delete a Path, Object, or Group Using Selection Tools ... 71
  - Special Text Selection Considerations 71
- Lesson: Penguin Selection 73

Chapter 5—Transformation Tools 81
- Not-So-Radical Transformation 82
  - Basic Transformations—Rotate, Scale, Reflect, and Shear 82
  - To Transform Objects Interactively 83
  - To Specify Exact Transformations 84
  - Transformations of a Different Color—Twirl and Reshape ... 87
  - To Twirl a Selection Interactively 87
  - To Specify a Twirl 88
  - To Reshape a Selection 88
- Lesson: I Could Have Transformed All Night 90

Chapter 6—Attributes: Applying Strokes and Fills 99
- Paint Attributes 100
- Stroke and Fill from the Toolbox 100
  - To Activate the Stroke or Fill Button to Edit Color Attributes 101
  - To Return to the Default Stroke and Fill Settings 101
  - To Swap Stroke and Fill Colors 101
  - To Set Fill or Stroke to None 102
  - To Use the Color and Gradient Buttons 102
- Gradient Extents 103
  - To Apply a Gradient Fill to an Object Using the Gradient Tool 103
- Copying Attributes: Eyedropper and Paintbucket Tools 104
  - To Sample with the Eyedropper Tool 105
  - To Paste Attributes onto an Object 105
  - To Sample or Apply Attributes Selectively 106
  - To Toggle Between the Eyedropper and Paintbucket tools .. 106
- Measure Tool 107
  - To Measure Between Two Points 107
- Lesson: Penguin Patchwork 108

Chapter 7—View Tools 119
- What Does a View Look Like? 120
- Panning and Zooming: Hand and Zoom Tools 120

Contents

    To Pan with the Hand Tool 121
    To Magnify with the Zoom Tool—Zooming In 122
    To Demagnify with the Zoom Tool—Zooming Out 123
    To Change Magnification with the Zoom Pop-up Menu 124
  Views without Windows: Screen Modes 125
    To Change Screen Mode 125
  The View from the Printer: Page Tool 127
    To Move Page Guides Using the Page Tool 128
Lesson: Mapping Views 129
Chapter 8—Blending, Tracing, and Graphing 137
  Shaping and Shading with Blends—Blend Tool 138
    To Blend Two Shapes 139
  Tracing the Easy Way—Auto Trace Tool 140
    To Convert Bitmap Shapes into Illustrator Paths 141
  Graphs Are Graphic, Too—Graph Tool 142
    About Illustrator's Graphs 142
    To Create a Graph Object 143
    To Enter Graph Data 144
    To Copy and Paste Data 145
    To Import Data 146
    To Edit a Worksheet Cell 147
    To Edit a Range of Cells 147
    To Enter Category and Value Labels 148
    To Transpose Rows and Columns in a Worksheet 149
    To Switch X and Y values for Scatter Graphs 150
    To Change Column Width in the Worksheet 150
    To Change Worksheet Cell Properties 151
    To Revert Data Values 151
    The Graph Type Dialog 151
    To Set Graph Options 152
    To Set Value Axis Options 155
    To Set Category Axis Options 156
    About Custom Graph Design 156
    To Create a Custom Graph Design 157
    To Manage Custom Graph Designs 158
    To Apply a Custom Graph Design 159
Lesson: Pain and Peppers 162
  Lesson 8, Part 1: The Pepper 162
  Lesson 8, Part 2: The Graph 169
  Lesson 8, Part 3: Integrating the Graph Design 173

Section III: Afloat with Palettes 179
Whither, Why, and Wherefore Palettes? 180
The Anatomy of Palettes 180
To Hide and Show Palettes 181
To Move Palette Windows 181
To Resize Palette Windows 182
To Regroup or Dock Palettes 182
To Use Palette Menus 183

Chapter 9—Shape and Position 185
Static Feedback—Info Palette 186
Interactive Adjustment—Transform Palette 187
To Edit Selections Using the Transform Palette 188
One-Click Adjustments—Align Palette 189
To Align or Distribute Objects 190
Lesson: A Lattice Transformed 191

Chapter 10—Appearance 199
Color Reproduction and Color Models 200
CMYK and RGB Become Equals—Color Palette 202
To Edit Fill or Stroke Color 203
To Change Color Models 204
Patchwork Color—Swatches Palette 205
To Use Swatches 206
To Add a Color Gradient or Pattern to the Swatches Palette . . 207
To Delete a Swatch from the Swatches Palette 208
To Replace a Swatch in the Swatches Palette 209
To Use the Swatches Palette Pop-Up Menu 209
Blended Color—Gradient Palette 210
To Define a Gradient 211
To Edit a Gradient 212
To Shrink the Gradient Palette 213
Perimeter Attributes—Stroke Palette 213
To Set Stroke Weight 214
To Set Cap and Join Attributes 214
To Create Dashed Lines 216
Where Do Custom Color Palettes Come From? 216
To Use Swatch Libraries 216
Attributes Palette 218

Contents

Lesson:Quilting and Coloring 221
Chapter 11—Layers 235
    About Layers and the Layers Palette 236
    Creating and Adjusting Layers 237
        To Create a New Layer 238
        To Duplicate Layers 240
        To Rearrange Layers 240
        To Delete Layers 241
    Objects and Layers 241
        To Move Objects Among Layers—Drag Method 242
        To Move Objects Among Layers— Cut/Copy and Paste Method
        242
        To Select All Objects in a Layer or Layers 243
        To Paste Multilayer Selections 243
    Using Layers While Working 244
        To Hide/Show Layers 244
        To Toggle Layers to Artwork View 245
        To Lock/Unlock Layers 246
        To Merge Layers 246
Dining with Layers 247

Section IV: Menu-Based Tools 255

    Menus and the Duplication of Functions 256
Chapter 12—Edit and Object Commands 257
    Edit Commands 258
        Undo and Redo Commands 258
        Cut, Copy, Paste, and Clear Commands 258
        To Define a New Pattern 259
        Selection Commands 260
        Macintosh Select Commands 261
    Object Menu in Brief 261
    Transform and Arrange Submenus 262
        To Transform Objects Separately in a Group 263
        Arrange Submenu Commands 264
    Group, Lock, and Hide Commands 265
        To Group and Ungroup Objects 265
        To Lock or Hide Objects 266
        To Unlock or Show All Objects 266

    To Convert Objects to Bitmap Images 267
  Path and Pathfinder Submenus 268
    To Join Two End points 269
    To Average Two Anchor Points 270
    To Outline a Path 270
    To Offset a Path 271
    To Clean Up a Drawing 272
    To Slice One Object with Another 272
    To Add Anchor Points Along the Entire Length of a Path . . 273
    To Use the Pathfinder Commands 273
  Mask, Compound Path, Cropmark, and Graph Commands . . . 276
    Masks in General 277
    To Turn Objects into Masks 277
    To Turn Off Masks 278
    To Add Objects to a Mask Group 279
    Compound Paths in General 279
    To Create a Compound Path 280
    To Release Compound Paths 280
    To Adjust Transparency in Compound Paths 280
    Cropmarks in General 281
    To Set Cropmarks 281
    To Release Cropmarks 282
    The Graphs Command in General 282
Lesson: Mixing Business and Pleasure 283

Chapter 13—Type Commands and Palettes 293
  Type Menu and Palettes in General 294
  Some Type Vocabulary 296
  Simple Character Formatting Commands 296
    To Set Font and Size Using Menu Commands 297
  Total Character Control—Character Palette 298
    Setting Fonts from the Character Palette 299
    Setting Character Options 299
  Indents, Spacing, and Hyphenation— Paragraph Palette 304
    To Use the Paragraph Palette 305
    To Set Paragraph Alignment 305
    To Set Paragraph Indents and Spacing 306
    To Set Word and Line Spacing 307
    To Set Paragraph Options 308

Contents

To Use Auto Hyphenation 308
Multiple Masters on the Fly—MM Design Palette 309
To Use the MM Design Palette 310
Tabs On Call—Tab Ruler 311
To Set Tabs 311
To Modify Tab Settings 312
To Move or Re-align the Tab Ruler 313
What to Make of a Text Block—Link, Wrap, and Fit 313
To Enter Text into a Block 313
To Link/Unlink Text Blocks and Reflow Text 314
To Flow Text Around Objects 315
To Fit Headlines 316
When Type Is Not Type—Create Outlines 317
To Convert Type to Outlines 318
To Turn Rectangles into Rows and Columns 318
Word Processing Commands 319
To Find/Change Text 320
To Find/Change Fonts 321
To Check Spelling 322
To Change Text Case 324
To Use "Smart Punctuation" 324
A Few Words About CJK Text 325
To Change the Orientation of Type 326
Lesson: Moby Typography 327

Chapter 14—Filter Menu and Submenus 339
Filters in General 340
Color Submenu Commands 341
To Adjust Colors 342
To Blend Filled Objects 343
To Convert Color Modes 343
To Invert Colors 344
To Add or Remove Black Overprint 344
To Adjust Color Saturation 345
Create Submenu Commands 345
To Fill and Stroke Masks 346
To Turn Bitmaps into Mosaics 346
To Create Trim Marks 348
Distort Filters Submenu Commands 348

Contents

- To Create Trim Marks 348
- Distort Filters Submenu Commands 348
  - To Distort Objects Freely 349
  - To Punk or Bloat Objects 350
  - To Roughen Objects 351
  - To Scribble and Tweak Objects 352
  - To Twirl Objects 353
  - To Create Zig Zags 354
- Ink Pen Submenu Commands 354
  - To Apply Ink Pen Effects 355
  - To Create a New Hatch Pattern 357
  - To Modify Hatch Patterns 358
- Stylize Submenu Commands 358
  - To Add Arrowheads to Paths 359
  - To Create Calligraphic Strokes 360
  - To Add Drop Shadows 361
  - To Apply Path Patterns 361
  - To Round the Corners of Objects 363
- Lesson: A Few Good Filters 365

Chapter 15—View and Window Menus 373
- Views and Windows in General 374
- Viewing Mode—Preview and Artwork 374
  - To Change Viewing Modes 375
  - To Preview a Selection Only 375
- Viewing Magnification—Zooming 376
- Edges and Tiles 377
- Rulers and Guides 377
  - To Show Rulers 378
  - To Reset the Ruler Zero Point 378
  - To Create Ruler Guides 378
  - To Create Object Guides 379
  - To Manipulate Guides 379
- Grid Commands 380
- Creating and Maintaining Views 381
  - To Name a View 381
  - To Edit Views 382
- Window Menu Commands 383
  - To Open Multiple Windows for a Single Document 383

Contents

Section V—Illustrator Environment 385
Illustrator in its Broader Context 386

Chapter 16—Files and File Commands . . . . — 387
Simple File Commands 388
    To Open a New Blank Drawing Window 388
    To Open an Existing Illustrator Document 388
    To Close an Open File Window 389
    To Save Illustrator Drawings 390
    To Discard Changes without Saving—Revert 390
    To Place Files into Open Documents 391
Importing Files and Artwork 391
    About Placing Text 392
    About Placing Graphics 392
    About Linked Files 392
Exporting to Other Formats 393
    To Export Drawings in Non-Native Illustrator Formats 393
    A Few Words about EPS Files 394
Interactive Import and Export 394
    The Clipboard 394
    Drag and Drop 395
    To Drag out of Illustrator and Drop Elsewhere 395
    To Drag into Illustrator from other Applications 395
Document/Object Info Window 396
    To View and Save Document/Selection Info 396

Chapter 17—Printing 399
Printing Terminology 400
Print Preparation 401
    To Set up Documents for Printing 402
Print Command 404
Color Separations 406
To Print Color Separations 406
Improving Print Performance 407

Chapter 18—The Web and Multimedia 409
The Screen As an Output Device 410
Working With Screen Resolution 410
Color: Palettes, Swatches, and Modes 411
File Formats: GIF, JPEG, and PNG 412

To Save Files as JPEG	415
About PNG Files	416
URLs and Browsers	416
To Create an Imagemap	417
Lesson: Brief Imagemap Lesson	419

Chapter 19—Performance, Preferences, and Help ... 425

A Few Words About Performance	426
Setting Preferences	427
Preferences in General	431
General Preferences Options	428
Keyboard Increments Preferences Options	430
Units & Undo Preferences Options	431
Guides & Grid Preferences Options	432
Hyphenation Options Preferences	433
To Add or Delete Hyphenation Exceptions	434
Plug-ins & Scratch Disk Preferences	434
To Reassign Illustrator's Plug-ins Folder	435
To Reassign Scratch Disks	435
Color Settings	436
Help System	436

Index ... 439

Section 1

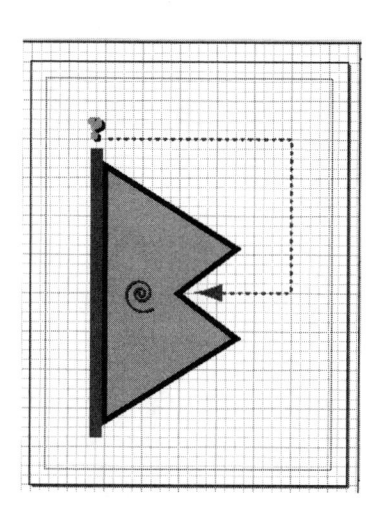

First Looking into Adobe's Illustrator

In this section...

- Chapter 1: What It Means to be a PostScript Drawing Program
- Lesson 1: Basic Drawing Vocabulary at Work
- Chapter 2: New Interface, New Features
- Lesson 2: Kicking Illustrator's Tires

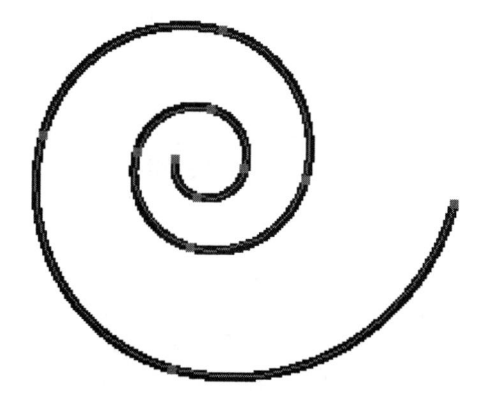

1 What It Means To Be a PostScript Drawing Program

In this chapter...

- Vector vs. bitmap graphics
- Illustrator vocabulary
- Getting help
- Lesson 1: Basic Drawing Vocabulary at Work

When Adobe released the first version of Illustrator in 1987, people didn't talk about killer-apps, yet this one fit the bill. Drawing programs were popular toys, good for simple diagrams, sketches, and organizational charts, but they weren't useful as serious tools for professional artists and designers. What made Adobe Illustrator different then we take for granted now.

Adobe was a small, young company that was growing rapidly because of PostScript's success as a page description language for printers. The desktop publishing revolution was just beginning, and its wide-ranging impact was not yet felt beyond the relatively few owners of Apple's first LaserWriters and those with access to Linotype's PostScript imagesetters. PostScript was something you needed to run Aldus PageMaker, or you could access PostScript directly by writing your own code. (People actually used to do that, and PostScript programming manuals were best sellers.)

It was not easy to put a friendly face on PostScript. PostScript is a collection of algorithms—mathematical formulae, which in this case are used to generate virtually any shape in any space and facilitate the translation of bits on a computer screen to different size bits on paper. Digital drawing tools, such as the pencil, rectangle, and oval tools, were easily adapted to Illustrator, but finding a tool to unlock the power of the Bezier equations used by PostScript to describe complex curves was a challenge.

Illustrator became the preeminent drawing program not because it was based on PostScript but because its Pen tool, the Bezier drawing tool, allowed computer users to draw any line directly by clicking and dragging the mouse. The Pen tool brought new power to computing, and it made it available through an intuitive, easy-to-learn metaphor.

It's curious that even though the Pen tool doesn't resemble an actual ink pen in any way, it has become the universal tool for drawing complex lines or paths. It seems as though every drawing program currently available has some variation of Illustrator's original Pen tool. We've come to take it for granted, just as we now tend to ignore PostScript.

These days you can print Illustrator images on just about any printer, whether it is PostScript-capable or not. But it's worth remembering that Illustrator is a PostScript drawing program and that your results will be more accurate if you use a PostScript printer.

VECTOR VS. BITMAP GRAPHICS

Adobe Illustrator is the premier drawing program for every computer platform. It is the ruler by which all other drawing programs are measured. It has the features and power to be the program of choice for illustration professionals, yet it is accessible to anyone who wants to create a professional-looking illustration for a simple newsletter or basic Web page. But it is not the preeminent tool for creating computer graphics in general. That title belongs to Adobe Photoshop.

Photoshop is a remarkable program, but it is not capable of creating the precise, smoothly rendered lines and images that Illustrator produces. This is because these two programs apply diametrically opposed paradigms to create images—one bitmapped, the other vector-based. To understand what this means, you need to know something about how images are drawn by computers and digital printers.

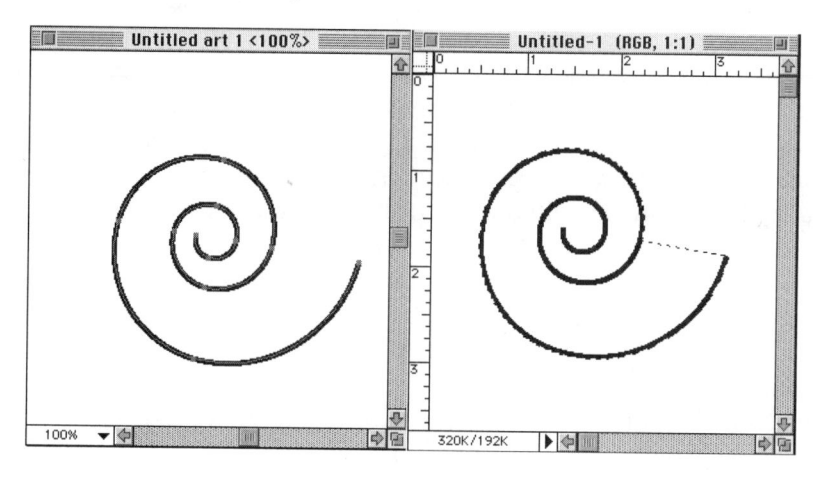

Figure 1.1 On the left is a simple spiral drawn as an object in Illustrator. On the right, the same spiral is painted as pixels and selected in Photoshop. The path anchor points in Illustrator allow you to manipulate the spiral without redrawing. You can do many things with this spiral in Photoshop, but you have to start over if you want to change the shape.

What you see on a computer screen is a matrix of dots called *pixels*. Most commonly, there are 72 dots for every inch of screen real estate. If you have a display that is 640 by 480 pixels, that means your screen is capable of displaying approximately 8.9 by 6.7 inches.

If you use a program such as Photoshop to "paint" on the screen, it changes each pixel individually depending on the tool or command you use. When you print your painting, it will look exactly like the screen image, but only if your printer is a 72-dpi (dots per inch) printer. The image will be more than four times smaller when printed on a typical 300 dpi laser printer, because 72 dots fits into less than a quarter of an inch. If you try to make the image the same physical dimensions, the program compensates by adding three and a fraction dots in between each one you created. This can make for very unsatisfactory results.

Illustrator is less literal-minded and ignores pixels in favor of vectors. A *vector* is a line with length and direction. You can define a vector with two endpoints, or you can add midpoints to create a more complex vector. It doesn't matter how many pixels your screen, printer, or any other device has, because the relationship of the points that make up your vector as well as the relationship of one vector to another remains the same at any pixel density.

In addition to scalability, "drawn" images remain editable. Endpoints, midpoints, and the vectors themselves can be selected, moved, or manipulated in numerous ways without affecting any other element of a drawing. You can build layers of discrete elements and still get at the middle of the pile to edit a vector.

If you've used a painting program like Photoshop, you probably know how difficult it is to work with text. Once type becomes part of an image, it's just bits and can only be edited as such. By contrast, type in a drawing program remains editable; each letter is treated as a distinct form.

The other major difference between bitmapped and vector images is in the resulting file sizes. You can calculate the file size of a bitmapped image by multiplying the height by the width in pixels and then by the number of color channels (one channel for gray, three channels for RGB, and four channels for CMYK color). A large, dense color image can quickly result in a file of several megabytes (millions of bytes).

With vector images, the output size does not affect file size. File size is determined by the number of control points and vectors. The complexity of the image and the resulting file size is determined by the number of drawn elements, including text elements. Even the most complex drawings result in smaller file sizes than equivalent bitmap images.

ILLUSTRATOR VOCABULARY

When the art of drawing became the craft of computer illustration, the vocabulary changed. It became important to identify the discrete elements

What It Means To Be a PostScript Drawing Program 5

of computer drawings. *Line* and *texture* have become *paths, strokes,* and *fills*—not so different except in the added rigor of their application.

Drawing in Illustrator involves the creation of open paths—vectors with two endpoints—or closed paths or objects— vectors with no endpoints. (Hybrid, single-endpoint objects are also possible.) The path itself has only a mathematical representation; you must define stroke and/or fill characteristics if you want something that will display on the screen and be printable.

Here is the briefest possible glossary of the basic vocabulary used by most drawing programs:

>**Anchor point**—The point at which a vector begins, ends, or changes direction is called an anchor or control point.
>**Path**—The vector or line between two or more anchor points is a path. All paths have a beginning anchor point and ending anchor, thus making them vectors.
>**Stroke**—The characteristic of a path is its stroke. A stroke has width and color. It can also be dashed.
>**Fill**—The space surrounded by a path can have a designated fill color or pattern. Filling a closed path or object is fairly obvious, while the fill for an open path can be less immediately apparent.

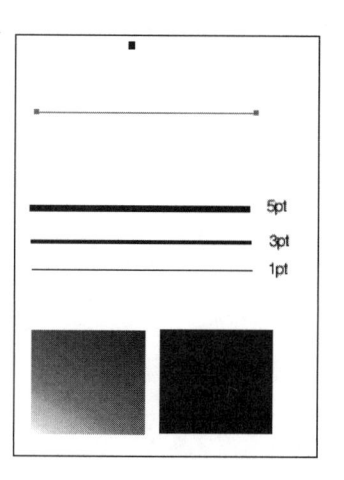

Figure 1.2 *A diagram illustrating some of the vocabulary unique to drawing programs. From the top down: an anchor point; a simple path between two anchor points; three paths stroked with three different thicknesses; a square object with a gradient fill on the left and a simple black fill on the right.*

GETTING HELP

In addition to its various manuals and this excellent book, Illustrator 7 provides some nearly instantaneous visual feedback via context-sensitive menus and pop-up help to guide you as you work. Complete on-line documentation is available either by using the Balloon Help menu (MacOS) or the Help menu (Windows).

To Use Context-Sensitive Help Menus

1. Move the cursor inside a drawing window or any of the palette windows.
2. Either hold down the right mouse button (Windows) or press **Control** and hold down the mouse button (MacOS). A menu will pop up at the point you click.
3. Use the mouse to choose one of the commands from the context-sensitive menu.

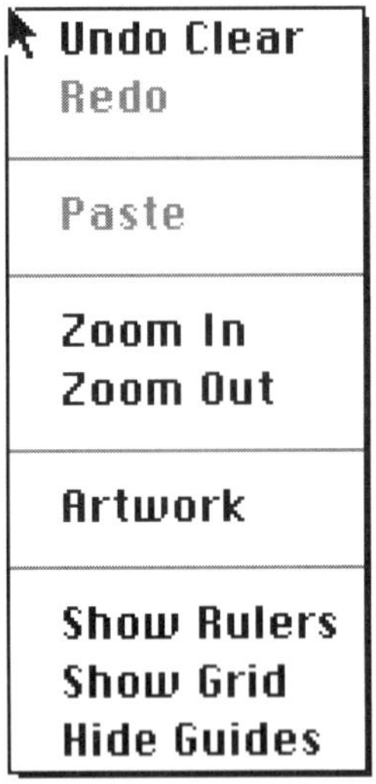

Figure 1.3 *The drawing window contains this context-sensitive menu. Press* **control***-click (MacOS) or the right mouse button (Windows) to access it.*

To View Pop-Up Help

1. Move the cursor over any tool in the Toolbox or any palette option.
2. After two seconds, a label will pop up indicating the name and keyboard shortcut for the tool. The label disappears after another 5 seconds.

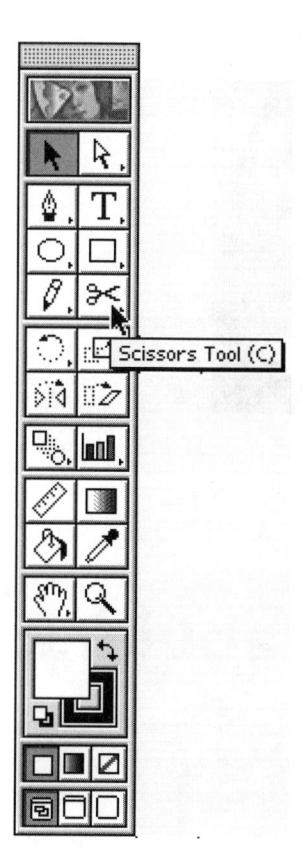

What It Means To Be a PostScript Drawing Program 7

Figure 1.4 When you let your cursor linger for two seconds over a tool or option, a label pops up to identify it.

Basic Drawing Vocabulary at Work

If you've never used Illustrator, it's best to start with the basics, and we'll cover some of them here. We haven't discussed Illustrator's tools and commands yet, so follow these very explicit instructions just to get a feel for what it's like to use a drawing program. We won't discuss operating system fundamentals of either the MacOS or Windows. You should already know how to launch applications and use your file system to open and save files.

1. Launch Illustrator 7. This opens a blank document window called **Untitled art 1**. Your drawing will be within this window. You can do all the usual things to this window, such as resize, zoom, or scroll. You can also have multiple active windows. The floating Toolbar should be in the upper-left corner of your screen.

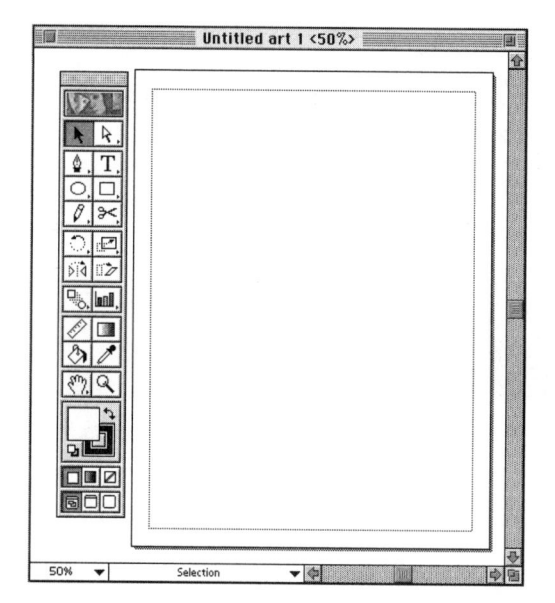

What It Means To Be a PostScript Drawing Program 9

Figure 1.5 When you first open Illustrator 7, the Toolbar should be in the upper-left corner of your display, as it is here.

2. Move the cursor over the Pen tool in the Toolbar. It's the one that looks like the nib of a fountain pen, and if you let the cursor linger over this tool for more than two seconds, a pop-up help label will tell you that this is indeed the Pen tool.

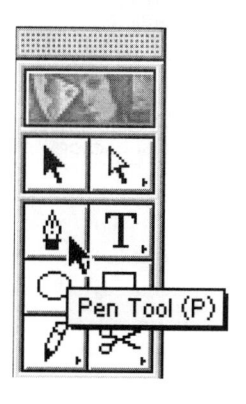

Figure 1.6 Leaving the cursor over an icon in the Toolbar for two seconds pops up a help label which, in this case, is the Pen tool. The label goes away after another five seconds.

3. Click the mouse button to select the Pen tool. The tool's square turns gray to indicate that it is the currently selected drawing tool.

10   CHAPTER 1

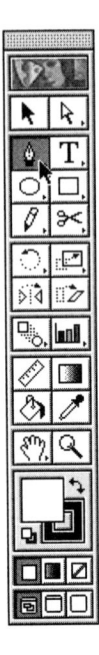

Figure 1.7 Clicking on a tool button makes that tool active, as indicated by the gray highlight. The tool remains active until another is selected.

4. Move the cursor into the Untitled window. The cursor is now pen-shaped to indicate that you are using the Pen tool. Click once with the mouse. You have just positioned your first anchor point.

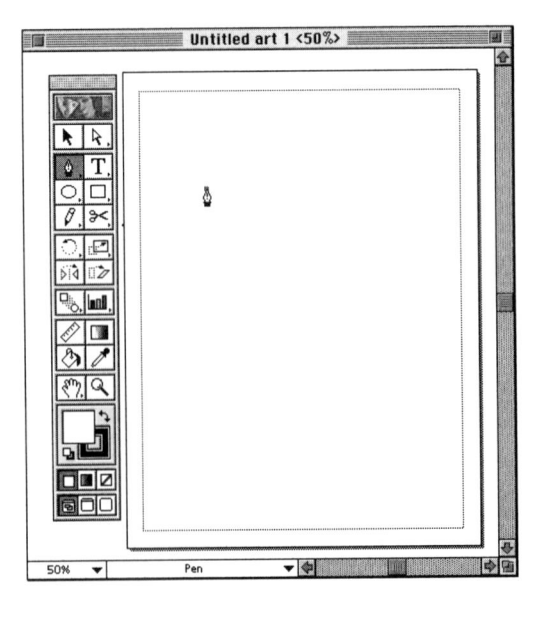

Figure 1.8 Clicking once with the Pen tool establishes a first anchor point.

What It Means To Be a PostScript Drawing Program 11

5. Move the cursor somewhere else in the Untitled window. Click the mouse again. You have now positioned your second anchor point. Illustrator connects these two anchor points with a path that has the characteristics of the default stroke—a black line with a thickness of one point.

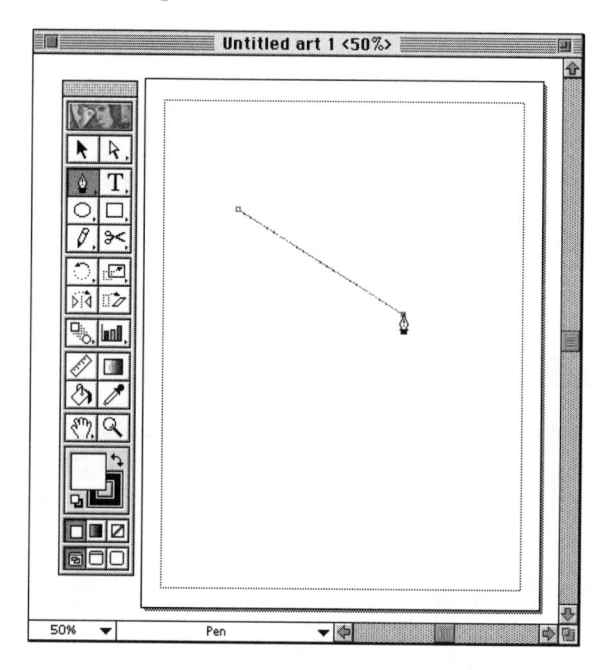

Figure 1.9 Because any two points describe a line, clicking a second time with the Pen tool defines a line in Illustrator.

NOTE Illustrator highlights the path and anchor points in blue, so it may not be immediately evident that you've created a black line. The highlight indicates that the line is selected and can be modified by any tool or command you choose. (Clicking on the background with any of the selection tools deselects all objects.)

6. You can continue moving the cursor with the mouse and placing anchor points by clicking. Illustrator extends the path by connecting the points. Every time you click, you create a new endpoint, and the previous point becomes a midpoint. This is an open path.

12 CHAPTER 1

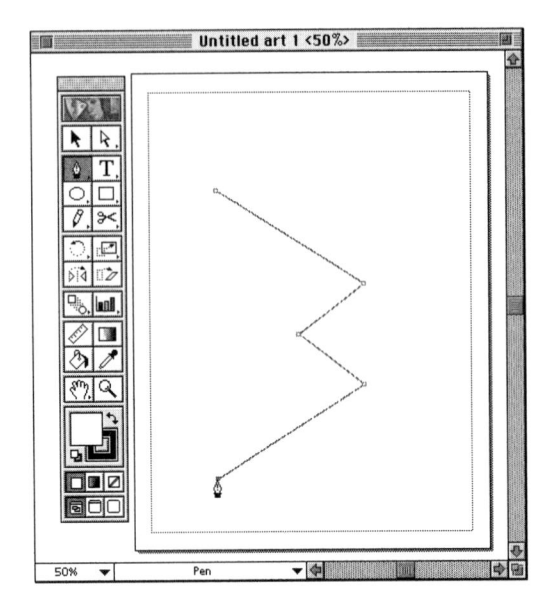

Figure 1.10 Every time you click with the Pen tool, Illustrator adds a new anchor point and extends the path to connect it.

7. Move the cursor near the first anchor point and click. Instead of adding another point, Illustrator draws a final path segment back to the starting point, thus closing the path. Every anchor point is connected by two path segments, and there are no endpoints.

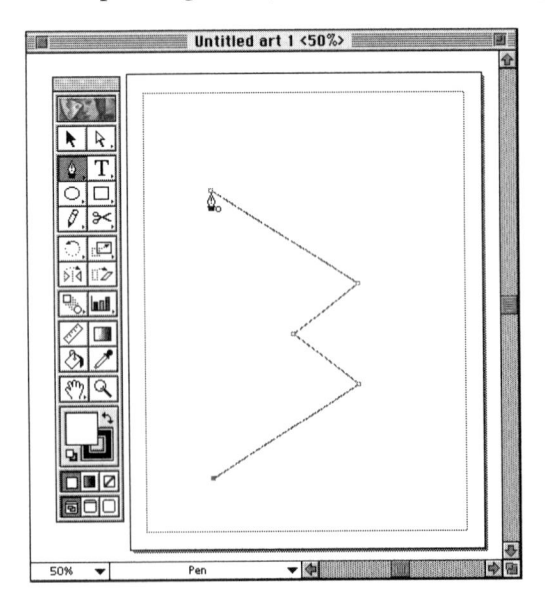

Figure 1.11 When you move the Pen tool's cursor back to the starting point of the path—the first anchor point—a small circle appears next to the cursor, indicating that clicking at this point will close the path.

What It Means To Be a PostScript Drawing Program 13

8. Of the several palettes that Illustrator scatters about the screen, there should be one with a tab labeled **Stroke**. Select this palette by clicking on its tab. If the palette is not on your desktop, choose **Window:Show Stroke** to reveal it. The Stroke palette is used to set the stroke width of the active path. To do this, move the cursor over the drop-down arrow, press the mouse button, and scroll to select a width of 10 points.

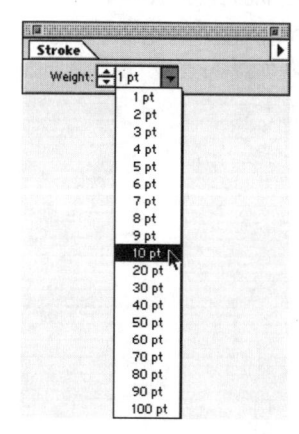

Figure 1.12 Setting the path width to 10 points using the Stroke palette's drop-down menu.

9. Choose the Swatches palette either by clicking on the **Swatches** tab to activate it or by choosing **Window:Show Swatches**. Click on one of the swatches in the top row that isn't white or black; yellow is fine. This changes the foreground color to yellow and fills our closed path.

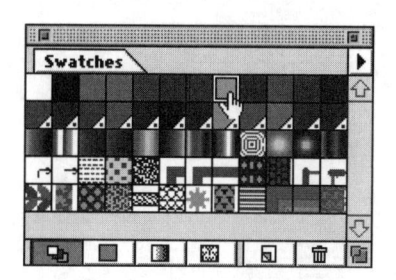

Figure 1.13 Clicking on a color in the Swatches palette changes the foreground color and fills any selected paths or objects with the same color.

10. Move the cursor back to the Toolbox and choose the Selection tool, which is shaped like an arrowhead and is in the upper-left corner. With the tool selected, click in the background of the artwork window away from the object you've drawn.

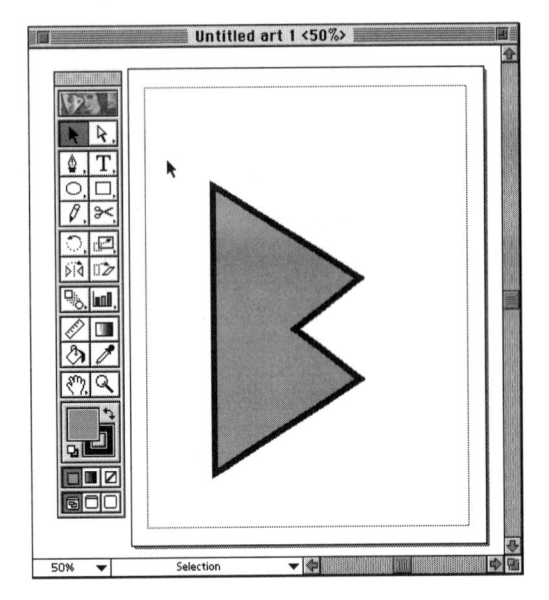

Figure 1.14 Clicking in the background of the window with the Selection tool deselects all paths and objects and reveals a true preview of the artwork without any selection highlights. Here, the object is a black, 10-point, closed path of straight line segments, with a solid yellow fill.

2 New Interface, New Features

In this chapter...

- The document window
- Floating windows
- The Toolbox window
- Menus
- Lesson 2: Kicking Illustrator's Tires

Like any major software upgrade, Illustrator 7 is faster and more capable than earlier versions. It also has an updated interface that incorporates Adobe's new product-wide application programming interface (API). To seasoned Illustrator users, version 7 will look less like the program we've grown used to over the past decade and more like the latest versions of Photoshop and PageMaker.

This will make life much easier for anyone who uses multiple Adobe products, but it also takes some getting used to because many commands have moved and shortcuts have changed. These short-term inconveniences should be outweighed by the efficiency of an API that allows Adobe to add new features across its product line and various computing platforms with a single programming effort. It also means that file formats and plug-ins can be shared among products.

Rather than dwell on the changes, this chapter discusses all the interface features of Illustrator as if everyone reading this book were a new user. Illustrator's interface is simple and straightforward. This makes it easy to become comfortable with a few features and begin using the program productively relatively quickly. It also makes it easy to learn additional features as you need them. In other words, once you've learned the basics, everything else works pretty much the same way.

The first time you launch Illustrator (which you should already have done in Lesson 1), a number of windows fill the space under the menu bar. There is a default document window and above that float the Toolbox and several palette windows.

DOCUMENT WINDOW

All of your drawing is done in a document window. The behavior of this window is the same as for any document window on your computer. You can drag it around, resize it, shrink or enlarge it, and close it. Illustrator lets you open as many document windows as memory allows. These can be new, blank windows, or windows for previously saved documents. (We'll discuss windows and views in greater detail in Chapter 7.)

NOTE   Due to the limitations of current operating systems, only one document window can be active at a time. You can *view* the contents of multiple windows simultaneously, and you can drag from one and drop in another, but you can draw in only one window at a time.

The document window shows not only your artwork but the size of your printed page and the imageable area of that page. It also shows page breaks and numbers for multipage artwork.

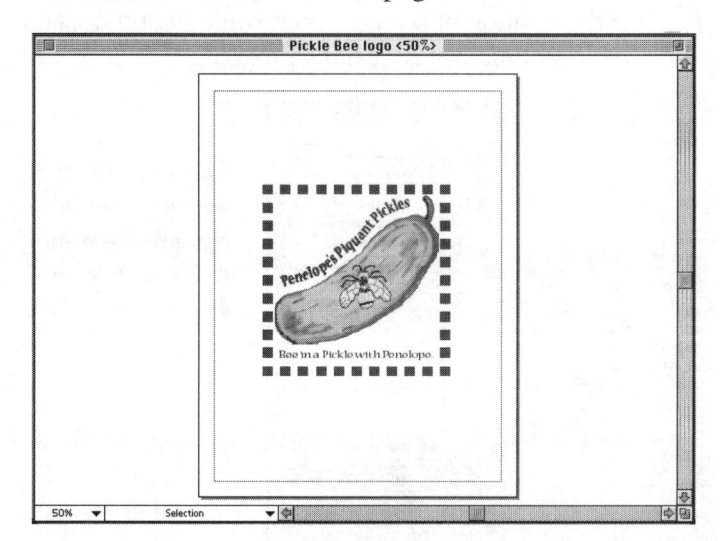

Figure 2.1 A single document window with a single drawing. The space within the window is known as the artboard, and it's where you do all your drawing.

The view within a document window is independent of the window itself. You can zoom in or out to reveal details or view the entire composition at once. When you scroll the contents of a document window, you see not only your artwork but the space around it, which Illustrator calls the *scratch area*. Every document has a maximum scratch area of 120" by 120".

You can draw whatever you like within this 100-square-foot scratch area, but you'll probably want to keep your creations within dragging distance of actual page margins. Everything you draw is saved with the document, but only objects within the imageable area for your specified page size and chosen printer will print.

FLOATING WINDOWS

Above the document windows are the Toolbox and palettes. Your artwork will never obscure Illustrator's controls, but the controls may obscure your artwork. Therefore, all of the floating windows can be dragged around and repositioned on your desktop.

The palette windows include tools that let you specify the appearance of all the objects you draw—their shape and position, their color, the properties of paths, and their sequencing. Palette windows behave like document windows in that they can be repositioned, resized (within certain restrictions), and closed. If you have plenty of screen real estate, you'll probably keep all the palettes open. If you have a small display, you'll want to keep open only the palettes you use most. Illustrator remembers the position of palettes when you quit and displays them in the same position the next time you launch the program.

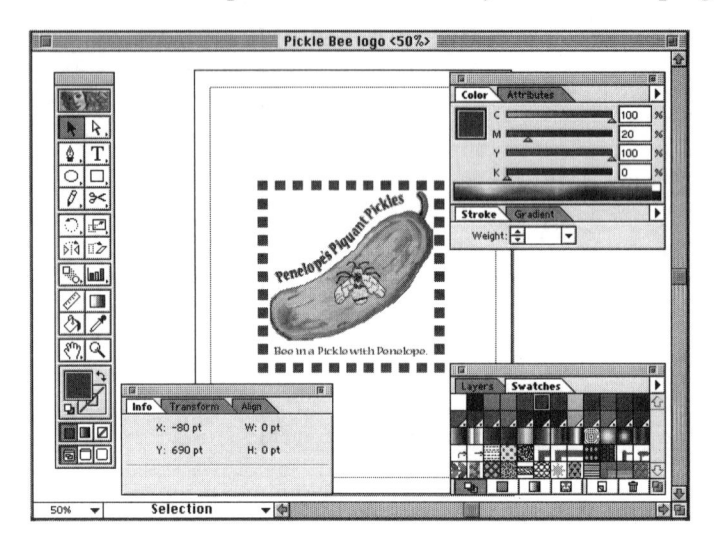

Figure 2.2 The same window shown in Figure 2.1 with the floating palettes in their default position.

Palettes have become a common feature of desktop applications, and they have been championed and refined by Adobe for many years. The palettes in Illustrator 7 are considerably different from previous versions. The windows themselves behave similarly, but they work slightly differently and look quite different—they're probably downright unfamiliar unless you also use the latest versions of PageMaker and Photoshop, which share the same palette design. (This is one of the advantages of the shared API mentioned earlier.)

As before, when you drag one palette near another, they snap to each other. You can customize palette groupings by dragging their tabs in or out of the palette window. Palettes can also be hidden or shown from the Window menu. It is mainly the contents of the palettes that has changed, and all of this is fully discussed in Chapters 9–11.

TOOLBOX WINDOW

Illustrator's Toolbox floats over the document windows like the palette windows, but it cannot be resized. It is either open or closed, and it is used to select the current drawing tool and mode. It, too, has changed to be more like PageMaker and Photoshop, with the tools now arranged in groups and the shortcut keys consistent across the Adobe product line.

Tools are chosen simply by clicking on them or by typing their shortcut key. The active tool is highlighted in gray, as is the current mode. (The details of the **Toolbox** and all its tools are discussed in Chapters 3–8.)

Figure 2.3 Illustrator 7's Toolbox window has been divided into logical categories. Each button represents a tool, and buttons with little left-facing triangles have pop-up hidden tools.

MENUS

Every application on every desktop computer has a menu bar. We're used to accessing commands heirarchically, and Illustrator holds no surprises here. The menu structure of version 7 hasn't changed, but commands have been added, dropped, and moved around to reflect new features and make Illustrator 7 more similar to other Adobe applications.

For instance, there is no longer a Paint Style command in the Object menu. All of its functions have been incorporated into the Color and Attributes palettes. Meanwhile, a brand-new Transform submenu has been added to the Object menu, and the Pathfinder commands have been moved from the Filters menu to the Object menu. (The specific menu commands and changes in Illustrator 7 are discussed in Chapters 12–15.)

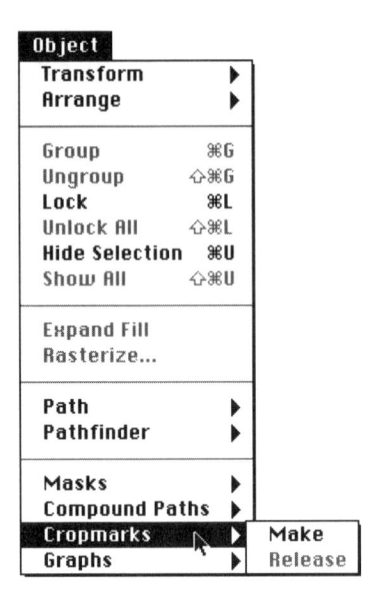

Figure 2.4 *The Object menu is typical of Adobe's design. Keyboard equivalents are shown, unavailable commands are grayed out, and other items hide sub-menus with more commands to choose from.*

Some commands found in the menu heirarchy can also be executed in palettes. This is especially true of the Type menu which controls its own menu-specific palettes.

NOTE Illustrator's menus are nonmodal, an impressive feat for a program of this complexity. This means the menu bar doesn't change to indicate different drawing or editing modes. Unavailable commands are grayed out when they can't be used, but the menu items and heirarchy are always the same.

LESSON 2

Kicking Illustrator's Tires

Rather than make anything particularly useful, we'll use this lesson to take a tour around Illustrator and see what it's made of. This will involve taking a look at a few tools, palettes, and commands. We haven't discussed any of these features yet, so you'll just have to muddle along. Full explanations will follow in later chapters. Be aware of the way we move around the different windows, tools, and menus. It is the efficient integration of these elements and the way we interact with them that makes Illustrator such a productive tool.

1. Open the file LESSON02.AI from the LESSON02 folder on the CD. Do not look for hidden significance in this illustration. It in no way reflects on the disarray of my inner state and was created solely for the purposes of this exploration. Elements of this illustration have to do with object creation and manipulation, the use of palettes to specify object attributes, and some commands that are available only from the menus.

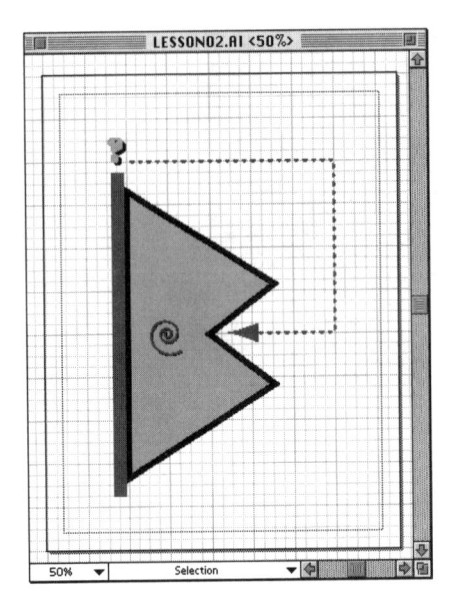

Figure 2.5 *The sample file for Lesson 2 is made up of objects, paths, shapes, and text created from Illustrator's Toolbox, palettes, and menus.*

2. In the Toolbox, make sure that the Selection tool is highlighted. (Click on it if it isn't.) Move the pointer over the yellow area of the filled shape and then click to select it.

   The outline of the shape—its path and anchor points—is highlighted. This shape was created using the Pen tool—I clicked in five places to specify the anchor points and then once more to close the path. Together, the path and the area it circumscribes are known as an *object*. You can fill and select an object as I have done here, or you can move, reshape, or otherwise transform objects individually or in groups. Objects have attributes of stroke, fill, position within a drawing, and sequence with respect to other objects.

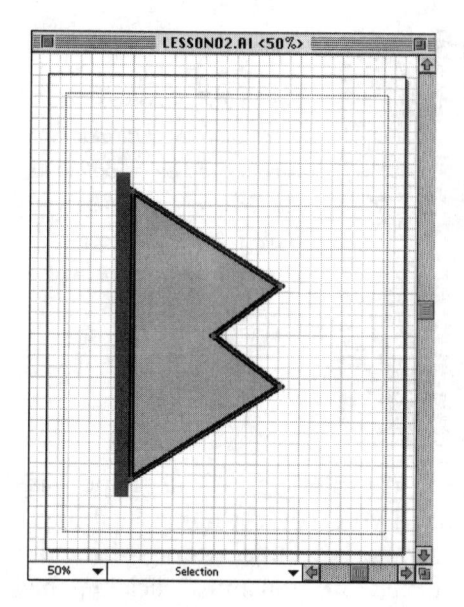

Figure 2.6 *A selected object is indicated by the highlighted path. Drawing and selecting are distinct activities in Illustrator. This shape was drawn as a path using the Pen tool but was selected by pointing and clicking in the filled area.*

3. Move the cursor up to the menu bar and choose **File: Preferences: General**.

    The ability of Illustrator to recognize filled areas as objects is an option in the General Preferences dialog. As shown in Figure 2.3, the Area Select option is checked, allowing you to click on a stroke or fill to select an object. Click on **Area Select** to deselect it, and click on the **OK** button to close the dialog box and change the option settings. (References are discussed in Chapter 19.)

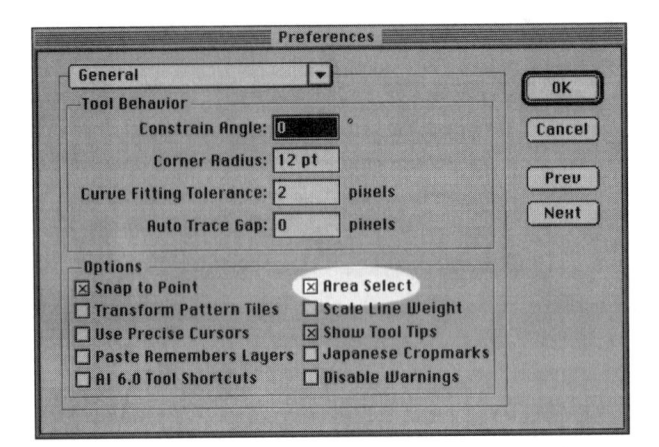

Figure 2.7 *Area selection is a feature of Illustrator that is controlled by an option in the **General Preferences** dialog. It makes objects more apparent, or at least easier to select.*

4. Click on the blue-green rectangle to try to select it. This shape was created using the Rectangle tool, and you would think that if anything were an object, a rectangle would be. Objects notwithstanding, if the Area Select option is turned off, you must click on the path that defines the perimeter of this rectangle to select it.

   This points out one of the basic differences between object-oriented drawing programs and pixel-oriented painting programs, as discussed in Chapter 1. You don't really see objects the way you see a collection of colored bits. Objects are merely mathematical definitions, and it is their properties—the stroke and fill at the simplest level—that make them visible.

   This quality is most apparent when you choose **View: Artwork**. Try it now and you'll see that Artwork mode shows the bare bones of the drawing—the skeleton devoid of any meaty color or other properties of interest. This is how PostScript sees objects, but it is not how we see them. You've got to click on a path to select an object.

   Let's undo the various mode changes so we can further our explorations. Choose **View: Preview** (it toggles on and off with the Artwork command) to return to living color, then choose **File: Preferences: General** again and click on the **Area Select** option to turn it back on. Click **OK** and we're ready to continue.

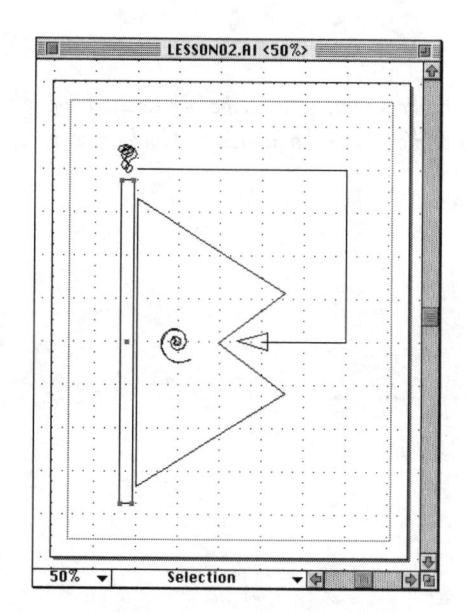

Figure 2.8 *The same illustration in Artwork mode with the rectangle selected. Artwork mode shows only the skeletal structure of the drawing—no color, no line thickness, no dashes or other distinguishing properties—just shape.*

5. Click on the dashed line to select it. (The Selection tool should still be highlighted in the Toolbox.)

    Like the first yellow-filled object, this line was created using the Pen tool. It has four anchor points, but it is an open path because it has two endpoints. Where do the dashes and arrowhead come from? Why can't you click in the area surrounded by this path to select it?

    Look at the **Toolbox**. Under the 20 tool icons is the Fill and Stroke selection area, which indicates that the line we selected has no fill (the red diagonal slash is the universal symbol for "no") and a red stroke. (See Figure 2.9.) When there is no fill, the area surrounded by a path is transparent. In other words, any object under a transparent (or no) fill object will show through and be available for selection.

    The arrowhead was added using **Filter:Stylize:Add Arrowheads**. I ungrouped the line and arrowhead for this lesson so that it would be a separate object.

Figure 2.9 The Fill and Stroke area of the Toolbox shows that the dashed line in this lesson's illustration has no fill and a red stroke (although it looks gray in this screen shot).

6. With the dashed line still selected, look at the Stroke palette. (If the palette isn't open, choose **Window:Show Stroke**.) This is the simplest of all palettes. Its only option sets the stroke width, which is 6 points in this example. But there's also something hiding here.

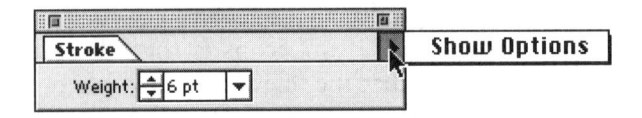

Figure 2.10 This is the Stroke palette, which is used to set the stroke width. By accessing the palette menu, as shown here, the palette can be expanded to include several other options.

7. Move the cursor over the right-pointing arrow as shown in Figure 2.11. This expands the palette menu, which has only one command, Show Options. Select it, and the palette enlarges to reveal the Dashed Line option that was used to turn the selected path into a dashed line.

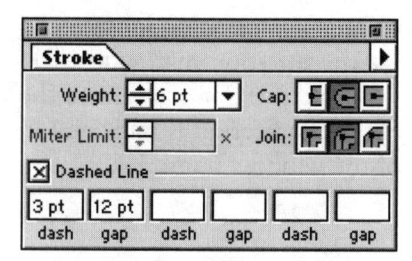

Figure 2.11 *The enlarged Stroke palette showing additional options.*

8. There are lots of clever tricks hiding under Illustrator's calm facade. Move the cursor over the Ellipse tool in the Toolbox—it's the one shaped like an oval. Instead of clicking to select, hold down the mouse button to pop up the hidden tools. While still holding the mouse button down, drag out to the end of the tools to select the Spiral tool.

   You can draw spirals simply by selecting this tool and dragging out shapes in the illustration. It's how the spiral in this lesson was created. I almost never use the Spiral tool, but it's really difficult to create a nice, even spiral without it.

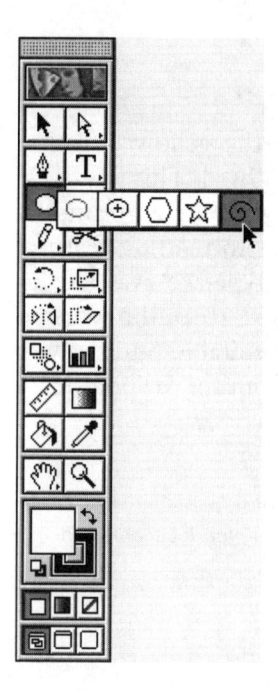

Figure 2.12 *The Spiral tool is hiding under the Ellipse tool's icon. Hold down the mouse button over the icon and this extended tool palette pops up. All of the tool icons with little triangles contain hidden tools.*

9. Choose the Zoom tool in the Toolbox. (It's the one that looks like a magnifying glass.) Move the cursor over the question mark and click. This enlarges the image. Keep clicking on the question mark until the image is enlarged to 200%. (The current magnification is indicated in the title bar and the lower-left border of the window frame.)

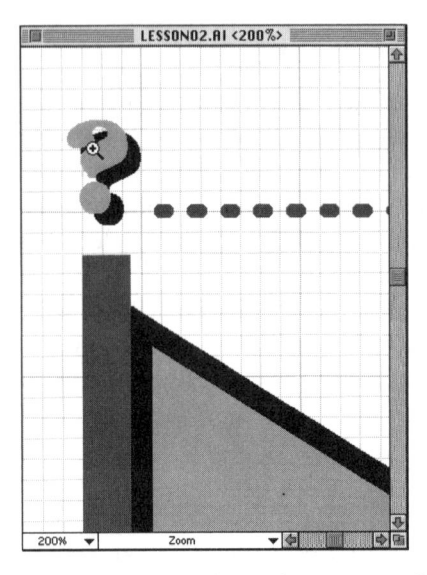

Figure 2.13 Clicking on an image with the Zoom tool enlarges it. In the lower-left corner of the window frame, it shows that this image is enlarged 200% and that the currently selected tool is the Zoom tool.

10. Choose the Selection tool again and click on the yellow question mark. The outline of the question mark is highlighted. This is a question mark from Adobe's Kepler typeface, and it was entered using the Text tool. As you will see later, Illustrator's text formatting features are extremely powerful. Since Kepler is not a typeface available to most readers of this book, I converted the text to outlines using **Type:Create Outlines**. That's why you see an editable outline with anchor points instead of text that you can edit from the keyboard.

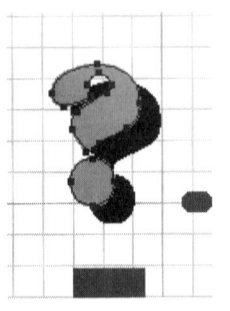

Figure 2.14 This selected object was once a question mark. When the text is converted to outlines, the question mark becomes an editable outline.

New Interface, New Features 29

11. Take a look at the View menu by holding it open with the mouse. Toward the bottom is the Hide Grid command. I previously selected **Show Grid** to turn on the grid that you see in the background of the image (see Figure 2.14). The grid is a new feature in Illustrator 7. This command, like several others in Illustrator, toggles between Show and Hide, depending on the state of the illustration. With the View menu still open, slide the cursor down to the **Fit In Window** command to return our illustration to its original magnification.

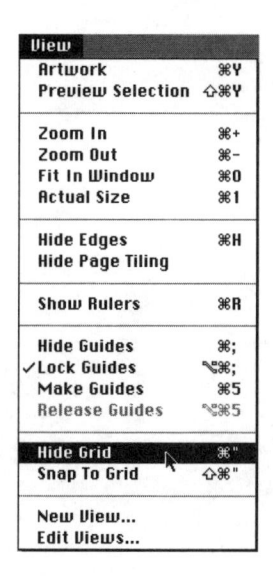

Figure 2.15 The View menu has a number of commands that toggle between Show and Hide, such as the Show/Hide Grid commands.

12. There's one more feature of this drawing you should know about. Both the question mark and spiral have drop shadows that were created using **Filter:Stylize:Drop Shadow**. We'll talk more about all of the filters, and drop shadows in particular, in Chapter 14.

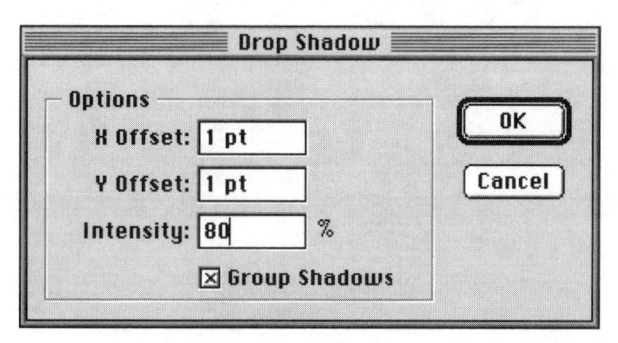

Figure 2.16 Illustrator can create drop shadows automatically using the Drop Shadow dialog box.

Section II

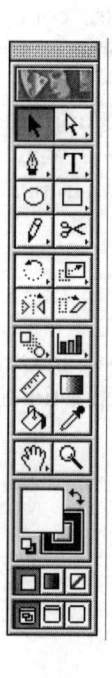

Looking Inside the Toolbox

In this section...

- Section Introduction: The Toolbox
- Chapter 3: Object Creation: Drawing and Text
- Chapter 4: Selection and Manipulation
- Chapter 5: Transformation Tools
- Chapter 6: Attributes: Stoking, Filling, and Blending
- Chapter 7: Windows and Views
- Chapter 8: Blending, Tracing, and Graphing

Section Introduction: The Toolbox in General

The Toolbox is the metaphorical heart of Illustrator. It contains pens, pencils, brushes, scissors, paintbuckets, and other familiarly named tools. For each object you create, you'll use one of these tools. The Toolbox also contains other tools that you'll use to manipulate objects and specify some of their attributes.

When you launch Illustrator, the Toolbox appears in the upper-left corner of your display. As mentioned in Chapter 2, the Toolbox window floats over any open image windows and can be repositioned simply by dragging.

To Reposition the Toolbox

The Toolbox is bordered at the top by a gray bar. Move the cursor into this gray bar, hold down the mouse button, and drag the Toolbox to reposition it.

NOTE The Toolbox cannot be resized.

To Show/Hide the Toolbox

- Select **Window: Hide Tools** to hide the toolbox.
- Select **Window: Show Tools** to show the toolbox.

NOTE This command toggles between Show and Hide.

Each button in the Toolbox represents a different tool, and each tool has its own cursor icon. This means that the cursor changes to reflect the currently selected tool. For example, the Pencil tool uses a pencil icon as its cursor. You can also set Illustrator's preferences to use "precise" cursors, which are described in Chapter 19.

Every tool is also represented by a shortcut letter—*p* for Pen tool, *t* for Type tool, and so on. Illustrator 7 shortcut keys have been made more consistent across the adobe product line., which means that the mnemonic connection between tool and letter is sometimes obscure.

To Select Tools in the Toolbox

There are two methods from which to choose:

- Move the cursor over a tool button and click to select it.
- Type the shortcut letter for the tool you wish to select.

NOTE The tool button is highlighted to indicate that it is the active tool, and the cursor changes shape to reflect your tool selection.

Illustrator's Toolbox also contains hidden tools. For the most part, these are variations of the basic tool set, but some represent specialty drawing tools. Hidden tools are found under tool buttons marked with a right-facing triangle, such as the Ellipse and Rectangle tools.

To Select a Hidden Tool

There are two methods from which to choose:

- Move the cursor over a tool button and hold down the mouse button. A button bar of hidden tools associated with the base tool pops up, with the base tool highlighted gray. Slide the cursor over the button bar to select one of the hidden tools.
- Type the shortcut letter for the base tool and then type the letter again to cycle through each of its hidden tools. All hidden tools share the shortcut letter of the base.

NOTE Selecting a hidden tool moves it to the base layer of the Toolbox and adds the base tool to the hidden tool pop-up palette.

Many of the tools have associated options. These are different from the options available from the various palettes in that they are tool-specific. We'll cover each option as we discuss the various tools.

To Select Tool Options

1. Double-click on a tool icon in the Toolbox to open the associated options dialog.
2. Set the options you wish within the dialog.
3. Click **OK** to change the option settings and close the dialog.
4. Use the selected tool and the options will be in effect.

NOTE: Tool options remain in effect, from document to document and from session to session, until you explicitly change them.

The new Toolbox in Illustrator 7 is divided into functional categories—selection, object creation, manipulation, and so on. A couple of the categories appear a bit random, but I have tried to stick with Adobe's organizational scheme in organizing the chapters of this book.

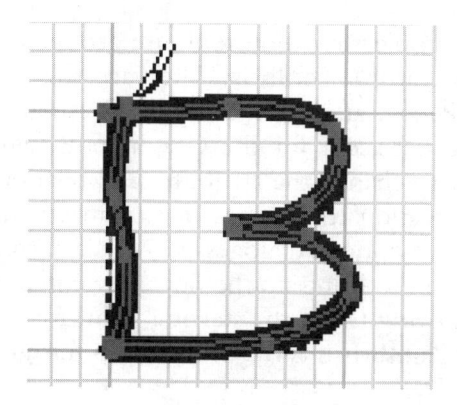

3

Object Creation: Drawing and Text Tools

In this chapter...

- Regular shapes—rectangles and ellipses
- Specialty shapes—polygons, stars, and spirals
- Making paths—pen, pencil, and paintbrush
- Editing paths—scissors, knife, and hidden pen tools
- Text—the Naked Text tool
- Lesson 3: Alphabet Paths

All of the basic object creation tools are grouped together as six buttons in Illustrator's Toolbox. They are the Pen, Type , Ellipse, Rectangle, Pencil, and Scissors tools. These are the tools you will use to create objects. Except for the Graph tools, which are special, all other tools are used to change the attributes and relationships of objects.

Each of these creation tools hides one or more additional tools, and most of the tools have options dialogues. However, instead of double-clicking on the tool button to bring up the object-oriented options dialog, you click once in the drawing to set the starting point for the object and bring up the dialog. The Paintbrush is the only tool in this group with a double-click option.

REGULAR SHAPES—RECTANGLES AND ELLIPSES

The simplest objects are squares and circles, or more generally, rectangles and ellipses. They are basic not only to visual perception but to PostScript. Both shapes consist of four anchor points and a closed path. Rectangles can have square or rounded corners.

Ellipses can be thought of as rectangles with the corners rounded to the midpoints of the sides. Both shapes can be drawn from corner to corner or from a center point. Illustrator shows you a preview of the shape as you drag. Releasing the mouse button sets the object in place, leaving it selected.

To Create a Rectangle or Ellipse

1. Click on the **Rectangle** tool (m) or **Ellipse** tool (n) to select one.
2. Move the cursor to the drawing window and hold down the mouse button where you want a corner of the object to be.
3. Drag to the opposite corner of the object and release the mouse button, as shown in Figure 3.1.

NOTE: It can be difficult to judge the placement of an ellipse using this method. If you imagine a rectangle circumscribing the ellipse and draw the corner points with this in mind, you'll find it easier to draw ellipses of predictable size and shape.

Object Creation: Drawing and Text Tools

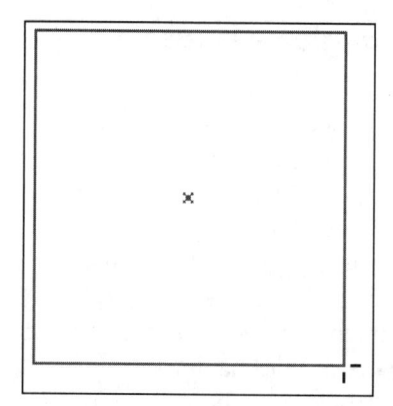

Figure 3.1 Illustrator shows a preview of the shape as you drag from corner-to-corner with the **Rectangle** tool. Releasing the mouse button sets the shape in place.

To Create a Centered Rectangle or Ellipse

The Centered Rectangle (m) and Centered Ellipse tool (n) are hidden.

1. Either click and drag on the tool button or use the shortcut key to select the hidden tool with the + in it. Repeatedly pressing the shortcut key for any tool will cycle through all the additional hidden variants of that tool.
2. Move the cursor to the drawing window and hold down the mouse where you want the center point to be.
3. Drag out from the center in any direction and release the mouse button when the object is the size you want.

NOTE Holding down the **Option/Alt** key before dragging a rectangle or ellipse toggles between corner-drawn and centered objects. In other words, you can draw a centered object with the standard tool selected by holding down the **Option/Alt** key before you click and drag, or you can switch from center to corner the same way.

Figure 3.2 This square-with-crosshairs cursor is used when creating a centered rectangle.

To Specify the Dimensions of a Rectangle or Ellipse

1. Click on the **Rectangle** tool or **Ellipse** tool to select one.
2. Move the cursor to the drawing window and click to set the upper left-corner of the object. If the Centered Rectangle or Centered Ellipse tool is selected, click to set the center point.
3. A dialog pops up that lets you specify the Height and Width of the object in any units you choose, as shown in Figure 3.3. The Rectangle dialog also includes a Corner Radius dimension, which is the same as the Rounded Rectangle tool discussed later in this chapter.
4. Click **OK** to dismiss the dialog. Illustrator draws the object to your specifications and leaves it selected. (Using the dialog always draws objects from upper left to lower right.)

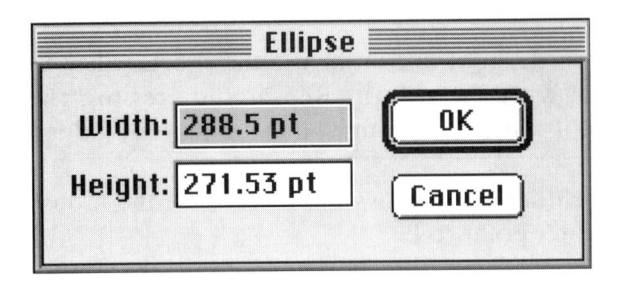

Figure 3.3 The Ellipse dialog lets you specify the Height and Width of the rectangle that forms the bounds of an ellipse.

To Create Rounded Rectangles

Creating rounded or centered rounded rectangles is the same as creating any rectangle. Follow the steps outlined earlier to choose the hidden tool, and either click and drag or click and set the object specifications in the dialog. The only way to reset or change the corner radius is in this dialog. (You can also change the default corner radius using the General Preferences dialog, discussed in Chapter 19.) Clicking and dragging always uses the last specified corner radius.

To Create Squares and Circles

Select any of the rectangle or ellipse tools and hold down the **Shift** key as you drag. This constrains the object to a square or circle.

SPECIALTY SHAPES—POLYGONS, STARS, AND SPIRALS

In addition to simple rectangles and ellipses, Illustrator includes three tools to draw polygons, stars, and spirals. Hidden under the Ellipse button, they share the **n** shortcut key and behave much like the Ellipse tool.

NOTE The specialty shape tools always draw from the center out.

To Draw Specialty Shapes by Dragging

1. Select the hidden Polygon, Star, or Spiral tools by clicking and dragging the **Ellipse** button or by using the **n** shortcut key to cycle to the tool. Figure 3.4 shows art created with each of these tools.
2. Move the cursor to the drawing. Click the mouse point at the center point of the shape and drag to the desired size.
3. Release the mouse button.

Figure 3.4 This polygon, star, and spiral were each created with a different specialty tool.

NOTE The shape you drag uses the last supplied specifications as described in the next section.

To Specify Specialty Shape Options

1. Select the hidden Polygon, Star, or Spiral tool as described earlier.
2. Move the cursor to the drawing and click.
3. In the dialog, fill in the options and click **OK** to draw the shape.

Polygon Options

- **Radius**—Specify a radius from 0 to 4320 points.
- **Sides**—Specify the number of sides from 3 to 1000.

Star Options

- **Radius 1 and Radius 2**—Specify two radii from 0 to 4320 points. These represent the inner and outer points of the star.
- **Points**—Specify the number of points from 3 to 1000.

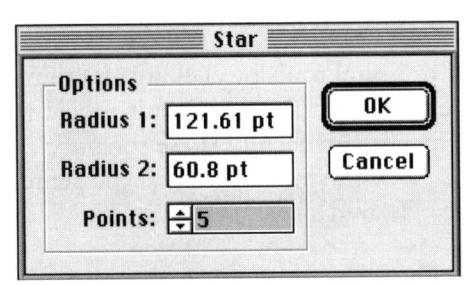

Figure 3.5 The Star Options dialog, like all the shape tool dialogs, is opened by selecting the tool and clicking in the drawing without dragging. When you click **OK** to dismiss the dialog, the shape is drawn from the point you clicked.

Spiral Options

- **Radius**—Specify a radius from 0 to 4320 points.
- **Decay**—Specify the rate of curve from 5% to 150%. A decay of 100% makes a circle equal to the radius specified, while a decay less than 100% will fit inside the circle. A decay greater than 100% exceeds the bounds of the circle.
- **Segments**—Specify the number of anchor points in the spiral from 2 to 1000. It requires four segments to complete one full revolution of a spiral.
- **Style**—Choose either a clockwise or counterclockwise spiral by clicking on one of the radio buttons.

NOTE

For any of the specialty shapes, if you specify a tiny radius, the shape will not be discernible. Similarly, too many sides, points, or segments will end up looking like a circle or a dark blob. If a blob is your goal, this is one way to achieve it.

Making Paths—Pen, Pencil and Paintbrush

Paths are fundamental to PostScript and therefore to Illustrator. You can call them *lines*, but even a line enclosing a shape has a starting and ending point, and this directionality makes it a vector, or path. As discussed in Chapter 1, paths are composed of two or more connected anchor points. Anchor points determine both the position and curve of a path.

Illustrator's Pen tool, originally called the *Path tool*, has expanded somewhat in functionality but remains essentially unchanged. With the Pen tool selected, you click to set anchor points, and click and drag to make curves. Its simplicity belies the enormous precision and flexibility that take some practice to master. We'll go into the details a little later in this chapter.

By contrast, the Pencil tool, formerly called the *Freehand tool*, is so flexible and imprecise as to be nearly flaccid, like limp spaghetti. Don't get me wrong, having a tool that you can use to make quick sketches or impart an informal look is extremely useful. You simply draw the line you want and Illustrator calculates the anchor points and path to follow.

The Paintbrush tool, formerly called the *Brush tool*, is similar to the Pencil tool in its freehand quality. It is used to make paths of varying thickness. In other words, the brush stroke you make with the Paintbrush tool is converted into a closed path surrounding the stroke. It becomes a filled rather than stroked path. This is especially effective if you have a pressure-sensitive drawing tablet.

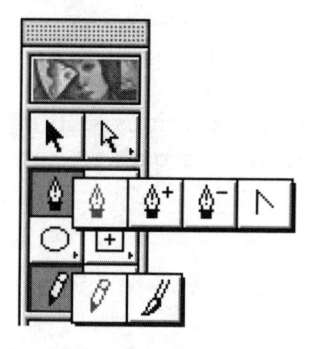

Figure 3.6 *The pop-up tools under the* **Pen** *and* **Pencil** *buttons.*

To Make Straight Path Segments

1. Select the **Pen** tool (p).
2. Click in the drawing window to set the starting anchor point.

3. Move the cursor and click again to set the second anchor point. Hold down the **Shift** key to constrain the tool to increments of 45°. Illustrator connects the two points with a straight line segment and strokes the line using the current specifications.
4. Continue clicking to set more anchor points. Illustrator continues connecting them as described earlier.
5. When the cursor is within a pixel or two of the starting anchor point, a small circle appears next to the Pen cursor indicating that clicking will close the path instead of setting a new anchor point.

NOTE The last anchor point you set is always the active one, as indicated by the solid square. All other anchor points in the active path become hollow squares.

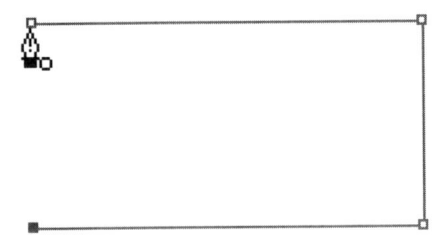

Figure 3.7 This rectangle is being drawn with the Pen tool in a clockwise direction. The circle next to the Pen cursor indicates that clicking will close the path.

To End a Path

Short of closing a path, as described in Step 5 in the previous section, there is no direct way to tell Illustrator that you want a path to end. Instead, use one of the following methods:

- Select another tool in the Toolbox.
- Click on the **Pen** tool in the Toolbox. This allows you to end one path and start another.
- Hold down the **Command/Ctrl** key, which is a shortcut way to toggle to the Selection tool, and click anywhere except the path. This ends and deselects the path.
- Choose **Edit: Deselect All**.

The Vocabulary of Curves

When you graduate from rectilinear paths (point and click) to curves (click and drag), the vocabulary becomes more complex. Anchor points sprout *direction lines* and become *smooth points* and *corner points*. Here's a brief lexicon:

- **Direction line**—Direction lines are attached to anchor points and control the direction and magnitude of connected path segments. An anchor point can have one or two direction lines.
- **Direction point**—The endpoint of a direction line opposite the anchor point is called the *direction point*. Moving the direction point away from or toward the anchor point changes the degree of curvature of the attached path segment.
- **Smooth point**—Paths that form a continuous wave or sine curve change curve direction at a smooth point.
- **Corner point**—Discontinuous paths that appear to bounce create a corner point when the path changes direction.

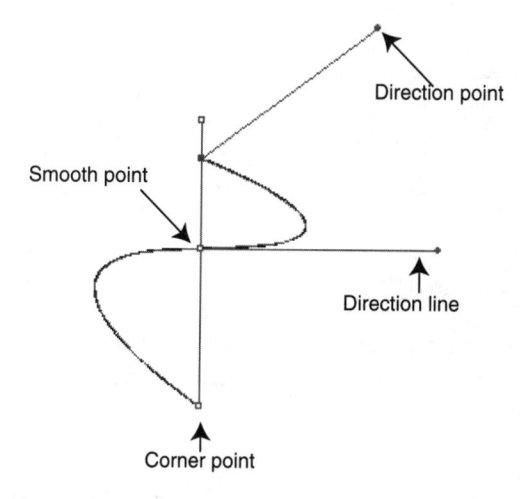

Figure 3.8 A diagram illustrating the basic terminology of curves.

To Make Smooth Curved Path Segments

1. Select the **Pen** tool (p).
2. Move the Pen cursor to the starting point of the curve. Hold down the mouse button (the cursor turns into an arrowhead) and drag in

the direction of the curve. Clicking sets the starting anchor point, and dragging creates the first direction line.
3. Release the mouse, move the cursor, and do it again. The length and angle of the direction line determines the properties of the curve that follows. Holding down the **Shift** key constrains the tool (in terms of the placement of anchor points) to multiples of 45°.
4. Ending curved paths is just like ending straight ones. Either close the path by returning to the starting anchor point or use one of the path ending methods described earlier.

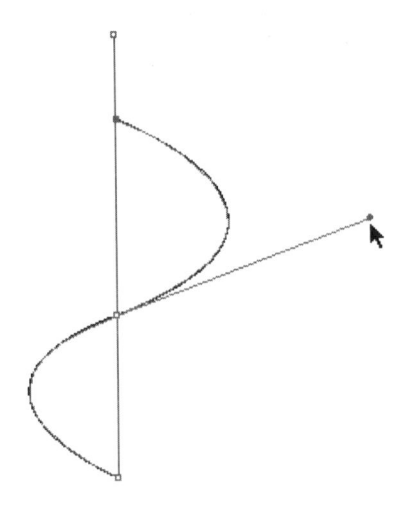

Figure 3.9 As shown here, a smooth curve is created when the path changes directions without making an angle.

To Make Angled Curved Path Segments

Drawing curved segments as described in the preceding section creates smooth points. To make curves that attach at angles rather than flowing from one to the next, you need to create corner points.

1. Create the first curved segment as described earlier.
2. Before setting the next anchor point, hold down the **Option/Alt** key and click on the last anchor point to convert it into a corner point.
3. Drag from the corner point to create an independent direction line.
4. Continue setting anchor points and direction lines as before.

Object Creation: Drawing and Text Tools 45

> **NOTE:** While **Option/Alt**-clicking turns smooth points into corner points, **Option/Alt**-dragging does the opposite.

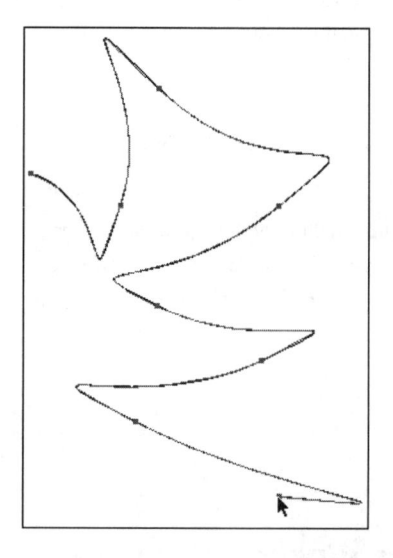

Figure 3.10 Curves attached at angles are created with corner points.

Mixing Straight and Curved Path Segments

Clicking with the Pen tool makes straight segments, while clicking and dragging makes curves. Within a path, it's possible to switch back and forth between straight and curved segments as you draw. The point at which the path changes is a corner point.

To Draw Freehand Paths—Pencil Tool

1. Select the **Pencil** tool (y).
2. Move the cursor where you want the path to start, hold down the mouse button, and drag. Illustrator follows the cursor with a dotted line to indicate the path you've drawn.
3. Pressing the **Command/Ctrl** key as you draw toggles the pencil cursor into an eraser and allows you to backtrack over your path to erase a portion of it.

4. Release the mouse button to stop drawing. Illustrator creates a path complete with anchor points and direction lines.

> **NOTE** The accuracy of paths created with the Pencil tool is dependent upon the Curve Fitting Tolerance setting in the General Preferences dialog. (See Chapter 19.)

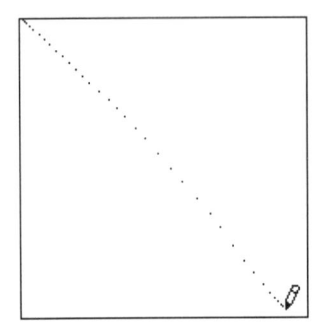

Figure 3.11 As you drag with the Pencil tool, Illustrator follows the cursor with a dotted line to show a preview of the path you are creating. The slower you draw, the closer the dots.

To Draw Closed Paths with a Single Stroke—Paintbrush Tool

1. Select the **Paintbrush** tool (y), which is hidden under the Pencil tool.
2. As you would with the Pencil tool, move the cursor where you want the path to start, hold down the mouse button, and drag. Illustrator follows the cursor with a black stroke of the thickness specified in the Paintbrush Options dialog (see the following note).
3. When you release the mouse button, the brush stroke is converted into a closed path of the currently specified fill and stroke.

> **NOTE** The use of the word *stroke* is unintentionally ambiguous when referring to the Paintbrush tool. There is the metaphorical brush stroke, which refers to a stroke of some thickness such as one would apply with an actual paintbrush, and there is also the usual meaning of *stroke* within Illustrator to refer to the properties of a path. The Paintbrush tool's stroke is converted into a path, which can then be stroked and filled.

Object Creation: Drawing and Text Tools 47

Figure 3.12 The streamers on the star are not strokes, but are closed and filled paths made by the Paintbrush tool.

To Set Paintbrush Options

1. To open the Paintbrush options dialog, double-click on the **Paintbrush** tool. (If the tool is hidden, you must first select it from the hidden button bar or type the shortcut key, **y**.)
2. Change the options and click **OK** to set the new specifications. The options remain in effect until they are changed.

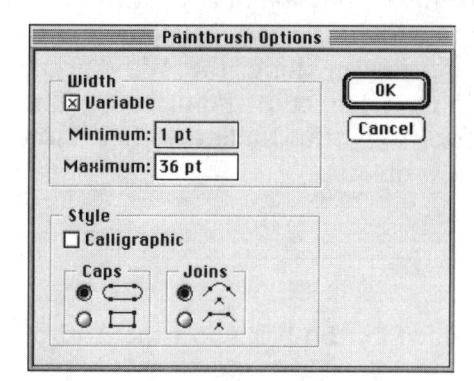

Figure 3.13 In the Paintbrush Options dialog you can set the Width and Style. The Variable option is available only if you have a pressure-sensitive drawing tablet.

Width Options

- **Variable**—Check this box if you have a pressure-sensitive drawing tablet and wish to specify a minimum and maximum stroke width. If the box is unchecked, specify a constant line width between 0 and 1296 points.

- **Minimum**—The width of the stroke when applying minimal pressure.
- **Maximum**—The width of the stroke when applying maximum pressure.

Style Options

- **Calligraphic**—Check this box to turn the Paintbrush into a chisel-tipped tool for creating calligraphic effects. Specify a brush angle from -360° to +360°.
- **Caps**—Select round-ended or flat caps to determine how Illustrator will treat line endings of paintbrush strokes.
- **Joins**—Select round or flat joins to determine how Illustrator treats line angles within paintbrush strokes.

EDITING PATHS—SCISSORS, KNIFE, AND HIDDEN PEN TOOLS

As you'll see as you progress through this book, there are many ways to create paths. Some are more precise than others which can be used to render quick approximations. But what good is a path that can't be adjusted? You'll also find that there are many ways to adjust paths. In this section, we'll discuss ways to edit anchor points, the foundation of any path.

Hidden under the Pen tool are three additional tools that allow you to alter anchor points without actually moving anything: the Add Anchor Point, Delete Anchor Point, and Convert Direction Point tools. The Scissors tool divides single paths in two, while the Knife tool can bisect paths or objects, resulting in multiple new objects.

To Add or Delete Anchor Points

1. Using the **p** key or the Pen's hidden button bar, select the **Add or Delete Anchor Point** tool.
2. Click on a path with the Add Anchor Point tool to add an anchor point. Click on an existing anchor point with the Delete Anchor Point tool to delete it. Adding an anchor point does not change the shape of the path, but deleting one will cause the path to be redrawn to fit the two anchor points adjacent to the one that was deleted.

Object Creation: Drawing and Text Tools 49

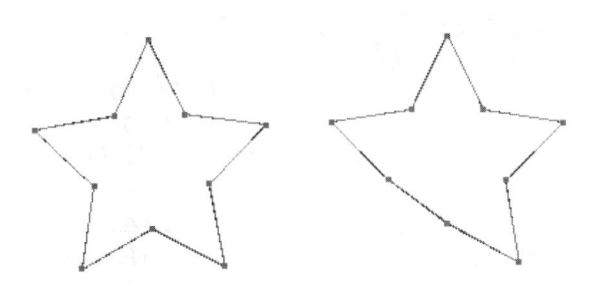

Figure 3.14 On the left, a five-point star, and on the right, the star after deleting one of its anchor points using the Delete Anchor Point tool.

To Convert Anchor Points Between Smooth and Corner

1. There are several ways to select the Convert Direction Point tool:

   - Use the **p** key or the Pen's hidden button bar to select within the Toolbar.
   - With the Pen tool selected, hold down the **Option-Alt** key alone to toggle to the Convert Direction Point tool.
   - With any Selection tool selected, hold down the **Command/Ctrl-Option/Alt** key combination to toggle to the Convert Direction Point tool.

2. The Convert Direction Point tool can be used for three different conversions, depending on where you click:

   - Click on a smooth point to convert it to a corner point. All direction lines are deleted for that anchor point.
   - Click and drag on a corner point to convert it to a smooth point and create new direction lines.
   - Click and drag on a direction point (the endpoint of a direction line) to convert its anchor point to a corner point while preserving the direction lines. For this method to work, you must first select the anchor point with the Direct Selection tool.

NOTE: While drawing a path, if you move the Pen cursor back over the last anchor point, the Pen becomes a conversion tool, so that you can convert points as you draw a path. This is a new feature in Illustrator 7.

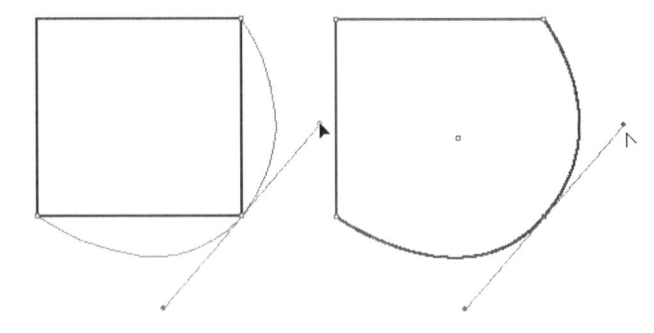

Figure 3.15 *By clicking and dragging on the corner point in the drawing on the left with the Convert Anchor Point tool, it becomes a smooth anchor point as shown on the right.*

About the Pen Cursors

The Pen cursor has many guises depending on the tool or hidden tool selected, the state of the selected path, and the position of the cursor with respect to the active path. Table 3.1 is a brief guide to Pen cursors.

Table 3.1 Pen Cursors

Cursor	Description
The vanilla Pen tool	Use to create anchor points and direction lines.
Continue a path	Click on an endpoint of an open path and continue drawing.
Rework path	Click on an endpoint to convert between corner and smooth points, allowing you to rework the path as you draw.
Close a path	Appears when the cursor is within two points of the starting anchor point.
Merge paths	Appears when clicking will cause the path being drawn to merge with another path.
Add anchor point	Click to add an anchor point in a pathsegment.
Delete anchor point	Click on an anchor point to delete it.
Start path	Appears when clicking will begin a new path.

To Make One Path Two

1. Select the **Scissors** tool (c).
2. Click on a path to divide it. If you click on an existing anchor point, it becomes two endpoints, and if you click between anchor points, two coincident endpoints are created.

NOTE The effect of applying the Scissors tool is not always immediately apparent. You must deselect the line and reselect one of the new endpoints with the Direct Selection tool. Then you can drag one point away from the other.

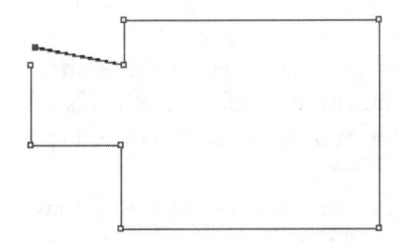

Figure 3.16 This shape was a closed path. By clicking on one of the anchor points with the Scissors tool, two end points were created. By then dragging one of the endpoints with the Direct Selection tool, it has been moved away from its closed position, as shown here.

To Divide Paths with the Knife

While the Scissors tool can divide a path at a single point, the Knife tool can be used to draw a dividing line that splits a path or paths at every intersection. It can also divide whole objects across the path you draw.

1. Select the **Knife** tool (c), which is hidden under the Scissors tool.
2. Click and drag a line across the path or paths you wish to divide. Every object crossed by the path you draw is divided.

TEXT—THE NAKED TYPE TOOL

One could write an entire book on Illustrator and typography. I've limited the discussion of typography in this book to Chapter 13 and will introduce the straightforward use of the Type tool and its hidden variations in this chapter. But first, it's important to realize that text in Illustrator is a special kind of object. The text itself, the letterforms, can be edited as you would any text in any application. But a group of text, a line or text block, is treated like an object. You use different tools and commands to manipulate letterforms and text objects. You can also convert letterforms into actual objects, but we'll discuss this in Chapter 13.

The Type tool has five variants, including three vertical type tools that were added for the Japanese market but are useful in their own right. With the plain vanilla Type tool, you click in the drawing and type. The text you enter flows into your drawing at the exact point where you click. (You'll sometimes see this referred to as point type.) You can set the type in innumerable ways; this is a function of the Type menu and its associated palettes and is discussed in Chapter 13.

In addition to straightforward text entry, the Area Type tool allows you to fill an object with text, the object acting as a typographic boundary for your text, while the Path Type tool lets you bind type to any shape path, one of Illustrator's first great tricks. The three vertical type tools are the vertical equivalents of the standard horizontal versions: Vertical Type, Vertical Area Type, and Vertical Path Type.

The type tools have a certain "intelligence" that allows them to behave differently depending on context. The unmodified Type tool also functions as an area or path type tool. When you move within a pixel or two of an object or Path, the standard Type tool icon automatically changes into an Area or Path tool icon. The Vertical Type tool behaves similarly.

The Area Type tools will fill the area under a curve if you click on a path. Clicking on an object with one of the Path Type tools uses the object perimeter as the type path. The icon does not change in either case, nor can you enter text without clicking on an object or path if these tools are selected.

> **NOTE** You can temporarily toggle between equivalent horizontal and vertical type tools by holding down the **Shift** key.

To Enter Type

1. Select one of the six Type tools (t).
2. Move the cursor to the point where you want to enter text and click. (The effect of clicking is dependent on the chosen type tool and the context: path, object, or blank space described earlier.)

Object Creation: Drawing and Text Tools 53

> **NOTE** If you click and drag with the unmodified Type tool, the area you drag defines the bounds of an area container for type.

3. Type in the text you want or paste it in from the Clipboard.
4. You can continue entering text until you click on the Text tool button in the Toolbox, which allows you to enter another text object or select another tool.

> **NOTE** The Text tool converts paths or objects into text containers, and once a path or object becomes a container, you can no longer stroke or fill it. If you want both, copy the path or object before using the Text tool. One copy becomes a container and the other can be stroked, filled, or manipulated in any way you choose.

To Edit Type

1. Select any Type tool (t).
2. Click on the text in an existing text object. The cursor changes to an I-beam, and all the standard editing features of your computer are available such as the Select, Cut, Copy, and Paste functions and commands.
3. You can continue editing text until you click on the Text tool button in the Toolbox, or select another tool.

> **NOTE** You cannot edit horizontal text to be vertical or mix text directions in a single text object.

Type tool | Type tool

Figure 3.17 On the left, clicking with the I-beam Text cursor to set the flashing insertion point. On the right, dragging the Text cursor over a word to select it.

Confusion Over Type Selection

As mentioned earlier, editing text and editing text objects are distinct activities in Illustrator. For instance, when editing text, you can't move the entire text block around, and, conversely, when positioning a text block, you can't edit the letters without changing tools.

Illustrator makes it clear where you are with regard to text through its interface. If a text object is selected, Illustrator underlines the text and places a single anchor point on the first text line. The placement of the anchor point matches the text alignment: left, centered, right, or vertical. If the text is bound to a container, the container and its anchor points are highlighted when the text object is selected.

Any of the selection tools can be used to select text objects as discussed in Chapter 4. Clicking on an existing text object with one of the text tools selects the text itself rather than the object. In this case, either a flashing I-beam is present to indicate that the text can be edited, or the text itself is highlighted to indicate that it is selected.

> **NOTE** You can't use the tool shortcut keys while editing text, because Illustrator enters all keystrokes into the drawing while in text mode.

Alphabet Paths

This lesson is not going to demonstrate all of the tools discussed in this chapter. Instead, we will concentrate on the Pen tool and compare it to the Pencil and Brush tools. You should try out the others. You will see them in later lessons.

We'll be using two templates for a monospaced font composed of straight lines and circles only. Illustrator 7 doesn't use templates the way previous versions did, so the template is on a locked layer, and you will draw on a layer above it.

Before tracing these letterforms with the Pen tool, you need to make some settings so that your drawings match the screen shots. We haven't discussed how to make these settings yet, but follow along for this lesson and they'll be explained soon.

ALPHABET LESSON: PART 1

1. Open the file ALPHA1.AI in the LESSON03 folder on the CD. This file contains the straight line letters.

56   CHAPTER 3

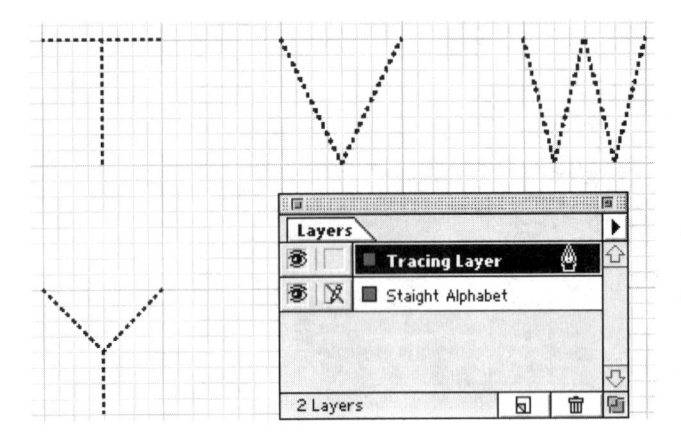

Figure 3.18 Part of the alphabet template along with the Layers template showing the locked template layer and the active drawing layer for tracing (see Chapter 11).

2. Set the width in the Stroke palette to 5 points. (If the Stroke palette isn't open, choose **Window: Show Stroke**.) You can type in a **5**, use the arrows to increment or decrement to 5, or choose **5** from the drop down menu.

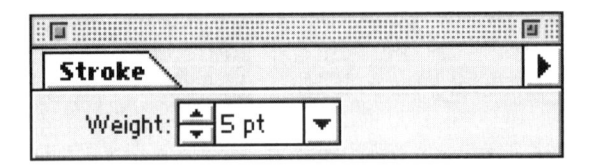

Figure 3.19 The Stroke palette sometimes looks like this (where you can set it to a 5-point stroke for this lesson), or it can be expanded. It might also be in a window with other Palette tabs. These palette properties are discussed in Section III.

3. Set the stroke to black and the fill to None. Stroke and fill colors are controlled from the painting section of the Toolbox shown in Figure 3.20. Click on the **Default** button or press the **d** key to set the stroke to black and the fill to white. (They may already be at their default settings.) If the white Fill box isn't on top of the black Stroke box, click on it. Click on the **None** button (the button with the red slash) or press the **/** key to set the fill to None.

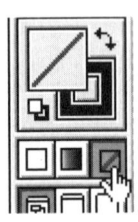

Figure 3.20 The painting section of the Toolbox shows you the current settings for fill and stroke. Here, the stroke is set to black, the default, and the None button was just clicked to set the fill to None.

Object Creation: Drawing and Text Tools 57

4. Two commands in the View menu (shown in Figure 3.21) make it easier to do this lesson: Show Grid and Snap To Grid. Neither is specific to the document, so select both from the View menu to turn them on. When they are selected, Show Grid toggles to Hide Grid, and Snap To Grid appears with a check mark next to it in the menu.

Figure 3.21 The View menu includes the Show/Hide Grid and the Snap To Grid commands, both of which make this lesson easier. When the Hide Grid command is active, it means that the grid is already on, as you can see in the illustration window. The Snap To Grid has a check mark next to it to indicate that it is on.

5. Choose the **Pen** tool (p). We'll start by tracing easy letters.

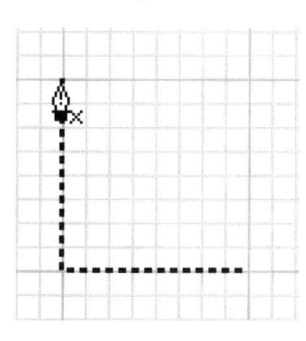

Figure 3.22 The Pen tool cursor is often modified by an additional figure to the right to let you know what action the Pen will initiate next. Here, the X in the cursor indicates that the Pen is ready to start a new path.

6. Trace the *L* by clicking first at the top, next at the left bottom, and last at the right bottom. Three clicks and you have drawn a path that looks like an *L*.
7. To finish the letter so that you can move on to another without continuing this path, click on the **Pen** tool button in the Toolbox or hold down the **Command/Ctrl** key (which toggles to the selection pointer) and click away from the path.

58 CHAPTER 3

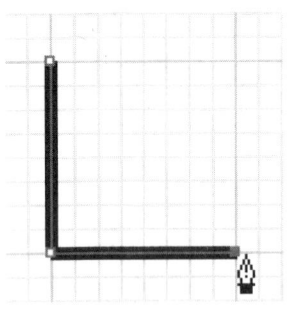

Figure 3.23 After tracing over the L with the Pen tool, you should have a path like this one, composed of three anchor points. You'll notice that the last drawn anchor point is solid and the other two are hollow.

Repeat Steps 6 and 7 for the *M*, *N*, *V*, *W*, and *Z*.. The remaining letters require multiple paths. For example, for the *A*, first make the path for the inverted *V*, and then hold down the **Command/Ctrl** key and click away from the path. Then draw the crossbar for the *A* and finish by **Command/Ctrl** clicking again.

Now you can complete the rest of the straight-line alphabet by clicking with the Pen tool, toggling to the Selection arrow to end the path, and finishing with the Pen tool again. You may save your traced alphabet if you wish.

ALPHABET LESSON, PART 2

Open the file ALPHA2.AI in the LESSON03 folder on the CD. This contains all the letters of the alphabet with curves. Instead of using only the Pen tool, this time you'll try some of the other tools.

1. Choose the **Ellipse** tool (n).

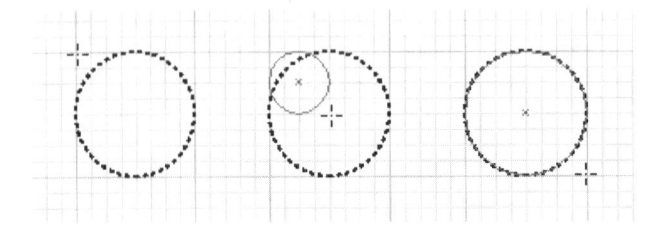

Figure 3.24 Draw a circle with the Ellipse tool. Start in any corner, drag through the center, and finish at the opposite corner.

2. Move the cursor to the upper-left corner of the *O*. Click and drag to the lower-right corner to trace the shape of the *O*.

  If this is the first time you've used the Ellipse tool, you probably missed the target by a bit. You have to imagine the rectangle around the object being traced and use it as a guide when you click and drag. The grid actually makes the circumscribing rectangle more evident as you'll see even more clearly if you try tracing the *D* with the Ellipse tool.

Also try tracing the O using the Centered Ellipse tool. Click in the center and drag a radius of the circle.

In either case, we could also hold down the **Shift** key while dragging to constrain the shape to a perfect circle. However, because Snap To Grid is turned on, it's pretty easy to get a circle without the Shift key.

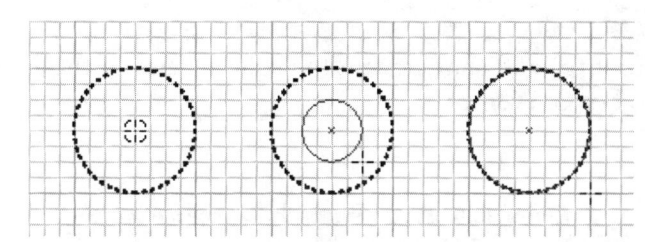

Figure 3.25 *Draw a circle with the Centered Ellipse tool: start at the center, drag in any direction, and finish at the corner.*

3. If you didn't already draw a circle over the *D*, do so now using the Ellipse tool.

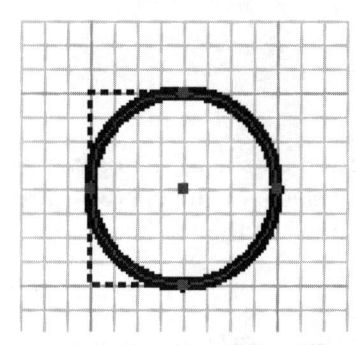

Figure 3.26 *An ellipse drawn over the D in the template shows that the bowl of the letter is a perfect circle.*

4. Choose the **Rectangle** tool (m) and draw a square over the *D*.

You'll notice that the *D* is half circle, half square. We could pick off pieces of the shapes we drew and delete them, but there's a more direct way to trace the *D*. Choose the **Selection** tool (v), click on the square and circle you just drew, and delete them by pressing the **Delete/Backspace** key.

60 CHAPTER 3

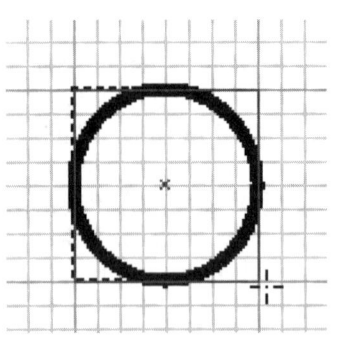

Figure 3.27 Adding a square over the circle covers all of the D in the template, but leaves some extra lines that have to be selected and deleted.

5. Choose the **Pen** tool (p) and start tracing the square parts of the *D* from top center to bottom center.

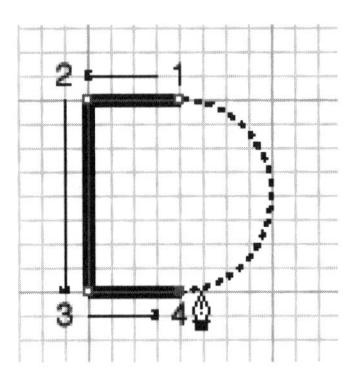

Figure 3.28 It takes four clicks to trace the straight portion of this D.

6. To trace the curved part of the *D*, move the cursor to the center of the curve, click and drag upward until the shape of the curve you're dragging matches the bottom half of the bowl of the D.

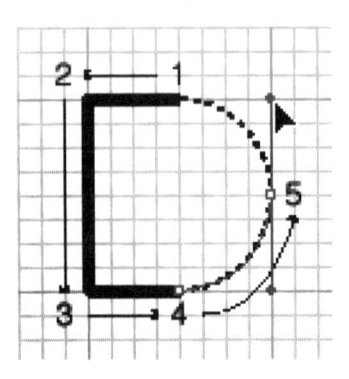

Figure 3.29 Changing from straight segments to curved segments is a simple matter of clicking and dragging. Here, clicking in the middle of the bowl of the D and dragging upward starts the curve.

Object Creation: Drawing and Text Tools 61

7. Close the path by clicking at the starting point. Illustrator completes the curve.

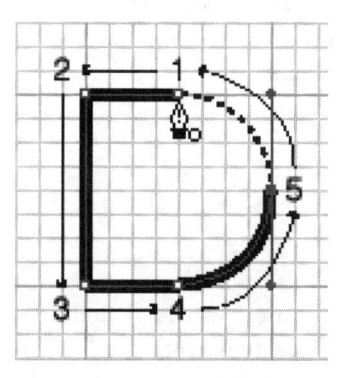

Figure 3.30 *The D is closed by clicking again at the starting point. The curve is continued from the previous drag, and a corner point is made to finish the letter.*

8. Try tracing the *C* using the same method. Start at the upper right. Click to set the first two anchor points for the straight line segment. Click and drag the third anchor point to start the curve. The fourth click finishes the curve, and the fifth click finishes the *C*.

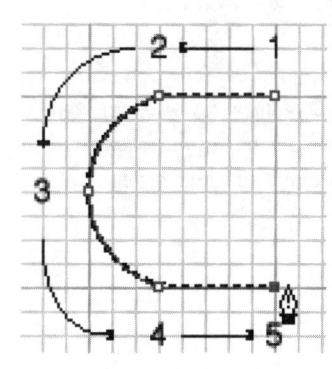

Figure 3.31 *Tracing the C requires 5 anchor points, only one of which, point 3, is a click and drag.*

Continue tracing the rest of the letters, except the *B*. The *J*, *R*, and *Q* require two separate paths. The *S* is the only letter that requires four drags.

9. The *B* requires slightly different treatment. Choose the **Pencil** tool (y) and try tracing over the *B* freehand. The results are pretty close, but that's because the Lock To Grid option is turned on. Try tracing again with this option toggled off. (You can delete these tracings either by choosing **Edit:Undo Typing**, or by using the **Delete/Backspace** key.)

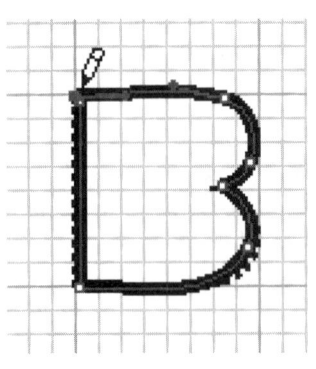

Figure 3.32 Tracing the B with the Pencil tool yields reasonable results when the Lock To Grid option is turned on, but it is not good enough in this case.

10. Choose the **Paintbrush** tool (y) and try tracing over the *B* again. (If you have a pressure-sensitive drawing pen, you may want to double-click on the Paintbrush tool button and try experimenting with the options.) The Lock to Grid option doesn't seem to affect the Paintbrush tool. The results are again interesting but even less accurate than with the Pencil tool. (Delete this tracing, too.)

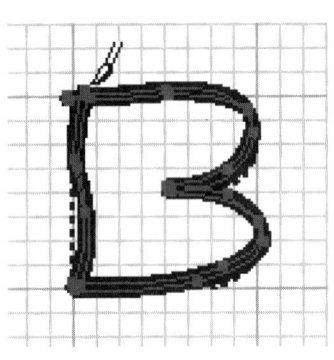

Figure 3.33 This is a tracing of the B made with the Paintbrush tool. The variable thickness resulting from the use of a pressure-sensitive pen makes the letter more calligraphic, but that is not the effect we are trying to achieve with this font.

11. Choose the **Pen** tool again and start tracing the *B*. Do all of the straight segments first. Follow the steps shown in Figure 3.17 until you get to anchor point 6.

Object Creation: Drawing and Text Tools 63

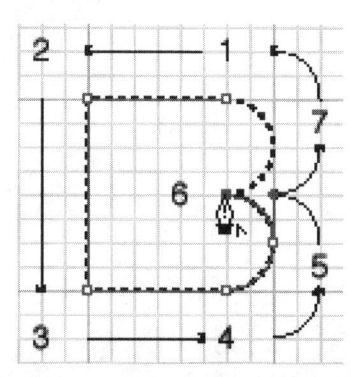

Figure 3.34 After clicking to set anchor point 6, hold down the **Option/Alt** key and click in the same spot again. (A small arrowhead appears next to the cursor to indicate that clicking here will convert the anchor point.) This converts the smooth point to a corner point.

12. Click to set anchor point 6, hold down the **Option/Alt** key, and click again at point 6 to convert the smooth point into a corner point. Now you can continue by clicking and dragging at point 7 and clicking again at point 1 to close the path.

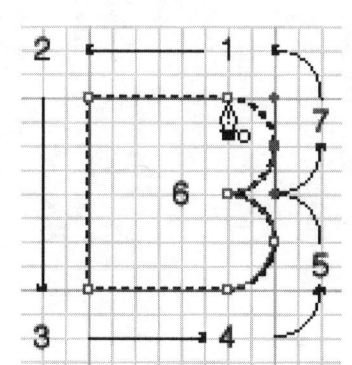

Figure 3.35 When you come around to anchor point 1 again, a small circle appears next to the cursor to indicate that clicking here will close the path.

You may save your work if you wish.

4

Selection and Manipulation

In this chapter...

- Selection—general, direct, and group
- Manipulation—move, copy, delete
- Special text selection considerations
- Lesson 4: Penguin Selection

We discussed image creation tools in Chapter 3—these are the tools you'll use for every line and shape you draw. But the value of these tools is negligible without the ability to refine, redraw, and adjust as you work. That's what this chapter is about—the tools used to select and modify the elements of your image.

All drawing programs require you to make a selection before you can edit or manipulate it. As mentioned in Chapter 3, as you draw paths and objects, the anchor points and segments remain highlighted or selected. These selection highlights mark the portions of the image that are available for editing. The processes of selecting, expanding or limiting selections, and deselecting are crucial to image creation.

The process of selection requires either clicking on an anchor point, segment, or object area with one of the selection tools or dragging over an area of an image to select several elements simultaneously. The latter method uses a temporary "marquee" as visual feedback so that you can see the area you're dragging over. All paths, objects, and groups within the marquee are selected.

Selection tools generally select what you click on and deselect everything else. However, you can extend any selection by holding down the **Shift** key while you make the selection. This adds the current selection to any previously selected items and leaves all items highlighted. You can mix any selection method or tool when extending selections with the **Shift** key.

If you **Shift-click** on a selected item, it is deselected without deselecting other selected items that may be highlighted.

SELECTION—GENERAL, DIRECT, AND GROUP

Illustrator provides three selection tools and numerous tool shortcuts. The three are distinguished by different cursors. The most general tool is called the Selection tool (v). The importance of this tool is evident from its primary location in the Toolbox.

Use the Selection tool to select entire paths, objects, or groups. Illustrator indicates current selections by highlighting the path and all anchor points within the path. When an entire path is selected, all of the anchor points have solid highlights. It's also possible to select single or multiple anchor points or segments using the Direct Selection tool. When only a segment is selected, all of the anchor points have hollow highlights. When a curved segment is selected, the direction lines of the adjoining anchor points are also highlighted.

Selection and Manipulation   67

When single or multiple anchor points are selected, the selected anchor points are solid, and other anchor points on the path have hollow highlights.

> **NOTE** Holding down the **Command/Ctrl** key while any tool is active temporarily toggles to the last chosen selection tool.

With Area Selection (the default) turned on, clicking anywhere within a filled object selects the entire object or group as seen in Figure 4.1.

Figure 4.1 Clicking on the cream-colored fill of the envelope's flap selects the envelope object and its grouped drop shadow. (The screen shots for this chapter are from an illustration by Nancy Stahl.)

To Make a Selection Using the Selection Tool

1. Choose the **Selection** tool (v).
2. Click on the path, segment, object, or group you wish to select or drag over an area of your illustration to select every path, object, or group within the selection marquee. (If the Area Select option is not checked in the General Preferences (see Chapter 19), you must click on a point or segment to select objects.)

The Selection tool selects entire entities only. Every segment is highlighted and every anchor point has a solid highlight. Direction lines are not selected. To select direction lines or portions of an object, use the Direct Selection tool.

To Select Single Segments or Anchor Points.

1. Choose the **Direct Selection** tool (a)—the hollow arrow.
2. Click on a segment or anchor point. The entire path or object is highlighted, but only the clicked elements are actually selected. In other words, anchor points with hollow highlights are not selected but are highlighted to show the extent of the path that is partially selected (see Figure 4.2). Direction lines for selected curved segments are also highlighted. If you drag to make your direct selection, selected anchor points have solid highlights, and the direction lines of selected curves are highlighted.

NOTE Direct selection entirely ignores any groups you have defined. (Grouped objects are discussed in Chapter 12.)

Figure 4.2 Using the Direct Selection tool, only the single anchor point is selected.

To Select Objects within a Group

1. Choose the **Group Selection** tool (a)—the hollow arrow with a plus sign.
2. Make selections just as you would using the Selection tool described earlier. The difference is that while the Selection tool selects grouped

Selection and Manipulation

objects, the Group Selection tool ignores any groups defined within your illustration as shown in Figure 4.3. (This tool seems misnamed to me. *Ungrouped* tool would be more descriptive.)

3. Clicking again with the Group selection tool adds grouped objects to the selection, effectively expanding the selection.

> **NOTE** Holding down the **Option/Alt** key temporarily toggles between the Direct and Group Selection tools.

Figure 4.3 *On the left, clicking with the Selection tool (v) selects all the grouped objects that make up the seal, while, on the right, clicking with the Group Selection tool (a) selects a single object regardless of grouping.*

MANIPULATION—MOVE, COPY, DELETE

Paths must be selected before you can do anything to them, including editing and manipulating. Editing paths involves the adjustment of anchor points or direction lines; this was discussed in Chapter 3. Here we'll discuss the larger issue of moving paths around.

To Move a Path, Object, or Group Using Selection Tools

1. Choose any selection tool or hold down the **Command/Ctrl** key.
2. Move the cursor over a path, anchor point, or area, hold down the mouse button, and drag the selection from its current position to a new one as shown in Figure 4.4. Hold down the **Shift** key to constrain the move to multiples of 45°. The item remains selected.
   - If you use the Selection tool (v), the entire path, object, or group will be moved.

- If you use the Group Selection tool (a), the entire path or object will be moved, but groups will be ignored.
- If you use the Direct Selection tool (a), only the segment or anchor point you click on will move, and the path will be adjusted accordingly.

NOTE If there is already an active selection, clicking and dragging with any selection tool will move all paths within that selection as described earlier. Also, double-clicking on the Selection tool opens the Move dialog box (see Chapter 9).

Figure 4.4 Moving an object group with the Selection tool (v). Notice that a "ghost" of the image follows the cursor to give you a preview of the move. The actual selection doesn't move until you release the mouse button.

To Copy a Path, Object, or Group Using Selection Tools

- Follow the preceding instructions to move a path, but hold down the **Option/Alt** key while you're dragging as shown in Figure 4.5. The only difference between this screen shot and Figure 4.4 is the double selection arrowhead, one solid and the other hollow. Release the key after you release the mouse button, and the selection will be copied to the new location.

NOTE This copying technique (Option/Alt-drag) also works if you use the **Command/Ctrl** key to toggle to a selection tool.

Figure 4.5 *The hollow arrowhead indicates that the Option/Alt key is being held down to make a copy of the selection.*

To Delete a Path, Object, or Group Using Selection Tools

1. Use any of the methods described earlier to make a selection.
2. Press the **Delete/Backspace** key or choose **Edit: Cut** (**Command/Ctrl-x**) or **Edit: Clear**. Cutting deletes the selection and makes a copy on the Clipboard. Clear simply deletes the selection.

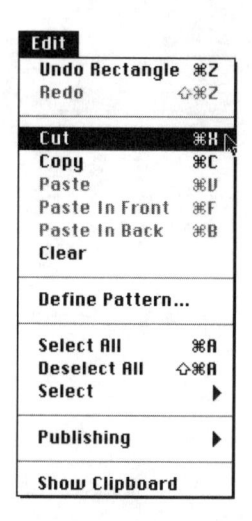

Figure 4.6 *Choosing **Edit: Cut** deletes the selection from the drawing and places it on the Clipboard.*

SPECIAL TEXT SELECTION CONSIDERATIONS

As described in Chapter 3, blocks of text are treated like any other object in Illustrator. The selection tools behave the same way with text objects.

Clicking on a text object selects its path and anchor point(s). The difference is that text objects either have a single anchor point or the anchor points of the path or object they are bound to. The text itself can only be selected using the Text tool.

With a single anchor point text object, you can move, copy, or delete the anchor point, and the text will be moved, copied, or deleted. If there is a path, you can select and adjust the anchor points as you would for any path or object. In this way, you can adjust a text path or reshape area type even after text is bound to it. The text automatically reflows as you make adjustments.

LESSON 4

Penguin Selection

For this lesson, open the file PENGUIN.AI from the LESSON04 folder on the CD. It is a simple line drawing of a king penguin that we will examine here and work with again in a later lesson to render the colors.

1. Choose the **Selection** tool (v) and click on the penguin. (You must click on one of the lines because there are no fills defined for area selection.)

    You'll notice that a single click has selected all the lines of this penguin (see Figure 4.7), and all of the anchor points are solid squares. (This penguin illustration is actually several paths grouped together for easy selection.)

Figure 4.7 *Clicking on an object with the Selection tool highlights the entire object and its anchor points.*

2. Click and drag the penguin around with the selection cursor. (Clicking off the line deselects everything, so once again, you must click on one of the lines.)

    The selection moves around the page as you drag, but the original lines stay put as shown in Figure 4.8. When you release the mouse button, the original moves to the new location and remains selected. You can move the selection anywhere, but you can't edit any of the lines or anchor points.

Figure 4.8 *The Selection tool can be used to drag any object, moving it to a new location without changing its shape.*

Selection and Manipulation 75

3. Hold down the **Option/Alt** key, then click and drag again.

   The same thing happens as in Step 2, except the cursor is now a double-headed pointer, one solid and one hollow (see Figure 4.9). This is the *copy cursor*. When you release the mouse button, a copy of the selection is made at the location you drag to, and it remains selected.

> **NOTE** You can press down (or release) the **Option/Alt** key at any time during a move operation. To assure that a copy is made, make sure you release the **Option/Alt** key *after* you release the mouse button.

*Figure 4.9 Holding down the **Option/Alt** key while moving a selection makes a copy. Note the two-headed copy cursor.*

Delete the copy you just made by pressing the **Delete/Backspace** key. You should be left with a single penguin and no active selections.

4. Choose the **Direct Selection** tool (a) and click on the belly line of the penguin. You have selected a single segment of one of the paths that make up this illustration. The two direction lines for this segment, one at each anchor point, are selected, while the entire path and its anchor points are highlighted. The Direct Selection tool ignores grouping (see Figure 4.10).

76 CHAPTER 4

Figure 4.10 A direct selection selects only a single segment and its direction lines, ignoring groupings.

5. Now click and drag on the same segment to move it. This lets you move a segment only so far, and it works better for small adjustments than for wholesale redrawing. Notice how the direction lines change as you move the line as shown in Figure 4.11. Try dragging one of the direction lines to adjust the curve. You can see that this gives you a different kind of control and lets you weight the adjustment of a curve to one side or the other.

Figure 4.11 You can adjust a single segment of a path by dragging with the Direct Select tool, but you can't move it far, because although the direction lines are adjusted, the anchor points remain fixed.

When you have finished experimenting, you may need to choose **File: Revert** to return the penguin to its pristine state.

6. With the Direct Selection tool (a) still active, click on an anchor point. You may have to click on a segment of a path first to show the anchor points and then click directly on the point.

    The anchor point highlights change from hollow to solid when selected, and the direction lines are also selected. Try dragging the anchor point around. Unlike the path segment we moved in Step 5, you can move an anchor point anywhere, and the attached segments will follow as shown in Figure 4.12. You can also adjust the direction lines just as you would if a segment were selected.

    You might be wondering if it's possible to copy a segment or anchor point by holding down the **Option/Alt** key. Perish the thought.

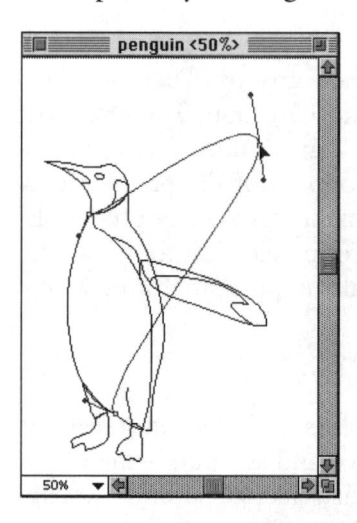

Figure 4.12 Moving a single anchor point.

7. Hold down the **Option/Alt** key. The Direct Selection cursor turns into the Group Selection cursor, indicated by a small plus sign.

    Try moving a segment or anchor point with the Group Selection tool (a). You can't do it, because the entire path moves. The Group Selection tool behaves just like the vanilla Selection tool, but it ignores grouping so that you can get at single paths within a group (see Figure 4.13).

78   **CHAPTER 4**

Figure 4.13 Moving with the Group Selection tool. The entire penguin is grouped, but this grouping is ignored when clicking with the Group Selection tool. Clicking gain with the Group selection tool would add the grouped objects to the selection.

It's time to digress a moment to explain groups. There are two commands in the Object menu, Group and Ungroup. The first links together any selected paths so that they can be moved and edited together. This command was used to group all of the paths in this penguin illustration. The Ungroup command breaks any previously defined link for a selected group. The Group Selection tool lets you make ungrouped selections without actually ungrouping or breaking the links.

8. If the Direct Selection tool (a) isn't active, choose it now and drag over the head of the penguin.

Dragging with any of the selection tools is indicated on screen by a selection marquee that follows the cursor and surrounds the selection range. Everything within the range is selected—every segment and anchor point as shown in Figure 4.14. Paths of the selected items are highlighted.

Figure 4.14 *Selecting the penguin's entire head with the Direct Selection tool.*

We haven't actually done anything to this penguin, but we now have the ability to select any part, make modifications or add color, which we'll do in Lesson 6.

5 Transformation Tools

In this chapter...

- Not so radical transformation
- Basic transformations—rotate, scale, reflect, and shear
- Transformations of a different color—twirl and reshape
- Lesson 5: I Could Have Transformed All Night

Not-So-Radical Transformation

It probably goes against the grain of many people who use it, but Illustrator is firmly based in classical geometry: angles, congruency, complements, and all the properties of Euclidean geometry that made ninth-grade math so much fun. Ninth grade may have been a horror, but using Illustrator's geometrical transformation tools is a delight.

The transformation tools—Rotate, Scale, Reflect, and Shear—have held a key place in Illustrator's Toolbox for a long time. Illustrator 7 has not changed these tools or how they work, but the way they are used has been streamlined. Instead of requiring you to click to define the source point for a transformation, Illustrator 7 automatically defines the source at the chosen object's center. This is very convenient, and it also lets you change the origin as needed without adding any extra steps.

Transforming has become even easier and more precise with the addition of the Transform submenu (discussed in Chapter 12) and a Transform palette (discussed in Chapter 9). But in this chapter we'll stick to the basics.

There are four other transformation tools. The Twirl tool, which is hidden under the Rotate button and works much like the Rotate tool, is used to twirl shapes around a fixed point. There is also a similar Twirl filter. (Filters are discussed in Chapter 14.)

The Reshape tool is new and lies under the Scale button. It doesn't work quite like the other transformation tools and is actually more similar to the selection tools. It can be used for subtly reshaping and smoothing paths while still retaining some semblance of their original form.

NOTE   While the four basic transformation tools can be used with text objects, the two hidden transformation tools, Twirl and Reshape, have no effect on them. You must convert text to paths to transform it with these tools.

Basic Transformations—Rotate, Scale, Reflect, and Shear

The four basic transformation tools—Rotate, Scale, Reflect, and Shear(shown in Figure 5.1)—all work identically. The final effect of each one is different, but the method of using them is the same. The tools even share the same source point.

Transformation Tools

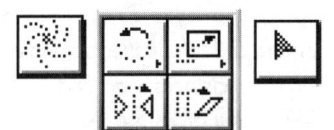

Figure 5.1 *The four basic transformation tools sit as a group in the Toolbox and hide two additional transformation tools.*

To Transform Objects Interactively

1. Make a selection in your illustration.
2. Choose one of the transform tools: Rotate (r), Scale (s), Reflect (o), or Shear (w). Illustrator automatically sets the source point for the transformation at the center of the selection.
3. Click anywhere to move the source point, or skip this step to use the centered source point.
4. Click away from the source point and drag. As you drag around the source point, the transformation is adjusted interactively. If you are using Rotate or Reflect, it doesn't matter how far from the source point you drag, but the effects of Scale and Shear increase in magnitude the farther from the source you drag.

NOTE Hold down the **Shift** key to constrain transformations to multiples of 45°.

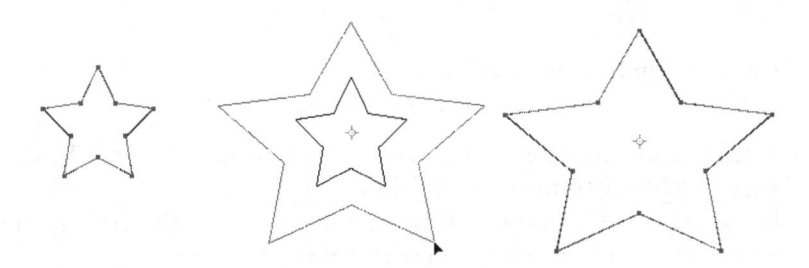

Figure 5.2 *Drag on an object with the Scale tool to change its size. (Note the default source point at the center of the star.)*

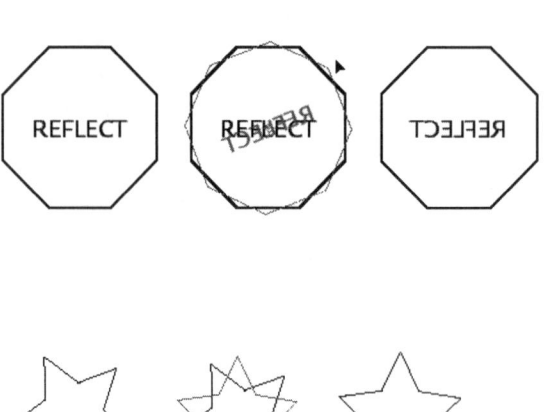

Figure 5.3 The Reflect tool mirrors objects across an axis. When you drag, the axis rotates and the mirrored object with it.

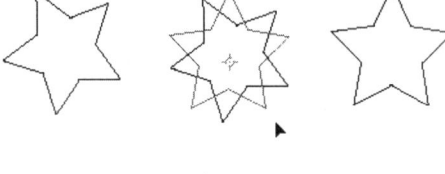

Figure 5.4 Drag on an object with the Rotate tool to spin it around the source point.

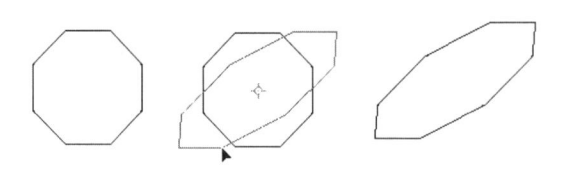

Figure 5.5 The Shear tool scales with respect to an axis and rotates at the same time. In this example, it's like squeezing the object flat so that it bulges at the sides.

To Specify Exact Transformations

1. Make a selection in your illustration.
2. There are three ways to open the transformation dialog boxes:
   - Double-click on one of the transform tools: Rotate, Scale, Reflect, or Shear to bring up a dialog.
   - Choose one of the transform tools and **Option/Alt**-click in the drawing to reset the source point and open a dialog.
   - Choose one of the transform commands from the Object: Transform submenu. (The Object menu is discussed in Chapter 12.)

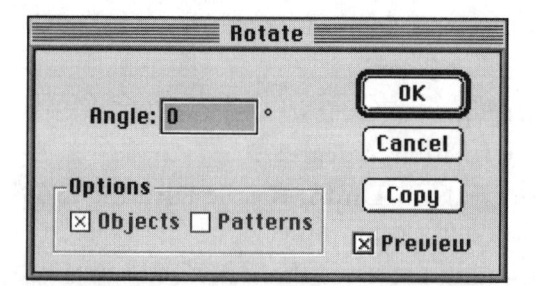

Figure 5.6 The Rotate, Reflect, Scale, and Shear dialogs can be used to specify exact transformations as opposed to the interactive transformations available using the tools alone.

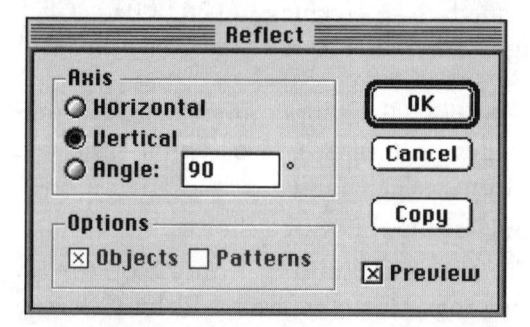

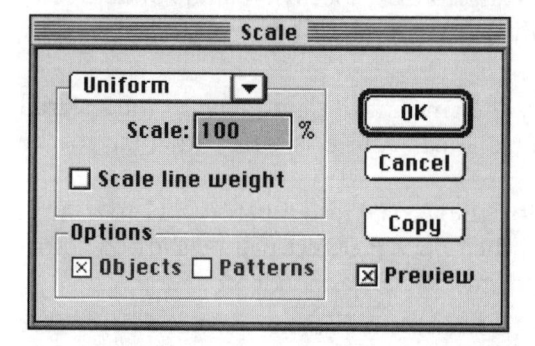

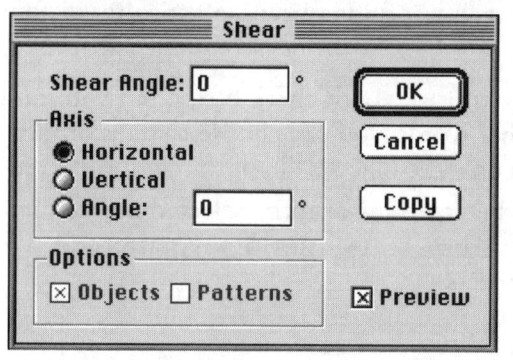

3. Fill in your specifications in the dialog. All angles must be in the range of ±360°.
   - **Rotate**—There is one setting.

     Angle: Set the angle of rotation in degrees.
   - **Scale**—Choose **Uniform** or **Non-Uniform** scale from the drop-down box and then make your specifications.

     Uniform—Uniform scaling preserves the aspect ratio of width and height and is specified as a percentage (±20,000%). Click on the **Scale line weight** check box to scale stroke widths with the object.

     Non-Uniform—Specify the Horizontal and Vertical scaling individually as percentages (±20,000%). You cannot scale line weight with a non-uniform scale.
   - **Reflect**—There is only one setting, but three choices.

     Axis— Choose one of the Axis radio buttons: Horizontal, Vertical, or Angle, and the selected object will be reflected across this axis. For an angled axis, specify an angle in degrees.
   - **Shear**—You must specify an Axis and a Shear Angle to calculate shear.

     Shear Angle—Specify the amount of slant given to the sheared object in degrees. The Shear Angle is perpendicular to the angle of reflection.

     Axis—Choose one of the Axis radio buttons: Horizontal, Vertical, or Angle and the selected object will be sheared across this axis. For an angled axis, specify an angle in degrees.
4. If the selection you wish to transform has any patterned fills (see Chapter 10), the two check box options become active in all four dialogs.
   - **Options**—You can select either or both check boxes, but you must select at least one. In other words, you can choose to transform the object only, to transform only the object's fill, or to transform both.

     Objects—Check this box to transform the selected objects.

     Patterns—Check this box to transform any patterned fills within the selected objects.

5. Click the **Preview** check box to see the effect of your specifications without dismissing the dialog. Use the **Tab** key after entering a specification to update the preview.

> **NOTE:** Setting the Preview and Options check boxes in one dialog sets them in all four of the Transform dialoges, so the next time you open a Transform dialog the previous check box settings remain.

6. There are three buttons that dismiss the dialog and either enact the specifications, cancel them, or create a copy.

    - OK—Click to enact the transformation as specified in the dialog. This is the default.
    - Cancel—Click to ignore the specifications in the dialog and leave the selection unchanged.
    - Copy—Click to make a transformed copy of the original selection. The copy remains selected.

Transformations of a Different Color—Twirl and Reshape

As mentioned earlier, the Twirl and Reshape tools are less like the classic transformation tools and more like special effects tools. Twirl used to be a plug-in tool, but Illustrator 7 has eliminated the plug-ins palette.

To Twirl a Selection Interactively

1. Make a selection.
2. Choose the hidden **Twirl** tool.
3. Click and drag using a circular motion around the selection in either direction. The object is twirled around its outermost points as you drag, the center twirling most.
4. Release the mouse button when you've achieved a pleasing twirl. Figure 5.7 shows the results.

Figure 5.7 Twirling a star results in a pleasing swirl.

To Specify a Twirl

1. Make a selection.
2. Choose the hidden **Twirl** tool.
3. Hold down the **Option/Alt** key and click in the illustration to set the twirling point.
4. In the dialog (shown in Figure 5.8), specify a degree of twirl (±3600°).
5. Click **OK** and the selection is twirled around the source point.

NOTE: The Twirl dialog is identical to the Twirl filter.

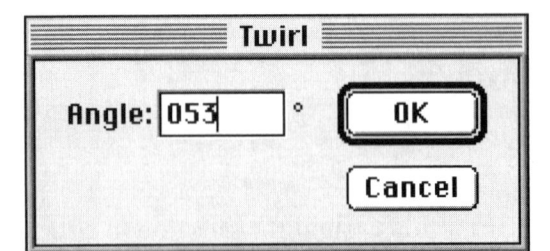

Figure 5.8 Enter the amount of twirl in degrees in the Twirl dialog.

To Reshape a Selection

1. Select only the anchor points of a path that you want to reshape. Unselected points within the same path will remain pinned to the artboard.

2. Choose the hidden **Reshape** tool (s).
3. Click, **Shift**-click, or drag to doubly select points. Clicking on a segment creates a new anchor point and doubly selects it. These points have an extra highlight and are the focal point for reshaping. You can add or remove focal points by **Shift**-clicking. If there are multiple focal points, they will retain their relationships to one another as you drag.
4. Drag one of the doubly selected points to reshape the path. All singly selected points are adjusted as you drag the focal point(s), while unselected points in the path remain pinned. Figure 5.9 shows an example.

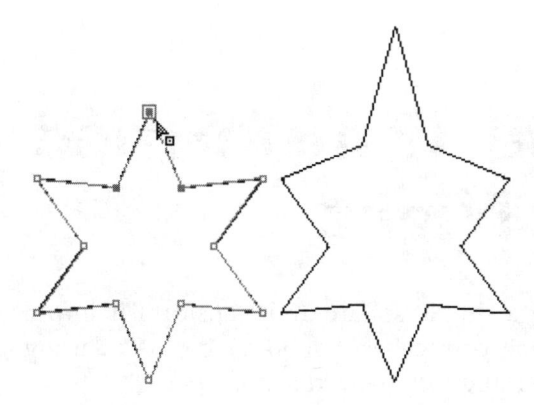

Figure 5.9 *The Reshape tool (s) can be used to drag anchor points, but it differs from the selection tools in that all other selected anchor points will also move, while unselected anchor points remain fixed*

LESSON 5

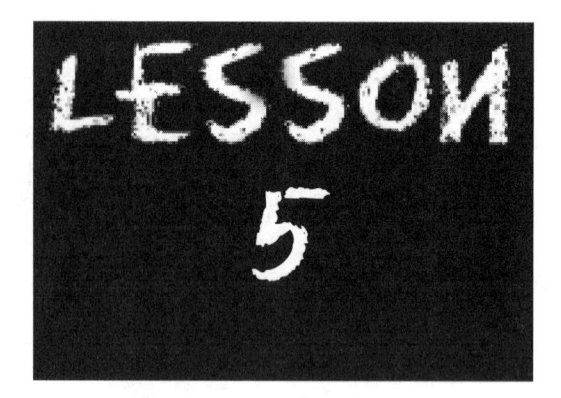

I Could Have Transformed All Night

In this lesson we will start with a simple square and transform it into a cube. This kind of exercise is one of the basic building blocks of using Illustrator effectively and has application in many kinds of work.

1. We will start this lesson with a blank slate, so choose the **File: New** command to open a new document. Click on the **Default** button (d) to set the stroke to black and fill to white, then click the **Swap Fill and Stroke** button to switch them, i.e. white stroke and black fill. See Figure 5.10.

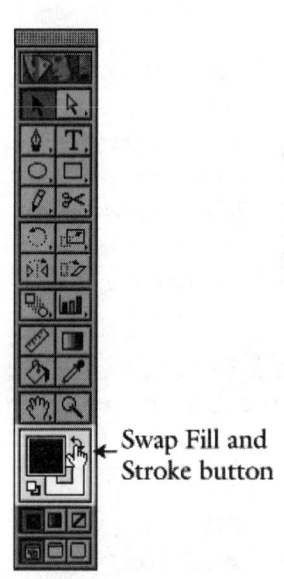

Figure 5.10 *Click on the **Swap Fill and Stroke** button to switch the stroke and fill colors. Here the defaults are being swapped, so that the stroke is white and the fill is black.*

Swap Fill and Stroke button

2. Choose the **Rectangle** tool, click anywhere in the middle of the artboard, and specify a square 2" × 2" in the Rectangle dialog shown in Figure 5.11. Click **OK** to dismiss the dialog and draw the black-filled rectangle.

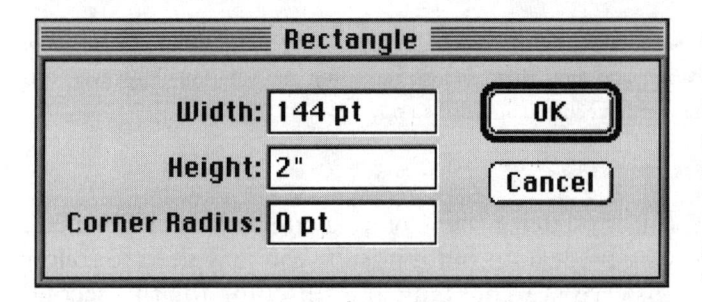

Figure 5.11 *You can enter an amount using any units in Illustrator's dialogs. The 2" amount entered here is automatically converted to 144 points when you tab to or click in the next field.*

3. Choose the **Rotate** tool, hold down the **Option/Alt** key, and click on the upper-left corner of the square to set the rotation point and bring up the Rotate dialog shown in Figure 5.12.

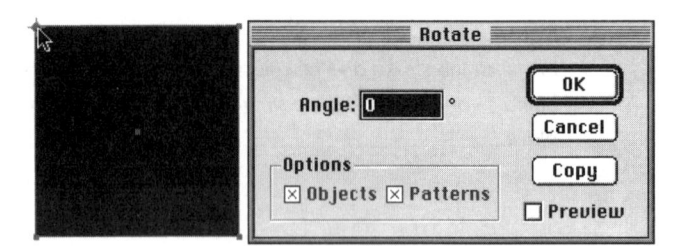

Figure 5.12 *Option/Alt-click on the upper-left corner of the square to set the rotation center point and bring up the Rotate dialog so that you can specify the exact rotation.*

4. Set the rotation to 90°, as shown in Figure 5.13. Then click the **Copy** button to dismiss the dialog and copy the first square on top of itself. The copied square is selected.

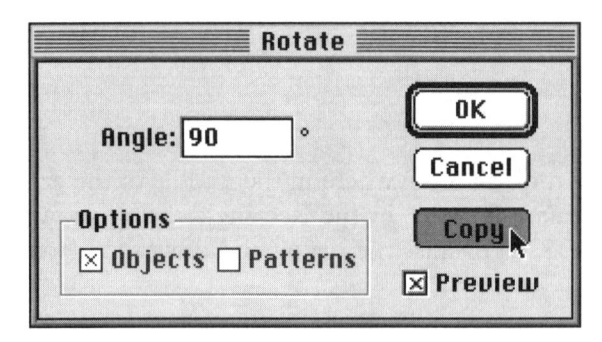

Figure 5.13 *When clicking* **Copy** *instead of* **OK** *in the Rotate dialog, the original selection is left unmodified and a copy is rotated. The copy remains selected.*

> **NOTE** If you check the Preview button before clicking **Copy**, you can see the results of your specification and alter them before executing the rotation. However, this previews a standard execution and not a copy.

5. Change the K (black) slider in the Color palette to 66%. This palette should be showing by default, but if it isn't, you may need to follow a few extra steps. We are changing the fill color for the second square, but we haven't talked about how to do this yet, so I'll be especially explicit about what to do next:
    - Make sure the Color palette is open. If it isn't, choose **Window: Show Color**.
    - Make sure that you are setting the Fill color and not the Stroke color. You can tell this by the color icon in the Color palette; solid for fill, perimeter line for stroke. If it's set for stroke, press the **x** key to toggle to fill or click on the **Fill** button in the Toolbox.

- Make sure that the Color palette is showing the CMYK sliders (see Figure 5.14). If it isn't, hold down the mouse over the right pointing arrow near the upper-right corner to open the palette options menu and slide the cursor to select CMYK.
- Either click in the specification box at the end of the K slider and type in **66** or drag the K slider until the value is 66%.

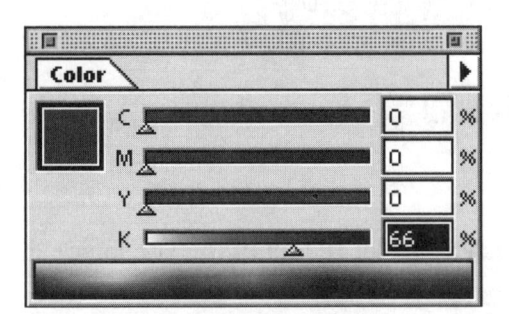

Figure 5.14 The Color palette. Note the CMYK sliders, which can be set independently to mix colors, and the solid icon, which indicates that you have set the fill color.

6. Choose the **Reflect** tool and **Option/Alt**-click anywhere along the right side of the second (gray) square to reset the reflection point and bring up the Reflect dialog. (We could have used the Rotate tool again, but it's nice to have the opportunity to use a different tool.)

*Figure 5.15 Option/Alt-click on the right side of the second gray square to set a new reflection point. Notice how the default reflection point is in the center of the selected square, also that the cursor has an ellipsis (three dots) attached to it to indicate that the **Option/Alt** key is engaged and a dialog will open upon clicking.*

7. In the Reflect dialog shown in Figure 5.16, click on the **Vertical** button to reflect across the vertical axis, then click the **Copy** button to dismiss the dialog and make a second copy of the square.

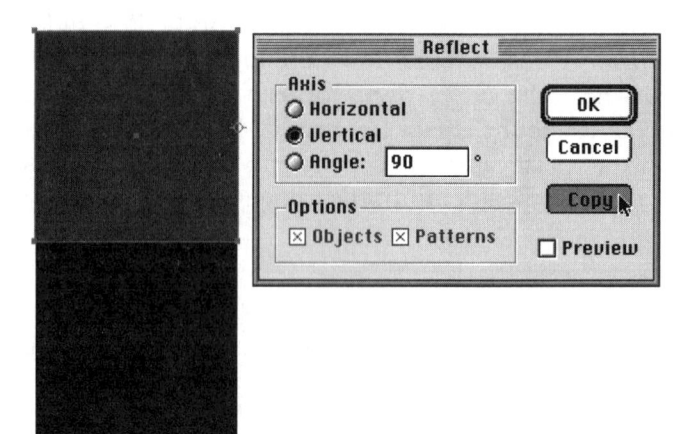

Figure 5.16 Make a reflected copy of the second square across the vertical axis.

8. As in Step 5, use the Color palette to set the fill of the last square to **33%**.

Figure 5.17 You should now have three squares with three shades of fill. The third square is selected, and all three share a single point of attachment.

9. Hold down the **Command/Ctrl-Shift** keys to toggle to the Selection tool and add to the current selection. Click on the second square. The two top squares should now be selected.

Transformation Tools 95

*Figure 5.18 After **Shift**-clicking with the Selection tool, the top two squares are selected. Note how the source point has automatically shifted to the center point of the combined selection.*

10. Choose the **Scale** tool and **Option/Alt**-click on the bottom line of the two selected squares.

*Figure 5.19 You can **Option/Alt**-click anywhere along the bottom line of the selection for this Scale operation.*

11. In the Scale dialog shown in Figure 5.20, choose **Non-Uniform** from the drop-down menu and specify a Vertical scale of **50%**. Leave the Horizontal scale at 100% and click **OK**.

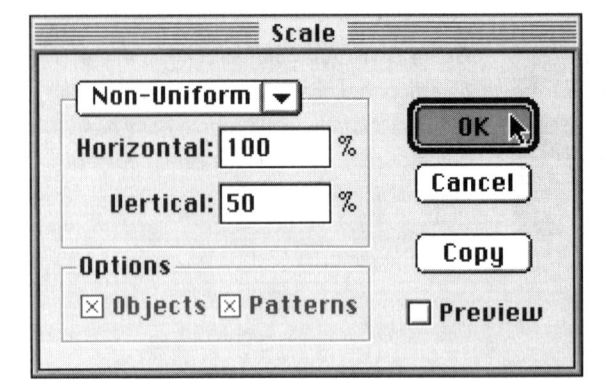

Figure 5.20 *A Non-Uniform scale specification allows us to maintain the horizontal dimension while foreshortening the vertical dimension so that it looks more realistic in perspective.*

12. Choose the **Shear** tool, then hold down the **Option/Alt** key and click on the bottom line of the selection again. (It would be nice if we could just double-click on the Shear tool to bring up the dialog, but the previous Scale operation set the source point back to the center.)

Figure 5.21 *Option/Alt-click to reset the source point back to the lower line after the previous Scale operation reset it to the center.*

13. In the Shear dialog, specify a Shear Angle of **45°** (see Figure 5.22) and leave the Horizontal radio button selected. Click **OK**.

Transformation Tools 97

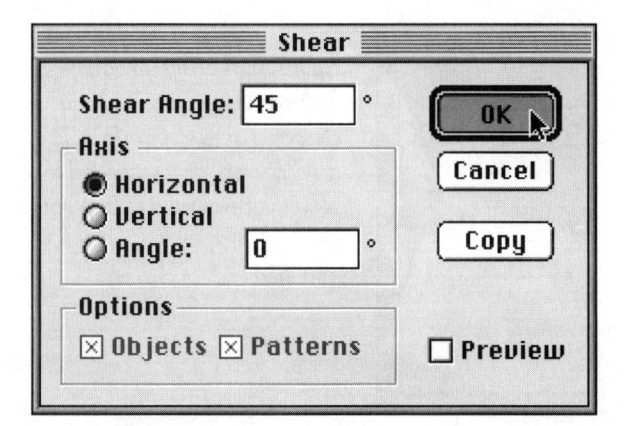

Figure 5.22 Specify a straightforward 45% shear along the horizontal axis.

14. Hold down the **Command/Ctrl-Shift** keys and click on the 66% gray parallelogram to deselect it. Only the 33% gray parallelogram should now be selected.

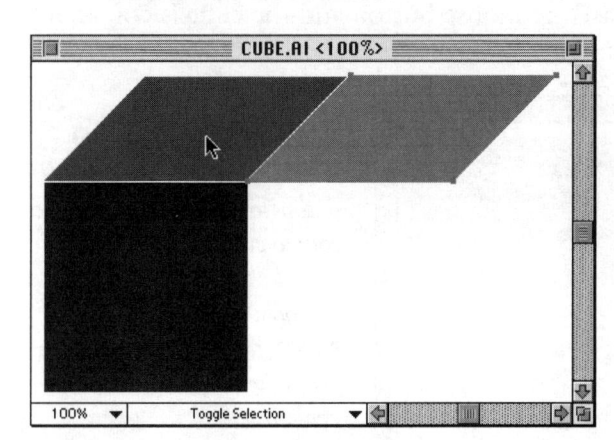

*Figure 5.23: **Shift**-clicking with the Selection tool will either add to the current selection, or, as is happening here, if you Shift-click on part of a selection, it is deselected. Notice how this is called **Toggle Selection** in the tool label along the bottom of the window.*

15. With the Shear tool still selected from Step 12, click in the lower-left corner of the selected parallelogram, this time without holding down any modifier keys. This resets the source point without opening a dialog.

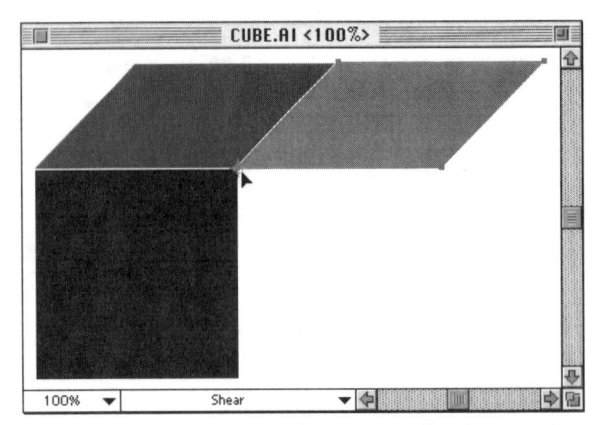

Figure 5.24 *With any of the four transform tools, you can click and drag to transform in a single step, or if you need to set an uncentered source point, you click first, as shown here, and then click and drag.*

16. Click and drag down on the lower-right corner until the cursor is lined up with the lower-right corner of the original black square. The cursor will turn hollow (or white) to indicate that the drag will snap to a point. Release the mouse button and the cube is complete. Save your cube if you wish.

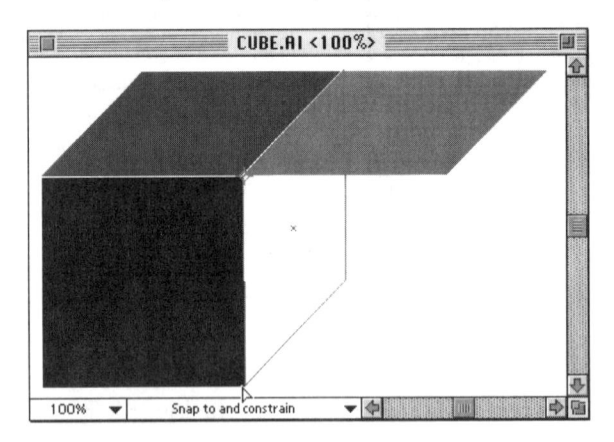

Figure 5.25 *Drag the right corner of the selected parallelogram to the right corner of the square until they meet. The cursor is hollow to indicate that two points will snap together. Notice that the tool label at the bottom of the window also confirms this.*

You can see a finished version of this lesson by opening the file CUBE.AI in the LESSON05 folder. If you'd like to play with transformation some more, open the file CYLINDER.AI and try to construct another cylinder just like it. You can do it with only a square and a circle of matching diameter. The gradient fill and drop shadow add an extra touch of realism.

6 Attributes: Applying Strokes and Fills

In this chapter…

- Paint attributes
- Stroke and fill from the Toolbox
- Gradient extents
- Copying attributes: Eyedropper and Paintbucket tools
- Measure tool
- Lesson 6: Penguin Patchwork

Paint Attributes

The Illustrator 7 *User Guide* includes a chapter devoted to painting. I find this confusing, because one thing Illustrator does not do is paint. You can achieve painterly effects, but not with typical painterly methods. This makes the use of a painting vocabulary inappropriate to Illustrator. Yet, we are stuck with Adobe's choice and will do our best not to strain the metaphor too much.

The objects you create with Illustrator's drawing tools have two distinct paint attributes—stroke and fill—which you use to edit and differentiate shapes. Every time you create a new path or object, the current settings for stroke and fill are applied to it. If you change the specification for stroke or fill, the selected paths and objects are updated. When there is no active selection, nothing is changed except the stroke and/or fill specifications, which are used the next time you create a path or object.

Strokes have color and width, but fill has only color. There are special strokes, such as dashed lines, and special fills, such as gradients and patterns, but there are really only two attributes for every path and object you draw. You can set an attribute to **None**, which effectively turns off the attribute, but it is still a part of the object.

Illustrator 7 includes a new Attributes palette, discussed in Chapter 11, but these attributes have nothing to do with the way color is applied to paths and objects, which is the subject of this chapter. While the primary stroke and fill tools are part of the Toolbox, the selection of colors, gradients, patterns, widths, and dashes is controlled from palettes discussed in Section III.

Stroke and Fill from the Toolbox

The largest division of the Toolbox includes the Stroke and Fill buttons along with the Default and Swap Fill and Stroke buttons. Just beneath this section are the Color, Gradient, and None buttons. The Stroke and Fill buttons have the unique property of changing to show the current color specification, so you can see the current stroke and fill colors by glancing at these buttons in the Toolbox.

Another unique property of these two buttons is the fact that they overlap slightly. One is always on top of the other. The button on top is active and will reflect any color choice changes you make in the Color or Gradient palettes. The default palette has the Fill button on top of the Stroke button, so if you pick a new color, it will change the fill without affecting the stroke. There are various ways to make one or the other active.

To Activate the Stroke or Fill Button to Edit Color Attributes

Click on either the **Stroke** or **Fill** button in the Toolbox. The **x** key toggles the active button. This is important when assigning colors, because only the active button can be edited. You have to toggle between the Stroke and Fill buttons to set the color for both. (There are a number of ways to assign attributes, and these are discussed in Chapter 10.)

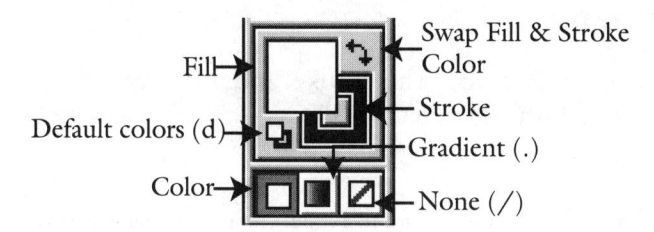

Figure 6.1 A diagram of the Toolbox highlighting the stroke and fill buttons area.

To Return to the Default Stroke and Fill Settings

Click on the **Default Fill and Stroke** button (d) in the stroke and fill area of the Toolbox. This returns the fill to white and the stroke to 1-point black.

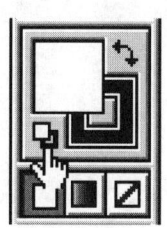

Figure 6.2 Clicking on the Default button to set the stroke and fill colors back to black and white, the default settings.

To Swap Stroke and Fill Colors

Click on the **Swap Fill and Stroke** button (the double-headed arrow) in the stroke and fill area of the Toolbox. This swaps the stroke and fill color attributes so that the fill color becomes the stroke color and vice versa.

NOTE The Swap Fill and Stroke button is the only button in the Toolbox without a shortcut key. Use the (x) shortcut key to exchange the active attribute, i.e., press the x key to make stroke active instead of fill and vice versa.

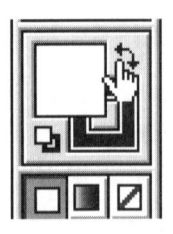

Figure 6.3 *Clicking on the Swap button to exchange the stroke and fill colors. This does not change the active button, only their colors.*

To Set Fill or Stroke to None

Click on the **None** button (/) below the stroke and fill area of the Toolbox. The active attribute button, Stroke or Fill, is set to none, which removes all attributes.

NOTE If both the stroke and fill attributes are set to **None**, the path remains part of the illustration, but it will not print.

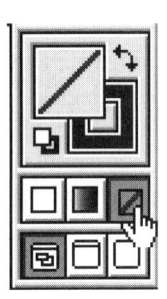

Figure 6.4 *Clicking on the None button (/) to assign the transparent attribute to the stroke or fill, whichever is active.*

To Use the Color and Gradient Buttons

- Click on the **Color** button(,) to assign the current color to the active attribute button (Fill or Stroke).
- Click on the **Gradient** button(.) to assign the current gradient to the Fill button.

NOTE If the Stroke button is active and you click on the Gradient button, it both assigns the current gradient to the Fill button and makes the Fill button active.

Both of these buttons refer to the current settings of palettes and should not be confused with any of the tools in the Toolbox. There is always a current color selection in the Color palette (shown in Figure 6.5) and a current gradient in the Gradient palette (see Chapter 10).

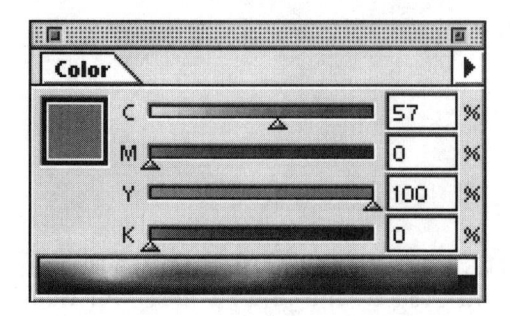

Figure 6.5 The Color palette, the place to mix colors, always displays the current color.

GRADIENT EXTENTS

Gradients are defined using the Gradient palette and assigned using the Color palette (as described in Chapter 10). You can also use the Gradient button in the Toolbox as a shortcut to assign the current gradient to the Fill button (as described earlier). There is also a Gradient tool that lets you define the extent or application of a gradient.

You don't need to use the Gradient tool to apply a gradient fill. Simply assigning a gradient as the current fill will apply that gradient to the current selection and to any objects you create while that fill attribute remains. A linear gradient will fill the object from left to right, while a radial gradient fill, the object from the center outward.

The Gradient tool allows you to set the starting and ending points for a gradient fill. Radial fills can be made asymmetrical, and linear fills can go in any direction: left to right, right to left, top to bottom, bottom to top, corner to corner, and so on.

To Apply a Gradient Fill to an Object Using the Gradient Tool

1. Make a selection to be filled.
2. Assign a gradient fill as the current fill either by clicking on the

Gradient button (.) or by choosing a gradient from the Color or Gradient palettes.

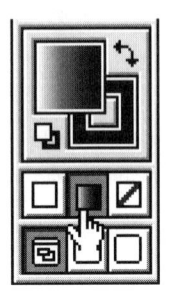

Figure 6.6 Clicking on the Gradient button to assign the most recent gradient as the fill attribute.

3. Choose the **Gradient** tool (g). Click in the illustration where you want the gradient to begin and drag to the point where you want the gradient to end. The gradient fills the active object(s) in the direction and to the extent you dragged.

NOTE: You needn't click within the active object(s). The extent of a gradient fill can go beyond the selection. Illustrator will fill the selection as though it were spreading the gradient over the full length you dragged, but it "paints" only within the selection.

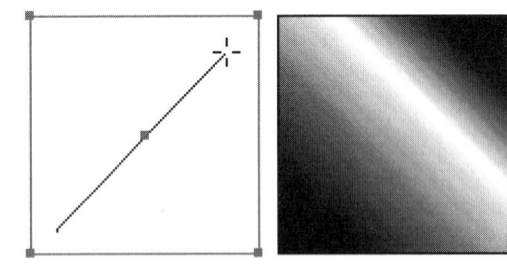

Figure 6.7 On the left, dragging across a shape with the Gradient tool to define the extent and direction of a gradient fill. On the right, the gradient applied.

COPYING ATTRIBUTES: EYEDROPPER AND PAINTBUCKET TOOLS

It's possible to copy paint attributes from one object to another just as you might copy and paste phrases into different paragraphs. The Eyedropper tool is Illustrator's sampler. Use it as an attribute copy command. Any item you touch with the Eyedropper is sampled and stored in an attributes buffer. In fact, you can use the Eyedropper to sample any color showing on your screen.

Attributes: Applying Strokes and Fills 105

Clicking on a path or object with the Paintbucket tool pastes any attributes that are stored in the attributes buffer onto that item. The item needn't be active when you click. Clicking with the Paintbucket tool pastes and activates at the same time.

To Sample with the Eyedropper Tool

1. Choose the **Eyedropper** tool (i).
2. You can sample attributes from anywhere on your display using one of the following methods:

   - Click on a path or object to sample all attributes. You can also click in any illustration window to sample attributes from another image without activating the window.
   - Click in the illustration window and drag to any place on your screen. Release the mouse button and the color at that point will be sampled. The color can come from any window or application, including your screen's background, but you must start dragging within an Illustrator window.

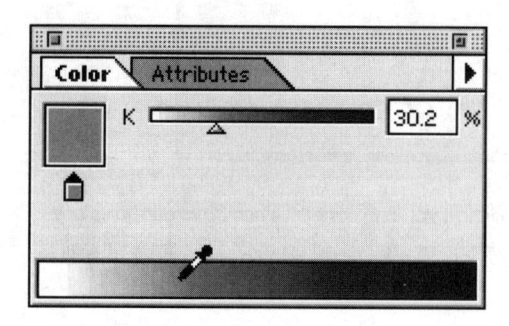

Figure 6.8 Sampling with the Eyedropper tool. Notice how the Eyedropper icon appears to "fill up" when you sample a color. You must click and drag from an artwork window to sample attributes from a palette window as shown here.

To Paste Attributes onto an Object

1. Sample the attributes you wish to paste using the Eyedropper tool as described earlier.
2. Choose the **Paintbucket** tool (k) and click on any object or path in the active window. The attributes are copied and the item is made active.

To Sample or Apply Attributes Selectively

1. Double-click on either the **Eyedropper** or **Paintbucket** tool button in the Toolbox. This opens the Paintbucket/Eyedropper dialog with checkboxes for all attributes of stroke and fill.
2. Click on any checkboxes you want to exclude or select. The default selects all attributes. You can select Eyedropper and Paintbucket attributes separately. For example, you may want to pick up the stroke attributes of a dashed path but apply the dash attribute without changing the color of another path.

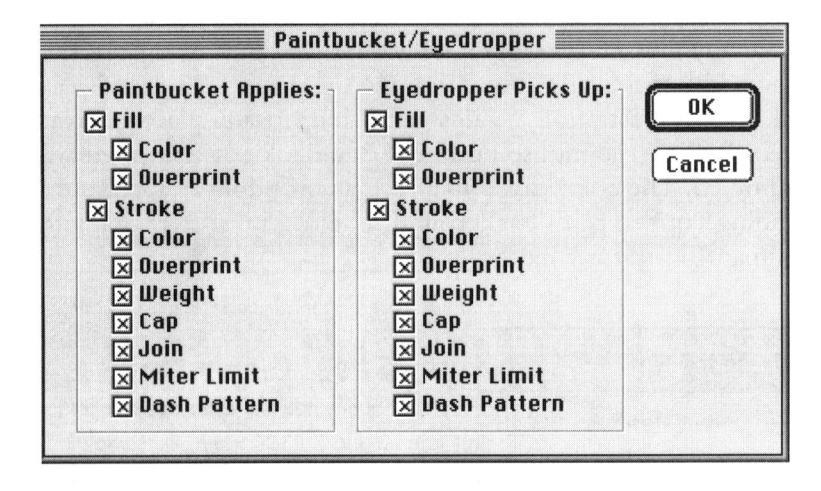

Figure 6.9 In the Paintbucket/Eyedropper dialog you can control which paint attributes are applied by the Paintbucket tool and which attributes are picked up by the Eyedropper tool.

To Toggle Between the Eyedropper and Paintbucket tools

1. Select either the **Eyedropper** (i) or **Paintbucket** (k) tool.
2. Hold down the **Option/Alt** key, the cursor toggles between Eyedropper and Paintbucket.

MEASURE TOOL

Illustrator's Measure tool is purely a feedback device. It does not create, edit, or manipulate objects in any way. Use it to find distances and angles and to calculate the length of blended fills so that you can avoid banding (see Chapter 8).

To Measure Between Two Points

1. Choose the tool **measure** (u).
2. Either click and drag or click once to define a starting point and click a second time to define the ending point. You can click anywhere in the work area; it needn't be on a path or object. The total distance, its vertical and horizontal components, and the angle are reported in the Info palette (see Chapter 9). To use the Measure tool you also need to open the Info palette to view the readouts.

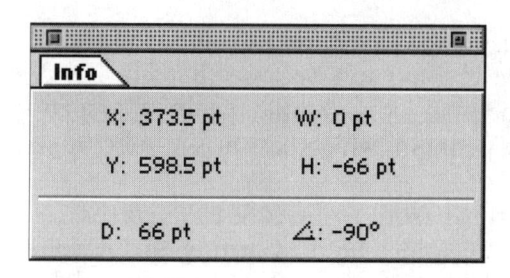

Figure 6.10 The Info palette showing feedback from the Measure tool.

LESSON 6

Penguin Patchwork

It's time to fill in the penguin we examined in Chapter 4. As we all know, penguins are frequently used in the graphic arts because they are pretty much black and white; this gives them an iconographic quality. Our penguin, however, happens to be a king penguin, which has splashes of orange on the head and neck.

I've altered the file slightly for this lesson, so be sure to open the file PENGUIN2.AI from the LESSON06 folder before starting this lesson. This file is the black silhouette of a king penguin. It has the paths of the penguin we used in Lesson 4, but all the paths have stroke and fill attributes of black. You'll see how much easier it is to select filled objects with area selection, as opposed to clicking directly on the stroked paths as we had to do in Lesson 4.

1. Choose the **Selection** tool (v) and click on the penguin. All the paths have been grouped and filled, so clicking anywhere selects everything.

Attributes: Applying Strokes and Fills 109

Figure 6.11 Click on this penguin silhouette with the Selection tool to select everything and reveal the paths and objects that make up this grouped image.

2. Click on the **Default** button (d) in the stroke and fill area of the Toolbox. This sets all paths to a black, 1-point stroke with a white fill. Our penguin is no longer a silhouette, but we need to find some middle ground here. Clicking on the Default Fill and Stroke button (d) in the Toolbox, as shown in Figure 6.12, sets the fill to white and the stroke to 1-point black lines. Because all the paths were selected before clicking, they all receive the new attribute assignment. (The pop-up label is showing in this screen shot.)

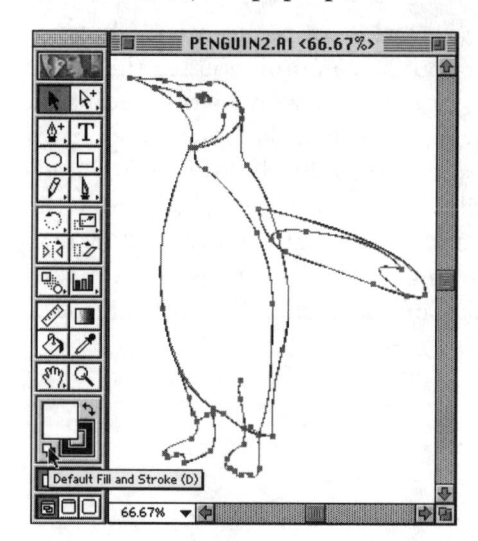

Figure 6.12 Assigning the default fill and stroke attributes sets all fills to white so we can see the black-stroked lines.

Before proceeding, check and make sure that the Fill button is on top of the Stroke button. If not, click on it or press the **x** key.

3. First deselect everything by clicking away from the penguin, then choose the **Group Selection** tool (a) hidden under the Direct Selection tool, and click on the penguin's back. This allows us to select individual objects without the extra step of ungrouping all paths.

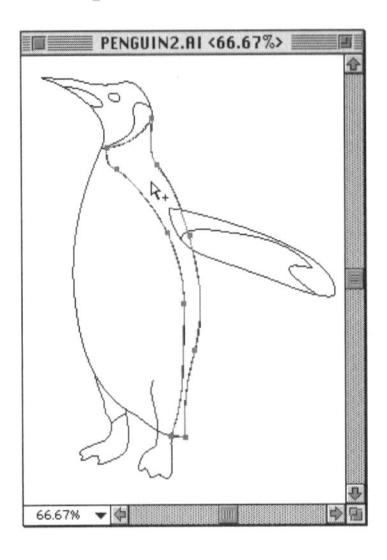

Figure 6.13 Click on the fill with the Group Selection tool to select this single object within a group

4. Choose the **Eyedropper** tool (i), hold down the mouse button, and drag to any black object on your screen until you see the Color button change to black. The penguin itself won't work because it has no black fills now, so try something like the black drop-down arrow at the bottom of your screen. Admittedly, this is a roundabout way to choose a black fill, but we haven't talked about the Color palette yet and this shows you an alternative. (You may notice that the Stroke button reset itself to None as you do this; just ignore it, as it doesn't make any difference for our purposes.) (See Figure 6.14.)

Attributes: Applying Strokes and Fills   **111**

Figure 6.14 It's not immediately obvious what's going on here, but you can see in the bottom of this figure that the Eyedropper tool is being used to sample the black color from the drop-down arrow in the image window's frame. Click-dragging the Eyedropper tool lets you sample colors from anywhere on your computer's display.

5. Choose the **Paintbucket** tool (k) or hold down the **Option/Alt** key as you complete this step. Click on the upper part of the wing, then on each of the feet, and finally on the penguin's head. This allows you to paste attributes without first making a selection.

Figure 6.15 Click on an object with the Paintbucket tool to paste the current attributes and leave the object selected. Here, the left foot is still selected, because it was filled last, and we are about to click on the penguin's head with the Paintbucket to finish all the black fills.

112　CHAPTER 6

6. Choose the **Group Selection** tool (a) again and click on the neck and ear area as indicated in Figure 6.16. The king penguin has yellow-orange markings on its neck, beak, and breast. We'll use gradient fills for these areas. This will require the use of the Swatches and Gradient palettes, both of which are discussed in Chapter 10.

Figure 6.16 Select the neck area with the Group Selection tool in preparation for a gradient fill.

7. Move the cursor to the Swatches palette. If the palette isn't open, choose the **Window: Open Swatches** menu command. The default Swatches palette includes a sunburst gradient at the right end of the sixth row. You may need to scroll down to find it (see Figure 6.17). Click on this swatch to make it the current fill. At the same time, the active selection is filled with this gradient.

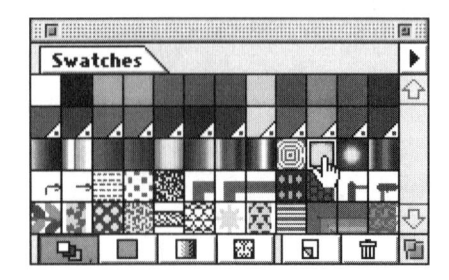

Figure 6.17 Clicking on this sunburst gradient in the Swatches palette makes it the current fill and fills any active selections.

Attributes: Applying Strokes and Fills 113

> **NOTE** When using a radial gradient, such as the one chosen in Step 7, to fill an unevenly shaped object, Illustrator calculates a center point for the object and starts the radial fill at this point.

8. Choose the **Gradient** tool (g). Click at the right side of the selected object (in this case, the penguin's neck area) and drag to the left, as indicated in Figure 6.18. This changes the way Illustrator applies the gradient. The point you first click becomes the starting point for the fill, and you drag and release at the endpoint.

Figure 6.18 Drag with the Gradient tool to set the start and endpoints for the gradient fill.

9. Choose the **Paintbucket** tool (k) and click in the white area of the penguin's beak. The beak should be more yellow than orange, so choose the **Gradient** tool (g), click at the right end of the beak's fill, and drag out to the tip of the beak, past the area that's being filled (as shown in Figure 6.19).

114   CHAPTER 6

Figure 6.19 When dragging past the selected area with the Gradient tool, only a portion of the gradient is used to fill the selection. Notice how the same gradient fill was used to produce subtly different results in Steps 8 and 9.

NOTE The gradient fills used in Steps 8 and 9 were radial fills, but they could just as easily have been linear fills. In most cases, this would make a big difference, but in this instance the difference is slight. (The differences are discussed in more detail in Chapter10.)

10. Hold down the **Command/Ctrl** key to toggle to the **Direct Selection** tool, and click on the penguin's belly. Then click on the **Gradient** button (.), not the tool, to choose the same gradient fill as used before.

Figure 6.20 Click on the Gradient button to apply the same gradient fill we used before, without switching tools.

This gradient is not right. We only wanted a little gradient color at the neck, and the rest of the breast should be white. You can try using the Gradient tool to define a short gradient ramp, but instead of a white breast, it will be filled with the end color of the fill, yellow. We could define a new smaller object that is just the penguin's neck (and don't say he doesn't have much of a neck—you'll offend him), but it's possible to achieve the effect we want without using the drawing tools.

We'll define a new gradient that does everything we want. Once again, this is jumping ahead to Chapter 10, but you'll find that we do that a lot in this book. It's more fun that way. Make sure that the Gradient palette is open. If it isn't, choose **Window: Show Gradient**.

The Gradient palette shows the current gradient: the start and end colors and the rate of color change as expressed by the position of these colors on the color ramp. We will change the order of the colors and add a white finish to this gradient.

11. Move the cursor inside the Gradient palette over the orange slider at the right end of the gradient scale. Hold down the mouse button and drag to move it all the way to the left side of the scale. Release the mouse button. This puts the orange slider on the other side of the yellow slider and interactively updates the gradient and the fill in the penguin's belly.

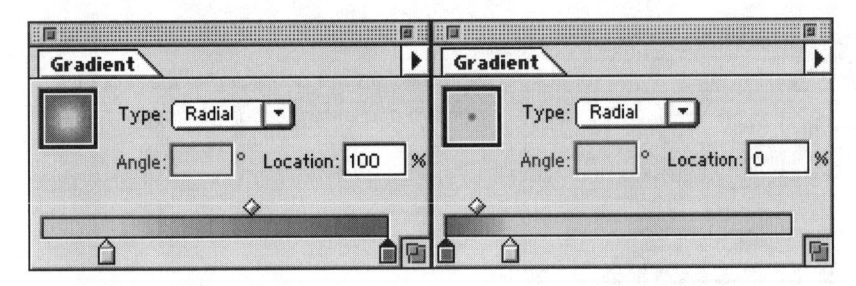

Figure 6.21 On the left, the gradient that we've used for the head of the penguin, and on the right, the same gradient after dragging the orange-filled slider from one end of the scale (100%) to the other (0%).

12. Click and drag in the opposite direction with the yellow slider, but instead of dragging it to the end, stop at about 80%. You can also click on the slider and type **80** into the percentage field. (If this field is not showing, click on the triangle at the right side of the palette and choose **Show Options**.)

116 CHAPTER 6

Figure 6.22 After moving the second gradient slider, the Gradient palette, Toolbox, and image will look like this, all showing the same newly edited gradient fill.

13. Click below the right end of the gradient ramp where the orange slider used to be, at 100%. This adds a new slider.

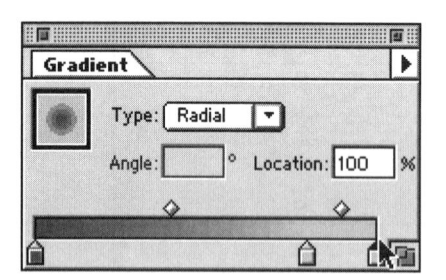

Figure 6.23 Click at the end of the gradient ramp to add a third gradient slider.

14. Hold down the **Option/Alt** key and click on one of the white swatches in the Swatches palette. This fills the new slider with white and completes our custom gradient.

Attributes: Applying Strokes and Fills   **117**

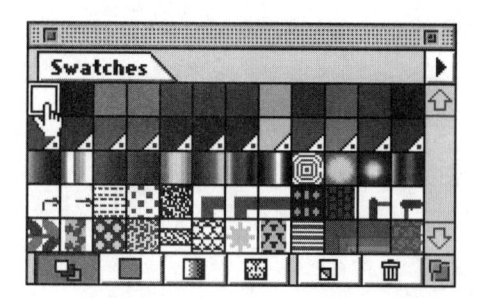

Figure 6.24 Option/Alt-clicking on a white swatch changes the third gradient slider to white. You can also drag a swatch to the Gradient palette to change colors.

15. The Gradient tool (g) should still be active in the Toolbox. If it isn't, click on it. Move the cursor to the top of the penguin's belly. Click and drag down no further than the top of his wing. Voilá, the gradient has done the trick. Everything after the end of the drag is white, and only the penguin's neck is yellow and orange.

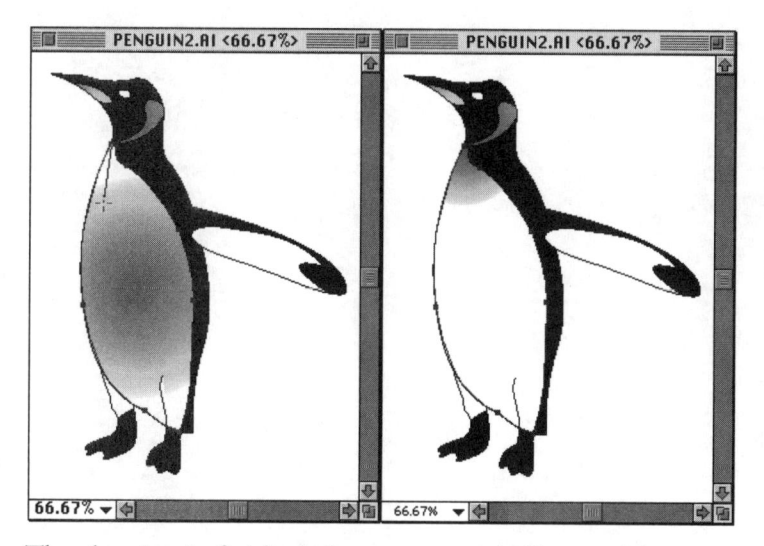

Figure 6.25 On the left, dragging a short gradient that ends in white produces the effect we're looking for, as shown on the right.

The drawing is finished. Save your work if you wish or open the file PENGUIN3.AI from the LESSON03 folder on the CD to see a finished version.

7

View Tools

In this chapter…

- What does a view look like?
- Panning and zooming: Hand and Zoom tools
- Views without windows: screen modes
- The view from the printer: Page tool
- Lesson 7: Mapping Views

What Does a View Look Like?

When you open an Illustrator document, you open a window and your drawing is viewed within it. This is true of all applications in all operating systems for which there are versions of Illustrator. This viewing window and the document exist independently of one another. Just as you can move and resize a document window, you can move and resize the view of your drawing within that window.

Illustrator provides two tools for adjusting the document view. The Hand tool is used to move the image within the window, which is sometimes referred to as *panning*. The Zoom tool changes the magnification of the view, which is like resizing a window without making it bigger or smaller.

In keeping with its policy of making the user interface of Photoshop and Illustrator 7 as similar as is reasonable, Adobe has added Screen Mode buttons to Illustrator's Toolbox. These allow you to change the entire contents of your screen so that you can view your drawing without the usual window elements.

There is one more viewing tool, the Page tool. It lets you preview and change the view from your printer. In other words, the Page tool is used to define the limits of the printed page in relation to your drawing.

Panning and Zooming: Hand and Zoom Tools

You don't need the Hand tool to pan your drawing. Instead, you can use the ubiquitous scroll bars. Scrolling is a function provided by the operating system that varies slightly from platform to platform but is consistent across applications on a single platform. You should know how your operating system implements scrolling, because we won't discuss it here.

Illustrator's Hand tool provides a faster and more direct alternative to scrolling. Clicking and dragging with this tool moves the drawing exactly the distance and direction you drag. Panning with the Hand tool becomes more important at higher magnifications when parts of your drawing aren't within the image window. Simply click and drag to bring the portion of your drawing you want into view.

The Zoom tool is used to change the document view by magnifying and shrinking the image. Illustrator has an absolute zoom range of 6.25% to 1600%, which is plus or minus a factor of 16. Unfortunately, Illustrator 7 has yet to implement infinite zooming. You cannot specify the exact zoom factor but are instead stuck with eight powers of magnification and eight of demagnification.

You can change the zoom factor by clicking to set the stationary zoom point or by clicking and dragging to select an area of the drawing to be zoomed. You can also pick a zoom factor from the drop-down menu along the bottom border of the image window, and there are a number of zoom-related commands in the View menu, discussed in Chapter 15.

> **NOTE** The current drawing magnification is displayed both in the window's title bar and in the magnification area at the lower-left corner of the window's frame. If the window itself is too small, this information may not be visible.

To Pan with the Hand Tool

1. Use either of the following methods to choose the Hand tool:

   - Click on the **Hand** tool (h) in the Toolbox to select it.
   - Hold down the **Spacebar** on your keyboard to toggle temporarily to the Hand cursor. This works when any tool is active, but not when a text object is active.

2. Move the Hand cursor over your drawing. Click and drag the mouse in any direction. Wherever you move the cursor, the drawing follows. Figure 7.1 shows the Hand tool in action.

> **NOTE** You will probably find that you use the Hand tool shortcut more often than you select the Hand tool from the Toolbox. It's extremely convenient, and it's the fastest way to move your drawing around within the document window.

Figure 7.1 *The Hand tool pans the entire image as though it were being grabbed and dragged by a physical hand. (The Mardi Gras image used for the screen shots in this chapter was created by Nancy Stahl.)*

To Magnify with the Zoom Tool—Zooming In

1. Use either of the following methods to choose the Zoom tool:

   - Click on the **Zoom** tool (z) in the Toolbox to select it.
   - Hold down the **Spacebar** and **Command/Ctrl** keys to toggle temporarily to the Zoom tool. This works when any tool is active, but not when a text object is active.

2. Use one of the following methods to magnify the drawing:

   - Click anywhere on the drawing. This sets the zoom point and increases the magnification by one step. The zoom point remains fixed at its position within the drawing window.
   - Hold down the mouse button and drag to surround an area of the drawing within a temporary marquee. Illustrator chooses the magnification factor that will enlarge this area to fill the window without cropping any of it, as shown in Figure 7.2.

Figure 7.2 On the left, dragging a marquee around an area to be magnified using the Zoom tool. On the right, Illustrator selects the appropriate magnification to fit the entire selection in the window, in this case, 200%.

> **NOTE**
> You can drag a zoom marquee from a center point outward, instead of corner-to-corner. Hold down the **Control** key after you start dragging. If you press the **Control** key before dragging, the context-sensitive menu pops up.

To Demagnify with the Zoom Tool—Zooming Out

The steps for demagnifying are identical to the steps for magnifying described earlier, except that you must hold down the **Option/Alt** key to toggle to the Zoom Out tool. The Zoom Out cursor is a magnifying glass with a minus sign in it (see Figure 7.3). Earlier versions of Illustrator had a hidden Zoom Out tool in the Toolbox, but it has been eliminated from version 7.

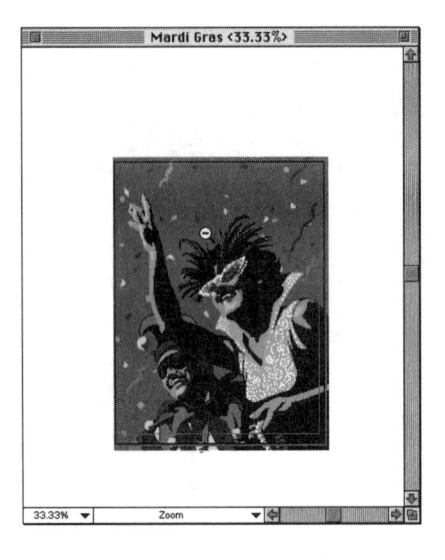

Figure 7.3 *To zoom out, hold down the* **Option/Alt** *key to toggle the Zoom tool from zoom in (+) to zoom out (-). The magnifying glass icon changes to indicate that clicking will zoom out.*

To Change Magnification with the Zoom Pop-up Menu

1. Move the cursor to the lower-left corner of the drawing's window frame. This area displays the current magnification and includes a pop-up menu (see Figure 7.4).
2. Click and hold down the mouse button to pop up the magnification menu, then slide the cursor over the magnification factor you want and release the mouse button. The drawing is zoomed at its center point within the window.

Figure 7.4 *You can always change magnification in either direction using the Zoom pop-up menu in the lower-left corner of every image window.*

VIEWS WITHOUT WINDOWS: SCREEN MODES

At the bottom of the Toolbox are three Screen Mode buttons: Standard Screen Mode, Full Screen Mode with Menu Bar, and Full Screen Mode. These control the way windows are displayed on your screen and share the f shortcut key. One of these buttons is always highlighted.

The two full screen modes eliminate all vestiges of the standard operating system window borders so that the image fills the screen, effectively hiding all other open document windows. You can still view other open windows by selecting them from the Windows menu.

To Change Screen Mode

Click on one of the Screen Mode buttons (f) to change the mode:

- **Standard Screen**—The left button displays all documents within the standard operating system-supported windows. This is the default mode. Figure 7.5 shows a document in standard screen mode.

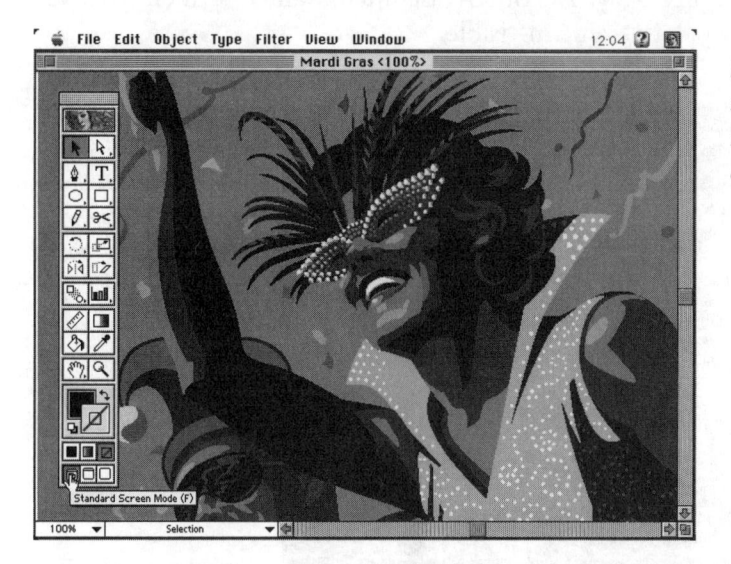

Figure 7.5 Standard screen mode with menu bar and window scroll bars.

- **Full Screen with Menu Bar**—Enlarges the current document to fill the entire screen area under the standard menu bar (see Figure 7.6). There are no window borders, scroll bars, or title bar. Palettes remain visible, but all other document windows are hidden.

126 **CHAPTER 7**

Figure 7.6 Full screen mode with menu bar, but no window elements, such as scroll bars.

- **Full Screen**—Enlarges the current document to fill the entire screen area (see Figure 7.7). All other documents and the menu bar are hidden, but palettes remain visible.

Figure 7.7 Full screen mode fills the entire computer screen with your drawing. There are no window or other operating system elements.

NOTE: Screen modes are document-specific, so that it's possible to have different documents set to different display modes.

THE VIEW FROM THE PRINTER: PAGE TOOL

Illustrator only prints objects and paths that fall within the delineations of the page. You may use all of the artboard for your drawings, but any artwork that falls outside the borders of the page definition will not be printed. Page definitions are made in the Document Setup dialog, discussed in Chapter 17, but page placement is adjusted by using the Page tool. The Page tool (h) is hidden under the Hand tool. Figure 7.8 shows the Page tool in use.

Every document window has a set of default guidelines that reflect the size of the printed page and the extent of its printable area. If you find that your drawing is not placed within these guides correctly, you can either select the paths and move them, or move the page guides using the Page tool.

Figure 7.8 When using the Page tool, the cursor drags by the inner page border, which represents the printable area of the image. The outer border represents the physical page size.

To Move Page Guides Using the Page Tool

1. Choose the **Page** tool (h), which is hidden under the Hand button.
2. Click in the drawing and drag to move the page guides. The Page cursor represents the lower-left corner of the page guides. When you click, the entire size of the page is shown, and this guide moves with the cursor, so that you can see what falls within the moved guides.
3. Release the mouse button and the page guides are repositioned.

NOTE: There are two dotted outlines that represent the page guides: the inner guide is the imageable area of the currently chosen printer, and the outer is the actual page size. The Page tool cursor points to the lower-left corner of the inner guide.

LESSON 7

Mapping Views

We'll examine a file in this lesson that is hard to see all at once, but it represents a single 8.5 × 11 inch page. It was supplied by American Custom Maps of Albuquerque, New Mexico, and it is one of many similar maps prepared for the 1996 Olympics in Atlanta.

1. Open the file OLYMPIC.AI from the LESSON07 folder on the CD (see Figure 7.9). You can see from the title bar that the magnification is 50%, but it's hard to see much else. Most of the text is greeked and the details are lost at this magnification, but you can see the entire composition and the placement of the image on the page, which actually isn't right. This kind of thing can happen when you are printing to different devices. For instance, this file was last printed on an imagesetter with completely different page guides.

130 CHAPTER 7

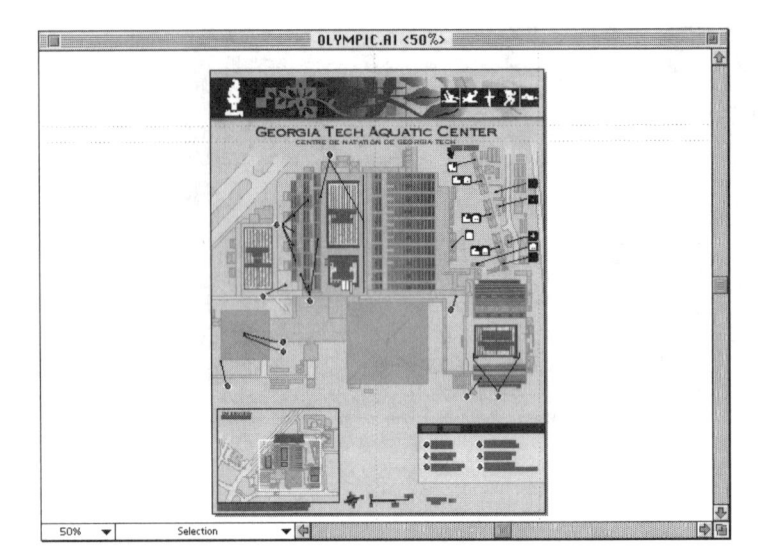

Figure 7.9 The Olympic image is at a 50% view which reveals the entire layout, but leaves the details and text indistinguishable.

2. Choose the **Page** tool (h) hidden under the Hand tool, then click and drag the page guides into place at the lower left corner of the image. (The page guides reflect the Page Setup for your printer. Most likely you have an 8 1/2 × 11 inch page size chosen, but the printable area of printers will vary, and this is reflected by the inner guide.) The Page tool is being used to create new page guides in Figure 7.10.

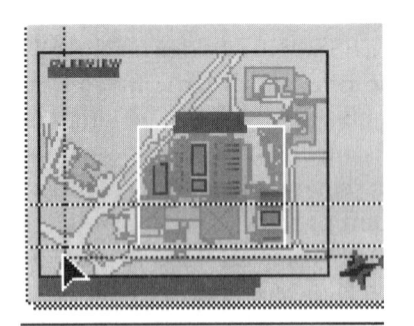

Figure 7.10 Drag new page guides into place using the Page tool. The crosshairs icon turns into an arrowhead when you click and drag, and the preview of the page guides follows the point of the arrow.

3. Change the screen mode by clicking on the **Full Screen** button or by pressing the **F** key twice (see Figure 7.11). You might expect that by taking over the full display area of your screen with this single image, you could see more of it. Not so. Full Screen mode eliminates the standard display window, but it doesn't change the magnification or placement of the image.

View Tools 131

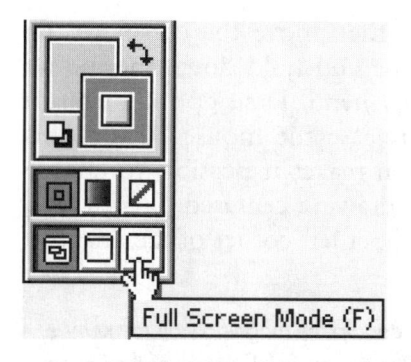

Figure 7.11 Click on one of the Screen Mode buttons to change the way images are displayed on your screen. The f shortcut key can be used as a three-way toggle among modes.

4. Choose the **Zoom** tool (z). Click outside one of the corners of the drawing and drag to the opposite corner. This will increase the magnification so that the area within the Zoom marquee fills the screen and is centered within it (see Figure 7.12).

    What you see at this point will depend on your monitor size. On a large display, at any resolution of a full page or greater, you will see this image at actual size. Medium-sized displays will enlarge the image to 66.67% magnification.

    One of the things you lose when viewing in Full Screen mode is the information that Illustrator displays in its window frames.

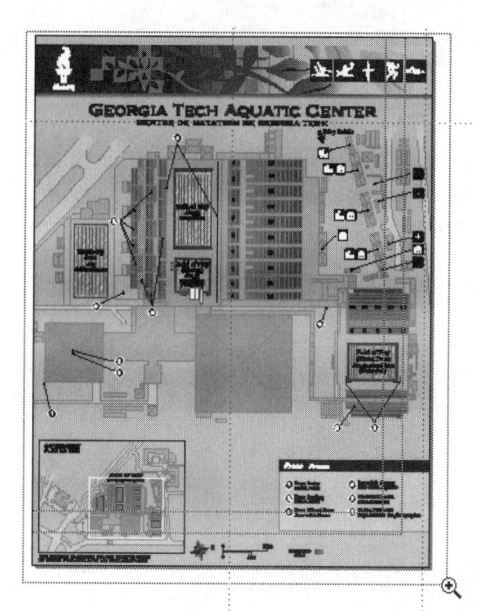

Figure 7.12 Drag a Zoom marquee over the image to select an area to be enlarged. Illustrator magnifies the selection so that it fills the window and is centered within it.

5. Switch back to **Standard Mode** (f), then move the cursor to the lower-left corner of the window frame and hold down the mouse button over the magnification pop-up menu. Drag up the menu to 300% (shown in Figure 7.13) and release the mouse button. This method of changing the magnification makes it possible to choose an exact percentage, and it leaves the drawing centered. In this case, we want to edit something near the upper left corner of the image.

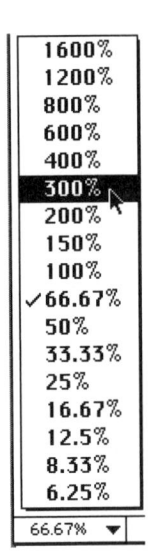

Figure 7.13 *At any time, you can pop up the magnification menu by holding down the mouse button over the lower-left corner of the image window. Here, the magnification is being increased to 300%.*

6. Choose the **Hand** tool (h). Click in the image and drag downward and to the right. This reveals more of the upper left corner of the image. When you have brought the word *Georgia* to the top of your view, release the mouse button.

    Panning like this with the Hand tool (shown in Figure 7.14) is a very effective way to move directly to any area of your drawing. However, some systems pan more slowly than others, so you may have to wait a moment or two after you drag for your screen to redraw.

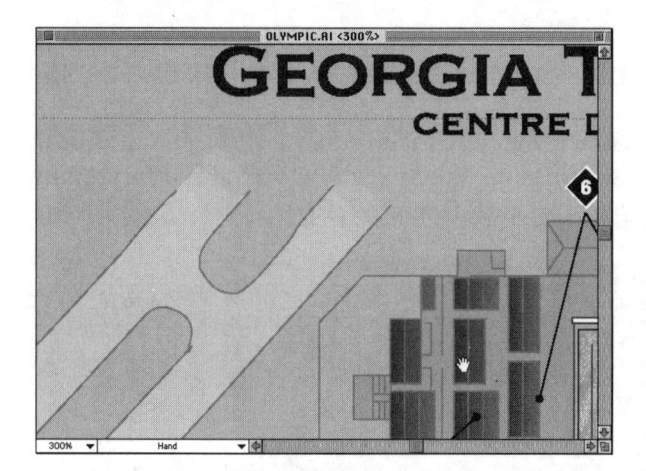

Figure 7.14 Pan down and to the right to bring the upper-left corner of the image into view. The Hand tool provides the quickest way to move an image around within its window.

7. Hold down the **Spacebar** and then the **Command/Ctrl** key to toggle to the Zoom tool. Under the word *Georgia* and to the left are the paths for a divided boulevard. Click and drag a magnification marquee over this boulevard to enlarge and center the view, as shown in Figure 7.15.

   You can see that one of the paths delineating the median strip is not perfectly drawn. There's a slight overlap where the path crosses itself. This probably wasn't even visible on the printed maps, but we'll fix it since we've found it.

Figure 7.15 Drag once more with the **Zoom** tool to enlarge the problem path and fill the image window.

8. Choose the **Direct Selection** tool (a) and click on the offending path. (If you wish, you can zoom in closer to get a better look at the problem.)

    You can see there are two anchor points in close juxtaposition. The lower anchor point has its direction point crossed, thus causing the inadvertent loop in this path (Figure 7.16).

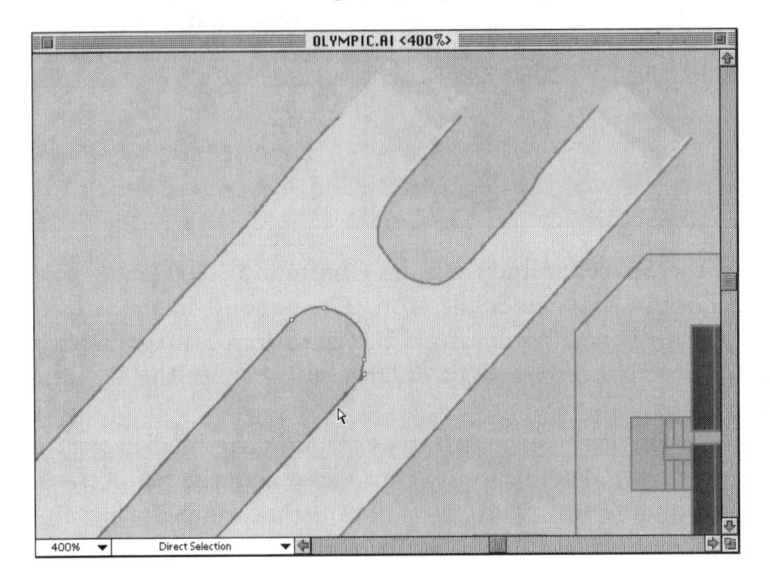

Figure 7.16 Clicking on this path, the median strip for a boulevard, selects it and shows that the direction line for one of the anchor points was inadvertently left pointing the wrong way.

9. Choose the **Delete Anchor Point** tool (also known as the Minus Pen tool, p), move the cursor over the lower anchor point, as shown in Figure 7.17, and click to delete it. This is the quickest and simplest way to smooth the wayward path.

View Tools 135

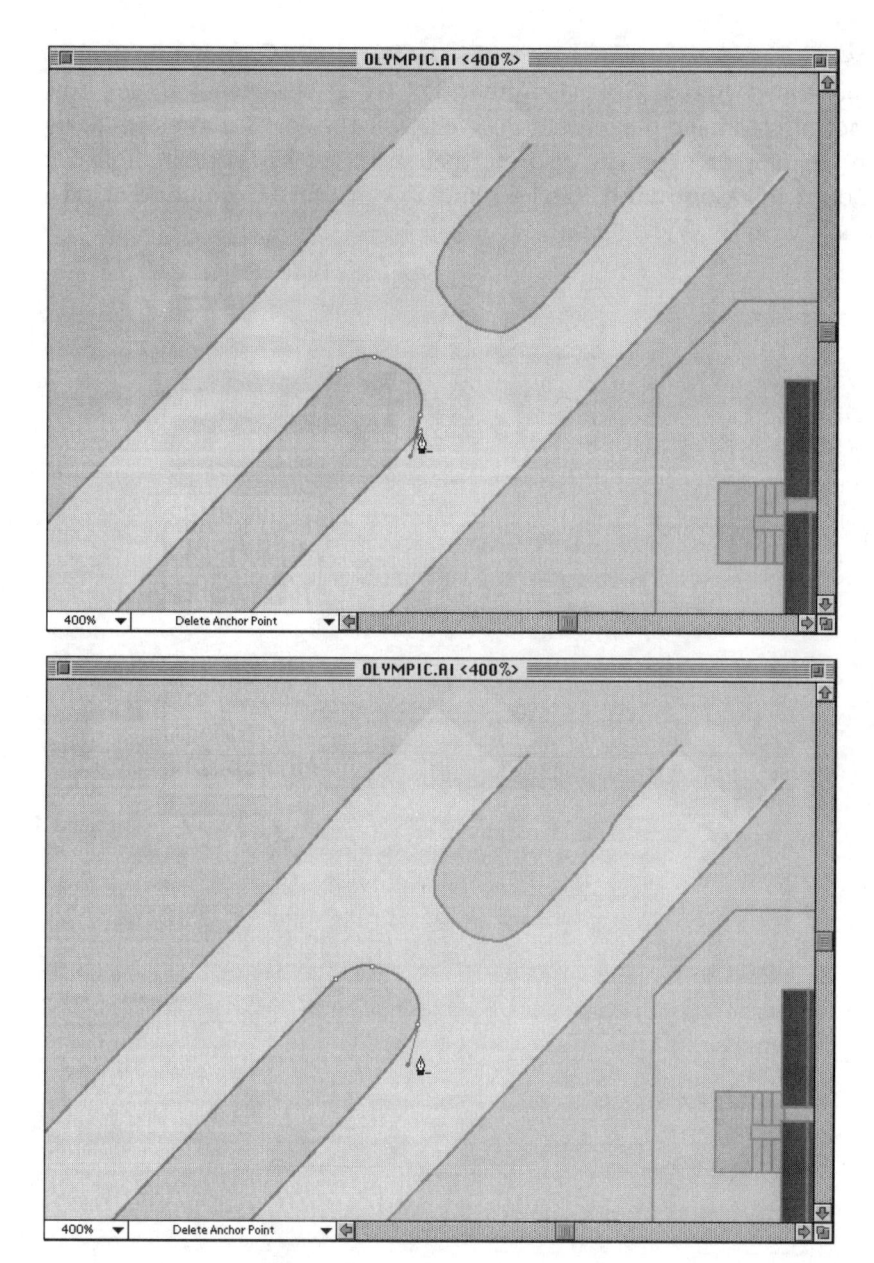

Figures 7.17 *and **7.18*** *Clicking on the misplaced anchor point (7.17) with the Minus Pen tool deletes it. Illustrator redraws the curve, and the median strip is repaired (7.18). If only all road repairs were this easy*

10. As a final step, choose the **View: Fit In Window** (**Command/Ctrl-0**) and **View: Actual Size** (**Command/Ctrl-1**) commands to see how they affect image magnification. We'll visit the View commands again in Chapter 15. You can also see that there are key combinations for Zoom In (**Command/Ctrl-+**) and Zoom Out (**Command/Ctrl-**-) available in the View menu.

8 Blending, Tracing, and Graphing

In this chapter…

- Shaping and shading with blends—Blend tool
- Tracing the easy way—Auto Trace tool
- Graphs are graphic, too—Graph tool
- Lesson 8: Pain and Peppers

You are thinking, *What do the Blend, Auto Trace, and Graph tools have in common?* Adobe, in its infinite wisdom, has grouped these three tools together in Illustrator's revamped Toolbox, and you want to know why. Is there some shared algorithm known only to programmers, or did the interface designers lump these tools together like a hash of yesterday's leftovers? The latter is the only explanation that makes sense to me, but we have made the best of this unfathomable decision by cooking up a spicy lesson to finish off this chapter.

SHAPING AND SHADING WITH BLENDS—BLEND TOOL

Not so long ago, Illustrator had no Gradient tool (see Chapter 6). Every shade of every color needed to be contained within a path. A simple blend from a white shape to a black shape required 254 intermediate shapes to create the requisite 256-step grayscale ramp to avoid banding problems. You can still use the Blend tool to create color ramps, but it is much easier to use the Gradient tool and palette.

Blends and gradients as defined by Illustrator are different. The term *blend*s (the older tool) refers not only to blending colors but shapes (a bimorphic blend of form and attributes), while *gradients* (the newer tool) are used strictly as fills. This is why you must select two shapes to create the intermediate steps when using the Blend tool, but the Gradient tool is used to define the attributes of direction and limits for the fill of a single selection.

Gradient fills can be defined and used as easily as custom colors. You can apply them to multiple items, edit the fill, and all items filled with that gradient will be updated. Blends must be defined individually and are difficult to change without deleting and starting from scratch.

Illustrator has always had the ability to blend one shape into another (this functionality is now popularly referred to as *morphing*). More importantly, the bimorphic nature of blending allows you to wrap color changes to any shape to create complex shading, highlighting, and contour effects.

Using the Blend tool is not Illustrator's most straightforward function and it has a number of limitations:

- You can blend two open or two closed paths, but you cannot blend an open path and closed path.
- You must blend two and only two objects.
- Groups cannot be blended, but objects within groups can be blended.

- Compound paths cannot be part of a blend.
- Spot colors are converted to process equivalents when blending, except when blending two shades of the same spot color.
- Patterned objects cannot be blended unless the pattern fills are the same.

Blends also have a number of printing limitations, which are discussed in Chapter 17.

To Blend Two Shapes

1. Select the two shapes to be blended. They must be in the correct relative position before you blend them.
2. Choose the **Blend** tool (b) and click on a single anchor point on each selected object. For open paths, these must be endpoints.
3. In the Blend dialog, shown in Figure 8.1, specify the number of intermediate steps Illustrator should create between the two selected objects and the Start and End percentages for the blended shapes. The number of steps must be between 1 and 1000, and the Start and End value must be between -100 and +200.

   - Steps—There is always a default value for the step count supplied by Illustrator. This is calculated automatically from the color values specified for the object fills and is based on a maximum range of 256 printable shades from any single color of ink. For instance, there are only 254 discernible gray shades between black and white. A blend from 50% gray to white requires only 126 intermediate steps to yield 128 total shades from start to finish. When there are colors involved, Illustrator uses CMYK values to calculate the maximum change within any single color channel.

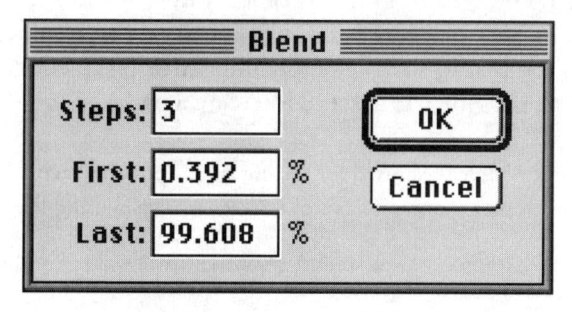

Figure 8.1 The Blend dialog is simple. Illustrator calculates the number of steps required to make a smooth blend given the color values. You can change this value as well as the First and Last blend step percentages.

NOTE There are several reasons you might want to reduce the number of blend steps. If your output device is not capable of reproducing 256 shades, you can reduce the number of blending steps without affecting image quality. If you are blending shapes for a special effect rather than to create a shading effect, the number of color steps is unimportant. If you intend to create a banding effect, you must reduce the number of steps.

- Start and End—Illustrator calculates the step values in even percentages, but you can change the calculated starting and ending percentages in the Blend dialog. Illustrator will recalculate the blend percentages based on the values you supply for Start and End. All intermediate blend values are evenly divided across the steps.

Click **OK**. Illustrator creates the blend steps and leaves them selected and grouped. The original two objects, shown in Figure 8.2, are not part of this group.

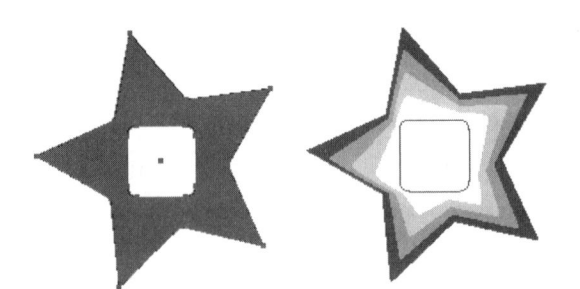

Figure 8.2 A white rounded rectangle and a gray five-pointed star, on the left, are blended in three steps to produce the image on the right.

TRACING THE EASY WAY—AUTO TRACE TOOL

The Auto Trace tool is useful for quickly turning bitmaps into paths. (The Auto Trace is hidden under the Blend button in the Toolbox.) In previous versions of Illustrator, you had to import bitmaps as templates before you could trace them. Illustrator 7 has no templates, so you simply import or place your image and click on it directly with the Auto Trace tool to create a path.

NOTE The Auto Trace tool is rather crude, best used for tracing simple or easily recognizable shapes. For more complex shapes, it's better to trace manually using the Pen or Pencil tool.

Blending, Tracing, and Graphing 141

The Auto Trace tool uses bit color to determine shape and is affected by the Auto Trace Gap and Curve Fitting Tolerance settings in the General Preferences dialog (see Chapter 19). Increasing the Gap and Tolerance settings creates a looser fitting tracing, while lowering these values creates a more precise fit. However, precision is gained at the cost of recognizability. If the settings are too tight, the Auto Trace tool won't recognize the shape. It's often better to use looser settings and make adjustments by editing the resulting path with Illustrator's other tools.

To Convert Bitmap Shapes into Illustrator Paths

1. Place or Paste a bitmap image into an Illustrator drawing.
2. Choose the **Auto Trace** tool (b), hidden under the Blend button.
3. There are two ways to trace a shape:

   - Move the cursor within 6 pixels of the shape you wish to trace, and then click the mouse button. Illustrator draws the entire outline of the shape to create a closed path.
   - Move the cursor within 2 pixels of the shape you wish to trace, and then click and drag from start to end point of the tracing. Illustrator traces along the contours of the shape from one point to the other, creating an open path.

NOTE: The Auto Trace tool always looks to the right of the point at which you click to find the shape to be traced.

Figure 8.3 *A placed bitmap image with a path created by the Autotrace tool.*

Graphs Are Graphic, Too—Graph Tool

In general, people use spreadsheets or dedicated graphing applications to create graphs. Illustrator makes no attempt to match the numerical power of these programs. Instead, it offers unparalleled graphic control of numerically based graphs. There is no better tool for adding graphs to annual reports, papers, or presentations.

There isn't really a single Graph tool; instead, nine graph types are hidden under a single Graph tool button. The use of each tool is identical. You click or click and drag where you want the graph to be (just as you would with the Rectangle tool), but the result is a different graph type. You can always change the graph type, so it's not important that you start with the right tool.

The nine graph types are:

> **Column**—This is the default type. It creates rectangular columns of length equal to the relative values.
> **Stacked column**—Stacks columns of values to create a cumulative length rather than displaying adjacent columns.
> **Bar**—A horizontally displayed column graph.
> **Stacked bar**—A horizontally displayed stacked column graph.
> **Line**—Represents values as points and connects points with a trend line.
> **Area**—Similar to a line graph, but with the area under the trend lines filled in.
> **Scatter**—Plots points without any connections.
> **Pie**—Divides a circle into percentage values or wedges of the pie.
> **Radar**—A circular representation of a line graph. Also known as a *web graph*.

About Illustrator's Graphs

If you plan to use the graph tools, it's important to understand how Illustrator creates graphs and maintains the integrity of graph objects. Illustrator maintains a simple spreadsheet-like database that stores the numerical information needed to produce a graph. This data entry and storage element is accessed automatically when you click with a graph tool, or it can be opened and edited at any time from the **Object: Graphs** submenu. Every graph object you create is linked to its own worksheet.

You can enter data directly into the rows and columns of a graph's worksheet, or you can import data from any source. You can also Cut and Paste from the Clipboard or drag and drop data from applications that support this feature. Illustrator's data import capability is especially important since you are unlikely to want to use Illustrator to store your actual data. In most instances, the information used to create a graph can be exported as summary data.

When you create a graph object, Illustrator takes all the elements of the graph and groups them into a single object. You can select the entire group or use the Group Selection or Direct Selection tools to select elements within the graph object. This gives you the ability to edit every line, dot, box, or label individually. As long as the integrity of the group remains intact, you can edit the data and elements and be assured that everything will update correctly. If you remove an element from the graph object by ungrouping it, that element will no longer update with the others.

To Create a Graph Object

1. Choose the **Graph** tool (j) or specify one of the specific graph types by choosing its hidden tool or by double-clicking on the Graph tool to open the Graph Type dialog, shown in Figure 8.4. (We'll get to this dialog a little later.)
2. Specify the size of the graph object in one of two ways:

   - Click in the drawing to open the Graph dialog. Specify a Width and Height for the graph object in any units from 0 to 8640 points. Click **OK**.
   - Click and drag from corner to corner where you want the graph object to be. Hold down the **Shift** key to constrain the shape of the graph to a square. Hold down the **Option** key to draw the graph object from center to corner. Entering a graph object into a drawing is just like creating a rectangle. Either drag the bounds of the graph using the Graph tool, or click and enter the Width and Height of the graph using the Graph dialog.

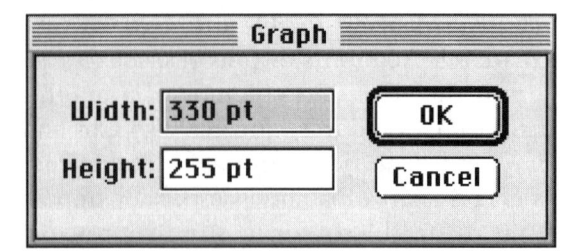

Figure 8.4 *The Graph dialog with Width and Height fields.*

In either case, the Graph Data worksheet opens so that you can enter or import data for the graph object. If you don't have to enter the data immediately, it's possible to create a graph object with an empty data set. You can edit the graph elements and enter the data later.

To Enter Graph Data

1. Create a graph object as described earlier to open the Graph Data worksheet, or select a graph object and choose **Object: Graphs: Data**, as shown in Figure 8.5.

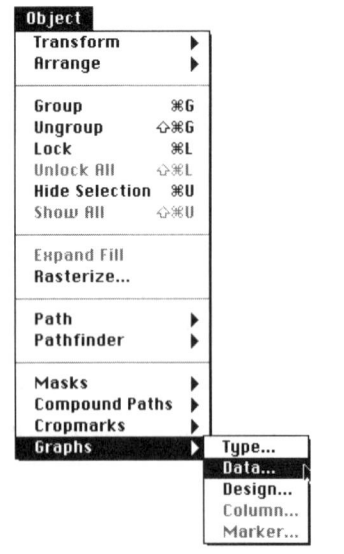

Figure 8.5 *You can always select a graph object and enter or edit data using the **Object: Graphs: Data** command.*

2. Type in the data, one data element per worksheet cell. Figure 8.6 shows the worksheet. You can move around the worksheet by clicking directly on a cell or by using the **Tab** key to move to the right

along a row, the **Return/Enter** key to move down a column, or the arrow keys to move in any direction one cell at a time. Illustrator highlights the active cell.

Data is typed into the data entry line at the top of the worksheet and entered into the active cell when you change cells using any of the methods described in the previous paragraph. If you need to change a value, you can't edit directly in the cells. You must select a cell and edit its contents in the data entry line.

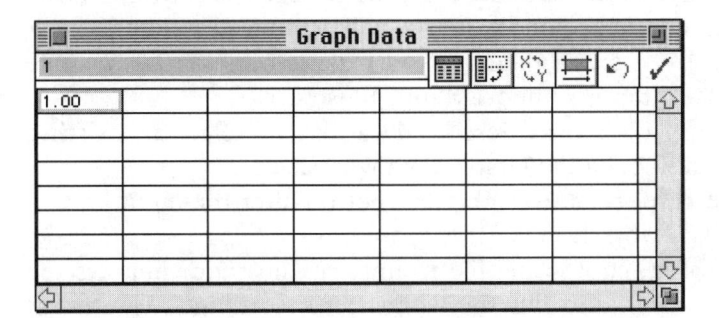

Figure 8.6 The Graph Data worksheet. The default state of the worksheet contains a 1 in the first cell. Actually, it's 1 and it's displayed with two decimals by default.

3. Click the **Apply** button (the checkmark icon in the upper right corner) to graph the data and leave the Graph Data worksheet open, or click on the close box to graph the data and close the worksheet.

To Copy and Paste Data

1. Prepare the data in any other application. Select the data and choose **Edit: Copy** to copy it to the Clipboard.
2. Create a graph object, as described earlier, leaving the Graph Data worksheet open, or open the Graph Data worksheet for an existing graph object.
3. Select the cell that will be the upper-left corner for the pasted data. Illustrator fills cells from left to right, top to bottom when pasting or importing and overwrites all existing data.
4. Choose **Edit: Paste**, and the data from the Clipboard fills the cells of the worksheet.
5. Click the **Apply** button to update the graph with the imported data.

To Import Data

1. Create the data in any application and use that application to create an export file. The file format must be text, and the data must be tab-delimited with carriage returns at the end of each line. (Read the manual for the exporting program if you don't know how to do this.)

    You must also make sure that there are no commas or other characters in numeric fields, or Illustrator will assume that they are text fields and will not graph them. If you make a mistake, it's possible to edit the data after it's imported into Illustrator.
2. Create a graph object, as described earlier, or select an existing graph object and open the Graph Data worksheet.
3. Click on the **Import** button, the first button after the input line, in the Graph Data worksheet.
4. In the file dialog, choose the file to import. Illustrator imports the file, reads the data, and fills the worksheet accordingly. Figure 8.7 shows data after being imported.
5. Click the **Apply** button and the graph is updated with the imported data. The values will always be displayed using the default number and decimal format.

Figure 8.7 The Graph Data worksheet showing values that have been imported from a text file.

NOTE You needn't restrict the creation of a worksheet to a single method. It's possible to use data from multiple sources and edit and arrange it within the worksheet.

To Edit a Worksheet Cell

1. Open an existing worksheet by selecting a graph object and choosing **Object: Graphs: Data**.
2. Click on the cell you wish to edit and change the data in the data entry line at the top of the worksheet. You may use any of the Edit commands—Cut, Copy, Paste, and Clear—to change the value of a cell (see Figure 8.8).
3. Move to another cell in the worksheet by using any of the navigation keys or by clicking to update the edited cell.
4. Click on the **Apply** button to redraw the graph to reflect the edited data.

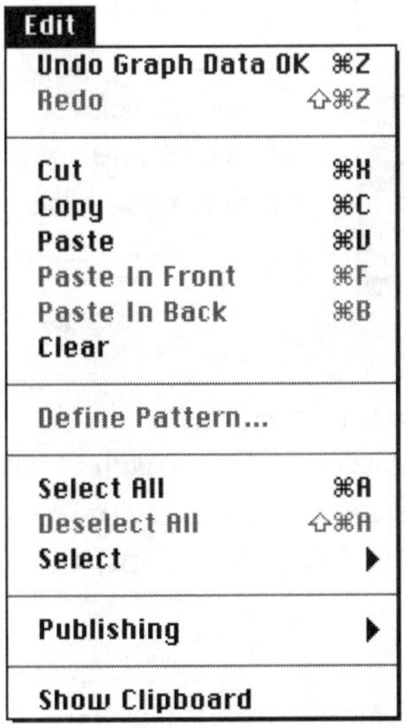

Figure 8.8 Use the standard **File: Edit** commands to edit worksheet values. Notice how the Undo command lists the last Graph command.

To Edit a Range of Cells

1. Open an existing worksheet by selecting a graph object and choosing **Object: Graphs: Data**.
2. Click and drag within the worksheet to select a range of cells.
3. Choose one of the commands from the Edit menu (Cut, Copy, Paste, or Clear).

NOTE: The cell you start dragging in is active and can be edited in the usual ways. Other cells in the range are selected for Edit menu commands only and will be deselected if you try to edit them in any other way.

To Enter Category and Value Labels

1. Create a new or select an existing graph object and open its worksheet as described earlier. Figure 8.9 shows a worksheet containing sample data.

Figure 8.9 Illustrator treats the text in the first column of this example as value labels and does not attempt to graph the ungraphable.

2. Type category labels into the first row and value labels into the first column. If there is already data in the first row or column, select all the data, choose **Edit: Cut**, select a cell one column and/or row over, and choose **Edit: Paste**. If you are using both value and category labels, the top left cell will be blank.

NOTE: Label values must have at least one non-numeric character. So if you want to use a numeric label, such as a date, enclose the value in double quotes. If you want to display quotes in a label, add an extra set of double quotes.

3. Click on the **Apply** button to draw the graph with the added labels. (A sample graph is shown in Figure 8.10.)

Blending, Tracing, and Graphing 149

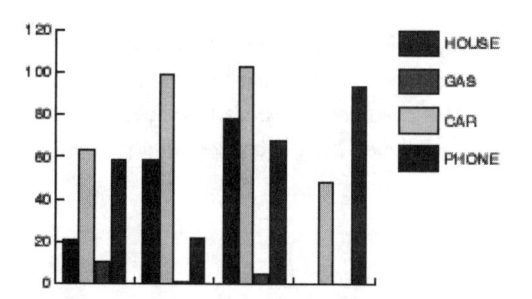

Figure 8.10 *A column graph of the data entered in Figure 8.9 should look something like this graph, with the value labels used to create the key.*

> **NOTE:** Labels are not appropriate for all graph types and are simply ignored when they can't be displayed with the graph.

To Transpose Rows and Columns in a Worksheet

1. Make sure the Graph Data worksheet is open as described earlier.
2. Click on the **Transpose** button (the second button after the input line). Row 1 becomes column 1, and so on, as shown in Figure 8.11.

Figure 8.11 *This is what the worksheet in Figure 8.9 looks like after clicking the Transpose button. Notice how the row values become column values.*

3. Click on the **Apply** button to draw the graph with the transposed values (see Figure 8.12).

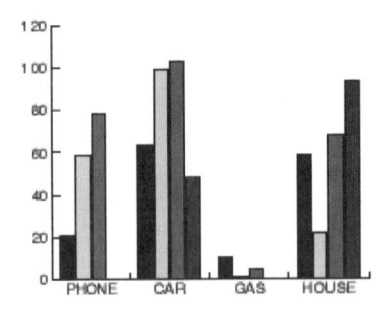

Figure 8.12 *This is the same column graph shown in Figure 8.10 after the worksheet values have been transposed. Notice how the value labels have become category labels.*

To Switch X and Y values for Scatter Graphs

1. Make sure the Graph Data worksheet is open as described earlier.
2. Click on the **Switch XY** button (the third button after the input line). The two columns of data for the scatter plot are switched so that the x-axis and y-axis values are switched.
3. Click on the **Apply** button to draw the graph with the switched values.

To Change Column Width in the Worksheet

1. Make sure the Graph Data worksheet is open as described earlier.
2. Move the cursor to the edge of a column. The cursor changes to a double arrow, as shown in Figure 8.13.
3. Click and drag left or right to adjust the column width. This setting affects only the data cell column widths and not the graph display itself.

Figure 8.13 *The double-arrow cursor appears when you drag a column boundary to change its width.*

To Change Worksheet Cell Properties

1. Make sure the Graph Data worksheet is open as described earlier.
2. Click on the **Cell Style** button (the fourth button after the input line) to open the Cell Style dialog, shown in Figure 8.14. There are two options:

   - **Number of Decimals**—Set the number of decimal digits from 0 to 10.
   - **Column Width**—Set the cell column width from 0 to 20 digits.

3. Click **OK** to update the Graph Data worksheet.

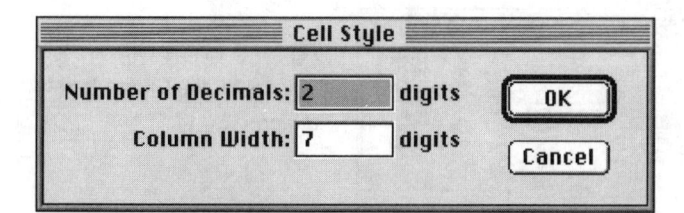

Figure 8.14 The Cell Style dialog is used to set the cell width and number of decimals for all cells in the worksheet.

NOTE All settings in the Cell Style dialog are global and override any individual column settings you may have made. Worksheet settings affect only the data cells and not the graph display itself.

To Revert Data Values

1. Make sure the Graph Data worksheet is open as described earlier.
2. Click on the **Revert** button (the curved arrow icon). Any changes made to the worksheet since last updating the graph revert to the values displayed in the drawing.

The Graph Type Dialog

The Graph Type dialog includes settings for graph style, axis settings, and type-specific options. It can be opened by double-clicking on the Graph button in the Toolbox or by choosing **Object: Graphs: Type**. The dialog either reflects the setting of the currently selected graph object or it can be opened to make settings before creating a new graph object. The dialog has three modes: Graph Options, Value Axis, and Category Axis.

The mode drop-down menu is always at the top left of the Graph Type dialog. Click on the box and choose one of the modes. All fields in the dialog change according to the mode.

To Set Graph Options

Choose Graph Options from the mode drop-down menu in the Graph Type dialog (Figure 8.15). This is the default.

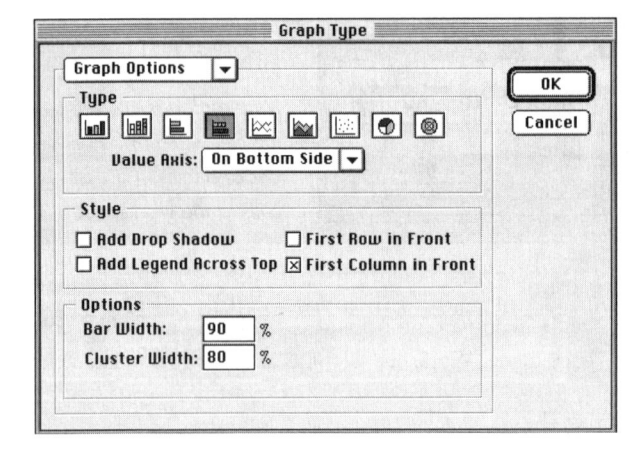

Figure 8.15 The default options for the Graph Type dialog.

The Graph Options mode divides the dialog into three functional areas: Type, Style, and Options.

Type

There are buttons for all nine graph types. Click on a button to change the graph type. The current type is highlighted. The Value Axis drop-down menu lets you select the location of this axis in the graph: left, right, top, bottom, both, or none, as appropriate to the graph type.

Style

There are four check boxes for graph style settings:

- **Add Drop Shadow**—Check this box to create drop shadows for column, bar, and pie graphs. Actually, you can add a drop shadow to

any type of graph, but it is not usually a good idea for line, area, and scatter graphs.
- **Add Legend Across Top**—Check this box to display legends horizontally across the top of a graph instead of vertically to the right, which is the default.
- **First Row in Front and First Column in Front**—Check one of these two boxes to set display precedence for overlapping chart elements. This only affects column and bar graphs when the Column Width option (described shortly) is set to a value greater than 100%. Column in Front is the default.

Options

This section changes depending on which Type button is selected in the top row. We'll break them down accordingly:

- **Column and Bar Graph Options**—These four types (including the stacked types) have the same options, but one applies vertically to columns and the other horizontally to bars.

    Column/Bar Width—Set the column/bar width from 1 to 1000%. A setting of 100% makes columns or bars flush, less than 100% creates gaps, and greater than 100% creates overlaps. (Use the Style options, described earlier, to set display precedence for overlaps.) The default is 90%.

    Cluster Width—A *cluster* is a group of columns or bars as represented by a row of values in the Graph Data worksheet. The cluster width is the total width of this group. The default is 80%.

NOTE: For Stacked graph types, a 100% Cluster Width is recommended.

- **Line, Scatter, and Radar Graph Options**—These three graph types share the same four option check boxes, except that the Edge-to-Edge Lines option is not available for scatter graphs and the default selections vary slightly:

    Mark Data Points—Check this box to display square markers at each data point. This is the default for scatter graphs.

Connect Data Points—Check this box to display connecting lines between data points. This is the default for all three graph types.
Edge-to-Edge Lines—Check this box to draw connecting lines to the left and right edges of the graph along the horizontal (x) axis.
Draw Filled Lines—This option is available only if the Connect Data Points option is selected. It allows you to specify the line width for connecting lines from 0 to 100 points.

- **Pie Graph Options**—Pie graphs have a unique set of three drop-down menu options.

  Legend—Choose a legend display option. Pie graph legends include a label and percentage:

  Standard Legend uses column labels outside the graph. It is the default.
  Legends in Wedge labels each wedge of the pie.
  No Legend omits all legend labels.

> **NOTE:** Pie graph legends are black by default. If a legend is unreadable over its pie wedge, use the Group Selection or Direct Selection tool to select the wedge and change its fill color.

  Position—These options determine the display method for multiple pie graphs:

  - *Ratio*—Sizes all graphs proportionally and is the default.
  - *Even*—Sizes all graphs to the same diameter.
  - *Stacked*—Stacks pie graphs and sizes them proportionally.

  Sort—These options set the clockwise order of the wedges starting at the top.

  - *All*—Sorts wedges from largest value to smallest.
  - *First*—Sorts wedges of multiple pie graphs in identical order based on the graph with the largest total value.
  - *None*—Leaves wedges and graphs in the order entered in the Graph Data worksheet.

- **Area graphs** have no options.

To Set Value Axis Options

Choose **Value Axis** from the mode drop-down menu in the Graph Type dialog, shown in Figure 8.16. This allows you to set the options for the vertical (y) axis.

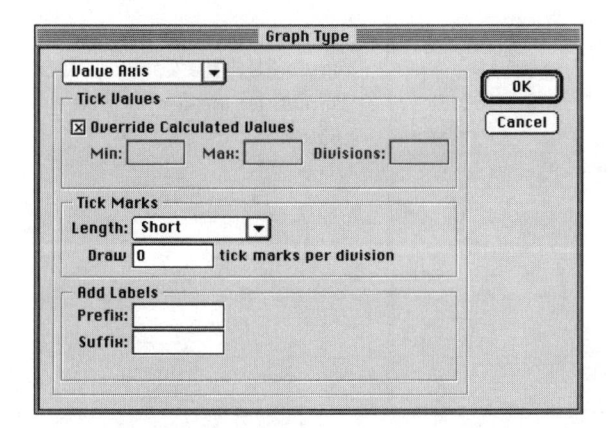

Figure 8.16 The Value Axis defaults for the Graph Type dialog.

The Value Axis mode divides the dialog into three functional areas:

- **Tick Values**—The values Illustrator displays with tick marks are calculated automatically depending on the minimum and maximum values and the number of values in the graph. You can choose to enter values manually by unchecking **Override Calculated Values**.

    Min—Specify a minimum tick value.
    Max—Specify a maximum tick value.
    Divisions—Specify the number of tick mark values displayed. Illustrator calculates an even distribution of values.

- Tick Marks—Allows you to set the appearance and number of tick marks as opposed to their associated value.

    Length—Choose **None, Short** (the default) or **Full Width** (from the left to right edge of the graph) from the drop-down menu.
    Draw # tick marks per division—Allows you to set the number of intermediate, unlabeled tick marks between each tick mark division.

- **Add Labels**—You can add a prefix and/or suffix to the tick mark value labels. This is useful for adding currency symbols. You can type any label into the Prefix and/or Suffix boxes and it will be added before and/or after the calculated tick mark label.

To Set Category Axis Options

Choose **Category Axis** from the mode drop-down menu in the Graph Type dialog (see Figure 8.17). This allows you to set the options for the horizontal (x) axis.

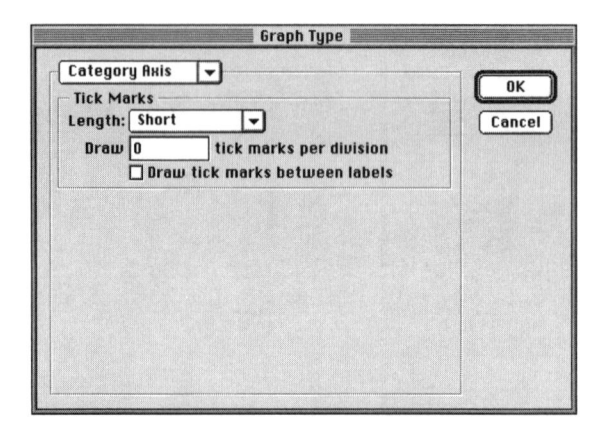

Figure 8.17 The Category Axis defaults for the Graph Type dialog.

The Category Axis mode has only a single option area:

- **Tick Marks**—Allows you to set the appearance and number of tick marks as opposed to their associated value.
- **Length**—Choose **None**, **Short** (the default), or **Full Width** (from the top to bottom edge of the graph) from the drop-down menu.
- **Draw # tick marks per division**—Allows you to set the number of intermediate, unlabeled tick marks between each tick mark division.
- **Draw tick marks between labels**—By default, category axis tick marks are centered under the category. Check this box to draw tick marks between categories instead.

About Custom Graph Design

One of Illustrator's nicest graphing capabilities is its graph design feature. This is not a way to reuse a styled graph you may have created. You can simply copy and paste to do that. A graph design lets you substitute graphic elements for the rectangles and squares used to indicate data values. Any

Blending, Tracing, and Graphing 157

Illustrator-drawn object can be used as a graph design element, which can be stretched in various ways or replicated to show relative value.

Graph designs can be used with column and bar graphs in place of the rectangular boxes or in line or scatter graphs in place of the point markers. You can use them with stacked types, but it can be difficult to create designs that stack well.

Graph designs are stored with the document and are accessed through the Graph Design dialog. You can import graph designs by saving them as custom libraries and using the **Window: Swatch Libraries: Other Library** command to open them. (See Chapter 10 to learn how to save libraries.)

To Create a Custom Graph Design

1. Draw a rectangle the size of the finished design. It's sometimes easier to do this after creating the design, or you can copy the smallest value rectangle from the graph and size the design to fit it. (See Figure 8.18.)

Figure 8.18 A custom graph design can start with something as simple as this pattern-filled rectangle.

2. Create the design using any of Illustrator's tools and commands.
3. Select the design and the rectangle.
4. Choose **Object: Group** (**Command/Ctrl-g**).
5. Choose **Object: Graphs: Design** (see Figure 8.19) to open the Graph Design dialog. This is where you actually turn the object into a graph design.

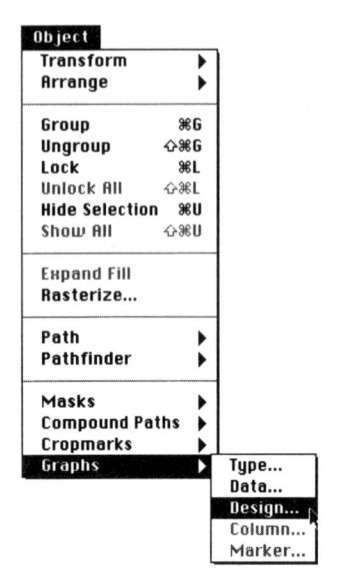

*Figure 8.19 The **Object: Graphs: Design** command is only available when there is an active selection in the drawing.*

6. Click on the **New Design** button. This turns the current selection into a new design and displays a preview of the design. You can click on the Rename button to change the name if you wish.
7. Click **OK** to add this design to the document and dismiss the dialog.

To Manage Custom Graph Designs

1. Choose **Object: Graphs: Design** to open the Graph Design dialog (shown in Figure 8.20), which lists all available graph designs for the current document.
2. Choose a graph design by clicking on it in the design list. The preview window displays the selected design. There are five buttons to choose from.

    - **Rename**—Click on this button to rename the design. Type in a new name in the Rename dialog.
    - **New Design**—Click on this button to create a new design from the current selection in the document. As discussed earlier, this button is not available if there is no selection.
    - **Delete Design**—Deletes the current design from the list.

- **Paste Design**—Pastes the current design into your document so that you can edit it and turn it into a modified graph design.
- **Select Unused**—Allows you to select all unused designs in the list.

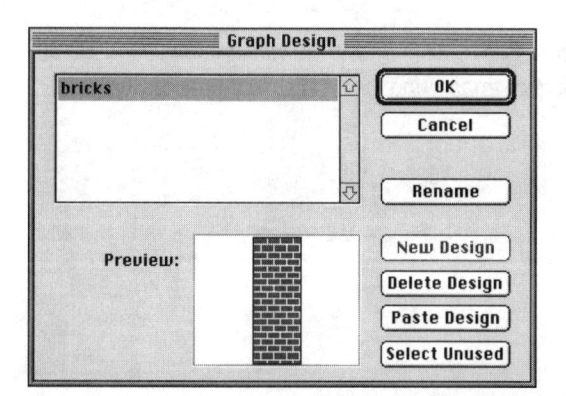

Figure 8.20 Once a design is defined, it is listed in the Graph Design dialog where it can be selected and previewed.

To Apply a Custom Graph Design

1. Define a graph design as described earlier.
2. Select a graph either by clicking on it with the Selection tool or by selecting part of it with the Group Selection tool. Figure 8.21 shows a graph that has been completely selected.

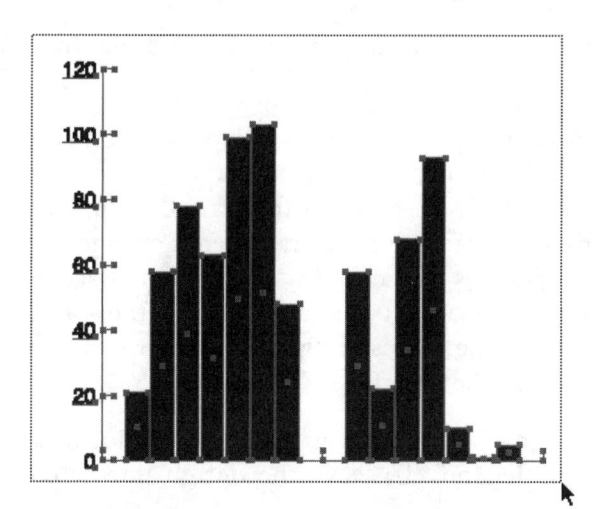

Figure 8.21 The graph must be selected, as shown here, to apply a custom graph design to it.

3. Choose **Object: Graphs: Column** (shown in Figure 8.22) or **Object: Graphs: Marker**, depending on the graph type. Choose **Column** for column or bar graphs or **Marker** for scatter or line graphs.

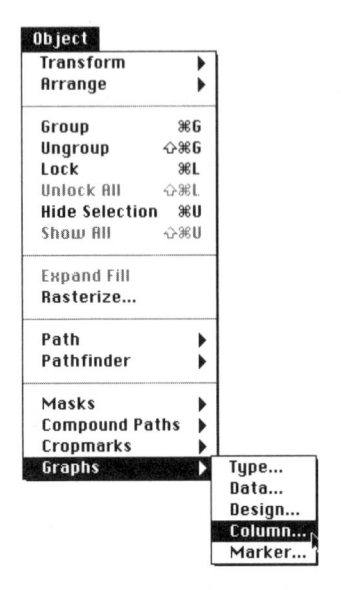

Figure 8.22 Custom graph designs are applied to a selected graph using the Column or Marker commands.

4. Click on a **Custom Design** in the list. The Graph Marker dialog has no options. The Graph Column dialog, shown in Figure 8.23, has several options.

    Column Type—There are four column types. Choose one from the drop-down menu.

    - **Vertically Scaled**—This type stretches or compresses vertically without changing width. It is the default.
    - **Uniformly Scaled**—This type scales both vertically and horizontally. The horizontal spacing of the graph is not changed.
    - **Repeating**—This type does not scale. Instead, each design represents a specified number of units and repeats to fill the scale.
    - **Sliding**—Instead of scaling, this stretches the design vertically at the point indicated in the design.

    - **Rotate Legend Design**—The design is rotated 90° clockwise when displayed in the legend. To leave the design unrotated, uncheck this box.

Blending, Tracing, and Graphing 161

- **Each Design Represents # units**—For repeating designs, it's necessary to specify the number of units that one design equals. The default is 1.
- **For Fractions**—Repeating designs are likely to have fractional units. Choose **Chop Design** or **Scale Design** from the drop-down menu, and the fractional unit will be treated accordingly.

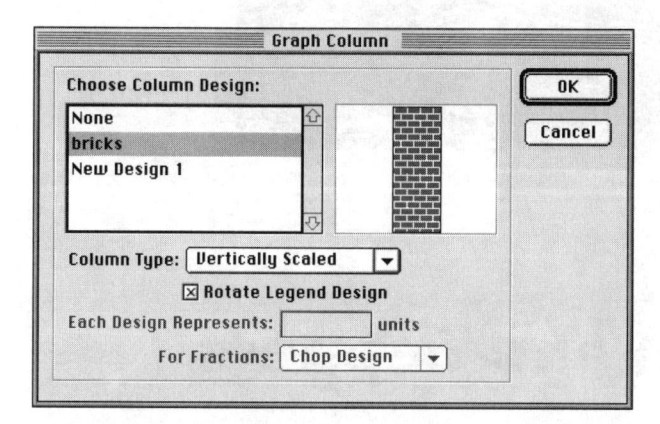

Figure 8.23 The Graph Column dialog used to define the application of a custom design to the graph columns.

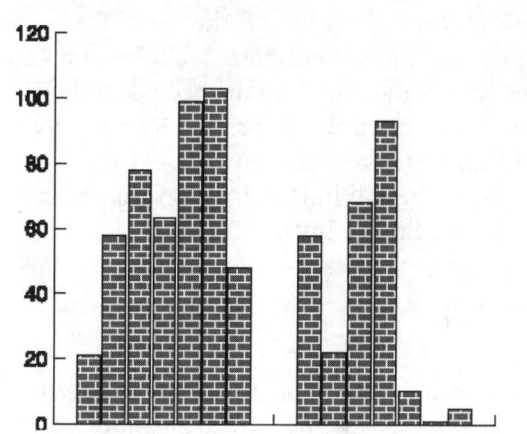

Figure 8.24 A graph with a custom column design applied.

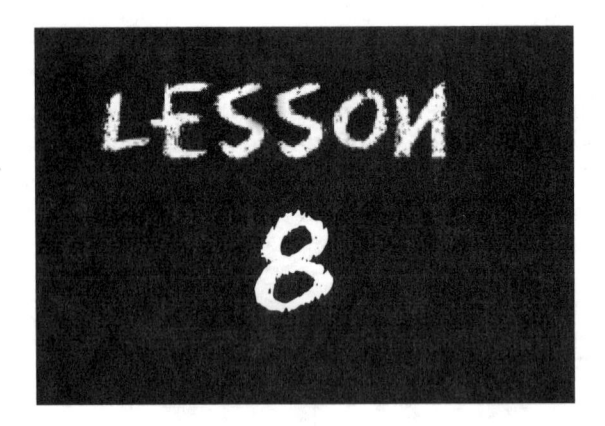

Pain and Peppers

In the first part of this lesson, we'll create an object with the Auto Trace and Blend tools to use as a graph design for the second part. We'll be graphing the relationship of chili peppers to pain as measured by the Scoville unit.

To get started, open a new blank document for this lesson (**New: Open**). Click on the **Default Fill and Stroke** button (d) to set the stroke and fill colors back to their defaults. If the Fill button isn't on top, click on it or press the **x** key so that it's over the Stroke button.

LESSON 8, PART 1: THE PEPPER

1. Choose **File: Place** and in the file dialog select the file PEPPER.PS from the LESSON08 folder on the CD, as shown in Figure 8.25. This is a grayscale file from Photoshop that we'll trace to make our graph design.

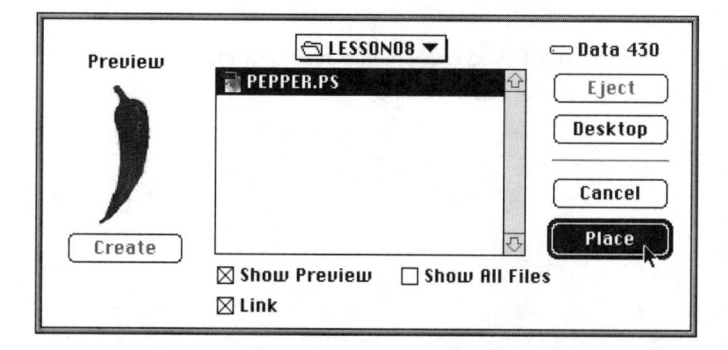

Figure 8.25 Pick your pepper from the standard file dialog and click **Place**. Illustrator places the image at the center of the active window on the current layer.

2. Choose the **Auto Trace tool** (b) hidden under the Blend button, and click on the jalapeno. (You may need to use **Edit: Undo** and click again if this doesn't work the first time.) This creates a path around the pepper, which we will fill and blend.

   We're already finished with the placed scan, so you can delete it if you wish. Move the new pepper path off the top of it so that you can see, select, and delete the bitmap scan.

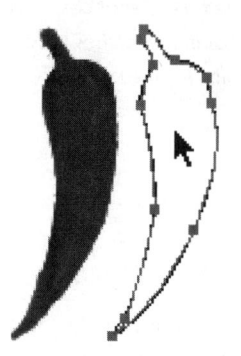

Figure 8.26 Click on the grayscale pepper with the Auto Trace tool to create a path with the shape of the pepper.

3. Choose the **Zoom** tool (z) and drag a marquee over the pepper path so that it fills the screen and you can work on it more easily, as shown in Figure 8.27.

164 CHAPTER 8

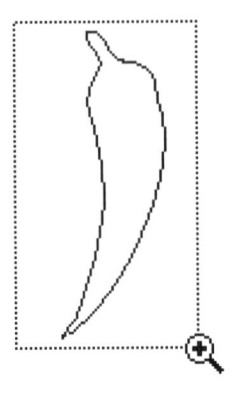

Figure 8.27 Drag a Zoom marquee over the pepper path to enlarge it for easier editing.

4. Choose the red spot color from the Swatches palette, shown in Figure 8.28, by clicking on it. It's second from the right in the second row. (If the Swatches palette isn't open, choose **Window: Show Swatches**.)

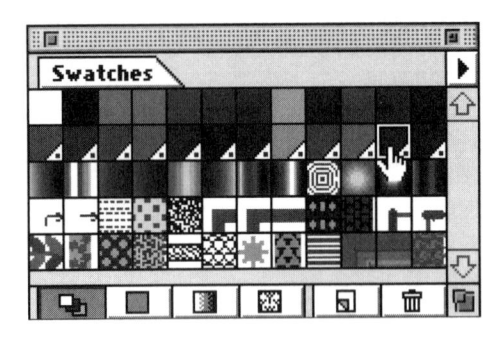

Figure 8.28 Pick the red spot color from the second row of the Swatches palette to use as the fill color for the pepper.

5. Click on the **Stroke** button (x) in the fill and stroke area of the Toolbox to bring it to the top, then click on the **None** button (/) (see Figure 8.29) to set the stroke to none.

Blending, Tracing, and Graphing 165

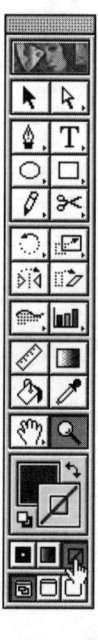

Figure 8.29 Set the stroke to none by clicking on the **None** button in the Toolbox.

6. Choose the **Pen** tool (p). Click near the top of the pepper toward the right side and drag down at about -30° (see Figure 8.30) to set the first anchor point and direction line of the highlight we're about to construct.

Figure 8.30 Drag the direction line for the first anchor point of the highlight path.

166   CHAPTER 8

7. Click near the tip of the pepper and drag down at about +30° (see Figure 8.31) to complete the path. The curve of the path should match the curve of the pepper.

Figure 8.31 Drag the direction line for the second anchor point. The highlight path matches the contour of the pepper.

8. Click on the **Swap Fill and Stroke** button to set the stroke to red and the fill to none.

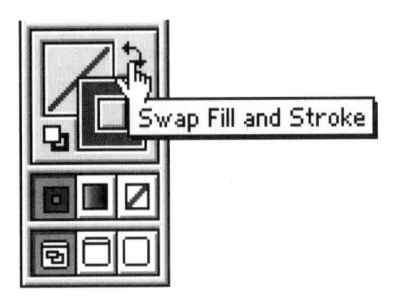

*Figure 8.32 Click on the **Swap** button to exchange the fill and stroke colors so that our path will be stroked with the same red used to fill the pepper.*

9. In the Color palette (shown in Figure 8.33), set the tint to **50%** by dragging the color slider to the left or typing the amount into the specification box.

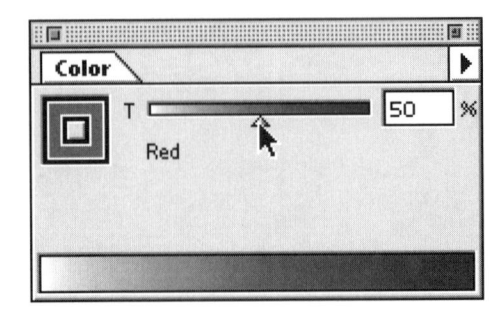

Figure 8.33 Change the tint of a spot color by dragging the slider, as shown here, or by typing the percentage into the specification box.

Blending, Tracing, and Graphing   **167**

10. Hold down the **Command/Ctrl** key to toggle to the Selection cursor and click on the path to select it, as shown in Figure 8.34. (Only the last point we drew was selected, and we'll be rotating the whole path.)

Figure 8.34 Click on the path with the Selection cursor. We need to select the entire path (i.e., both anchor points) so that we can transform and copy it.

11. Choose the **Rotate** tool (r) and click on the bottom anchor point to set the source point. Click and drag the top anchor point to the left several degrees. Hold down the **Option/Alt** key after you start dragging and before you release the mouse button to make a rotated copy, as shown in Figure 8.35.

Figure 8.35 Rotate the highlight path by clicking on the bottom anchor point to set the source point and dragging the top anchor point a few degrees while holding down the **Option/Alt** key to create a copy.

12. Set the tint in the Color palette (Figure 8.36) back to **100%**, and set the stroke width in the Stroke palette to 6 points. (If the Stroke palette isn't open, choose **Window: Open Stroke**.) The highlight will blend into the pepper.

168 CHAPTER 8

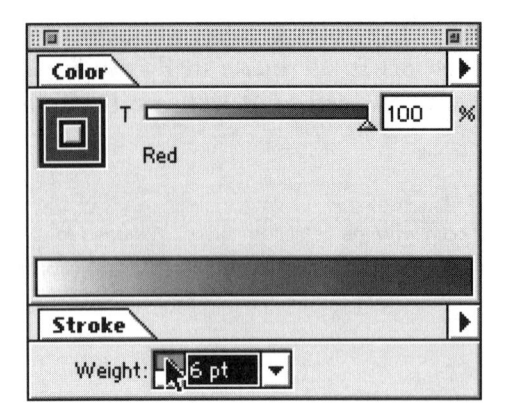

Figure 8.36 The Color and Stroke palettes with the spot color tint set back to 100% and the stroke width set to 6 points for the rotated and copied highlight path.

13. Hold down the **Shift-Command/Ctrl** keys to toggle the Selection cursor again and add to the current selection (which should be the rotated red path only) and click on the first pink path.

*Figure 8.37 Both objects of a blend must be selected before blending. Here, **Shift**-clicking on the first path leaves both highlight paths selected.*

14. Choose the **Blend** tool (b). Click on the anchor point of one selected path and then the other. The order doesn't matter in this case. In the Blend dialog (shown in Figure 8.38), set Steps to **9** and click **OK**. Illustrator blends the two lines and the highlight is finished.

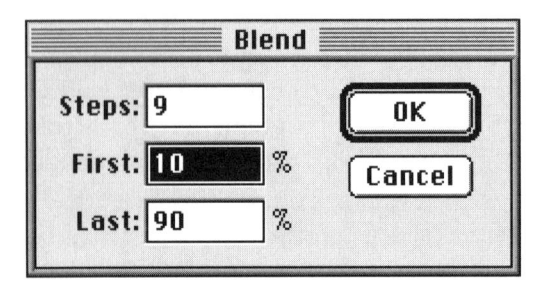

Figure 8.38 After clicking on the equivalent anchor points of two objects, specify a nine-step fill in the Blend dialog.

Blending, Tracing, and Graphing 169

15. Choose the **Edit: Select All** (**Command/Ctrl-a**) to select the pepper and its highlight, then choose **Object: Group** (**Command/Ctrl-g**), shown in Figure 8.39, to group the paths into a single object.

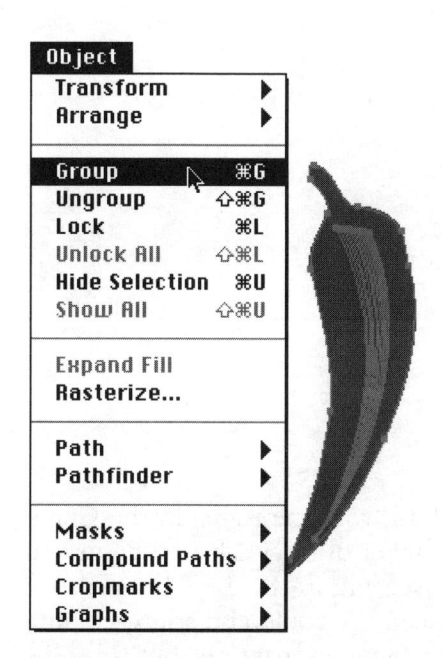

Figure 8.39 Choose **Object: Group** with the pepper and highlight gradient selected to turn this collection of paths into a single object.

Before going on, choose **View: Fit In Window** (**Command/Ctrl-0**) so that you can view the entire document. Then choose the **Selection** tool (v) and drag the pepper to the bottom of the image window so that it's out of the way when you create the graph in part two. This completes the first part of the lesson, so save your work if you wish.

LESSON 8, PART 2: THE GRAPH

Continue using your image from Part 1 or open the file PEPPER2.AI, from the LESSON08 folder on the CD, which contains the finished image from Part 1 of the lesson.

1. Choose the **Column Graph** tool (j). Click near the upper left corner of the screen and drag down and to the right as shown in Figure 8.40. When you release the mouse button, a blank Graph Data worksheet is opened. The first step in creating a graph is simply to indicate where you want it to go.

170 **CHAPTER 8**

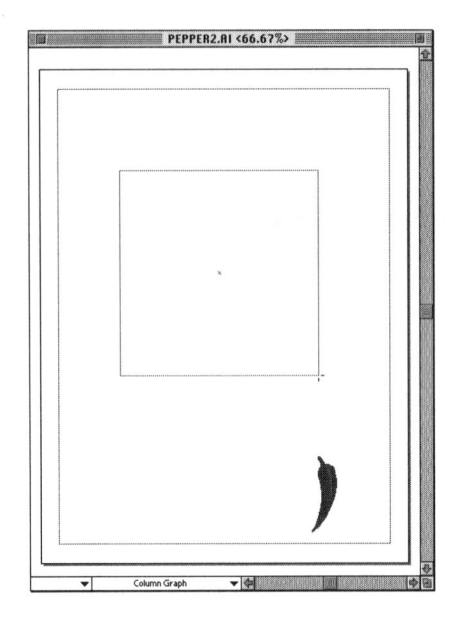

Figure 8.40 The Column Graph tool is selected and a graph marquee is being dragged across the drawing.

2. Click on the **Cell Style** button (third from the right) in the Graph Data worksheet and change the Number of Decimals to 0 digits and the Column Width to 15 digits (see Figure 8.41). This makes a global change to the entire worksheet. We could also adjust column widths individually by dragging the column separators, but this time it's easier just to set them all the same.

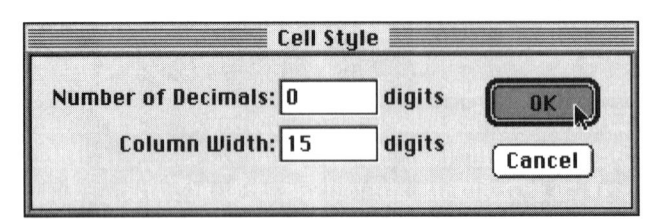

Figure 8.41 Use the Cell Style dialog to set a global worksheet style.

3. In the Graph Data worksheet, press the **Delete/Backspace** key to delete the default value of 1 from the first cell, then press the **Return/Enter** key to leave the first cell blank. Type the following headings, pressing the **Return/Enter** key after each to enter the value and go to the next cell in the column: **Thai Dragon**, **Super Cayenne**, **Charleston Hot**, **NuMex Bailey**, **Habanero (red)**. Then click on the first cell in the second column and enter the following values: Scoville

Blending, Tracing, and Graphing   171

Units, 35000, 50000, 70000, 97000, 285000. Click on the **Apply** button (checkmark) to enter the data and have Illustrator draw the graph.

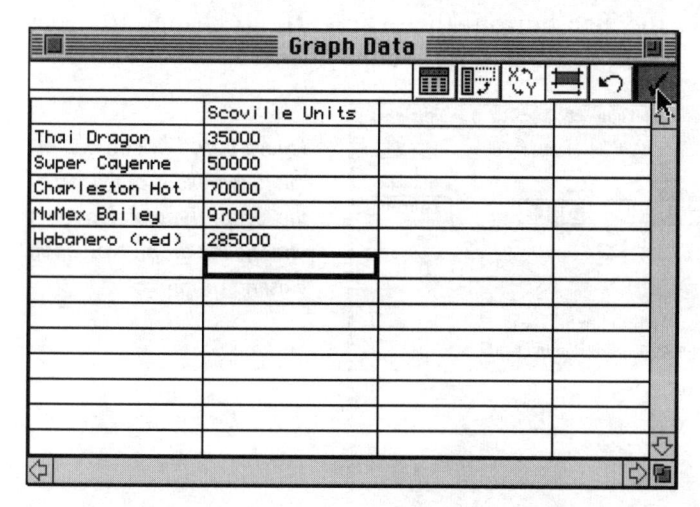

Figure 8.42 This is what the Graph Data worksheet looks like after entering the data. The Apply button is being clicked to enter the data into the graph.

4. Click anywhere on the drawing window to make it active and put the Graph Data worksheet in the background. The graph is selected. You'll notice in Figure 8.43 that Illustrator's defaults don't work very well with this data. We'll have to make some changes.

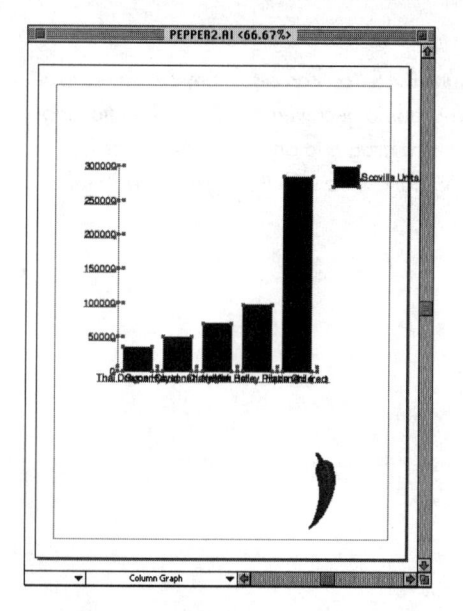

Figure 8.43 Illustrator graphs the data correctly but has no intelligence about sizing labels or fitting information on the page. These elements must be edited to complete this graph.

5. Choose **Object: Graphs: Type** or double-click on the Graph button in the Toolbox to open the Graph Type dialog shown in Figure 8.44. Click on the **Bar** button, then click **OK** to change to a bar graph. This is better, but it still needs adjustment.

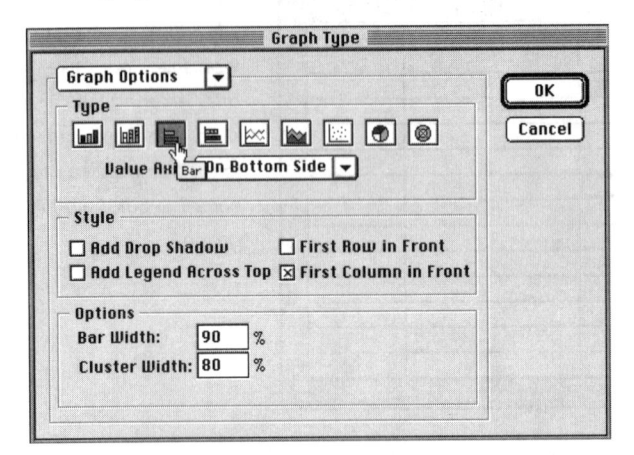

Figure 8.44 Click on one of the nine buttons at the top of the Graph Type dialog to change the graph type of an existing graph.

6. Choose the **Direct Selection** tool (a). Click outside the graph to deselect everything, then click and drag around the legend and its label, Scoville Units, to select both. Then click on the selection and drag the legend under the graph as shown in Figure 8.45.

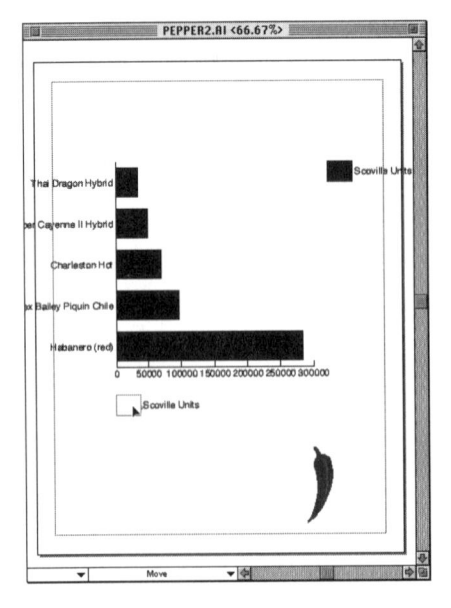

Figure 8.45 You can select any single element in a graph object with the Direct Selection tool and then drag it to another location, as is being done here with the legend and its label.

Blending, Tracing, and Graphing 173

7. Choose the **Selection** tool (v), click anywhere on the graph to select the entire graph object, then drag to center the graph on the page. We could change many other cosmetic aspects of this graph to make it look better, but we'll limit ourselves to adding the graph design next.

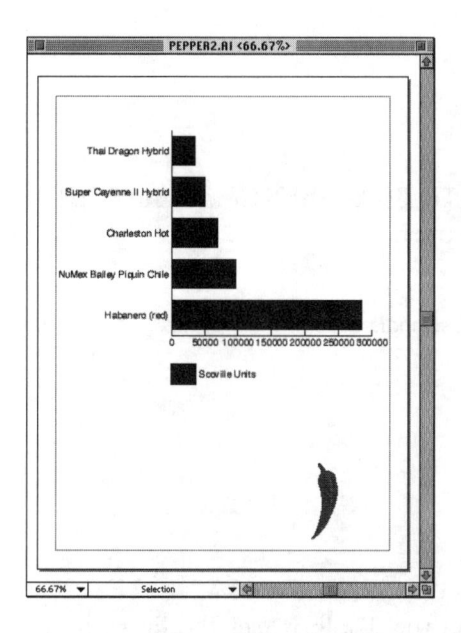

Figure 8.46 Moving the graph more to the center of the page makes all of the elements readable.

This completes part 2 of the lesson, so save your work if you wish.

LESSON 8, PART 3: INTEGRATING THE GRAPH DESIGN

Continue using your image from Part 2, or open the file PEPPER3.AI, from the LESSON08 folder on the CD, which contains the finished image from Part 2.

1. Choose the **Rectangle** tool (m) and drag a rectangle around the red chili pepper as shown in Figure 8.47. You must group an object with a rectangle to create a graph design. Don't worry that the rectangle obliterates your view of the pepper.

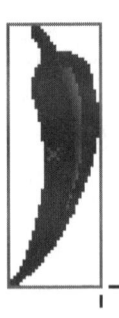

Figure 8.47 Draw a rectangle around the pepper to create a graph design.

2. Choose **Object: Arrange: Send To Back (Shift-Command/Ctrl-])** to put the rectangle under the pepper.

Figure 8.48 Arrange the black rectangle under the red pepper.

3. Click on the **None** button (/) in the Toolbox, set the fill to none. Figure 8.49 shows the resulting image. (The stroke should already be set to none. If it isn't, click on the **Stroke** button (x) and then on the **None** button (/).)

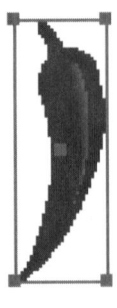

Figure 8.49 The rectangle, still selected, but with fill and stroke attributes of none.

4. Choose the **Selection** tool (v) and drag a selection marquee around the rectangle and pepper so that both are selected. Then choose

Blending, Tracing, and Graphing   **175**

Object: Group (**Command/Ctrl-g**) to create a single object for the graph design (see Figure 8.50).

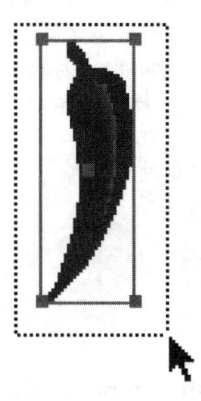

Figure 8.50 Drag a selection marquee over the rectangle and pepper so that they can be grouped together.

5. Choose **Object: Graphs: Design** to open the Graph Design dialog shown in Figure 8.51, then click on the New Design button. Illustrator previews the selection.

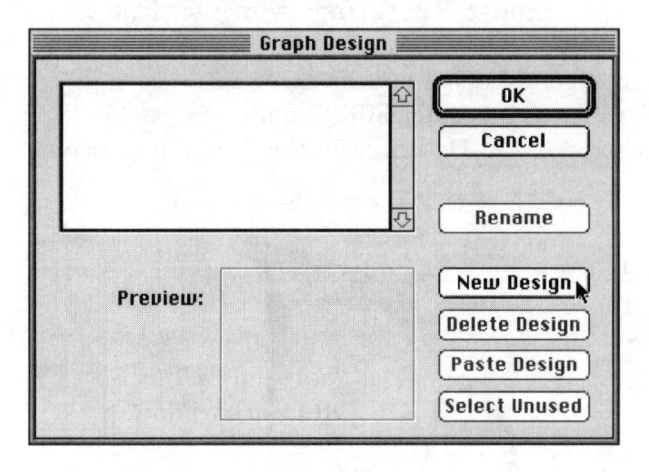

Figure 8.51 The Graph Design dialog doesn't know that you want to create a new graph design until you click on the New Design button.

6. Click on the Rename button, type "pepper" for the graph design (see Figure 8.52), then click **OK** twice to name the design and close the dialog.

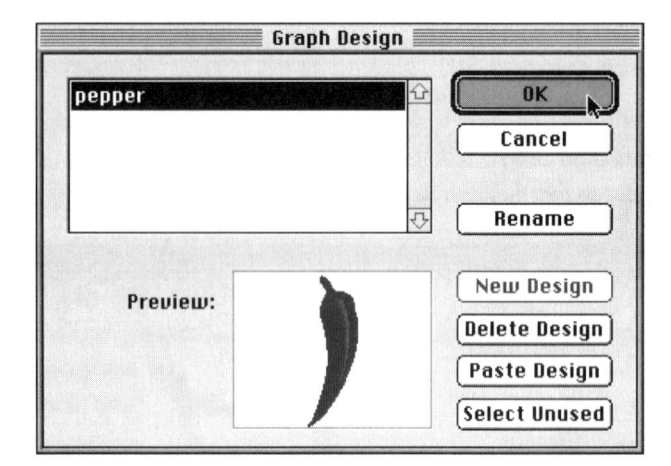

Figure 8.52 *After clicking on the **New Design** button to preview the selection and the **Rename** button to name the design **pepper**, you're ready to close the Graph Design dialog by clicking **OK**.*

7. The Selection tool should still be active, so click anywhere on the graph to select it, then choose **Object: Graphs: Column** to open the Column Design dialog:

- For Choose Column Design, click on **pepper**.
- For Column Type, choose **Repeating** from the drop-down menu.
- Leave the Rotate Legend Design box checked.
- For Each Design Represents, enter **50000** units.
- For Fractions, choose **Chop Design** from the drop-down menu.
- Click **OK**.

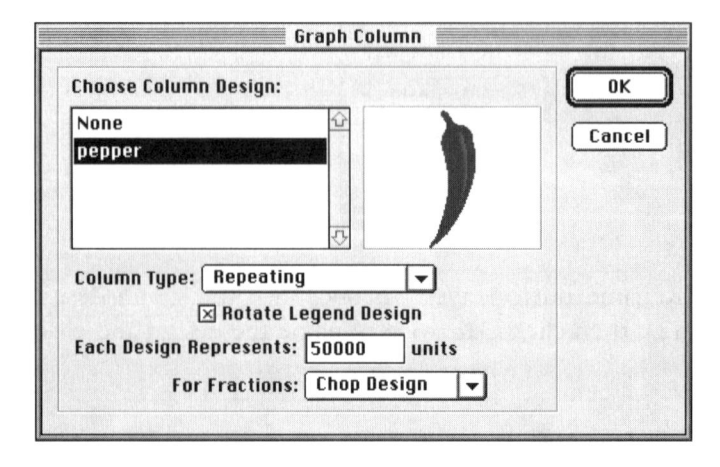

Figure 8.53 *The Column Design dialog with the appropriate settings.*

There's a lot that could be done to make this graph even nicer. We could select the pepper in the legend with the Group Select tool and rotate it 180° so that it faces the same direction that the peppers in the bars do. We could add a title and some notes about the relative heat of a Scoville unit. The type could look better. We could add a background.

This is the beauty of having a graphing module within Illustrator. We can do anything to the visual representation of numbers that we would do with any other visual element.

Save your work if you wish. You can also open PEPPER4.AI in the LESSON08 folder to view a finished version of this lesson.

Section III

Afloat with Palettes

In this section...

- Section Introduction: Palettes
- Chapter 9: Shape and Position—Info, Transform, and Align Palettes
- Chapter 10: Appearance—Color, Swatches, Gradient, Stroke, and Attributes Palettes
- Chapter 11: Layers

Whither, Why, and Wherefore Palettes?

If the Toolbox is the heart of Illustrator, the palettes must be its brain. Generally, you pick a tool and then draw or manipulate the drawing with it directly. With the palettes, you select a path or object in the drawing and then adjust it from the palette. Or you can pick a tool and then adjust its behavior from the palettes before you draw.

The point is, palettes provide a way to execute commands without having to open a menu, select a command, and fill out a dialog box. Palettes remain open on top of all document windows so that you can see at a glance what the current settings are and then change them in a single step if necessary.

There are nine palettes, and the default groupings and screen placements are somewhat baffling to me. It doesn't matter, because it's easy to adjust these to suit your personal working style. There are also two type palettes, but Adobe has segregated them under the Type menu. The other nine palettes can all be found under the Window menu. The type palettes behave like all other palettes, but we'll discuss them more fully in Chapter 13.

As mentioned in Chapter 2, Adobe has put considerable effort into refining Illustrator's palettes and making them more consistent with its other applications. This means that the palettes in Illustrator 7 look considerably different from previous versions, but they function the same way. There are also some new features and behaviors, which we'll cover in this section.

The Anatomy of Palettes

Each palette contains unique information and options that reflect the current selection in the drawing or active tool. All palettes are viewed in a palette window, which can contain multiple palettes.

It's important to understand that palettes are different from palette groups and palette windows. The *palette window* contains palettes for display on the screen. The size and placement of this window is independent of the palette itself. Within the window can be one or more palettes—this is a *palette group*. You can also "dock" multiple palettes to a single palette window, as described shortly.

The mechanism for maintaining order among palettes, groups, and windows is the palette tab. The name of the palette is displayed on a tab that can be clicked to activate the palette or dragged to move the palette out of or into palette windows. In other words, you can drag a palette window to reposition it on screen, or you can drag a palette tab to move a palette to a different window.

Each palette group has a single active palette, which is indicated by a white palette tab. All other tabs in the group are gray. In addition to dragging, windows can be resized or closed like any document window in your operating system, although there are some fixed-width palettes, such as the Swatches palette, and some fixed-size palettes, such as the Info palette, that limit your ability to resize the palette window when they are active.

One additional feature of palettes is the small right-pointing arrow near the upper-right corner of the palette window. Clicking at this spot opens the Palette menu with additional palette-specific options and commands. We'll cover specific palette options in each of the chapters of this section.

To Hide and Show Palettes

- Each of the nine palettes can be shown or hidden from the Window menu. Each palette-specific command toggles between Hide and Show depending on the current state of the palette.
- You can click on the close box (upper-left corner in MacOS and upper-right corner in Windows) of any palette window to close the window and hide all of its palettes.
- Click on a palette tab within a palette window to show its palette and hide the previously showing palette.

To Move Palette Windows

- Click and drag on the title bar of a palette window. (I call this a title bar, because it's where the title bar for most windows is, but there's no actual title.) You can drag a window anywhere on screen.
- When you drag near another open window in Illustrator, within one or two pixels, the window you're dragging snaps to the other window. This is a nice way to align windows and reduce screen clutter.
- It's possible to drag windows so that they overlap each other. The active window displays on top. Click on a window to bring it to the front.

- Illustrator remembers the screen position (and settings) of all windows when you quit and reopens all palettes where you left off.

To Resize Palette Windows

- Click on the **Zoom** box in the upper-right corner of the title bar (MacOS) or the **Minimize/Maximize** box next to the upper-right corner of the title bar (Windows). This operation is essentially the same for any window in your operating system. For palette windows, it reduces the size of the window to just the title bar and tab bar. The palette itself is not visible. Click again on the **Zoom** or **Min/Max** box or click on a palette tab to expand the window to its default size and display the palette.

NOTE: If you have resized a palette window, the first click on the Zoom or Min/Max box returns the palette to its default size and the second click collapses it.

- Drag on the **Resize** box (MacOS) or **Drag** corner (Windows), both of which are at the lower-right corner of the window, to resize the window. Some size restrictions apply to specific palettes, as noted earlier.

To Regroup or Dock Palettes

- Click and drag on a palette tab. As soon as you drag the tab out of its palette window, it is removed from the group.
- Drag the tab to any free area of the desktop and release the mouse button. Illustrator creates a new palette window containing this single palette.
- Drag the tab to another palette window, release the mouse button, and the tab is added to this palette group. Palette windows are highlighted when you drag in a tab.
- Drag the tab to the bottom of any palette window. Release the mouse button when the bottom of the window is highlighted to "dock" the palette. Docking is a way to display two palettes in a single window.

It's like snapping palette windows underneath each other, except that there is only a single window. This brings up another palette classification, the docked palette group. Undock simply by dragging the docked tab to a new location.

To Use Palette Menus

1. Move the cursor over the right-pointing arrow at the right side of the tab display area. (This includes docked palettes.)
2. Press down the mouse and the palette menu pops up.
3. Slide the mouse button over the command you wish to choose and release it.

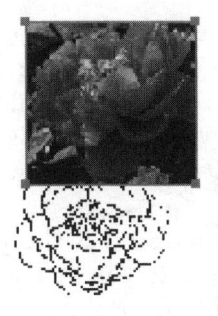

9 Shape and Position

In this chapter…

- Static feedback—Info palette
- Interactive adjustment—Transform palette
- One-click adjustments—Align palette
- Lesson 9: A Lattice Transformed

Illustrator has always been vaunted for its precision and control. I wouldn't argue with this, but since I began working with the first version ten years ago I have felt that there should be a way to edit the size and position of objects simply by typing in the specifications. Programs such as PageMaker have had this capability for years, and now, finally, Illustrator 7 has it too.

The new Transform palette takes the basic feedback Illustrator has always supplied through the Info palette and lets you work with the numbers directly. What could be more precise? We'll also discuss the redesigned Align palette in this chapter, which lets you set the vertical and horizontal alignment for a group of selected objects with a single click.

Illustrator's default palette groups combine the Info, Transform, and Align palettes in a single window. For me, the Info palette is of limited usefulness, but it does provide interactive numerical feedback for the drawing and selection tools. This same numerical information—width, height, position, etc.—can be edited using the Transform palette, while the relative position of objects can be adjusted using the Align palette.

STATIC FEEDBACK—INFO PALETTE

Every time you move the cursor across the screen, the numerical coordinates of its position are being tracked. This information is displayed interactively within Illustrator's Info palette. With any drawing tool selected, the Info palette shows the exact *x* and *y* coordinates of the cursor within the drawing window. When you click and drag, the Info palette (shown in Figure 9.1) provides additional information depending on the tool chosen. With a selection tool chosen you can view the size and position of any object or group by clicking on it. When there is no active selection, the Info palette tracks the cursor position in the drawing window. Since the default zero point for rulers is the upper-left corner of the window, x values for the cursor are usually negative.

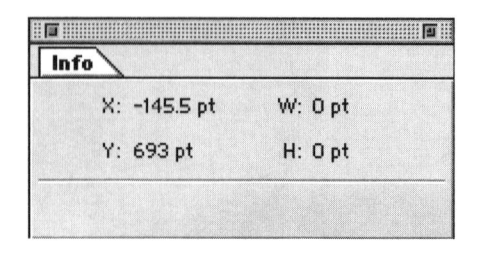

Figure 9.1 The Info palette.

The Info palette shows all information in degrees, percents, or in the default units set in the **File: Preferences: General** dialog. The tool-specific information displayed in the Info palette is exactly what you'd expect. In addition to x and y coordinates displayed for the Pen, Pencil, Scissor, Paintbucket, Eyedropper, Blend, and Auto Trace tools, Rectangle, Oval, and Graph tools display width and height. No information is displayed for the Polygon, Star, or Spiral tools.

All the transform tools—Rotate, Twirl, Reflect, Scale, and Shear—display x and y coordinates for the source point. No information is displayed for the Reshape tool.

- *Rotate*, *Spiral*, and *Reflect* show the angle.
- *Scale* shows the percentage change in width and height.
- *Shear* shows the angles of the shear axis and shear.
- *Measure* and *Gradient* tools display the length (or delta) and the angle.
- *Zoom* shows the magnification in percent.

The Type tool displays positional information—x, y, w, and h—only when dragging a type rectangle. Otherwise, it displays the type size, font name, and kern setting.

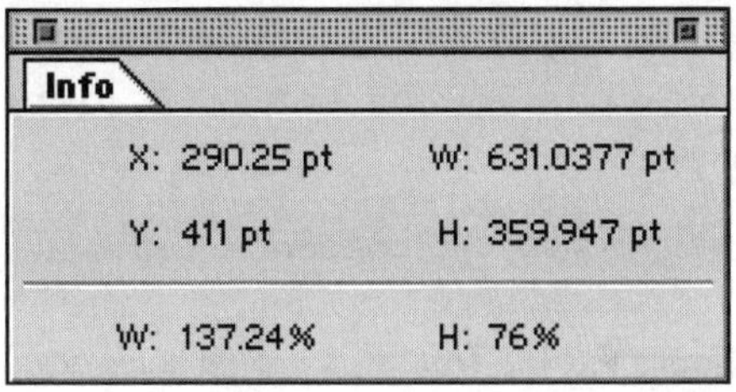

Figure 9.2 When a selection is being transformed in any way, the Info palette gives complete feedback. Here, a selection is being scaled as indicated by the W and H percentages at the bottom of the palette.

INTERACTIVE ADJUSTMENT—TRANSFORM PALETTE

You could say that while the Info palette is *cursor oriented*—it shows coordinates, distances, and deltas—the Transform palette is *object oriented*—it shows position and dimensions for selections only. The major difference is that the information displayed in the Transform palette can be edited; it's interactive rather than static.

When you select an object or group of any shape, Illustrator calculates a rectangular bounding box that surrounds the selection as though you were dragging a selection marquee that exactly circumscribed the selection. The position and dimensions of the bounding box are displayed as x, y, w, and h dimensions. There are two additional specification fields, angle and shear. These fields are always 0° until you edit them to make an adjustment.

The other feature of the Transform palette is a 3 × 3 matrix of small hollow squares representing the bounding box. (This feature will be familiar to users of PageMaker.) The nine squares represent the reference points for adjustment, so you can adjust relative to any of the four corners, the middle of any side, or the center of the bounding box.

> **NOTE** The capabilities of the Transform palette are very similar to the commands in the **Object: Transform** submenu (see Chapter 12) and the transform tools in the Toolbox (see Chapter 5). Choosing which method to use when transforming a selection is more a matter of circumstances and personal preference than the desired result.

You can use the Transform palette (see Figure 9.3) to calculate moves or resize objects by using the **+** and **-** keys in the specification fields to add or subtract amounts with existing values. You don't even have to match units, so it's possible to have a value of 360 points and type **+ 1** in after it to add an inch, which Illustrator converts to 72 points.

> **NOTE** Once a specification field has been edited, clicking on another field or clicking on the reference point matrix applies the change. That means that you can enter only one value at a time, which isn't really a hardship because the palette remains open and it's easy to undo any errors.

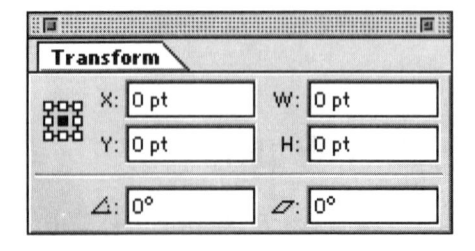

Figure 9.3 The Transform palette fields are all 0 when no selection is active.

To Edit Selections Using the Transform Palette

1. Make sure the Transform palette, shown in Figure 9.4, is open (**Window: Show Transform**).
2. Make a selection to be transformed.

3. Click on one of the nine reference points to set the source point for transformations.

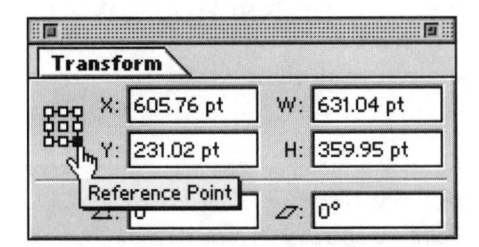

Figure 9.4 Changing the Reference Point by clicking on one of the nine points of the reference grid in the Transform palette.

4. Type the specification for the transform into any of the six transformation fields:

   - X—Moves the selection horizontally.
   - Y—Moves the selection vertically.
   - W—Changes the width of the bounding box and scales all objects within accordingly.
   - H—Changes the height of the bounding box and scales all objects within accordingly.
   - —Rotates the bounding box and its contents 0° to 360°.
   - —Shears the bounding box and its contents 0° to 360°.

5. Press the **Tab**, **Return**, or **Enter** key to apply the transform.

NOTE Hold down the **Option/Alt** key while applying a transformation to transform a copy. The copy is selected, and the original is left unaltered, although it is grouped with the copy. (This grouping is a bug acknowledged by Adobe and should be fixed in the next update to Illustrator 7.) Be sure not to hold down the **Option/Alt** key until you are finished typing in your change, or you will enter special characters instead of numbers.

ONE-CLICK ADJUSTMENTS—ALIGN PALETTE

Illustrator has many tools to help you position objects precisely where you want them within a drawing. You can also position objects relative to one another with one or two clicks using the Align palette (shown in Figure 9.5).

This includes aligning objects to a shared axis or distributing them equally along an axis. Relative alignment or distribution can be vertical or horizontal, left, right, or centered. The Align palette does all its work visually, with six alignment and six distribution buttons. The buttons act either on the vertical or horizontal axis and align or distribute to the left, center, or right.

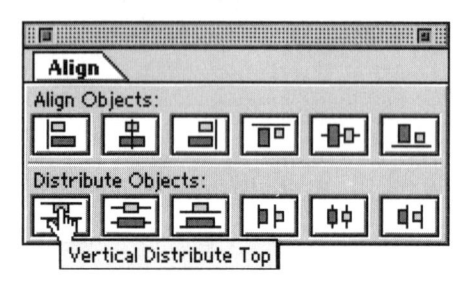

Figure 9.5 The Align palette has two rows of six buttons each that allow you to align or distribute objects with a single click.

To Align or Distribute Objects

1. Make sure the Align palette is open (**Window: Show Align**).
2. Select two or more objects.
3. Click on one of the 12 buttons in the palette to establish the relationship among the objects.

NOTE Aligning objects and aligning type are distinct. You can select a type object and align it with other objects, or you can select type using the Type tool and edit it as you would in a word processor to align the type relative to itself.

LESSON 9

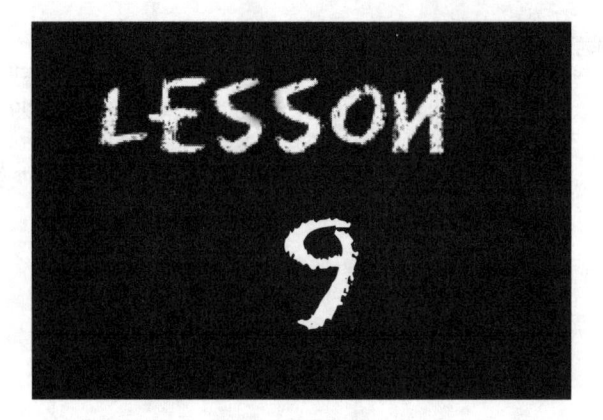

A Lattice Transformed

We will be using the Transform and Align palettes to lay out a page for a Web site devoted to Chinese tree peonies. We'll be placing predesigned objects and manipulating them with the palettes. In a later lesson, we'll revisit this project to add links.

To get started, open the file LATTICE.AI from the LESSON09 folder on the CD. If the image doesn't fit on your monitor, choose **View: Fit in Window** to reduce the magnification. Make sure the Info/Transform/Align palette group is open before beginning this lesson; any of the three appropriate **Window: Show** commands will open the entire group. (If you've rearranged your palette groupings, make sure that both the Transform and Align palettes are open.) The Selection tool (v) should be the active tool. It's the only tool used in this lesson.

1. Choose **Edit: Select All** (**Command/Ctrl-a**) and look at the Transform palette to see the specifications for this selection, shown in Figure 9.6.

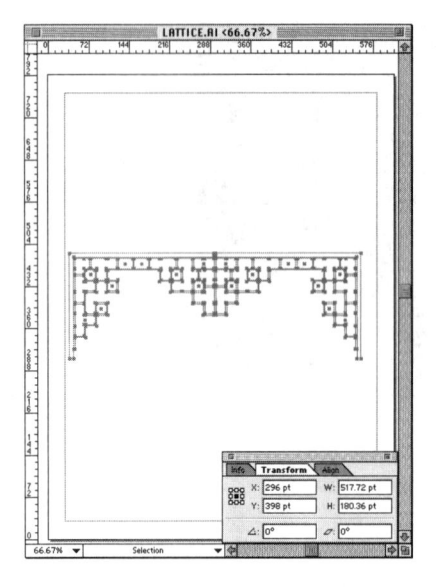

Figure 9.6 *The Transform palette in its default palette group window, showing the position of the selected Chinese latticework drawing with respect to the center point of its bounding box.*

2. Click on the top center reference point in the nine-point matrix in the Transform palette, then click in the Y field and type **756**. Press the **Tab**, **Return**, or **Enter** keys to apply the transformation (see Figure 9.7). The selection moves to the top of the window.

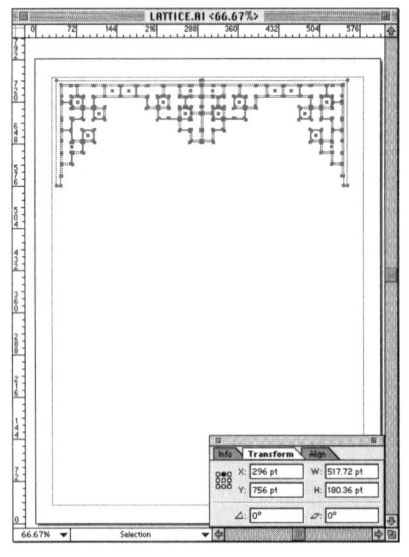

Figure 9.7 *The reference point has been changed to the top middle and a new Y specification has been entered to move the selection with respect to the top of its bounding box.*

3. Click on the bottom center reference point in the Transform palette, then click in the Y field and type **36**. Hold down the **Option/Alt**

key before applying the transformation. This makes a copy of the lattice and leaves it selected (see Figure 9.8).

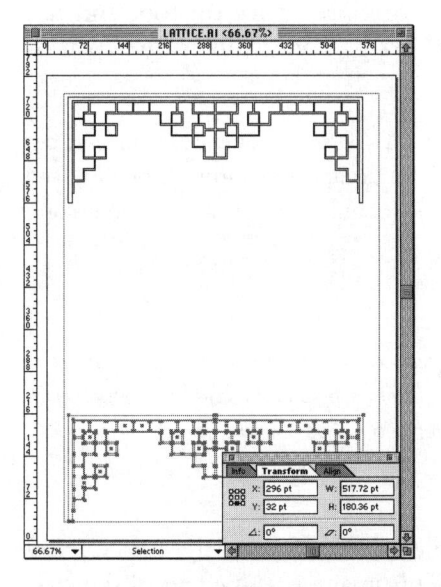

Figure 9.8 Two lattices positioned using the Transform palette: the original at the top and the copy, still selected, at the bottom of the image window.

4. Click on the center reference point in the Transform palette, then click in the rotate field and type **180**. Apply the transformation by pressing **Tab**, **Return**, or **Enter**, and the selection is flipped across the horizontal axis (see Figure 9.9).

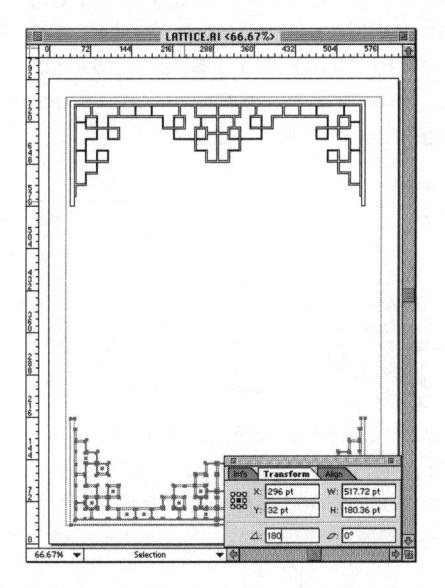

Figure 9.9 Flip the lattice copy about its center point by specifying an angle of 180° in the Transform palette.

5. Choose **Object: Group** (**Command/Ctrl-g**) to keep the lattice lines together when we use the Align palette later in this lesson. Drag a Selection marquee over the original lattice on top, and use the **Object: Group** (**Command/Ctrl-g**) command to group it as well, as shown in Figure 9.10.

> **NOTE** I would have liked to group the lattice for you in the original document, but there's a bug in the Transform palette that groups copies to their original, and this would interfere with the rest of the lesson. None of the other transform tools or commands have this bug.

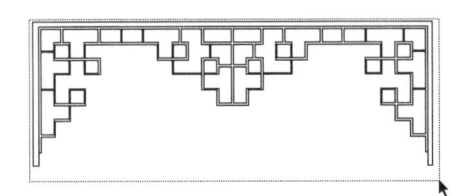

Figure 9.10 Drag a selection marquee over the top lattice so that it can be grouped and later aligned as a single object.

6. Choose **File: Place**, and select the file **SEMI.PS** from the LESSON09 folder on the CD, and click **Place**. This image is a drawing of the classic, semi-double form of the Chinese tree peony.

   We'll place two more images right on top of the first and move them later. Choose **File: Place**, select **ENSLAVE.PS**, a Chinese ink stamp meaning, *enslaved by peonies*. Click **Place**, then click the **Don't Replace** button in the warning dialog (see Figure 9.11).
   Choose **File: Place**, and then select **PAPERCUT.PS**, a reproduction of a very fine Chinese paper cut of a peony blossom. Click **Place**, and then click **Don't Replace** again.

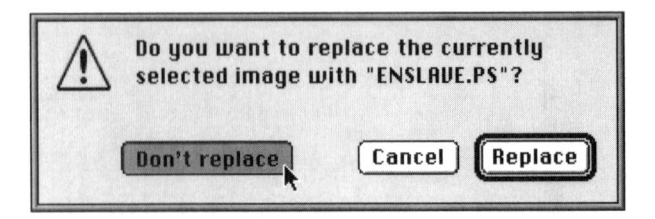

*Figure 9.11 When you place a file while a previously placed object is selected, this warning dialog gives you the choice of replacing the existing object or ignoring it. For this lesson, click the **Don't Replace** button and worry about arranging the placed objects later.*

Shape and Position 195

7. Click in the **X** field of the Transform palette to put the insertion point after the current setting. Type **+2in** and press the **Tab**, **Return** or **Enter** keys to apply the move. Figure 9.12 shows the result.

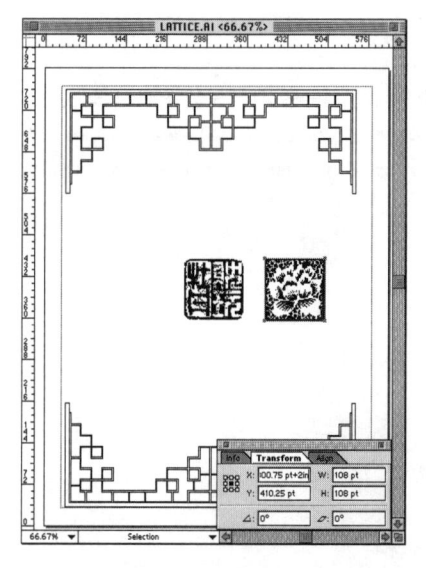

Figure 9.12 Move the selection to the right by adding two inches to the current X value in the Transform palette.

8. Click on the placed papercut image back in the center of the drawing to select it. Click in the X field of the Transform palette to put the insertion point after the current setting. Type **-2in** and press the **Tab**, **Return**, or **Enter** keys to apply the move. Figure 9.13 shows the result.

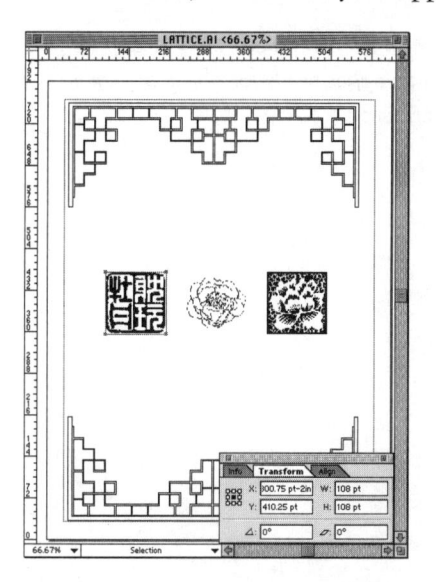

Figure 9.13 Move another selection to the left by subtracting two inches from the current X value in the Transform palette.

9. Drag a selection marquee around the three placed images to select them, then choose **Object: Group (Command/Ctrl-g)** (see Figure 9.14). Drag the group down slightly. For now, precision isn't important; we'll take care of it later.

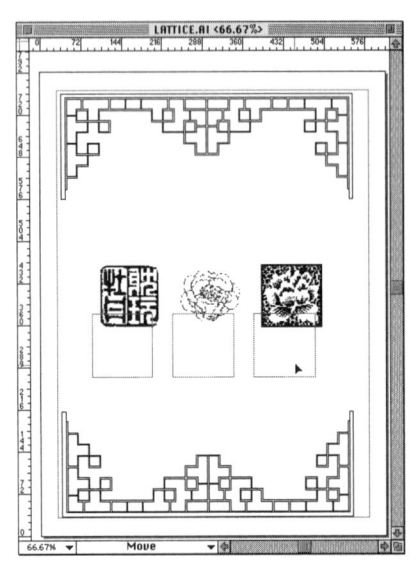

Figure 9.14 A less precise move: use the Selection tool to drag the group of three placed images out of the way to await later, more careful alignment.

10. Choose **File: Place**, select **CINNABAR.PS**, and click **OK**. This is a photograph of the Chinese tree peony, Cinnabar Red (see Figure 9.15).

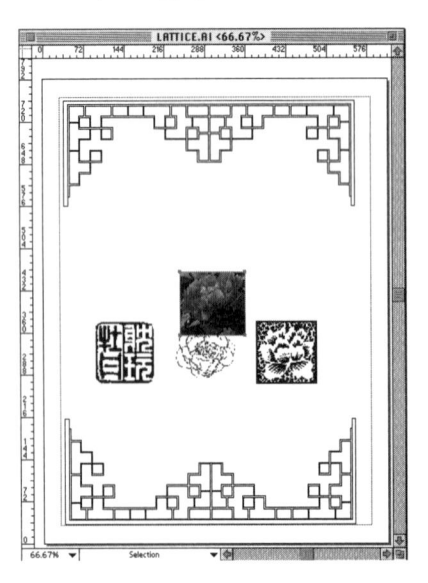

Figure 9.15 An unfinished composition, but with all placed images ready for object alignment and distribution.

11. Choose **Edit: Select All**, click on the Align palette tab, then click on the Vertical Distribute Center button, the second button on the Distribute Objects line. This evenly spaces the group of three buttons and the peony photograph between the two lattice drawings, as shown in Figure 9.16.

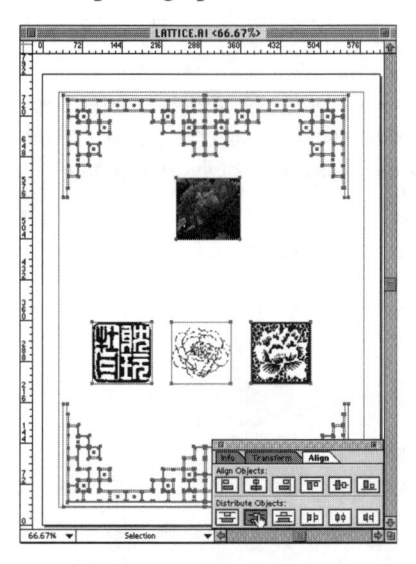

Figure 9.16 Distribute the objects between the two lattices by clicking on the Vertical Distribute Center button. The three drawn squares are treated as one object because they are grouped.

12. Click on the **Horizontal Align Center** button, the second button on the Align Objects line in the Align palette. This aligns the center points of the three groups and the photograph (see Figure 9.17), but it doesn't center the objects on the page.

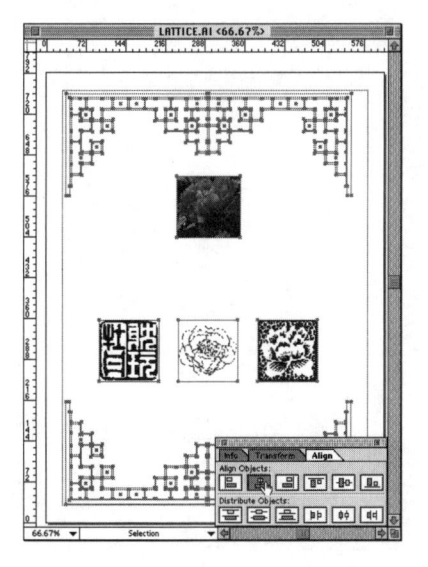

Figure 9.17 Align the selected objects by clicking on the Horizontal Align Center button. Now they share the same vertical center line.

198 **CHAPTER 9**

13. Click on the **Transform** tab and then select the **X** field. Type **4.25 in** (half of an 8-1/2 inch page) and press the **Tab** key to apply. Everything is now centered on the page and evenly distributed, as shown in Figure 9.18.

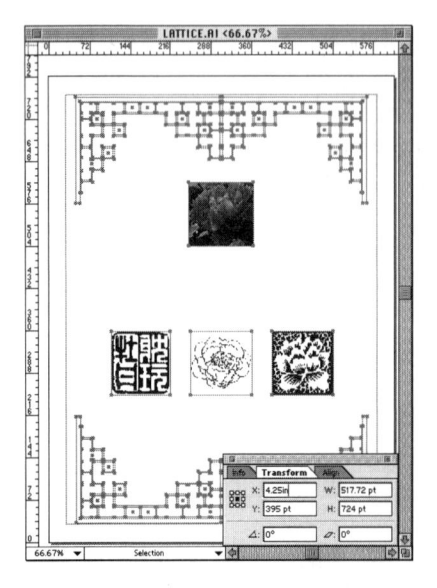

Figure 9.18 Center the composition horizontally on the page by entering the halfway point of an 8 1/2" page in the X field of the Transform palette.

Save your work if you wish. A finished version of this lesson can be found in the LESSON08 folder as LATTICE2.AI.

10 Appearance

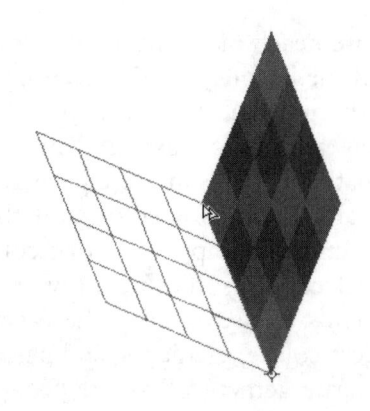

In this chapter...

- Color reproduction and color models
- CMYK and RGB become equals—Color palette
- Patchwork color—Swatches palette
- Blended color—Gradient palette
- Perimeter attributes—Stroke palette
- Where do custom color palettes come from?
- Attributes palette
- Lesson 10: Quilting and Coloring

We've already used each of the four palettes discussed in this chapter in some of the lessons. That's because they control the attributes of all paths and objects. The Toolbox provides the means to create objects and apply attributes (discussed in Chapters 3 and 6), but you define and manipulate attributes in these palettes.

The most basic of all attributes is color, and there are three palettes concerned with the selection and application of color. The **Color** palette allows you to mix and select colors in different ways. The **Gradient** palette lets you build color blends to use as fills. The **Swatches** palette lets you store, organize, and select colors, gradients, and patterns.

Illustrator's default arrangement of palette groups has the three color-concerned palettes in three different groups. I suspect the thinking here is that this makes it easy to have all three open at once, whereas if they were in the same group, you'd constantly be clicking on tabs.

The Stroke palette is used to define stroke width and dashed line attributes. In their default configuration, the Stroke and Gradient palettes are grouped, and this group is docked under the Color and Attributes palette group. Docking displays the groups in a single palette window so that all palettes can be moved around on the screen together, allowing you to see and work with two or more palettes within one window.

COLOR REPRODUCTION AND COLOR MODELS

The problem in a nutshell: there's no such thing as WYSIWYG (What You See Is What You Get) color. The green tree frog on your display isn't quite the same green tree frog on somebody else's, and it's altogether another green tree frog when you go to print it using process inks on an offset press.

Aligning the electron beams of all monitors to be within the limits of human perception is difficult enough, but developing four colors of ink (CMYK) that can reproduce the same colors that three beams of light (RGB) produce defies the laws of physics. Blasting beams of light onto the phosphors coating the inside of your monitor screen produces the *additive* color spectrum, whereas darkening paper by building up inky residue produces the *subtractive* color spectrum, and ne'er the twain shall meet.

Until now, Adobe has assumed that everything you created in Illustrator was headed for a process color printer, so why would you want to bother with anything but the CMYK process inks (cyan, magenta, yellow, and black) or spot color inks? But Illustrator has become an important tool for Web site designers, and the Web lives in an RGB (red, green, blue) display-oriented world.

Appearance 201

Illustrator 7 supports three process color models, CMYK, RGB, HSB (hue, saturation, and brightness), and grayscale (see Figure 10.1). HSB is theoretically closer to the way people perceive color. The thinking here is that editing colors the way we perceive them is more natural and perhaps easier. It's nice to have the choice.

- CMYK color is represented by cyan, magenta, yellow, and black measured from 0% to 100%.
- RGB color is represented by red, green, and blue measured from 0 to 255.
- HSB color is represented by hue, saturation, and brightness. Hue is a measure of position on a color wheel from 0° to 360° starting at red. Saturation and brightness are measured from 0% to 100%.
- Grayscale has a single slider measured from white, 0%, to black, 100%.

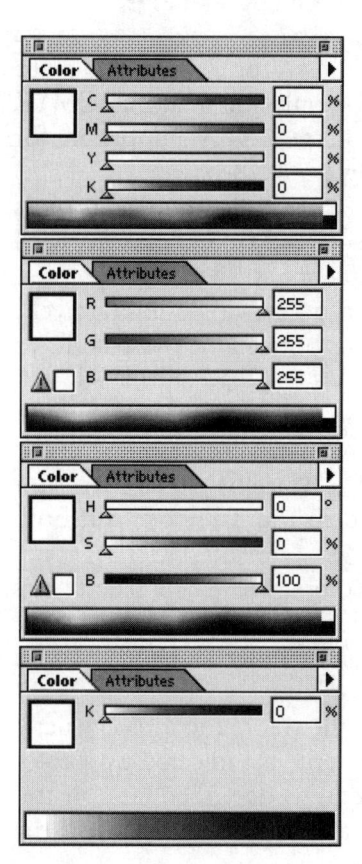

Figure 10.1 The Color palette in its four modes for CMYK, RGB, HSB, and grayscale.

Unlike Photoshop, Illustrator does not restrict the way you use the color models. You can mix and match or switch back and forth within a single drawing, but it doesn't make sense to do it this way. If you know an illustration is Web-bound, use only RGB colors. If it's print-bound, use only CMYK or spot colors. Use HSB to help you create the colors you want, but convert them to RGB or CMYK before finishing the illustration.

> **NOTE** If a single illustration is being used for multiple purposes, and it will be both printed and displayed, you should consider creating two versions. This allows you to control the way colors are converted between color modes, and you can avoid any unpleasant surprises.

CMYK AND RGB BECOME EQUALS—COLOR PALETTE

One of the most important new features of Illustrator 7 is its ability to work with RGB colors. (Previously, Illustrator only knew about CMYK process colors and spot colors.) The RGB palette is very important for working with Web-bound images, which are always RGB-based.

Illustrator's Color palette is now very similar to Photoshop's, and it is similarly easy to use. There are sliders with associated value fields for each color variable: four sliders for CMYK color, three for RGB and HSB color, and one for grayscale. You can drag sliders to adjust color interactively, type in values, or click on the color bar at the bottom of the palette to select a color.

The Color palette affects either the fill or stroke setting depending on which button is active in the Toolbox. The active tool is represented in the Color palette as a solid square icon for fill or as a hollow square icon for stroke. These are the same icons that are used in the Toolbox, and both icons always display the current color.

In addition to mixing your own process colors, the Color palette lets you edit the tint of spot colors. When you choose a spot color in the Swatches palette, the Color palette displays a Tint slider and specification box instead of process color sliders and the color bar.

When a gradient is chosen as the current fill color, the Color palette shows one of the specified colors from the gradient, as indicated by a color pointer under the Fill icon. Editing the gradient, as described later in this chapter, changes the Fill icon in the Color palette, just as changing the Color palette settings will update the gradient.

> **NOTE** Unlike other color drawing programs, Illustrator provides no mechanism to access the standard system or custom color pickers, except as custom swatch libraries.

To Edit Fill or Stroke Color

1. Make sure the Color palette is open (**Window: Show Color**).
2. The Color palette displays the Stroke or Fill icon depending on which is active. Click on the Fill (x) or Stroke (x) button in the Toolbox if you wish to edit the other attribute.
3. Use one of three methods to edit the current color:
   - When you move the cursor over the color bar across the bottom of the Color palette, the cursor turns into an Eyedropper cursor, as shown in Figure 10.2. Click anywhere in the color bar to select that color.

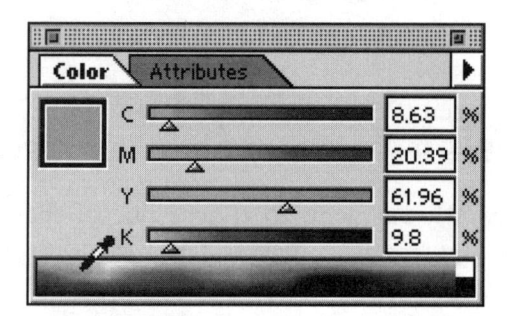

Figure 10.2 When you move the cursor over the color bar at the bottom of the color palette, you can sample color directly from the bar.

   - Drag the triangles beneath the color sliders to adjust color interactively, as shown in Figure 10.3. You can also click anywhere underneath a slider, and the triangle will jump to that point.

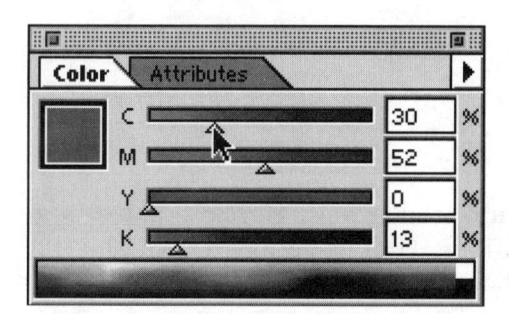

Figure 10.3 Dragging a triangle beneath any color slider interactively adjusts the color and updates all the information in the **Color** palette.

204 CHAPTER 10

- Type numbers into the color value fields to the right of each color slider to edit color directly (see Figure 10.4).

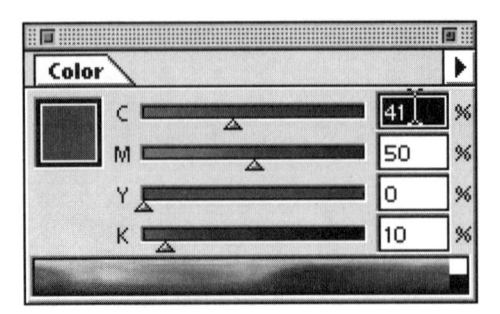

Figure 10.4 *Typing a number into a color field allows you to set precise color values.*

NOTE: Both the icon in the Color palette and the matching button in the Toolbox are updated as you edit a color. There is no "Apply" button or technique. If there is an active selection in the drawing, it is updated.

To Change Color Models

1. Make sure the Color palette is open (**Window: Show Color**).
2. Move the cursor over the palette menu arrow and hold down the mouse button.
3. Drag in the Color palette drop-down menu to choose one of the four color models (shown in Figure 10.5); then release the mouse button. The sliders in the Color palette change to match the current model chosen.

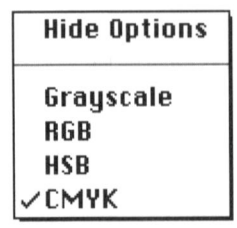

Figure 10.5 *The commands of the Color palette's drop-down menu.*

The Color palette drop-down menu has one additional selection that toggles between Hide and Show Options. Hiding options leaves only the color bar showing in the palette. Showing expands the palette to show the Stroke/Fill icon and the color sliders.

Patchwork Color—Swatches Palette

The ability to create color is worthless if you can't store and reuse colors, so Illustrator has supplied us with a Swatches palette. It's a the place to store not only colors but also gradients and patterns. (Gradients are discussed in this chapter, and patterns are discussed in Chapter 12.) You don't have to use the Swatches palette, but it does provide a convenient way to store swatches for reuse and it allows you to update all instances of a swatch within a drawing.

Illustrator comes with a default palette with one row of process colors, one of spot colors, one of gradients, and two of patterns. You'll most likely want to expand the color choices, but this is not difficult to do.

NOTE The color, gradient, and pattern swatches you create with a drawing are saved with the drawing only. This differs from the way Photoshop collects swatches and saves them with the program.

The Swatches palette can expand to accommodate years' accumulation of custom swatches. Unfortunately, the additions and modifications you make to the swatches are stored only with the current document. To make permanent changes, you must modify Illustrator's startup document, discussed in Chapter 16.

Like so much else in Illustrator's version 7 facelift, the Swatches palette has been rearranged to conform to Adobe's application-wide standard. This isn't bad, it's just different for experienced Illustrator users. There's even a Photoshop-like arrangement of command buttons across the bottom of the Swatches palette: Show All Swatches, Show Color Swatches, Show Gradient Swatches, Show Pattern Swatches, New Swatch, and Delete Swatch.

Clicking on the Show buttons changes the display of swatches so that only one swatch type is displayed, or all three types—color, gradient, and pattern—are displayed. Three new display-mode options are also available from the Swatches palette pop-up menu (see Figure 10.6):

- Name lists colors with their name, color model, and a process or spot color designation. Since there is only one color to a line, this list can get rather long.
- Small Swatch, which is most similar to earlier versions of Illustrator, displays small swatches in rows and columns. Spot colors are indicated by a small spot in the lower-right corner of the swatch. This is the most space-economical display mode.

- Large Swatch, which is similar to the swatches used in previous versions of Illustrator to display gradient swatches, displays large swatches in rows and columns. This is useful for displaying patterns, which may not show clearly in small swatches.

Figure 10.6 The commands of the Swatches palette's drop-down menu.

Functionally, the Swatches palette still provides a way to store colors, gradients, and patterns and then apply them to objects simply by clicking on the swatch.

To Use Swatches

1. Make sure the Swatches palette is open (**Window: Show Swatches**).
2. Click on any swatch:
    - If the Fill button is active, the color, gradient, or pattern you click on becomes the current fill color. The Fill icon in the Color palette and the Fill button in the Toolbar are updated, and any selection in the currently active drawing is filled.

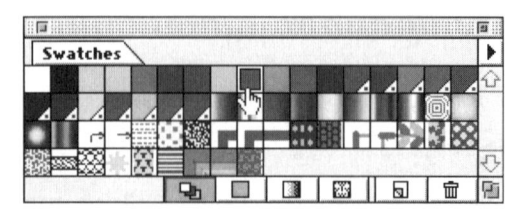

Figure 10.7 Clicking on a swatch selects that color and makes it the active fill or path color depending on which attribute is active in the Toolbox.

- If the Stroke button is active, the color you click on be
  rent stroke color, and the Stroke icon in the Color pal
  button in the Toolbar, the stroke color of any selection
  active drawing are updated. Clicking on a gradient swat
  Fill button and does not affect the stroke. Clicking on a
  applies the pattern as it would a color, but Illustrator cannot display
  patterned strokes. Instead, it displays a gray stroke, but the pattern will
  print correctly. (Use the **Filter: Stylize: Path Patterns** dialog to convert strokes to tiled patterns; see Chapter 14.)

To Add a Color Gradient or Pattern to the Swatches Palette

1. Make sure the Swatches palette is open (**Window: Show Swatches**).
2. In the Color or Gradient palette, or in the active drawing, select the color, gradient, or pattern you want to add to the palette.
3. Choose one of two swatch creation methods:
   - Click the New Swatch button at the bottom of the Swatches palette or choose **New Swatch** from the palette pop-up menu. In the New Swatch dialog (shown in Figure 10.8), fill in a Swatch Name. For colors, choose **Process Color** or **Spot Color** from the Color Mode drop-down menu, and click **OK**. A new swatch is created in the first open space at the bottom of the Swatches palette.

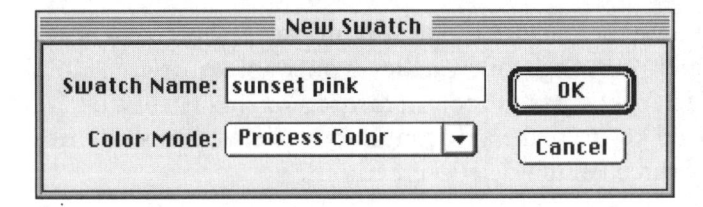

Figure 10.8 The New Swatch *dialog lets you name a swatch and designate it as a process or spot color.*

NOTE Swatch names need not be unique.

- Drag from the icon square of the Color or Gradient palette or from the Fill or Stroke button in the Toolbar to the Swatches palette. An insertion icon indicates where the new swatch will be inserted. Release the mouse button to create a new, unnamed swatch. You can also use this method to replace swatches by holding down the **Option/Alt** key before dropping the swatch.

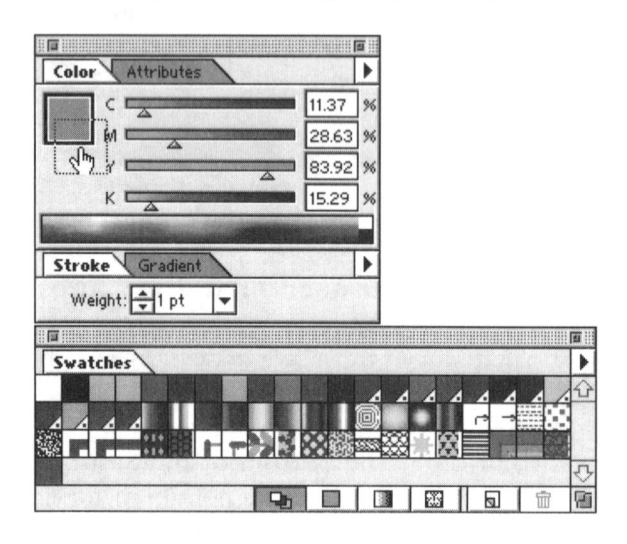

Figure 10.9 You can create a new color swatch by dragging from the Color palette and dropping in the Swatches palette.

To Delete a Swatch from the Swatches Palette

1. Make sure the Swatches palette is open (**Window: Show Swatches**).
2. Select the swatch, or range of swatches, you want to delete. Hold down the **Shift** key to select a range, or hold down the **Command/Ctrl** key to make a discontinuous selection of swatches.
3. Choose one of three swatch deletion methods:

    - Click the **Delete** button at the bottom of the Swatches palette.
    - Drag the swatches to the Delete button at the bottom of the Swatches palette.
    - Choose **Delete Swatch** from the palette pop-up menu.

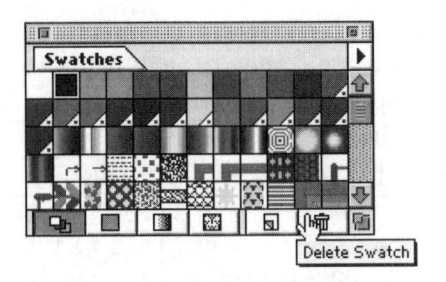

Figure 10.10 *Clicking on the **Delete** button permanently removes the active swatch from the Swatches palette.*

To Replace a Swatch in the Swatches Palette

1. Drag a color, gradient, or pattern to the Swatches palette as described previously.
2. Hold down the **Option/Alt** key as you drag and move the cursor to the swatch you wish to replace.
3. When you release the mouse button, the swatch is updated.

NOTE This is an indirect method, but it is the only way to edit swatches. It is an important technique to know, because replacing spot color swatches updates all instances in a drawing that use a particular color as an attribute.

To Use the Swatches Palette Pop-Up Menu

We've already mentioned some of the commands in the Swatches palette pop-up menu. Here is a more complete list with descriptions.

- **New Swatch, Duplicate Swatch, and Delete Swatch**—These are straightforward. Choose **New Swatch...** to create a new swatch from the currently selected color, gradient, or pattern. Select a swatch or swatches and choose **Duplicate Swatch** or **Delete Swatch...** to replicate or remove swatches.
- **Name, Small Swatch, and Large Swatch**—As described previously, these change the display within the Swatches palette to a list of swatches with names or a matrix of small swatches or large swatches.

- **Swatch Options**—Choose a swatch and select this command to open the Swatch Options dialog. You can change a swatch name or designate a swatch to be a process or spot color. You can use the latter feature to change a group of swatches to process or spot color in a single step. You can also double-click on a swatch to open its options.
- **Select All Unused**—Selects all swatches that are not used in the active drawing. As far as I can tell, the only reason to do this is to delete unused colors and reduce the palette size.
- **Sort by Kind and Sort by Name**—You can sort swatches by kind, color, gradient, pattern, or name. The latter is more useful for Name view.

NOTE: By default, Illustrator converts spot colors to their process approximations when printing separations. Deselect the **Convert to Process** option in the Separation Setup dialog to print spot colors (see Chapter 17).

BLENDED COLOR—GRADIENT PALETTE

A gradient is a graduated blend of color that can be used as a fill for any object. (You cannot use a gradient fill as a stroke.) We talked about the application of gradients and the Gradient tool in Chapter 6. Here we will discuss the creation of the gradient blend itself—the sole function of the Gradient palette.

The Gradient palette is to gradients as the Color palette is to colors—the cauldron for concocting new gradient combinations. Instead of adjusting sliders of colors, you select colors from the other palettes or your artwork and use the gradient bar to blend these chosen colors. Gradients can be saved as swatches and applied as fills just as you would any color, except that you can use the Gradient tool to define the extents and direction of a gradient fill.

The simplest method is to choose a starting color and an ending color, and then let Illustrator create an even blend of color from one end to the other. The Gradient palette also lets you select any number of intermediate blend colors and place them at any point along the gradient bar. You can also set the blend percentages and the midway point for every step of a gradient.

To Define a Gradient

1. Make sure the Gradient palette is open (**Window: Show Gradient**), then activate the gradient editor in one of three ways:

   - Click in the Gradient palette on the gradient icon or gradient bar.
   - Click on the Gradient button (.) in the Toolbar.
   - Click on a gradient swatch in the Swatches palette.

2. Click on one of the color squares below the gradient bar to select it. The first square to the left is considered the starting point, and the last on the right, the ending point. Since the Color palette's fill icon does not show gradients, it shows the color of the active color square and indicates this by displaying a color pointer beneath the icon.

3. Set the color of the selected square one of three ways:
   - Edit the color in the color square interactively by using the controls in the Color palette.
   - **Option/Alt** click on any color in the Swatches palette.
   - Drag a swatch from the Swatches palette directly to any color square beneath the gradient bar (shown in Figure 10.11).

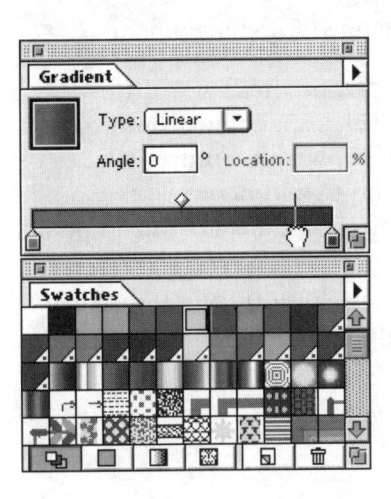

Figure 10.11 You can drag a color from the Swatches palette and drop it anywhere on the Gradient slider to add to or modify the gradient. A vertcal box appears to indicate where the new color will be added to the current gradient.

4. As you define a gradient fill, the Fill button in the Toolbar and Gradient button in the Gradient palette are updated, and the gradient is applied to any active selection.

5. To save a gradient, drag the gradient icon to the Swatches palette, click on the New Swatch button, or choose **New Swatch** from the Swatches palette pop-up menu, as already described.

To Edit a Gradient

Editing a gradient is just like creating one, because you always start with a base gradient to create a new one.
1. Select a gradient by clicking on it in the Swatches palette or on a gradient-filled object in your drawing.
2. There are several aspects of the gradient that can be edited:

   - Edit existing color points by clicking on their squares as described earlier or create new color points by clicking under the gradient bar to create multicolored gradients.
   - Change the position of color points by dragging their color square along the gradient bar or by selecting the color square and typing a position into the Location field as a percent.
   - Change the midpoint of any step of a gradient by clicking on one of the midpoint diamonds above the gradient bar and dragging or entering a Location specification.

3. There are three options that can be changed for any gradient:

   - **Type**—Choose **Linear** or **Radial** from the Type drop-down menu. Gradients can either be Radial, expanding from a center point equally in all directions as shown in Figure 10.12, or Linear, blended in a line from one end to another.
   - **Angle**—Set the direction of linear blends from start to end points in degrees.
   - **Location**—This is used to specify the location of color squares and midpoint diamonds along the gradient bar from 0% to 100%, as described earlier.

> **NOTE** If you fill an object before editing its gradient, you can see the effects on this object as you make changes in the Gradient palette.

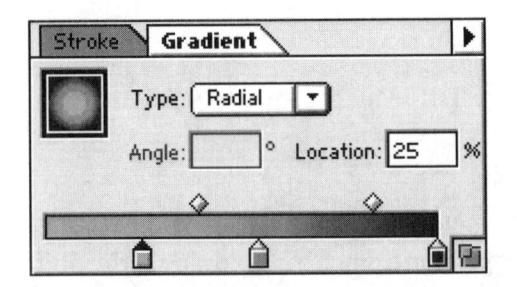

Figure 10.12 *When you select **Radial** from the Type drop-down menu in the Gradient palette, the gradient spreads from a point as indicated in the gradient swatch.*

To Shrink the Gradient Palette

1. Make sure the Gradient palette is open (**Window: Show Gradient**).
2. Open the Gradient palette pop-up menu. There is only one command: Hide Options.

Hiding options shrinks the Gradient palette so that only the gradient bar and the color points are displayed. The Hide Options command toggles to Show Options to return to the expanded display.

PERIMETER ATTRIBUTES—STROKE PALETTE

The Stroke palette does not affect fill color. Stroke colors are chosen from the Color or Swatches palette. The four attributes of Stroke are Weight, Cap, Join, and Dashed. (A fifth attribute, Miter Limit, applies only to the Miter Join setting, which is discussed later.) As with all the appearance palettes, if you change a setting when a selection is active, the selection is changed and any new objects you draw will have the changed attributes. If you change a setting when nothing is selected, the changes affect only newly created objects.

> **NOTE** The Stroke button in the Toolbar does not need to be active to edit stroke attributes.

The Stroke palette can be viewed either shrunken or expanded as controlled by the Show/Hide Options command in the Stroke palette's pop-up menu. Only the Weight field is shown in hidden mode.

214   CHAPTER 10

To Set Stroke Weight

1. Make sure the Stroke palette (shown in Fibure 10.13) is open (**Window: Show Stroke**).
2. Set the stroke weight in one of three ways:

   - Click on the up or down arrows in the Weight field to increase or decrease the weight in one-pixel increments. Hold down the Shift key while clicking to adjust line weight in equal increments of 10 points.
   - Type a weight directly into the specification field.
   - Click on the pop-up arrow to the right of the field and slide to select a weight from the list.

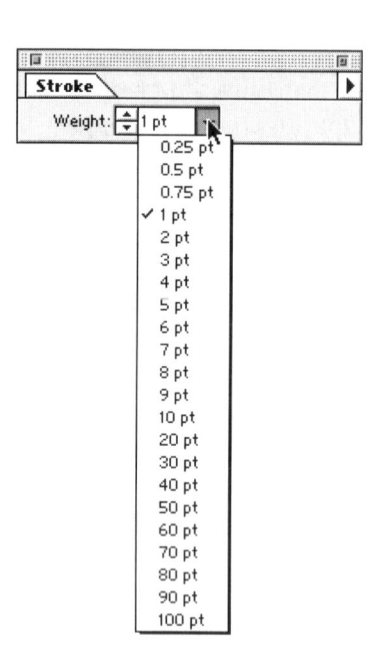

Figure 10.13 The Stroke Weight drop-down menu with many pre-set line weights to choose from.

To Set Cap and Join Attributes

1. Make sure the Stroke palette is open (**Window: Show Stroke**) and that the Stroke options are expanded as described earlier.
2. Click on one of the Cap buttons to set the treatment of endpoints as shown in Figure 10.14:

- Butt Cap creates square-ended strokes and is the default.
- Round Cap creates round-ended strokes.
- Projecting Cap creates square-ended strokes that project past the endpoint the distance of the stroke weight.

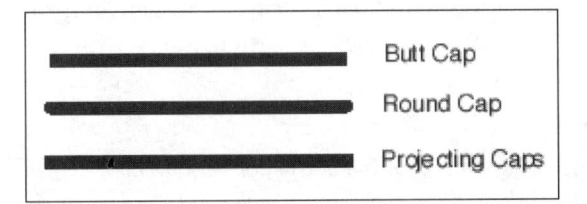

Figure 10.14 *The three types of caps. The line is the same in all three, only the cap option in the Stroke palette has been changed.*

3. Click on one of the Join buttons to set the treatment of midpoints (as shown in Figure 10.15):

- Miter Join creates angle-cornered strokes and is the default. Miter joins are controlled by the Miter Limit, which switches to beveled joins when exceeded. A Miter Limit of 1 always uses a bevel. The default limit of 4 switches to beveled when the length of the miter is four times the stroke weight.
- Rounded Join creates round-cornered strokes.
- Bevel Join creates square-cornered strokes.

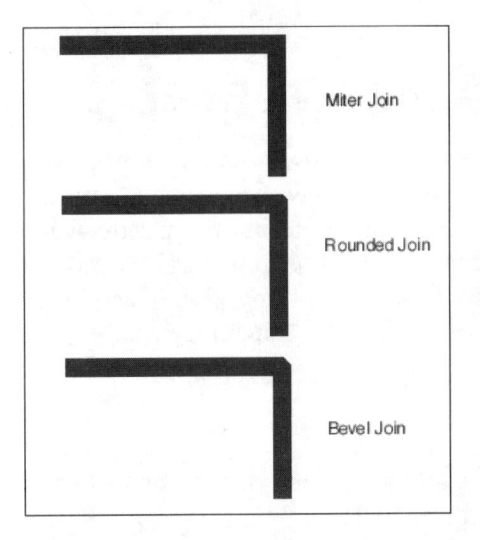

Figure 10.15 *Three joins with three different join options set in the Stroke palette.*

To Create Dashed Lines

1. Make sure the Stroke palette is open (**Window: Show Stroke**) and that the Stroke options are expanded as described earlier.
2. Click the **Dashed Line** check box to activate the dashed line editor.
3. Specify the dash sequence as dash length followed by gap length. The pattern can have one to three dashes and then repeats for the length of the path being stroked.

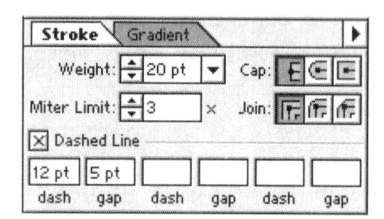

Figure 10.16 The Stroke palette showing a dashed line specification with the dashed line itself showing in the drawing underneath.

Dashes are affected by the cap style chosen. For instance, Projecting-Cap dashes are always longer than their Butt-Cap counterparts.

NOTE: There is no way to save dash patterns (or stroke styles in general) other than applying them to a path and saving the document.

Where Do Custom Color Palettes Come From?

The problem with the Swatches palette is that it includes no mechanism to save custom swatch palettes and reload them. You must save a document with the swatches you want to save and reopen the document to use this palette again. In fact, previous versions of Illustrator came with documents that included the various commercially-available color systems and nothing else. This kludgy workaround has a partial solution in Illustrator 7—the Swatch Libraries.

To Use Swatch Libraries

- Choose **Window: Swatch Libraries** and select one of the libraries from the drop-down list, shown in Figure 10.11.

Appearance 217

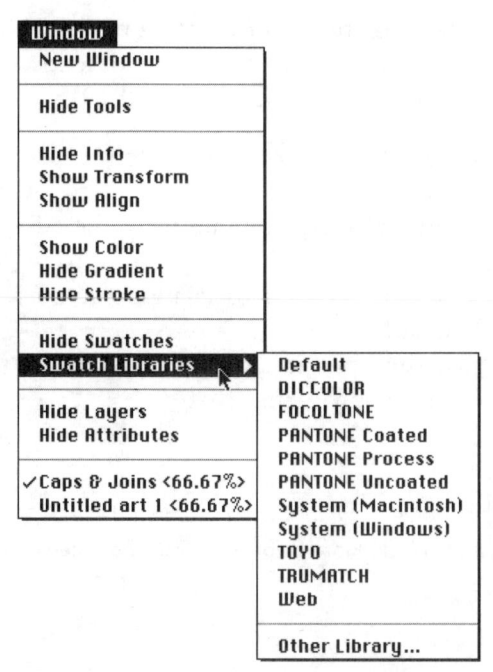

Figure 10.17 The Swatch Libraries submenu lets you pick among several predefined libraries of swatches.

Illustrator comes with ten Swatch Libraries: DICCOLOR, FOCOLTONE, PANTONE Coated, PANTONE Process, PANTONE Uncoated, System (MacOS), System (Windows), TOYO, TRUMATCH, and Web (see Figure 10.18). You can also choose **Other Library** to load other libraries, but there's no indication in the manual of where these other libraries might come from, or choose Default.

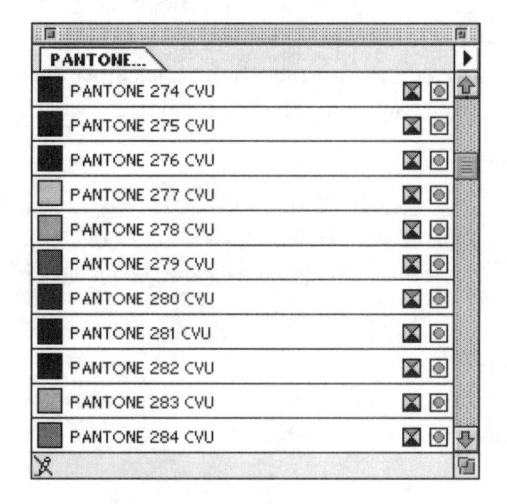

Figure 10.18 Each Swatch Library that you select will open in a special swatches palette like this one for Pantone swatches.

Loading a Swatch Library opens it in a new palette window with a tab of the library's name. The palette behaves exactly like the Swatches palette described earlier with slightly different pop-up menu commands (see Figure 10.19):

- Name, Small Swatch, and Large Swatch control the swatch display as described earlier.
- Add to Swatches allows you to copy selected swatches from the custom library palette to the Swatches palette.
- Sort by Kind and Sort by Name can be used to change the sort order of the swatches as described earlier.
- Persistent can be selected so that the open swatch library will load with Illustrator each time you open the program.

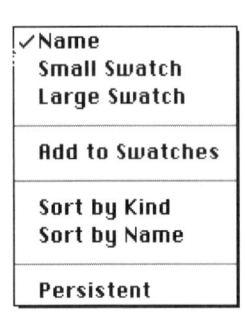

Figure 10.19 The pop-up menu for Swatch Library palettes is slightly different from the standard Swatches palette pop-menu.

ATTRIBUTES PALETTE

There is one more palette that affects the appearance of objects, but in more subtle ways. The Attributes palette, shown in in Figure 10.20, is new with version 7, and it has an eclectic mix of capabilities that defies summarization; instead, I'll list them in the order they appear in the palette.

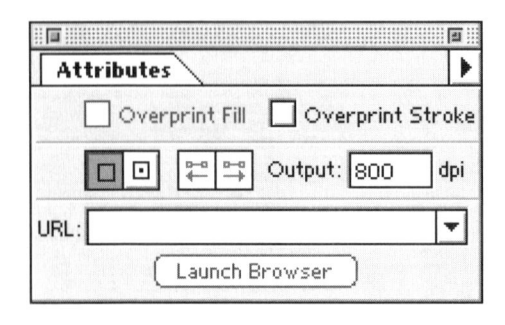

Figure 10.20 The Attributes palette has an odd collection of options that don't seem to fit anywhere else, including the new URL specification field.

- **Overprint Fill and Overprint Stroke**—These two check boxes allow you to control the way colors overprint when printing color separations. On screen, the top color "knocks out" all colors beneath it. But the transparent effect of overprinting inks to produce a third color is sometimes desired. You cannot preview the effects of overprinting on screen, but you can achieve a similar effect by using the **Object: Pathfinder: Hard command**.
- **Don't Show Center and Show Center**—These two buttons toggle from one to the other and replace the Attributes Show Center Pointer command option from previous versions of Illustrator. When on, selected objects include a highlighted center point. When off, no center point is displayed.
- **Reverse Path Direction On/Off**—These two buttons also toggle from one to the other. They control the way compound paths are filled. Sometimes the figure/ground relationship of a compound path (see Chapter 12) is ambiguous, and these buttons allow you to toggle between ambiguous states to choose the one you want.
- **Output**—Illustrator automatically calculates the flatness setting that controls the size of the segments used to draw curves. Lower flatness values use smaller segments that demand much higher processing overhead. This calculation is based on the Output resolution set in the Attributes palette, which the manual states is most efficient at 800 dpi. If you receive limit check errors when printing because paths are too complex, you can lower this value.
- **URL**—This new feature of Illustrator 7 allows you to create imagemaps for use with Web pages. Select an object and type in the name of an URL, or choose one that you have previously used from the drop-down menu. The URL is linked to the image. (Creating Web-bound images is discussed in Chapter 18.)
- **Launch Browser**—Click on this button when there is an Internet address in the URL field to launch your Web browser and preview the image.

There are three commands in the **Attributes** palette pop-up menu:

- Show Overprint Only collapses the Attributes palette so that only the two overprint check boxes are visible. The command toggles to Show All.
- Show Note expands the Attributes palette to include a notes field at the bottom. You can type information into this field to accompany any Web links you create. This command toggles to Hide Note.

- Palette Options opens the Palette Options dialog, where you can set the number of URLs saved in the URL drop-down menu. The range is 1–30, and 30 is the default.

LESSON 2

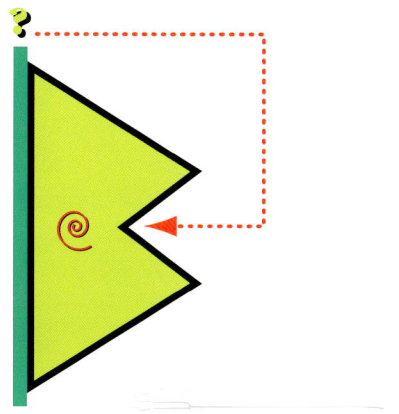

LESSON 5

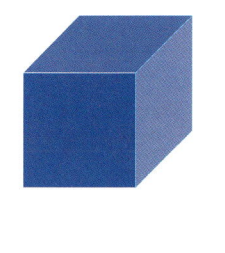

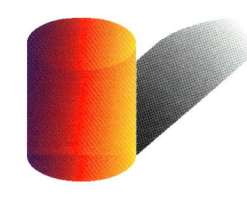

Creating 3D objects from 2D drawing tools: Cubes and cylinders, though not basic, are as much a part of Illustrator's vocabulary as rectangles and ellipses.

What is it? Merely an exploration of Illustrator's basic drawing vocabulary, with paths, objects, strokes, fills, dashes, arrowhead, spiral, text, and drop shadows.

LESSON 3

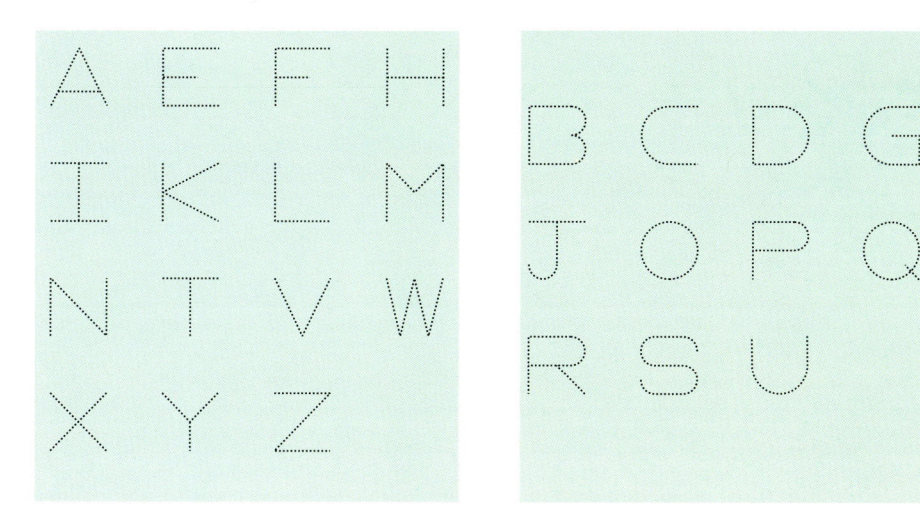

Two alphabets of basic shapes for tracing. Learning to construct shapes using Illustrator's tools is the first step toward understanding the workings of the program.

LESSONS 4 & 6

A line tracing of a penguin becomes a silhouette or a color rendering by adding color and gradient fills.

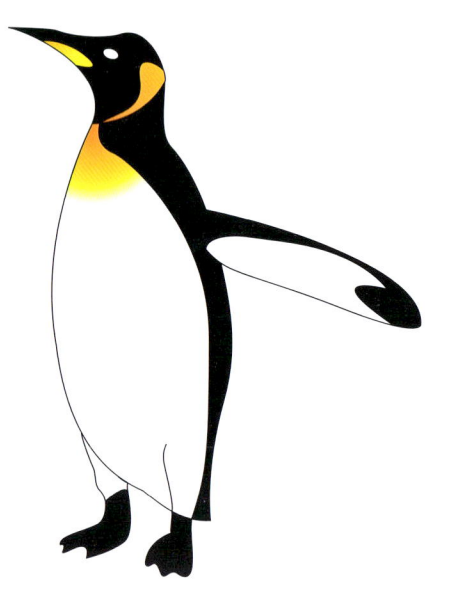

LESSON 7

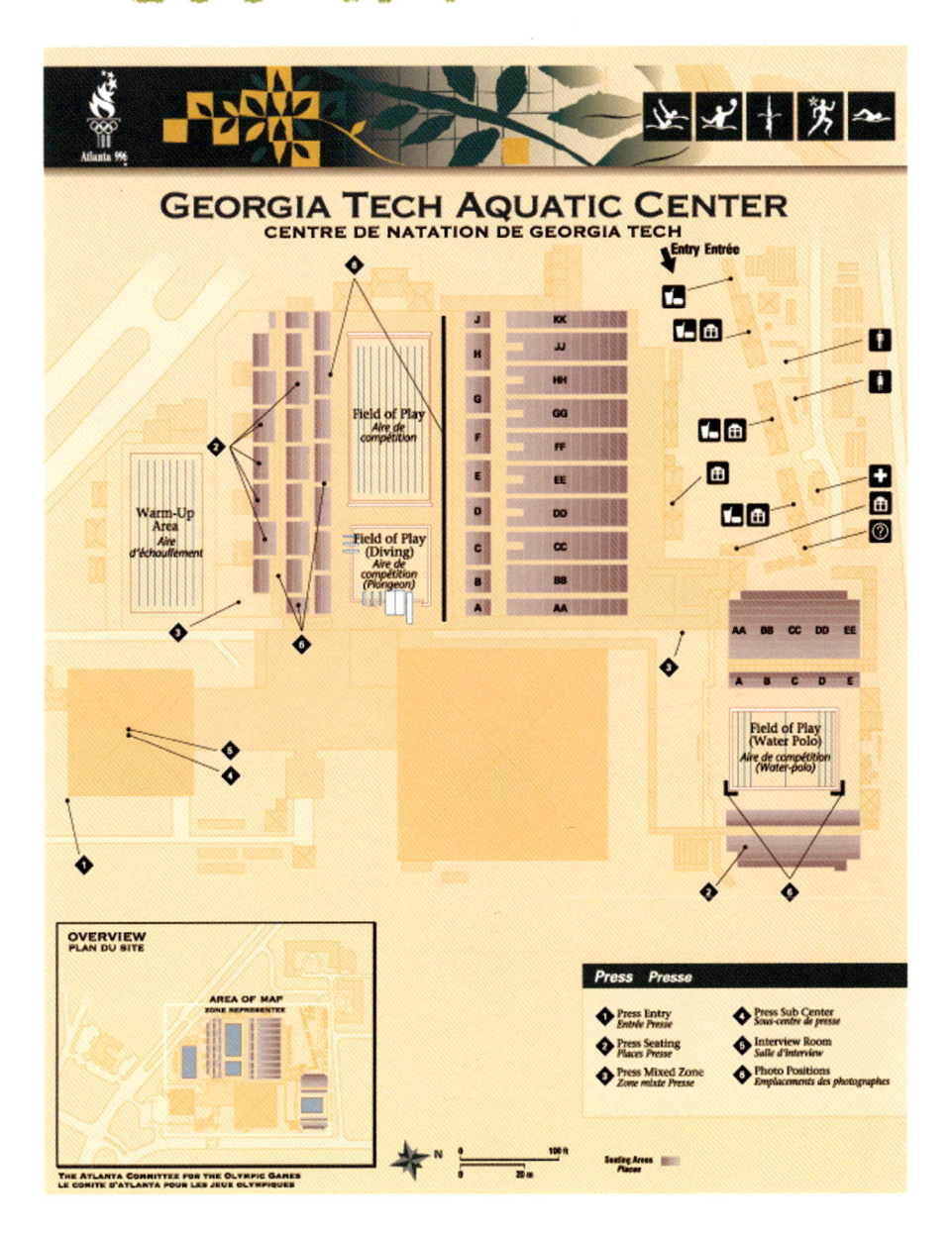

A large complex image like this multi-layered Olympic site map is much easier to work with using Illustrator's various tools to pan, zoom, and create custom views.

LESSON 10

A diamond becomes a classic multi-colored quilt pattern when copied, transformed, and aligned through numerous permutations.

LESSON 11

Dinner is set in layers from the sideboard for easy digestion. The tablecloth lays the foundation for place settings, food and drink, and is finished off with some text on top for dessert.

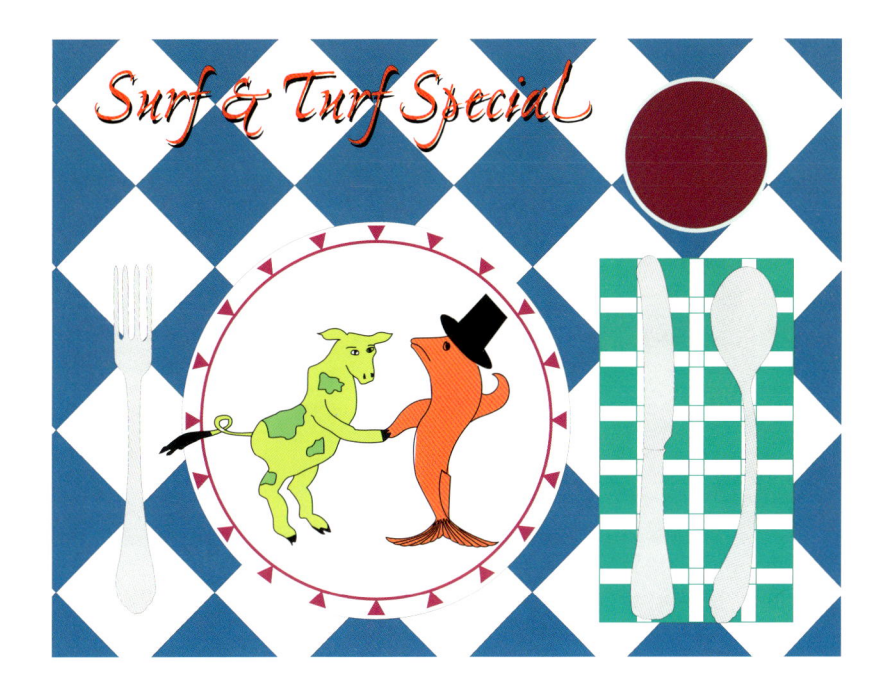

Surf & Turf Special

LESSON 12

Illustrator's Pathfinder commands make it possible to weave shapes over and under each other and blend colors to create transparent effects.

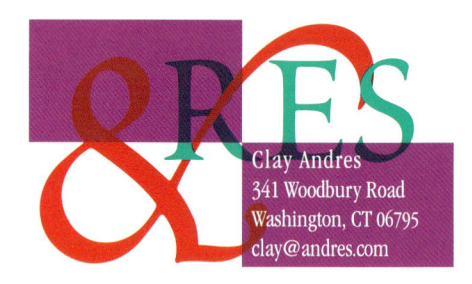

LESSON 14

A very different logo resulting from the application of several filters to adjust colors and create texture.

Lesson 13

Moby Dick; or the Whale

Herman Melville

Call me Ishmael.

Some years ago – never mind how long precisely – having little or no money in my purse, and nothing particular to interest me on shore, I thought I would sail about a little and see the watery part of the world. It is a way I have of driving off the spleen, and regulating the circulation. Whenever I find myself growing grim about the mouth; whenever it is a damp, drizzly November in my soul; whenever I find myself involuntarily pausing before coffin warehouses, and bringing up the rear of every funeral I meet; and especially whenever my hypos get such an upper hand of me, that it requires a strong moral principle to prevent me from deliberately stepping into the street, and methodically knocking people's hats off – then, I account it high time to get to sea as soon as I can. This is my substitute for pistol and ball. With a philosophical flourish Cato throws himself upon his sword; I quietly take to the ship. There is nothing surprising in this. If they but knew it, almost all men in their degree, some time or other, cherish very nearly the same feelings towards the ocean with me.

An exercise in typesetting: choosing fonts, setting size and leading, creating text blocks, making a runaround, using hyphenation, substituting typesetter's characters, and generally refining the look of the type to create a successful layout.

LESSON 8

It's very easy to turn a bland graph into something spicier using tools like Illustrator's custom graph design facility.

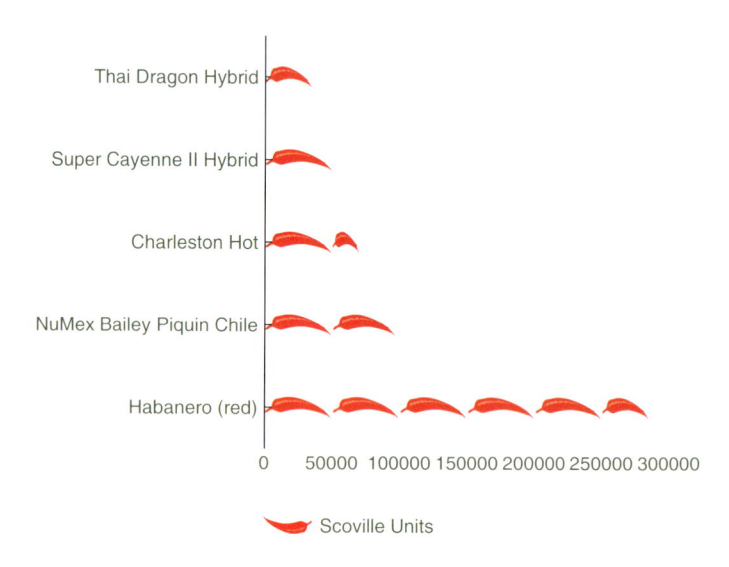

Thai Dragon Hybrid	🌶
Super Cayenne II Hybrid	🌶
Charleston Hot	🌶🌶
NuMex Bailey Piquin Chile	🌶🌶
Habanero (red)	🌶🌶🌶🌶🌶🌶

0   50000 100000 150000 200000 250000 300000

🌶 Scoville Units

LESSONS 9 & 18

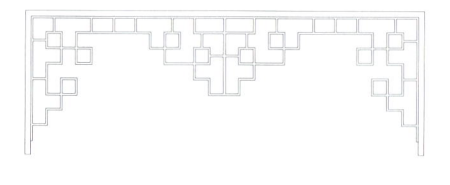

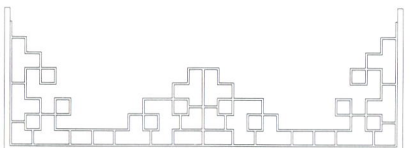

Creating a Web page by moving elements around and carefully aligning them. The icons are actually buttons that link to other related Web pages—one of Illustrator 7's important new capabilities.

LESSON 10

Quilting and Coloring

Pull up your rocker, because we will reproduce a fine old American quilt in this lesson. We'll make thorough use of the Swatches palette to gather quilting materials, which we will manufacture ourselves using the Color, Gradient, and Stroke palettes.

To get started, make sure all four of the aforementioned palettes are open, but not necessarily active, before joining our quilting circle. (Use the various Show commands in the Window menu if they aren't.) Set the Stroke and Fill buttons to their default colors (d) with the Fill button on top. I've supplied the first piece of the quilt to use as a template as QUILT.AI, which you can open from the LESSON10 folder on the CD.

1. Select the first four spot colors from the second row of the Swatches palette. (Click on the first, then hold down the **Shift** key and click on the fourth to select the range.) In order to avoid confusion later, make sure your Swatches palette is set so that there are 12 colors showing in each row before you make your selections. Figure 10.21 illustrates how to select a range.

222   CHAPTER 10

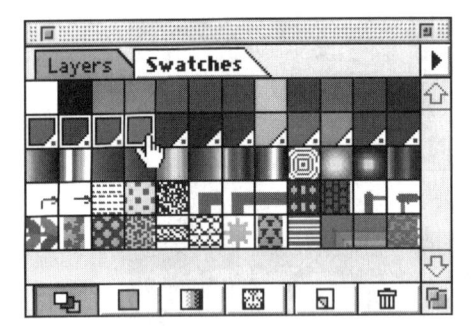

*Figure 10.21 Select a range of swatches just as you would a range of words in a word processing document. **Click** at one end, then **Shift**-click to extend a selection range to the end.*

2. Drag the range to the New Swatch button at the bottom of the palette window. Illustrator adds the duplicates to a blank row at the bottom of the palette.

NOTE Dragging a range of swatches to the New Swatch button to duplicate reverses the order of the swatches, while choosing the Duplicate Swatches pop-up command does not. It doesn't make any difference, except that you'll be able to duplicate this lesson only by dragging the swatches.

We'll be using duplicates so that we can edit the colors after we apply them to the quilt squares and have all like-filled squares update simultaneously. This will allow us to play with combinations of colors and patterns to find a pleasing mix.

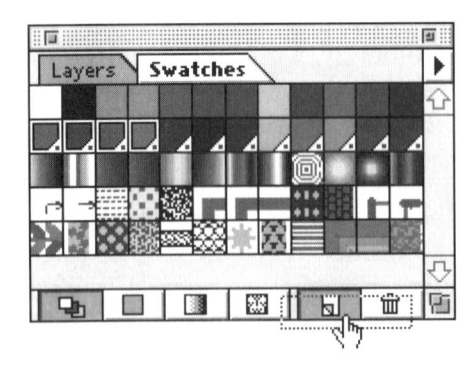

Figure 10.22 Drag a range of swatches to the New Swatch button to create duplicate swatches and place them in the first open spaces of the Swatches palette.

3. Choose the **Selection** tool (v) and click on the diamond in the drawing. Then click on the first copied swatch (not the original) to change the triangle's fill.

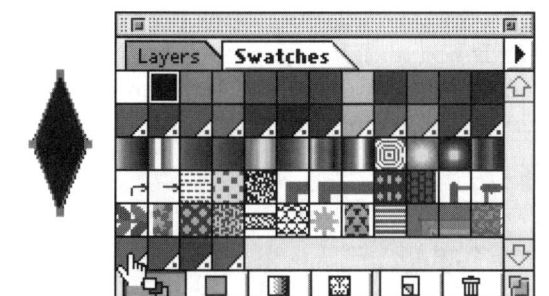

Figure 10.23 *Click on the first copied (Blue Sky) swatch to fill the selected diamond.*

4. Drag and copy the diamond by clicking on the bottom point, holding down the **Option/Alt** key, and dragging until the cursor is over the right point of the diamond. Release the mouse button. The diamond is copied, snapped to the first diamond, and left selected.

    The cursor becomes a double pointer when you press on the **Option/Alt** key and begin dragging to indicate that you are making a copy (see Figure 10.24). The black pointer turns white when you are within a pixel of the diamond's right anchor point to indicate that the copy will snap to this point. Precision is very important when quilting, so make sure that you "snap to" when copying.

Figure 10.24 **Option/Alt** *drag to snap a copy of the diamond to the right anchor point.*

5. In the Swatches palette, click on the second copied swatch to change the fill of the copied diamond, as shown in Figure 10.25.

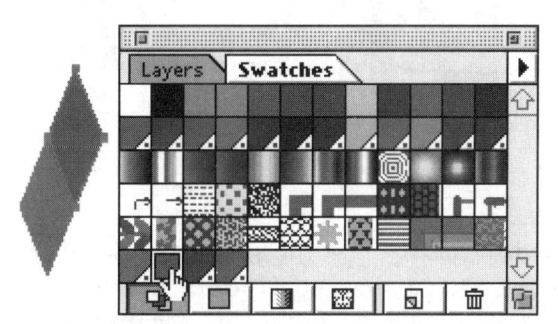

Figure 10.25 *Change the fill of the second diamond by clicking on the second copied (Blue Gray) swatch in the Swatches palette.*

224 CHAPTER 10

6. Drag and copy the second diamond by clicking on its bottom point. holding down the **Option/Alt** key, and dragging horizontally to the left until it snaps to the left anchor point of the original diamond (see Figure 10.27). Release the mouse button.

Figure 10.26 Option/Alt-drag to the left to create the third diamond, which remains the same color as the second.

7. Drag and copy the third diamond just as before, this time snapping to its own left anchor point, as shown in Figure 10.27.

Figure 10.27 Option/Alt-drag to copy from the second row and start the third row of diamonds.

8. In the Swatches palette, click on the third copied swatch to change the fill of the fourth diamond (see Figure 10.28).

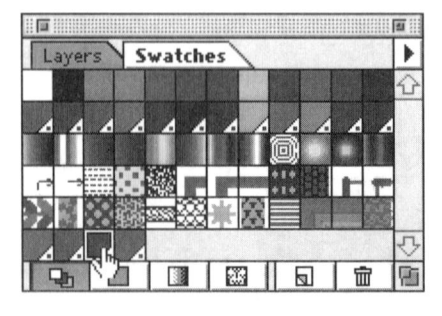

Figure 10.28 Click on the third copied spot color, Blue, in the Swatches palette to fill the first diamond of the third row.

9. Create the third row of diamonds. Copy the first diamond in the row by clicking on its left anchor point and **Option/Alt** dragging to its right anchor point. Then, instead of dragging again to create

Appearance 225

the third diamond in the row, use the **Object: Transform: Transform Again** (**Command/Ctrl-d**) command to repeat the last action, as shown in Figure 10.29.

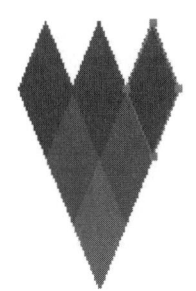

Figure 10.29 The finished third row created by **Option/Alt** dragging one diamond copy and then using the **Object: Transform: Transform Again** command to create the third.

10. For the fourth and last row, drag and copy diagonally up and to the right to snap to this most recent diamond's own right anchor point, as shown in Figure 10.30.

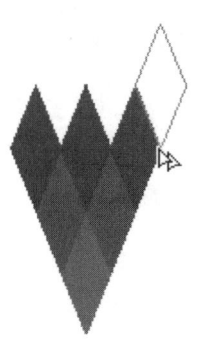

Figure 10.30 **Option/Alt**-drag diagonally again to start the fourth row of diamonds.

11. In the Swatches palette, click on the fourth copied swatch to change the fill for this, the fourth row of diamonds.

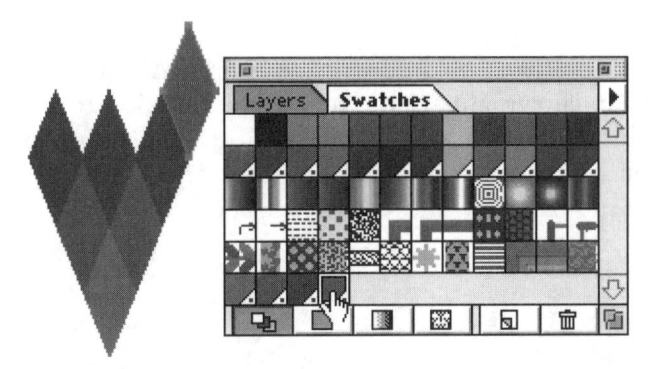

Figure 10.31 Click on the fourth copied swatch (Aqua) to fill the first diamond of the fourth row.

12. As before, drag and copy one anchor point to the left. It's faster to use the control keys, so press **Command/Ctrl-d** twice to copy the diamond twice more to complete the last row of four diamonds.

Figure 10.32 Four diamonds in the fourth row—two by cloning (**Option/Alt**-drag), two by duplicating (**Command/Ctrl-d**).

13. The Selection tool (v) should still be active. Use it to drag over the bottom three rows of diamonds without selecting the top, fourth row.

Figure 10.33 Drag a **Selection** marquee over the bottom three rows of diamonds to select them and deselect any previous selection.

14. Choose the **Reflect** tool (o). Hold down the **Option/Alt** key and click on any of the anchor points at the top of the selection to set the reference point and open the Reflect dialog. Click on the **Horizontal** button and then on the **Copy** button. This copies the selection across the fourth row and completes our first large diamond, as shown in Figure 10.34.

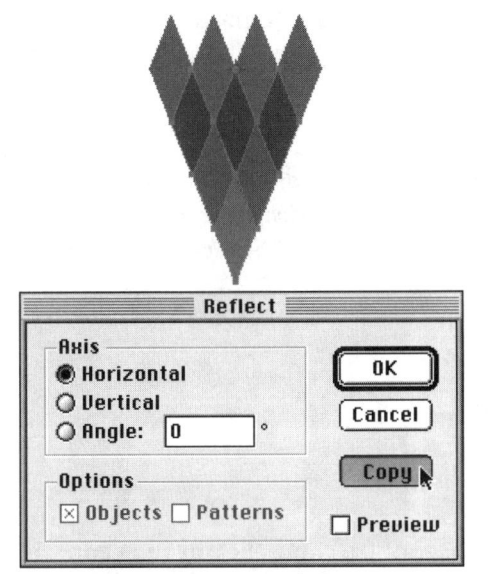

Figure 10.34 *Copy a reflection of the bottom three rows across the fourth row to create this diamond of 16 smaller diamonds.*

15. Swtich to the **Selection** tool (v) and drag a marquee over the entire large diamond to select it. Then choose the **Rotate** tool (r) and click on the bottommost point of the large diamond to set the source reference. Click and drag on the rightmost point of the large diamond. Hold down the **Option/Alt** key to make a copy and continue dragging in a counterclockwise direction until the black cursor arrow turns white to indicate that the copy will snap to the leftmost point of the large diamond. Release the mouse button.

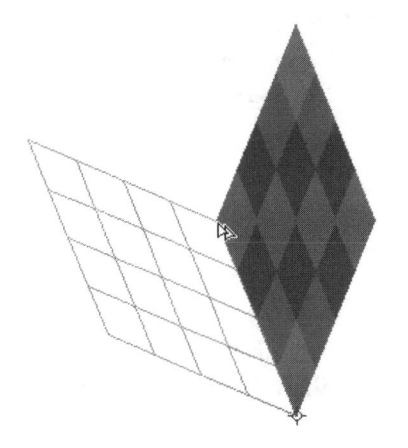

Figure 10.35 *Another kind of Option/Alt-dragging that uses the Rotate tool to copy the large diamond and have it snap alongside the original.*

228 **CHAPTER 10**

16. Make six more copies using the **Command/Ctrl-d** key combination to Transform Again six times (see Figure 10.36). This should complete an eight-pointed star.

Figure 10.36 *The nearly complete eight-pointed star. One more invocation of the **Transform Again** command will complete the shape.*

17. Choose the **Centered-Rectangle** tool (m) and click in the center of the star to open the Rectangle dialog. Enter 8 inches for both Width and Height, and click **OK**. Click on the Yellow and Orange Radial gradient, third from the right on the third row of the Swatches palette to fill the square with this gradient.

    If you wish, choose **Name** from the Swatches palette pop-up menu and you will see that this gradient is indeed named Yellow and Orange Radial.

Figure 10.37 *It would be difficult to judge the exact center point to click with the Centered-Rectangle tool, except that the last Transform-Again command left the eighth point selected, including the anchor point at the center of the star.*

18. Choose **Object: Arrange: Send to Back** (**Shift-Command/Ctrl-[**) to put the square beneath the star.

Figure 10.38 A square filled with a radial gradient sent to the back to set off the star quilt pattern.

19. Click on the **Stroke** button (x) in the Toolbar. In the Stroke palette (shown in Figure 10.39), set the Weight to **18** points, which automatically changes the stroke from none to white. Click in the **Dashed Line** check box and specify a dash of **9** points and a gap of **27** points. (If the Dashed Line check box isn't visible, choose the Show Options command from the Stroke palette options pop-up menu.)

    This white dash is only half visible—the half over the gradient filled square. Because the other half is a white dash over a white background, it doesn't show.

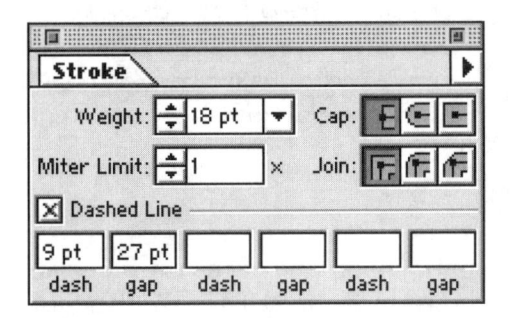

Figure 10.39 The Stroke palette showing the Weight and Dashed Line specifications for the gradient filled square.

20. Click on the **Gradient palette** to activate the gradient editor. (If the palette isn't fully expanded, choose the **Show Options** command from the Gradient palette pop-up menu.) Because most of the yellow of this gradient is covered over by the star, click on the midpoint diamond above the gradient bar and drag it to about 70% to increase the spread of yellow, as shown in Figure 10.40.

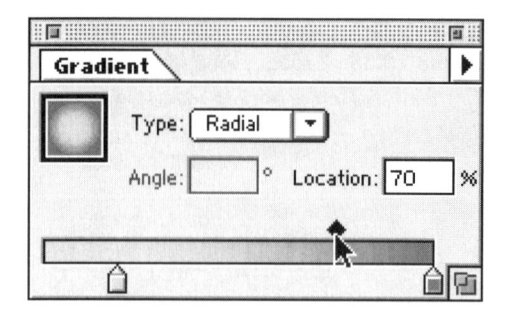

Figure 10.40 *Drag the midpoint diamond to 70% along the gradient bar to increase the coverage of yellow over the length of the gradient fill.*

21. Click on the orange color square under the right end of the gradient bar. The Color palette indicates that a process orange color is selected in the Gradient palette. In the Color palette, move the Y (yellow) slider to **100%** (as shown in Figure 10.41) to give this orange a bit more punch. The gradient is adjusted automatically with this change.

    This slightly altered gradient used as a background fits somewhat better with a quilt star. If you wish, click on the **New Swatch** button at the bottom of the Swatches palette to save this customized gradient. This step is optional, because we won't be using this gradient again.

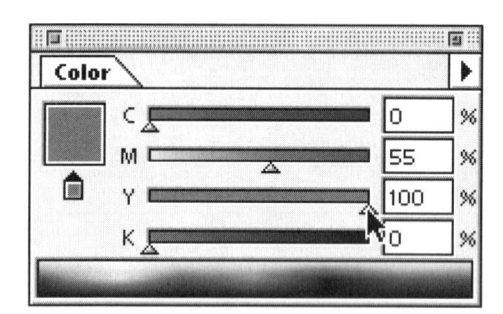

Figure 10.41 *Drag the Y (yellow) slider in the Color palette to 100% to change the orange that is the end color of the gradient. Notice that the fill icon in the palette has a color square beneath it.*

22. Choose the **Selection** tool (v) and click on one of the sky blue diamonds at the tips of the star (shown in Figure 10.42). We'll adjust this somewhat anemic-looking color to make it more striking and then update all the blue diamonds at once.

Figure 10.42 *Nothing in this drawing has been grouped, so clicking at the tip of a larger diamond selects the smaller diamond. Yet this sky blue color can be updated globally, because it is controlled from its swatch, regardless of object groupings.*

23. In the Color palette, choose **CMYK** from the palette pop-up menu to show the process color equivalents of the sky blue spot color. Drag the M (magenta) slider to **100%** to create a deep purple color.

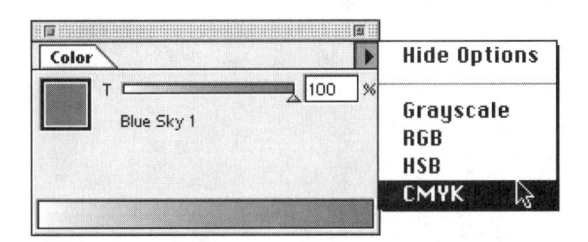

Figure 10.43 *Because this color swatch is a spot color, the Color palette is set to adjust its tint. We'll edit it using CMYK sliders.*

NOTE Editing a spot color swatch with the process color sliders does not convert the color to a process color or change the swatch name. You must update the Swatch Options by double-clicking on the swatch or choosing the command from the palette pop-up menu to do this.

24. Click on the **Fill** icon in the Color palette and drag it to the Swatches palette. Hold down the **Option/Alt** key while you drag and drop the color on the copy of the sky blue swatch we used to fill this diamond originally.

232 CHAPTER 10

The Swatch color is replaced, and all objects filled with it are updated with the new color. At the same time, Illustrator converts this process color to a spot color, since it's replacing a spot color, and names it Sky Blue 2. We would have to consider issues like this if we were going to send this image for color separations.

If you wish, double-click on the Swatch or choose **Swatch Options** from the palette pop-up menu and change the name to something more descriptive like Deep Purple.

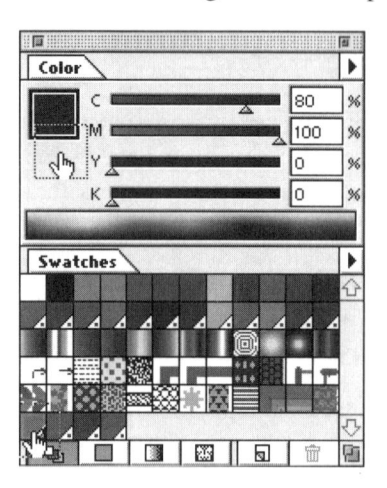

Figure 10.44 Drag the Fill icon from the Color palette, then holding down the **Option/Alt** key drop it on the sky blue swatch to modify the swatch and update all objects filled or stroked with the sky blue color to the new deep purple color.

25. Click on one of the blue gray diamonds. We'll replace these with a pattern. To make it easier to choose a pattern, click on the **Show Pattern Swatches** button at the bottom of the Swatches palette, and then choose **Large Swatches** from the palette pop-up menu, as shown in Figure 10.45.

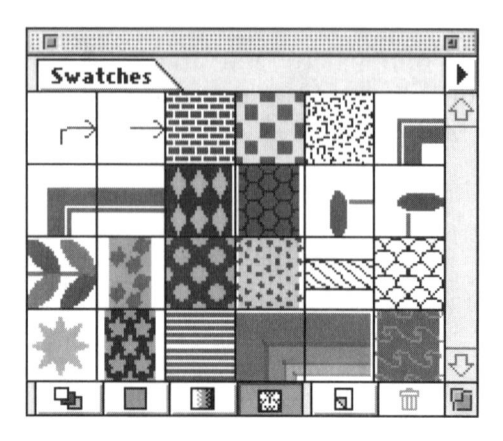

Figure 10.45 The Swatches palette showing pattern swatches only in Large Icon mode. Notice that the Pattern Swatches button at the bottom of the palette is gray to show that it's selected.

26. Click on the blue waves-scroll pattern to select. Now we're in a slightly awkward position, because the original swatch isn't visible for us to replace it. So click on the **Show All Swatches** button and then choose **Small Swatch** from the palette pop-up menu, as shown in Figure 10.46.

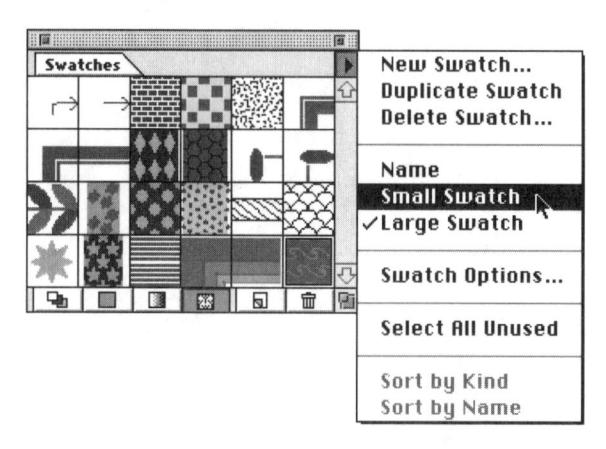

Figure 10.46 Switch back to Small Swatches mode using the Swatches palette pop-up menu.

27. Duplicate the pattern swatch either by dragging it to the New Swatch button or by choosing **Duplicate Swatch** from the palette pop-up menu.

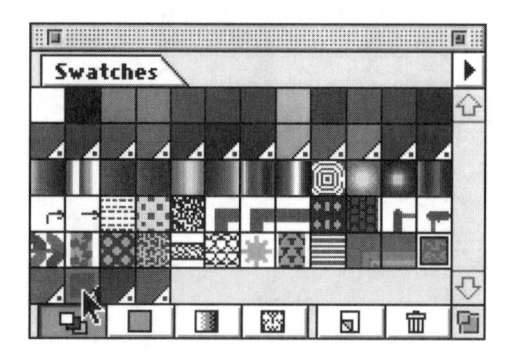

Figure 10.47 Drag the copied pattern swatch over the color swatch to replace all instances of the color in the drawing with the pattern.

We could have dragged the pattern swatch over the color swatch to replace it directly, but that would have rearranged the palette. Instead, drag the pattern swatch copy of the blue gray spot color while holding down the **Option/Alt** key to make a swatch replacement. All of the blue gray diamonds will be updated with the pattern fill.

We've run out of gossip at the quilting bee, so save your work if you wish. There's a copy of the completed lesson saved as QUILT2.AI in the LESSON10 folder, if you'd like to have a look.

11 Layers

In this chapter…

- About layers and the Layers palette
- Creating and adjusting layers
- Moving objects among layers
- Using layers while working
- Lesson 11: Dining with Layers

About Layers and the Layers Palette

Layers and the **Layers** palette became a part of Illustrator fairly recently, yet it's hard to imagine working without them. The sequencing of objects—one on top, another beneath—has always been an important aspect of drawing programs. But the ability to assign an order directly through layers has made it much easier to create complex compositions with many and diverse elements and to edit and manipulate these elements as work progresses and is refined.

Layers allow you to work on related objects without affecting other parts of a drawing. The comparison is often made to transparent sheets of acetate. But you can have as many drawing layers as memory allows without the bottom layer ever becoming dim. You can lock, hide, create nonprinting, or change the order of layers and the objects contained within them.

Layers determine the sequence Illustrator uses when drawing to the screen and printing and for certain filter effects. Because Illustrator does not support transparency directly (except as a null fill), this is very important. When objects overlap, the top object's fill will obscure anything beneath it. Illustrator also maintains an order of objects within layers, which can be controlled from the Adjust submenu (see Chapter 12).

The mechanism for working with layers is the Layers palette. Since this is another key feature of Adobe's Application Programming Interface (API), Illustrator's Layers palette has been changed to look and feel like Photoshop's and PageMaker's. Yet functionally, the Layers palette is essentially unchanged from previous versions.

In its default configuration, the Layers palette is grouped in the same palette window with the Swatches palette (see Chapter 10). The Layers palette lists each layer on a line within the palette and orders them from top to bottom. Every drawing has at least one layer, and the default name is Layer 1. As you add layers, the default layer's name is incremented by one, but you can quickly render these names meaningless by moving layers around in the stack. You're better off giving each layer you create a meaningful name.

NOTE Unlike Photoshop, Illustrator does not attach any special meaning to a background layer. All layers in Illustrator are created equal. You can call a layer "Background" and make it the top layer if you wish.

Within the layers list, each layer has a visibility check box and lock box to the left of its name. To the right appear icons that indicate an editable layer and an active selection on a layer. At the bottom of the **Layers** palette, shown in Figure 11.1, are two buttons: Create New Layer and Delete Selected Layers. All of these features are discussed later in this chapter.

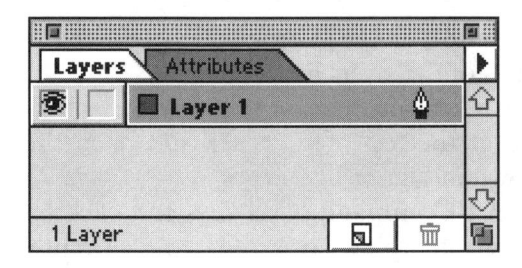

Figure 11.1 The Layers palette in its default state, with just a single layer.

NOTE Adding layers requires minimal overhead in terms of additional processing and memory. This differs from "painting" programs, like Photoshop, where adding a layer can make significant memory demands. In Illustrator, there's rarely a need to flatten layers to save memory and streamline the printing process.

As in any palette, layers are selected by clicking on the layer name in the palette. You can select a range of layers by **Shift**-clicking. Selected layers are highlighted in the Layers palette. Selecting a layer does not affect the drawing or make a selection within the drawing.

CREATING AND ADJUSTING LAYERS

Sometimes it's obvious when you need a new layer to simplify your work. For instance, I find that it's almost always a good policy to segregate text on a separate layer. It makes it easy to pick out text on top of objects and edit it later. This is especially helpful because text is often the last element of a project to be specified.

It's also a good idea to put placed objects, especially bitmapped images, on their own layer. Then you can lock them into place and avoid the nuisance of selecting them inadvertently. Blends, which can be difficult to edit, are simplified if kept confined to a separate layer. In fact, there are so many opportunities to use layers, that it's a good thing they're so easy to use in Illustrator.

To Create a New Layer

1. Make sure the Layers palette is open (**Window: Show Layers**).
2. As with most palette-oriented operations, there are several ways to create a new layer. (The new layer is always active after creation.)

   - Click on the New Layer button at the bottom of the palette to create a new layer at the top of the layers list.
   - Hold down the **Option/Alt** key and click on the New Layer button to create a new layer at the top of the stack and open the Layer Options dialog, shown in Figure 11.2.
   - Hold down the **Option/Alt-Command/Ctrl** keys and click on the New Layer button to create a new layer above the currently active layer without opening a dialog.

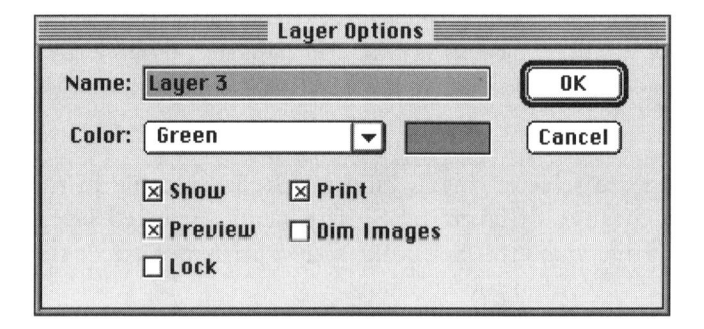

Figure 11.2 Whether you're creating a new layer or modifying an old one, you can always change the name and options associated with layers in the Layer Options dialog.

   - Hold down the **Command/Ctrl** key and click on the New Layer button to create a new layer below the currently active layer.
   - Choose the **New Layer** command from the Layers palette pop-up menu (shown in Figure 11.3) to create a new layer at the top of the stack and open the Layer Options dialog.

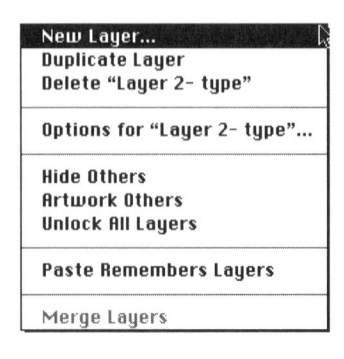

Figure 11.3 The **Layers** palette pop-up menu commands.

3. If you've chosen one of the methods that opens the **Layer Options** dialog, fill in the following options:

> **Name**—Illustrator increments layer names automatically, or you can type in any name. The name appears in the Layers palette.
>
> **Color**—Illustrator assigns colors used for highlighting selected objects within layers (see Figure 11.4). This helps identify which object is on which layer. Change the default color highlight assignment by choosing one of the colors from the drop-down box. Choosing **Other** allows you to define a color using RGB or HSB color sliders.

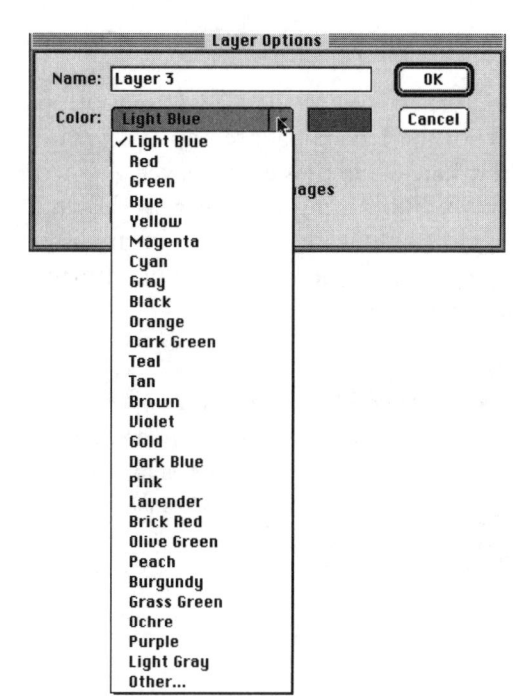

Figure 11.4 There are 27 default layer colors to choose from in the Layer Options dialog's Color drop-down menu. (This sets the highlight color when you select an object within the layer, and does not affect colors in the artwork at all.)

> **Show**—Deselect this check box to hide a layer. Show is the default and can be changed directly in the Layers palette. Hidden layers do not print.
>
> **Print**—Deselect this check box to make a layer nonprinting. Print is checked by default. This option allows you to prevent visible layers from printing.
>
> **Preview**—Deselect this check box to display objects in this layer in Artwork view instead of Preview mode. Preview is checked by default.

Dim Images—Check this box to dim placed or bitmapped images within a layer. Dim Images is unchecked by default.
Lock—Check this box to lock the objects within a layer so that they cannot be edited. Lock is unchecked by default.

4. Click **OK** to dismiss the dialog and apply its settings. When you avoid the dialog, the default values are used to create a new layer.

To Duplicate Layers

1. Make sure the Layers palette is open (**Window: Show Layers**).
2. Choose one of three methods:
   - Click in the Layers palette and drag a layer to the New Layer button.
   - Choose **Duplicate Layer** from the Layers palette pop-up menu.
   - Hold down the **Option/Alt** key, while dragging a layer. A + icon appears to indicate that you are duplicating this layer, as shown in Figure 11.5. When you drag the duplicate anywhere in the list of layers, it is added at the point you release the mouse button. (This method is an undocumented feature.)

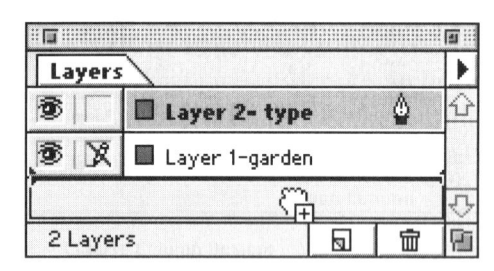

Figure 11.5 When you drag a layer within the palette while holding down the **Option/Alt** key, a plus sign appears next to the hand icon to indicate that the layer will be duplicated.

To Rearrange Layers

1. Click on a layer or layers to select.
2. Drag layers to another position in the layers list. As you drag, a highlighted line appears between layers to indicate where the selected layer(s) will be repositioned (see Figure 11.6). Moving layers changes the sequence Illustrator uses to draw and print objects, but not the objects themselves.

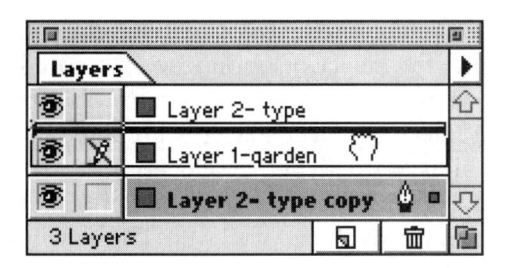

Figure 11.6 *When you drag a layer within the palette to reorder it in the layers stack, a dark bar appears between layers to indicate the new position of the layer.*

To Delete Layers

1. Make sure the Layers palette is open (**Window: Show Layers**).
2. Choose one of three methods:
   - Click in the Layers palette and drag a layer or layers to the Delete button (see Figure 11.7). Confirm the deletion.
   - Choose a layer or layers and click on the **Delete** button.
   - Choose **Delete Layer** from the Layers palette pop-up menu. Confirm the deletion.

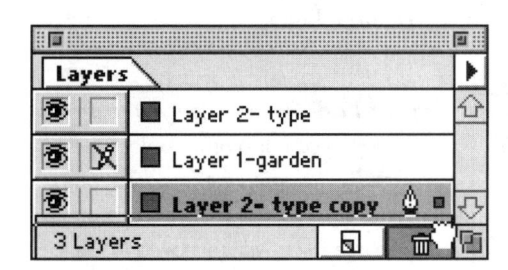

Figure 11.7 *Of the several ways to delete a layer, dragging it to the trash is perhaps the most straightforward.*

NOTE It's sometimes useful to hide all layers except the one being deleted so that you can see what's being deleted before it's gone.

OBJECTS AND LAYERS

More important than the layers themselves are the objects on them. The ability to lock and hide layers makes it easier to select and edit objects, especially in complex drawings or for detailed work. And just as it's possible to rearrange the order of layers, it's possible to move objects from layer to layer.

When you make a selection in a drawing, the layer of that selection is highlighted in the **Layers** palette, and the selection indicator (a colored dot) appears to the right of the layer name. If a selection contains objects on more than one layer, only the first selected object's layer is highlighted, but the selection indicator appears in all layers with active selections.

The distinction between active layers and selection layers is important because any new object you create is drawn to the active layer. This is why there can be only one layer active at a time. Layers can be activated either by clicking directly on the layer name or by selecting an object to activate its layer.

To Move Objects Among Layers—Drag Method

1. Make a selection in the drawing. Even though it's possible to make a selection that includes objects on multiple layers, you can only move from one layer to another in any single drag (see Figure 11.8).
2. Click on the selection indicator and drag it to another layer. This moves the selection to a new layer. Hold down the **Option/Alt** key while dragging to copy a selection to a new layer.

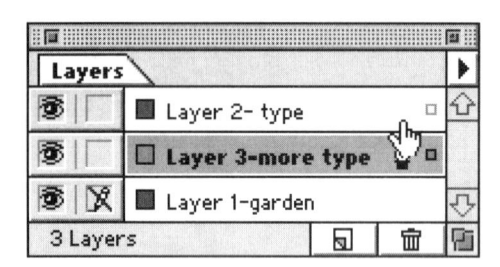

Figure 11.8 Not only can you rearrange layers, you can also move objects among layers. By dragging the icon from one layer to another, any active selection in the source layer will be moved to the target layer.

To Move Objects Among Layers— Cut/Copy and Paste Method

1. Make a selection in the drawing. In this case, the selection can include any number of objects on any number of layers.
2. Choose **Edit: Copy** or **Edit: Cut**.
3. Activate a different layer by clicking on its name in the Layers palette.

4. Choose **Edit: Paste**. The selection is pasted (or copied) from the **Clipboard** back into the drawing as part of the newly activated layer. (This behavior can be altered somewhat by using the **Paste Remembers Layers** command described later in this chapter.)

> **NOTE** You can also paste using the Paste in Front or Paste in Back commands. This affects the placement of pasted objects within a layer, but not which layer receives the pasted objects (see Chapter 12).

To Select All Objects in a Layer or Layers

Hold down the **Option/Alt** key and click on the layer name in the Layers palette. This makes the layer active and selects all objects in it. There are a couple of tricks you can use with this method:

- If you continue to hold down the **Option/Alt** key and drag slowly through other layers in the palette, all objects in these layers will also be selected. This behavior is a little unpredictable because if you drag more quickly, you can skip over selections in adjacent layers and make discontinuous selections. The first selected layer remains active.
- Another way to achieve multiple-layer selections is to make an **Option/Alt** selection and then hold down the **Shift-Option/Alt** keys and click on any other layer. This adds to the selection without changing the active layer.

To Paste Multilayer Selections

Choose **Paste Remembers Layers** from the Layers palette pop-up menu to toggle this command on. (You can also turn this option on from the General Preferences dialog; see Chapter 19.) A check mark appears next to the command to indicate that it is on and that selecting it again will toggle the command off.

When on, any multilayer selection you copy to the Clipboard retains information about its layer placement and even the layer name. So if you copy from one drawing to another, Illustrator will paste the objects from the Clipboard and either put the objects on layers with the same name or create new layers for them.

Using Layers While Working

Layers allow you to edit and view selectively, which can be very useful when working with complex drawings with many overlapping elements. Hiding a layer makes it invisible and unavailable for editing or printing. Locked layers are visible but uneditable. You can also choose to view layers in **Artwork** rather than the default **Preview** mode to see just the paths and anchor points with no fills or strokes.

The Hide, Preview, and Lock check boxes are part of the New Layer dialog, and they can always be opened and edited for preexisting layers using the **Options for...** command in the palette pop-up menu. But it's usually easier to change these options directly in the palette.

The **Layers** palette list displays one layer per line, and there are several columns of information on each line:

- The first column shows an eye icon when layers are visible and an empty check box when they are hidden. An outline of the eye icon appears when the layer is in Artwork mode.
- The second column shows an empty check box when a layer is unlocked and a pencil with a slash through it when the layer is locked.
- The third column shows the layer's name.
- The fourth column is not visible except when the layer is active. Then it displays a pencil icon to indicate that the layer can be edited and a pencil with a slash through it when a layer is locked and/or hidden.
- The fifth column is not visible except when there is an active drawing selection within the layer. Then a colored square is displayed to indicate the presence of **a** selection.

The first two columns, visibility and accessibility, can also be controlled from the Layers palette pop-up menu, which includes three commands that toggle between Others and All:

- Hide Others/Show All Layers
- Artwork Others/Preview All Layers
- Lock Others/Unlock All Layers

To Hide/Show Layers

There are several ways to show/hide layers:

- Click on the box with the eye icon in the first column to hide a layer. Click again to show the layer.

Layers 245

- Click and drag through the eye icon of several layers to hide a range of layers. Click and drag again to show a range.
- Hold down the **Option/Alt** key and click on the eye icon of a layer to hide all other layers leaving only the layer you click on showing and active. **Option/Alt** click again to show all layers.
- Choose **Hide Others** from the Layers palette pop-up menu to hide all but the currently active layer. This command toggles to Show All Layers, which makes all layers visible.
- Double-click on the layer name or choose **Options for...** from the pop-up menu, then deselect the **Show** check box to hide a layer.

NOTE: Hidden layers do not print. Objects must be showing to be printed. To prevent a visible layer from printing, deselect the **Print** check box in the Layers Options dialog as described earlier in this chapter.

To Toggle Layers to Artwork View

There are several ways to toggle between Artwork and Preview modes:

- Hold down the **Command/Ctrl** key and click in the first column next to a layer name. The eye icon changes to an outlined icon, and all drawing objects in this layer are displayed in **Artwork** view, rather than Preview mode (see Figure 11.9).

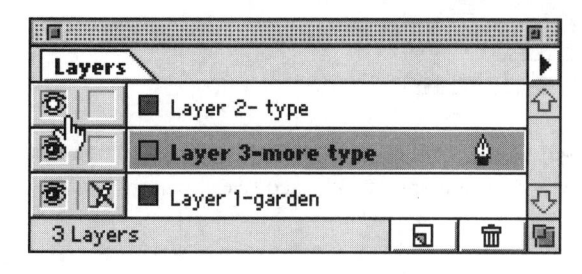

*Figure 11.9 Click while holding down the **Command/Ctrl** key to toggle layers between the Artwork and Preview modes.*

- Hold down the **Command/Ctrl** key; then click and drag through two or more visibility check boxes. The eye icons change to outlined icons, and all drawing objects in these layers are displayed in Artwork view.
- Hold down the **Option/Alt-Command/Ctrl** keys and click in the first column next to a layer name. The eye icon of all other layers changes to an outlined icon, and the objects of those layers is dis-

played in Artwork view. The layer you click on remains in Preview mode. **Option/Alt-Command/Ctrl** click again, and all layers return to Preview mode.
- Select a layer or layers and choose **Artwork Others** from the palette pop-up menu to leave the chosen layers in Preview while displaying all other layers in Artwork view. This command toggles to Preview All to return all layers to Preview mode.
- Double-click on the layer name or choose **Options for...** from the pop-up menu; then deselect the **Preview** check box to display a layer in Artwork view.

To Lock/Unlock Layers

Locking and unlocking layers works exactly the same way as hiding and showing layers, except that the lock icon is in the second column of the layers palette list. Follow the instructions for hiding and showing using the second column or the **Lock/Unlock** commands in the pop-up menu, as shown in Figure 11.10. The pencil with a slash through it indicates that a layer is locked and the objects within the layer can't be selected or edited.

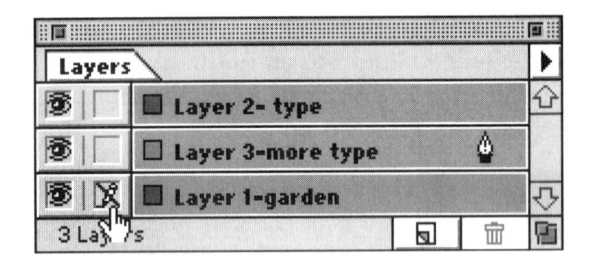

Figure 11.10 Click in the second column to toggle the layer lock on and off.

NOTE Locked layers can be moved around in the Layers palette, but no selection can be made in the layer, and you cannot paste into a locked layer.

To Merge Layers

1. Select two or more layers as described earlier in the chapter.
2. Choose **Merge Layers** from the palette pop-up menu. The selected layers are merged into a single layer retaining the name of the topmost layer. All objects retain their relative order from front to back.

Dining with Layers

This lesson will be a test of your table manners. Open the file DINNER.AI from the LESSON11 folder on the CD. All the elements we need to set the table are present. This lesson starts out using the Selection tool (v) several times, so select it, and then make sure the Layers palette is open before proceeding.

1. Choose **New Layer** from the Layers palette pop-up menu. In the New Layer dialog, type **on the table** for the name, leave all other options at their defaults, and click **OK**. (See Figure 11.11.) This creates a new layer and leaves it selected in the Layers palette, but there is nothing on the new layer, yet.

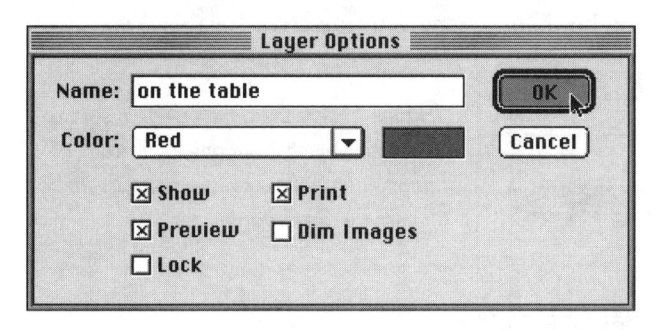

Figure 11.11 Assign a name and then click **OK** in the New Layers dialog.

248 CHAPTER 11

2. Hold down the **Option/Alt** key and choose the first layer by clicking on its name table in the **Layers** palette. Then hold down the **Shift** key and click on one of the blue diamonds of the tablecloth (see Figure 11.12). This selects all of the objects and then deselects the tablecloth.

Figure 11.12 All objects except the checkerboard tablecloth are selected. The Layers palette shows that there are two layers with the first chosen and containing an active selection.

3. Move the cursor over the selection square to the right of the "table" layer. Hold down the mouse button and drag the square to the "on the table" layer. Notice how the highlight color of the selection changes as you move the selected items to a new layer (see Figure 11.13). When you release the mouse button, the selection square moves to the new layer and the selection highlight changes to the color for this layer.

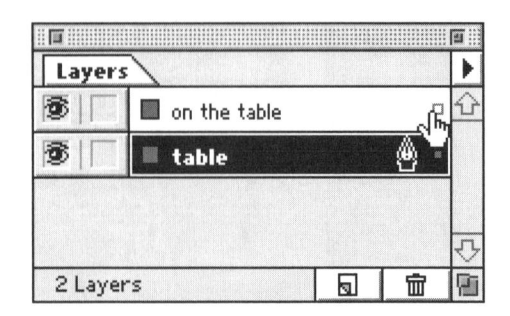

Figure 11.13 Drag the selection square to move objects from one layer to another. A hollow square appears in the layer you are dragging to.

Layers 249

4. Click in the second column of the table layer to lock it (as shown in Figure 11.14) and prevent accidental selection or modification of the tablecloth. The lock icon appears in the column. This will make it much easier to move the table settings on to the tablecloth.

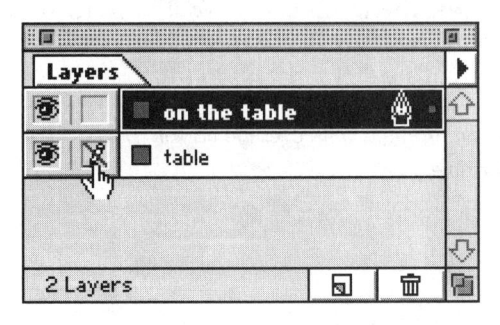

Figure 11.14 Lock the bottom layer by clicking in the second column.

5. Click in the drawing, but not on any objects to deselect everything. Then click, drag, and drop the plate, followed by the napkin, wine glass, and fork on their appropriate spots on the table. We can move objects without worrying about moving the tablecloth, because the tablecloth layer is locked.

Figure 11.15 Set the table by dragging objects into place.

6. Click and drag the knife so that it is positioned on the napkin. Notice when you release the mouse button that something different happens. Illustrator thinks the knife is under the napkin. It remains highlighted, but the stroke and fill are not visible. Choose **Edit: Undo** (**Command/Ctrl-z**) to put the knife back. We'll have to try something else.

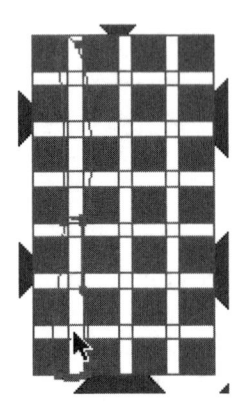

Figure 11.16 We can drag the knife over the napkin, but only the selection outline is visible.

7. The knife should still be selected, so hold down the **Shift** key and click on the spoon to add it to the selection (see Figure 11.19). We'll put these two on a layer together.

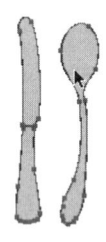

Figure 11.17 Select the knife and spoon together to move them to a new layer.

8. Hold down the **Option/Alt** key and click on the **New Layers** button at the bottom of the Layers palette. Type **on top** in the name field and click **OK**, as shown in Figure 11.19.

Layers 251

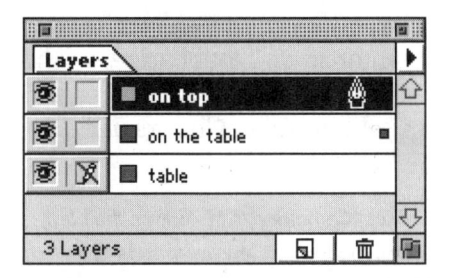

Figure 11.18 There are now three layers shown in the Layers palette. The bottom one is locked, the middle has an active selection, and the top is highlighted and ready to be edited.

9. Drag the selection square from the middle layer to the top layer to put the knife and spoon on a layer above the napkin (see Figure 11.19). Now drag the knife and spoon together over the napkin.

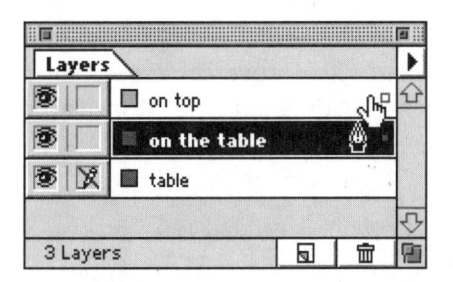

Figure 11.19 Drag the selection square from the middle layer to the top layer to move the knife and spoon up a layer.

10. Select the cow and fish and drag them to the plate. Once again, we find an incorrect sequencing of objects for our purposes (see Figure 11.20). But since we already have another layer to work with, simply drag the selection icon from the middle layer to the top layer. Voilá! The dancing couple is now on top of the plate ready for dining.

Figure 11.20 With the cow and fish moved partially to the plate, you can see that even though they are above the checkerboard tablecloth, they are lying under the plate. Moving them to the top layer fixes this problem.

11. Hold down the **Command/Ctrl** keys and click on the **New Layer** button to create a new layer beneath the top layer. Double-click on the new layer to open the Layer Options dialog. Name this layer **mask** and click **OK**. (We haven't discussed masks yet but will in Chapter 12.)

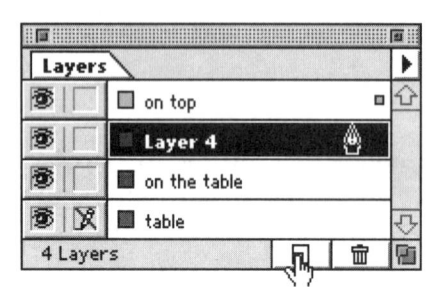

Figure 11.21 Command/Ctrl-click on the New Layer button to create a new layer under the active layer and assign it the default layer values.

12. This layer isn't exactly where we want it, so move the cursor over the layer name in the Layers palette and drag until it is one layer down, just above the table layer.

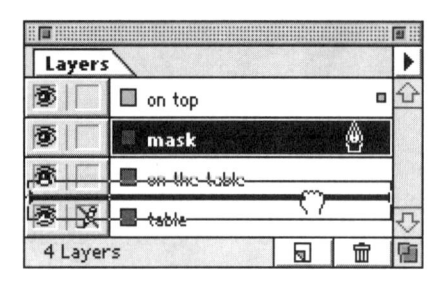

Figure 11.22 Drag the mask *layer down so that it is directly above the* table *layer in the Layers palette.*

13. Choose the **Rectangle** tool (m) and drag from the upper-left corner just within the page border to the lower-right corner within the page border. (See Figure 11.23.) Don't worry that this rectangle obliterates the background. We're going to turn it into a mask.

Layers 253

Figure 11.23 Drag a rectangle over the checkerboard tablecloth to use as a mask. (The dotted lines in the screen shot represent the page border.)

14. Click in the second column of the "table" layer to unlock the layer. Hold down the **Shift-Option/Alt** keys and click on the "table" layer to select it and the tablecloth object along with the "mask" layer. Then choose **Object: Masks: Make (Command/Ctrl-7)**, as shown in Figure 11.24. This masks the edges of the tablecloth and completes our composition.

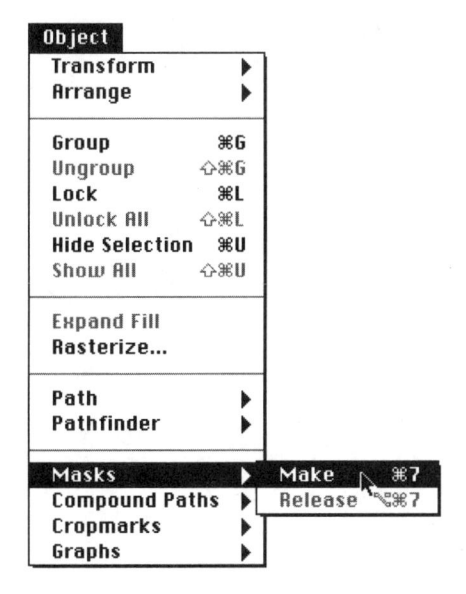

Figure 11.24 The Object: Masks: Make command turns the rectangle into a frame that reveals the tablecloth in the middle and masks the edges that are outside the view.

The table is set. If you wish, create another layer on top of everything (simply click on the **New Layer** button) and add some type to identify this as the "Surf & Turf Special." I used Adobe's multiple master typeface Ex Ponto in the finished version of this lesson, which is saved as EATUP.AI in the LESSON11 folder on the CD.

Section IV

Menu-Based Tools

In this section…

- Menus and the duplication of functions
- Chapter 12: Edit and Object commands
- Chapter 13: Type
- Chapter 14: Filters
- Chapter 15: Windows and Views

Menus and the Duplication of Functions

Making program commands available from menus was one of the great interface innovations developed at the Xerox Palo Alto Research Center, in the 1970s. Those were the halcyon days before John Warnock and Craig Geshke left to found Adobe. Since then, it has become such standard fare that it doesn't require any explanation any more.

Adobe's application programming interface (API) expands on the standard menu command structure by adding palettes (discussed in Section III). For historical and/or practical reasons, many of the functions of the palettes are duplicated in the menus. And while most menu commands have no palette equivalent, many can be executed using **Command/Ctrl** key shortcuts. Commands without palette or keyboard equivalents must be selected specifically.

Some menu commands change, or toggle, between two commands depending on their state. For instance, most of the Window menu commands toggle between Show and Hide depending on the state of the windows. The state of the drawing can also affect commands. For instance, many commands are grayed and unavailable when there is no active selection.

Multiple ways of achieving the same result can be confusing, but it needn't be. Use the method you find most convenient. If your hand is on the mouse, it may be more convenient to click on a command in a palette. From the keyboard, a shortcut key may be quicker. For commands you use less frequently, it's often easiest to remember where they are in the menu hierarchy. You'll discover what works best for you as you use Illustrator more.

12 Edit and Object Commands

In this chapter...

- Edit commands
- Object menu in brief
- Transform and Arrange submenus
- Group, Lock, and Hide commands
- Expand and Rasterize commands
- Path and Pathfinder submenus
- Mask, Compound Path, Cropmark, and Graphs commands
- Lesson 12: Mixing Business and Pleasure

Edit Commands

Illustrator's Edit menu is much like the Edit menus of other applications. There are the standard Cut, Copy, and Paste commands, plus a few additional commands. Most of the edit commands have Command/Ctrl key equivalents.

Undo and Redo Commands

- **Edit: Undo (Command/Ctrl-z)**—Undo eliminates the effect of the last executed operation and restores your drawing to its previous state. Illustrator maintains a stack of each operation you execute—creating objects, moving, editing, executing commands or filters. The maximum size of this stack is 200 operations, but the default is five. (Use the **File: Preferences: Units and Undo** dialog box to set the size of the undo stack from 0 to 200, see Chapter 19.)

    Repeated execution of the Undo command steps further back in the operations stack in order. This stack is deleted when you quit Illustrator, but not when you save a document. The command is grayed-out and unavailable when there are no operations in the undo stack.
- **Edit: Redo (Shift-Command/Ctrl-z)**: Once a command has been undone, it can be reexecuted using the Redo command. Redo shares the undo stack. Any number of undone steps can be redone in order, but execution of a Redo command must immediately follow an Undo execution. Executing another operation or command removes the previously undone steps from the stack so that they are no longer available. The command is grayed-out and unavailable when there are no undone operations on the top of the undo stack.

Cut, Copy, Paste, and Clear Commands

The Cut, Copy, and Clear commands require an active selection in the drawing, while the Paste command requires that there be an object in the Clipboard. Paste in Front and Paste in Back require both an active selection and an object in the Clipboard. When these conditions are not met, the commands are grayed-out and unavailable.

- **Edit: Cut (Command/Ctrl-x)**—Cut removes the active selection from the drawing and replaces the contents of the Clipboard.

Edit and Object Commands

- **Edit: Copy** (**Command/Ctrl-c**)—Copy copies the active selection in the drawing to the **Clipboard**.
- **Edit: Clear: Clear** removes the active selection from the drawing but does not change the contents of the Clipboard. Pressing the Backspace/Delete is a shortcut for the Clear command.
- **Edit: Paste** (**Command/Ctrl-v**)—Paste copies the contents of the Clipboard to the center of the drawing. The pasted object becomes topmost on the active layer and remains selected
- **Edit: Paste in Front** (**Command/Ctrl-f**)—Paste in Front maintains an object's original position in the drawing while moving or copying it up to the topmost position in the active layer.
- **Edit: Paste in Back** (**Command/Ctrl-b**)—Paste in Back maintains an object's original position in the drawing while moving or copying it down to the bottommost position in the active layer.

To Define a New Pattern

1. Create the pattern using Illustrator's drawing tools and leave it selected. It sometimes helps to create a square bounding box around the intended pattern. The bounding box should be beneath the pattern and without paint attributes.
2. Choose **Edit: Define Pattern** to open the New Swatch dialog.
3. Specify a Swatch Name and click **OK**. Illustrator adds the swatch to the Swatches palette where it can be used like any other swatch (see Figure 12.1).

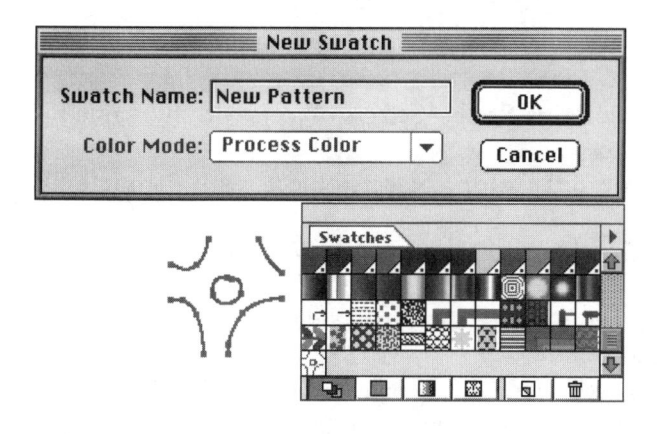

Figure 12.1 Adding a new pattern to the Swatches palette.

> **NOTE:** The Illustrator *User Guide* includes very good guidelines for creating patterns. Rather than duplicate this section, I refer you to it.

Selection Commands

There are two straightforward commands that let you select all or nothing as well as a Select submenu that lets you select objects by their characteristics—Paint Style, Fill Color, Stroke Color, Stroke Weight, Masks, Stray Points, and Inverse. The commands in the Select submenu were part of the Filter menu in previous versions of Illustrator.

- **Edit: Select All** (**Command/Ctrl-a**)—Select All selects all objects in all showing layers. Hidden objects and objects on hidden layers are not selected.
- **Edit: Deselect All** (**Shift-Command/Ctrl-a**)—Deselect All, formerly the Select None command, deselects any active selection and leaves no objects in the drawing selected.
- The **Edit: Select: Same** group of commands select all objects (except hidden ones) that match the current selection. If there is no selection, these commands will match the active settings in the Color, Gradient, and/or Stroke palettes:

> **NOTE:** When selecting objects with the same spot color, the color must have the same tint. To make global changes to spot-colored objects with different tints, use the Color palette (see Chapter 10).

> **Edit: Select: Same Paint Style**—Selects objects with the same fill and stroke attributes.
> **Edit: Select: Same Fill Color**—Selects objects with the same fill attributes.
> **Edit: Select: Same Stroke Color**—Selects objects with the same stroke color.
> **Edit: Select: Same Stroke Weight**—Selects objects with the same stroke weight.
> **Edit: Select: Masks**—Selects all mask objects. This is distinct from the objects masked and is discussed later in this chapter.

Edit: Select: Stray Points—Sometimes the process of creating a drawing leaves stray points around on the artboard. A stray point is one that has no connecting path. This command selects these points so that they can be deleted.

Edit: Select: Inverse—This is actually a *reverse* command, since all active selections are deselected and all unselected objects are selected, but we needn't quibble about semantics.

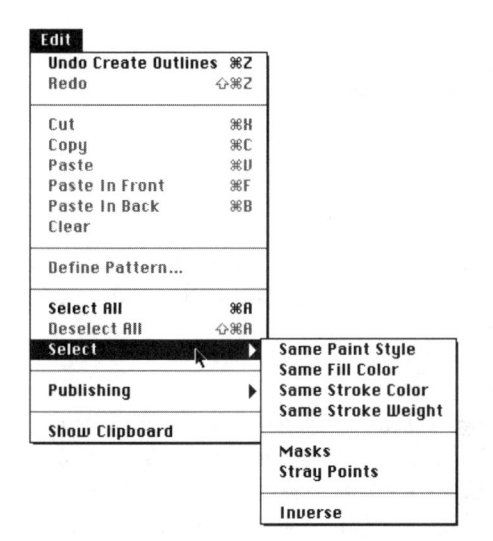

Figure 12.2 The special selection commands of the Edit: Select submenu let you select items that might otherwise be difficult to find.

Macintosh Select Commands

The Mac OS includes Publish and Subscribe capability. Illustrator supports this feature through the **Edit: Publishing** sub-submenu. It works exactly as it does in all Macintosh applications to publish shared documents that can be subscribed to by other applications. To find out more about Publish and Subscribe, read your operating system manual.

You can also view the contents of the Macintosh Clipboard within Illustrator. Choose **Edit: Show Clipboard** to preview what you are about to paste into an Illustrator document or overwrite by copying or cutting.

OBJECT MENU IN BRIEF

In Illustrator 7, the Object menu has lost several commands to other menus, and has gained some important new commands such as those in the Transform submenu. The actual changes need not concern us too much. It's more interesting to see the wide range of commands available for manipulating drawn objects.

Some of these commands actually change the way objects look, such as those in the Pathfinder submenu, while others change the way objects are drawn, like the Expand Fill and Rasterize commands. There are also commands that make simple groups or more complex groups that create masks and compound objects.

TRANSFORM AND ARRANGE SUBMENUS

Most of the Transform commands duplicate the operations of the Transform palette, which is discussed in Chapter 9, and the Toolbar tools, which are discussed in Chapter 5. These are the Move, Scale, Rotate, Shear, and Reflect commands. Accessing any of these commands from the Transform submenu, shown in Figure 12.3, opens a dialog that allows you to transform the current selection.

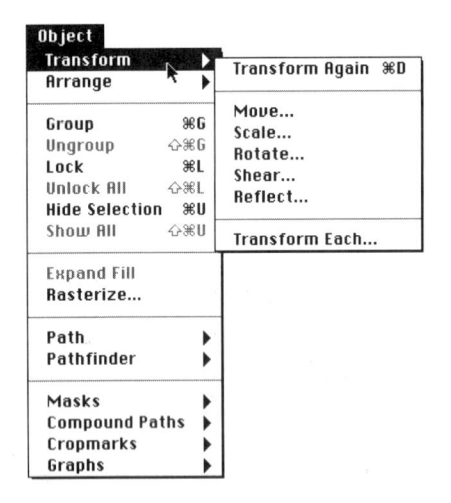

*Figure 12.3 The **Object: Transform** submenu includes the dialog-based methods for transforming objects. These duplicate the functions of the Transform tools and Transform palette, with the addition of a Transform Again and Transform Each command.*

Two other commands are not available anywhere else:

- **Object: Transform: Transform Again (Command/Ctrl-d)**—The Transform Again command allows you to apply the same transformation multiple times. This command is available only if the last command executed was a transformation.

NOTE: The Transform Again command is available after executing a transformation from the **Object: Transform** submenu, the Transform palette, or by using one of the transform tools.

- **Object: Transform: Transform Each**—The Transform Each command opens the Transform Each dialog.

To Transform Objects Separately in a Group

1. Select the objects you wish to transform. There must be more than one.
2. Choose **Object: Transform: Transform Each.**
3. In the Transform Each dialog, shown in Figure 12.4, either type in the specifications or use the sliders to make settings. Not all transformation types are available.

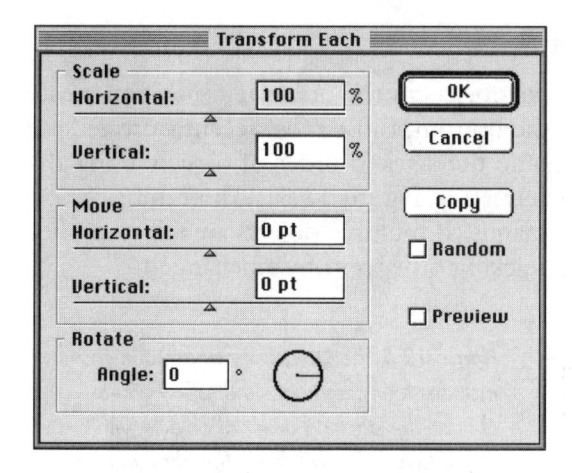

Figure 12.4 The Transform Each dialog applies multiple transformations to the entire selection, but it applies them individually to each object within the selection.

Scale—Specify Horizontal and/or Vertical scaling. The sliders' range is ±200%, but the data field range is ±4000% if you type the number in directly.

Move—Specify the distance for a move using Horizontal and/or Vertical distances. The sliders' range is ±200 pt, but the data field range is ±4000 pt. The default unit is points, but you can enter values in any supported units.

Rotate—Enter an angle of rotation in the range ±360°. Dragging the slider around the circle has a range of 0 to 359°.

Random—Check this box to randomize the transformation. Illustrator uses the specifications you set as the limits of randomization.
Preview—Check this box to preview transformations interactively while setting specifications.

4. Execute the transformations as specified by clicking the **OK** button or the **Copy** button to copy the selection and transform the copy. Each object within the selection is transformed independently of the others. Click **Cancel** to dismiss the dialog without changing the selection.

> NOTE: Transform Each treats each object within a selection independently. Any object grouping you may have set is also ignored. This differs from a standard transformation which treats the entire selection as a single object.

Arrange Submenu Commands

Within each layer, Illustrator stacks objects in the order in which you create them—those created first are at the bottom; those most recently created are at the top. It's possible to rearrange the stacked order of objects using the commands in the Arrange submenu (see Figure 12.5). There must be an active selection to use these commands. If multiple objects are selected, they are all affected, but their relative stacking order remains unchanged.

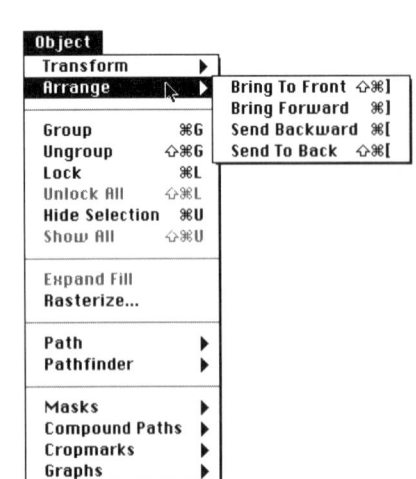

*Figure 12.5 The **Object: Arrange** submenu includes four commands that allow you to change the stacking order of objects within a single layer. You will likely find that you use them often and that it's worth learning the keyboard shortcuts.*

- **Object: Arrange: Bring to Front** (**Shift-Command/Ctrl-]**) puts all selected objects at the top of the layer stack.
- **Object: Arrange: Bring Forward** (**Command/Ctrl-]**) brings the selection up one level in the layer stack.
- **Object: Arrange: Send Backward** (**Command/Ctrl-[**) sends the selection down one level in the layer stack.
- **Object: Arrange: Send to Back** (**Shift-Command/Ctrl-[**) puts all selected objects at the bottom of the layer stack.

GROUP, LOCK, AND HIDE COMMANDS

The Object menu includes six commands that allow you to control the nonvisible attributes of objects. These attributes are group, lock, and hide. They don't affect the visible characteristics of objects (although hide makes them temporarily invisible) but aid in the process of creating artwork.

To Group and Ungroup Objects

1. Make a selection. Grouping requires that more than one object be selected, while ungrouping requires that at least one grouped object be selected.
2. Choose **Object: Group** (**Command/Ctrl-g**) or **Object: Ungroup** (**Shift-Command/Ctrl-g**).

The Group command creates an association between objects so that they can be easily selected and manipulated together. The Selection tool can be used to select an entire group with a single click (see Chapter 4).

NOTE Grouped objects must be contiguous in the stack on a single layer. Therefore, when you group noncontiguous objects, Illustrator moves all the objects so that they stack contiguously under the top object. This can affect the way overlapping objects are displayed.

Ungrouping objects breaks the link between them, but it does not change their order in the stack. Once ungrouped, objects will not be selected together with a single click of the Selection tool.

> **NOTE:** It's possible to have groups within groups, which means that it is also possible to ungroup objects more than once.

Use the Group Selection or Direct Selection tools (see Chapter 4) to select individual objects within groups.

To Lock or Hide Objects

1. Make a selection.
2. Choose **Object: Lock (Command/Ctrl-1)** or **Object: Hide Selection (Command/Ctrl-u)** to lock or hide the selected object. Hold down the **Option/Alt** key while choosing **Object: Lock** or **Object: Hide Selection** to lock or hide all unselected objects.

Locking objects prevents them from being selected, moved, or manipulated. Hiding objects makes them invisible. There is no way to see or select them. Hiding and locking have the same effect on objects that hiding or locking a layer has on a layer of objects (see Chapter 11).

To Unlock or Show All Objects

Choose **Object: Unlock All (Shift-Command/Ctrl-1)** or **Object: Show All (Shift-Command/Ctrl-u)** to unlock all locked objects or show all hidden objects.

If you select a visible or unlocked object within a group, hold down the **Option/Alt** key and then execute the **Object: Unlock All** or **Object: Show All** command to unlock or show objects that are part of the group.

EXPAND AND RASTERIZE COMMANDS

The Expand Fill and Rasterize commands create very specialized transformations. Expand Fill lets you convert gradients and patterns into objects. This is useful when you're having trouble printing certain drawings. Rasterize allows you to convert objects into raster images so that you can apply Photoshop or other raster-oriented filters to the objects.

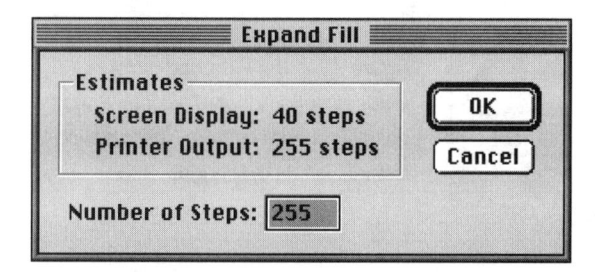

Figure 12.6 *The Expand Fill dialog is used to convert gradient fills into a sequence of graded objects. Photoshop suggests the optimum number of steps for screen or printed output.*

To Expand a Gradient or Pattern Fill into an Object

1. Select the object that contains the gradient or pattern fill you wish to convert.
2. Choose **Object: Expand Fill** to open the Expand Fill dialog, or hold down the **Option/Alt** key while choosing **Object: Expand Fill** to skip the dialog and use the last entered values. Any patterns selected are automatically expanded.

    The Expand Fill dialog supplies an estimate for the number of steps to specify if you intend to use the object for **Screen Display** or **Printer Output** (the default). The recommended number of steps should produce a smooth gradient. Type in the amount you wish, or use the default.
3. If you are using the dialog, click **OK**. The gradient is expanded into the number of objects specified in the dialog.

To Convert Objects to Bitmap Images

1. Select an object or objects.
2. Choose **Object: Rasterize**. This opens the Rasterize dialog with the following options:

    Color Model—Choose a color model from the drop-down menu: RGB, CMYK, Grayscale, or Bitmap.
    Resolution—Click on one of four radio buttons: Screen (72 ppi), Medium (150 ppi), High (300 ppi), or Other. You can set Other to any resolution you wish.
    Options—There are two check boxes:
    Anti-Alias—Check this box to anti-alias the raster image.
    Mask—Check this box to turn unfilled areas of the selection into a transparent bitmap mask.

268   CHAPTER 12

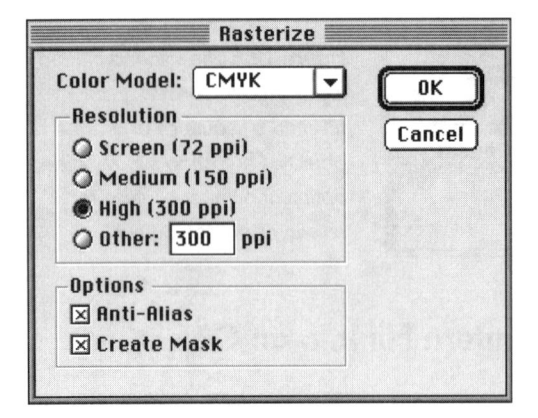

Figure 12.7 The Rasterize dialog includes options that affect the way an object is converted from Illustrator vectors into a bitmap image.

The object is turned into a bitmap or raster image and can be edited like any placed image, but it can no longer be manipulated as a vector-based object.

PATH AND PATHFINDER SUBMENUS

The Path and Pathfinder submenus contain commands that manipulate anchor points, paths, and objects precisely. In other words, the effects are calculated by Illustrator and applied to the selection or drawing. Many of these commands had other homes in previous versions of Illustrator, but they are now combined in two subgroups of the Object menu.

The commands on the Path submenu operate on paths and anchor points. All require a selection except for the Cleanup command, which makes and deletes selections. Most include dialogs.

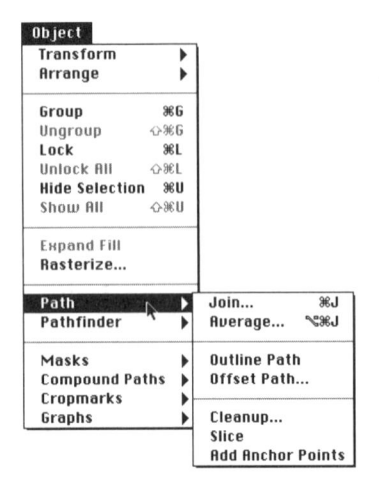

Figure 12.8 The commands of the Object: Path submenu give precision to operations that might otherwise be difficult or impossible to perform reliably.

The Pathfinder commands are used with multiple objects to combine, isolate, subdivide, or extract new objects. The intersection of paths and the stacking order of objects determines the results of a Pathfinder command.

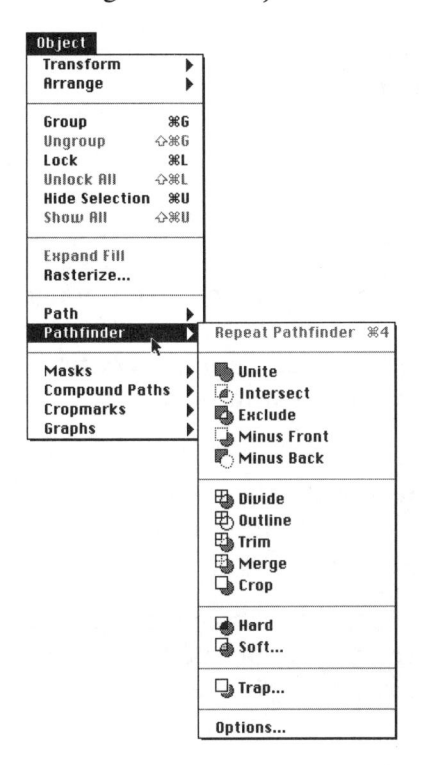

Figure 12.9 The Pathfinder submenu contains a unique set of commands that blend objects in various ways. The list of possibilities is long and some of the commands are easily confused, but this is one of Illustrator's most powerful features.

To Join Two End points

1. Select two open endpoints either by selecting them with the Direct Selection tool (drag to select coincident points) or by selecting an open path with the Selection tool.
2. Choose **Object: Path: Join** (**Command/Ctrl-j**). If the two points are coincident, the Join dialog opens. Click the **Smooth** radio button to turn the two points into a single smooth point or **Corner** to make a single corner point. (See Chapter 3 for corner and smooth points.) Click **OK** to dismiss the dialog and create the new anchor point.

    If the two points are not coincident, Illustrator attaches them with a straight path segment. The anchor points do not change.

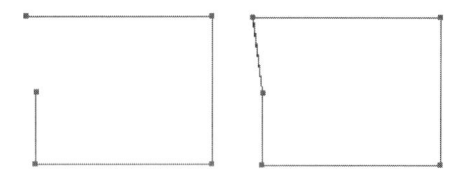

Figure 12.10 On the left, a selected open path before joining. On the right, the same path after executing the **Object: Path: Join** command is closed by a straight path segment.

To Average Two Anchor Points

1. Choose the Direct Selection tool (a) and click on or drag through two or more anchor points.
2. Choose **Object: Path: Average (Option/Alt-Command/Ctrl-j)**. The **Average** dialog has a single **Axis** option with three radio buttons. Choose one:

    Horizontal—Averages the two points along the horizontal axis.
    Vertical—Averages the two points along the vertical axis.
    Both—Averages the two points along both axes.

3. Click **OK**. Illustrator calculates the midpoint between the selected points and moves them accordingly so that they line up horizontally, vertically, or on both axes, which makes them coincident.

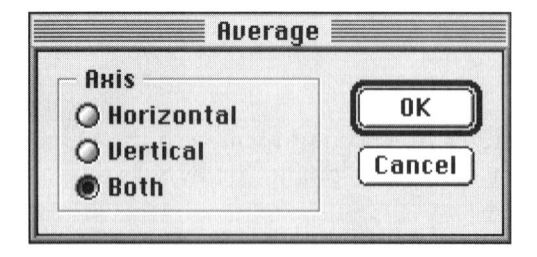

Figure 12.11 The Object: Path: Average *dialog lets you average the placement of multiple objects in relation to the vertical, horizontal, or both axes.*

To Outline a Path

1. Make a selection.
2. Choose **Object: Path: Outline Path**. The path is converted into a filled path by surrounding the old path width with a new filled path. Any previous object fills are discarded. There are no options.

Edit and Object Commands 271

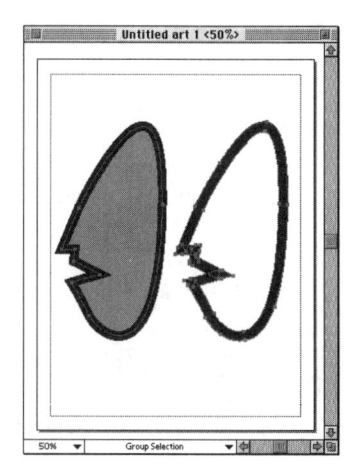

Figure 12.12 The Object: Path: Outline Path command makes a copy of the selected object but without the fill. This can be useful when you want to create a mask or some other special effect. Here the original figure with 20-point stroke and fill is on the left and the outlined path has been moved to the right.

To Offset a Path

1. Make a selection.
2. Choose **Object: Path: Offset Path**. This opens the Offset Path dialog which has three options.

    Offset—Specify the width of the offset from ±16000 points.
    Joins—Choose Round, Bevel, or Miter (the default) from the drop-down menu.
    Miter Limit—Set the miter limit as described in Chapter 3.

3. Click **OK** and Illustrator creates a new object at the specified offset from the first. The new object remains selected.

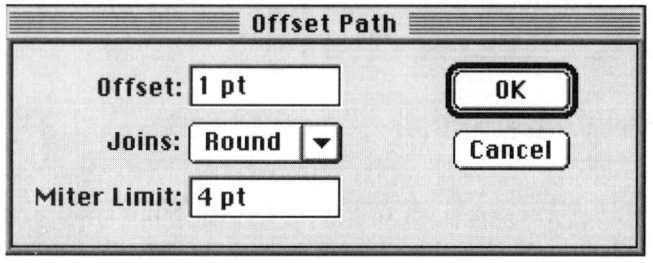

Figure 12.13 The Offset Path dialog lets you create object offsets of essentially any distance from the original. It's another way to copy and scale and object simultaneously with the advantage that you can adjust the joins and miters.

To Clean Up a Drawing

1. Choose **Object: Cleanup**. This is the only Path submenu command available when there is no active selection.
2. The Cleanup dialog has three options. You may select any or all of them.

    Delete Stray Points—Check this box to have Illustrator find and delete points that are not attached to any paths.
    Delete Unpainted Objects—Check this box to have Illustrator find and delete objects with no stroke or fill attributes.
    Delete Empty Text Paths—Check this box to have Illustrator find and delete text paths that have no text attached.

3. Click **OK**. Illustrator will execute the cleanup options you've selected.

NOTE It may look as though the Cleanup command hasn't done anything. This is because all of the objects it finds and deletes are invisible unless they are selected or viewed in Artwork mode. It's a good practice to clean up before sending files out for production.

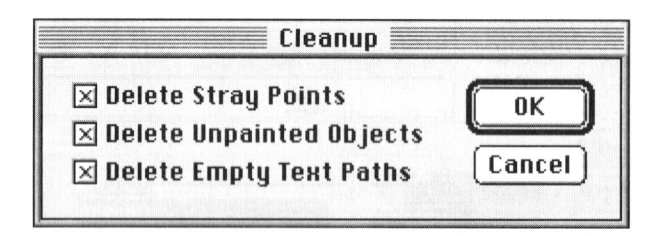

Figure 12.14 The Cleanup dialog with its three options.

To Slice One Object with Another

1. Draw or select the object you wish to use as a cutting die and move the die into position. The die must be on top of the object(s) to be cut, and it must be the only object selected.
2. Choose **Object: Path: Slice**. The die cuts all objects beneath it along its path. The die is deleted, and the resulting objects are ungrouped and selected.

Edit and Object Commands   **273**

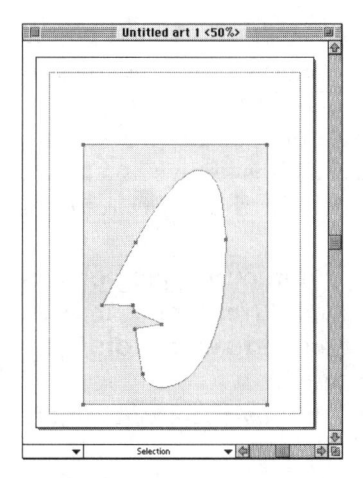

Figure 12.15 *This could be two objects or a compound object, but it is actually a single object created out of two with the Object: Path: Slice command.*

NOTE The Slice command will cut all objects lower in the stack or on a lower layer. However, all sliced objects end up on the same layer the die was on.

To Add Anchor Points Along the Entire Length of a Path

1. Make a selection.
2. Choose **Object: Path: Add Anchor Points**. Illustrator bisects the distance between each pair of selected anchor points and adds a new anchor point. A closed path will end up with twice as many points, while an open path will end up with 2X-1 points.

Figure 12.16 *Using the Object: Path: Add Anchor Points command on any selected object adds intermediate anchor points between each original anchor point.*

To Use the Pathfinder Commands

1. Select two or more objects.
2. Choose a command from the **Object: Pathfinder** submenu.

- **Unite** traces around the outside perimeter of all selected objects to create a single united object. This is known as a logical *and*. The fill color of the topmost object is used for the united object.
- **Intersect** traces only the overlapping portions of two selected objects to create a single smaller object. This is known as a logical *or*. The fill color of the top object is used for the object resulting from the intersection.
- **Exclude** traces around the perimeter of non-overlapping objects. It is the inverse of the Intersect command. Overlapping areas are left transparent, except for areas where an odd number of objects overlap, where the topmost fill color is used.
- **Minus Front** traces the back object minus the front object, which is deleted.
- **Minus Back** traces the front object minus the back object, which is deleted.
- **Divide** traces perimeters and intersections to turn the selection into filled objects that abut rather than overlap. The resulting objects may be ungrouped and manipulated independently.
- **Outline** is similar to Divide, but the resulting objects are outlined and not filled. The former fill colors are used as the path segment stroke colors.
- **Trim** maintains the integrity of the topmost object and deletes any overlap from objects beneath so that each object cuts the one beneath it in the stack. No fill colors are affected, but the stroke (if any) is deleted.
- **Merge** trims the topmost object and unites all objects underneath.
- **Crop** uses the back images to crop the topmost image successively by finding the intersections. The fill of the cropping object is used in the resulting image.
- **Hard** simultaneously divides overlapping objects and mixes the fill colors. The resulting color uses the highest value of color component, so that a magenta fill of 25% cyan, 100% magenta, 25% yellow, and 0% black mixed with a deep blue fill of 100% cyan, 90% magenta, 10% yellow, and 0% black yields a purple of 100% cyan, 100% magenta, 25% yellow, and 0% black. The result appears to be the addition of color and is always darker.
- **Soft**, like Hard, also simultaneously divides overlapping objects and mixes colors. Soft makes the top fill appear translucent by mixing color values at the rate you set using the Mixing Rate percentage value in the Pathfinder: Soft dialog.

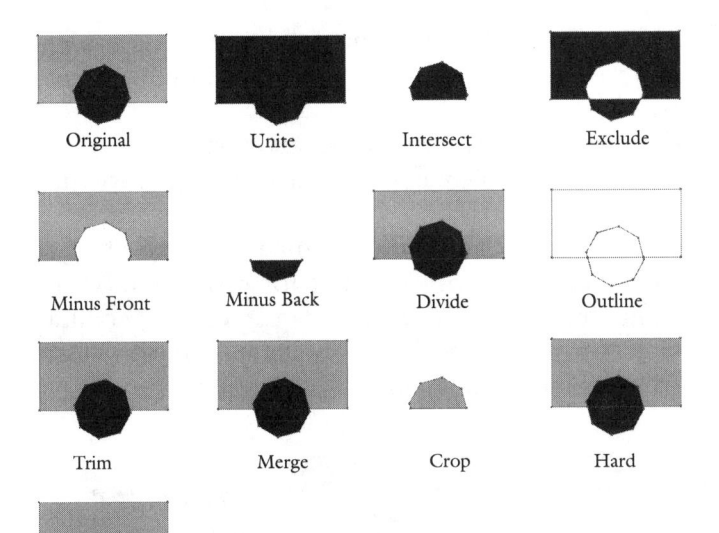

Figure 12.17 Each Pathfinder subcommand has a slightly different effect when combining these two objects.

To repeat a Pathfinder command, choose **Object: Pathfinder: Repeat Pathfinder (Command/Ctrl-4)**.

Choose **Object: Pathfinder: Options** to change the preference settings for all Pathfinder commands. The Pathfinder Options dialog includes three options and a Defaults button so that you can reset the options to their default settings. Click **OK** to set the options (Figure 12.18).

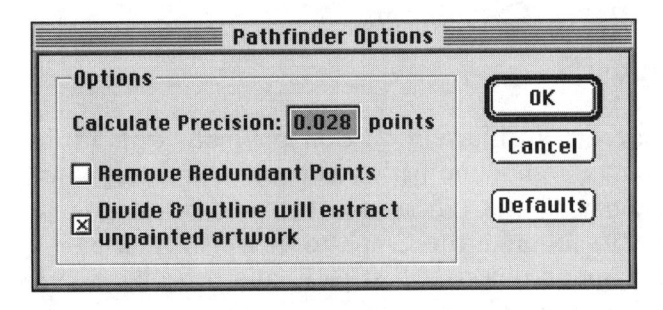

Figure 12.18 The setting and check boxes in the Pathfinder Options dialog affect the way all the Pathfinder commands calculate their results.

- **Calculate Precision**—Enter a value between .001 and 100 points. A setting of 0.028 points is the default. The lower the value, the more precisely Illustrator calculates Pathfinder effects, but the longer it takes to calculate them.

- **Remove Redundant Points**—Check this box to have coincident points combined into a single point after executing Pathfinder commands. Unchecked is the default.
- **Divide & Outline will extract unpainted artwork**—This box is checked by default so that unfilled artwork is deleted after executing these two Pathfinder commands.

There is one additional Pathfinder command, Trap (Figure 12.19). The issue of creating printing traps for process color artwork is discussed in Chapter 17. In brief, a trap extends or confines the borders of objects to compensate for misaligned printing plates so that unwanted colors don't show up in the resulting gaps.

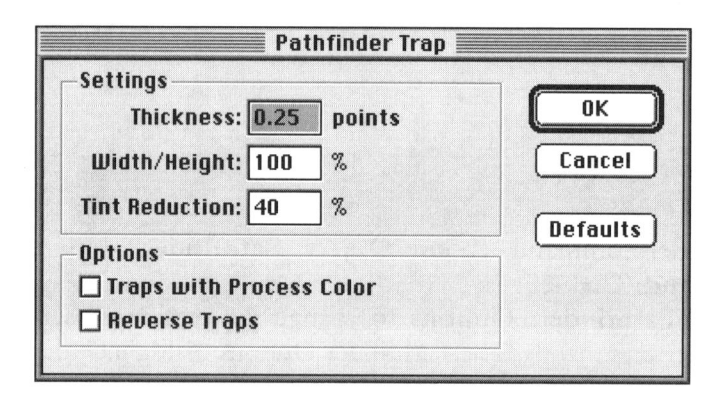

Figure 12.19 The Pathfinder Trap dialog allows you to create traps for individual selections.

MASK, COMPOUND PATH, CROPMARK, AND GRAPH COMMANDS

Most of the objects you create in Illustrator are simply paths with attributes of stroke and fill. Masks, compound paths, cropmarks, and graphs are special objects with unique attributes. These are all created by using commands in the Object menu, although the Graph tool (see Chapter 8) is a more direct way to create graph objects. (Text paths and text objects, see Chapters 3 and 13, are also special objects.)

Masks in General

The Mask submenu lets you turn objects into transparent masks that act like window frames. Everything beneath and inside the frame is revealed, while objects outside the mask window are blocked or cropped.

Creating a mask creates a special group in which the top object is the mask object and all other objects in the group are masked. Mask groups do not behave like other Illustrator groups. In other words, the objects aren't selected together and don't move together, but by using the **Object: Group** command, they will.

> **NOTE** Overly complex masks or drawings with many masks may cause printing problems. In this case you can unmask, group objects, and use the Pathfinder commands to achieve similar results and a simplified image.

To Turn Objects into Masks

1. Draw or select the object that will be the mask. Make sure it is above the objects to be masked.
2. Add the object(s) to be masked to the selection by **Shift**-clicking or by dragging a selection marquee across mask and masked objects.

> **NOTE** Mask and masked objects can be on separate layers, but if they are not on adjacent layers the unwanted side effect of masking everything on all layers in between can occur.

3. Choose **Object: Masks: Make (Command/Ctrl-7)**. Illustrator creates a mask group, converting the topmost object into a mask object with fill and stroke attributes set to none. All lower objects in the group are cropped by the mask.

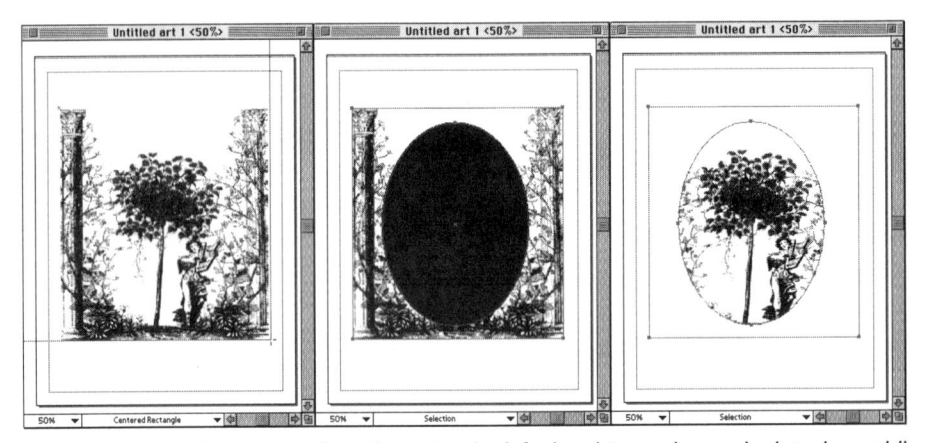

Figure 12.20 *The process of masking. On the left, the object to be masked. In the middle, creating the object to become the mask. On the right, after using the Object: Mask: Make command, the top oval masks the image beneath.*

To Turn Off Masks

1. Select the mask object. If you can't find it, choose **Edit: Select: Masks**. If there is no active selection, this will find all the masks in the document. **Shift**-click to deselect masks you don't want to release, or drag a selection marquee over those you do wish to release. If there is a selection, **Select: Masks** will deselect all objects in the selection that are not mask objects.
2. Choose **Object: Masks: Release** (**Option/Alt-Command/Ctrl-7**). The mask group is released and the former mask object is left selected, but with no fill or stroke. It's a good idea to apply attributes to it now because it may be hard to find this "invisible" object later.

NOTE It's possible to give mask objects attributes other than none, but you must use the Fill and Stroke for Mask filter (see Chapter 14).

To Add Objects to a Mask Group

1. Position the object you wish to add to the mask group over the mask and leave it selected.
2. Choose **Edit: Cut** (**Command/Ctrl-x**).
3. Select one of the masked objects by clicking on it with one of the selection tools.
4. Choose **Edit: Paste in Front** (**Command/Ctrl-f**) or **Edit: Paste in Back** (**Command/Ctrl-b**). This pastes the object into the mask group so that it is also cropped by the mask object.

> **NOTE** It's possible to find out which objects are part of a mask group by clicking on a mask repeatedly with the Group Selection tool. The first click selects the mask object, and subsequent clicks add the masked objects to the selection.

Compound Paths in General

Compound paths are created by grouping two objects so that any overlapping portion is left outside the combined object. In other words, two objects are grouped leaving the overlapping area of fill transparent.

Doughnuts are the archetypal compound object. If you tried to draw one in Illustrator, you would be hard pressed to combine two circles in such a way that you could see through the hole in the middle. The Compound Path submenu makes it easy.

> **NOTE** The same precaution that applies to masks applies to compound paths. If there are too many, or the paths are too complex, you may have trouble printing the file. Try using one of the Pathfinder commands to achieve a similar effect.

To Create a Compound Path

1. Draw the objects for the compound path making sure that the object that will create the transparency is on top.
2. Select the objects you wish to turn into a compound path.
3. Choose **Object: Compound Paths: Make (Command/Ctrl-8)**. This groups the objects and knocks a hole through at the point where the objects overlap. The fill of the bottom object is used for the non-transparent areas of the compound object.

Figure 12.21 Turning these two objects into a compound path has the effect of making a single object with a whole in it.

To Release Compound Paths

1. Select a compound path.
2. Choose **Object: Compound Paths: Release (Option/Alt-Command/Ctrl-8)**.

To Adjust Transparency in Compound Paths

1. Use the Direct Selection tool (a) to select the path you wish to change in the compound object.

   NOTE: Compound paths are "real" groups. To select part of a compound path, you must use the **Direct Selection** tool.

2. Choose **Window: Show Attributes**. In the Attributes dialog, click the **Reverse Path Direction On** button or the **Reverse Path**

Direction Off button. Reversing the direction in which a path is drawn reverses its transparency within a compound object.

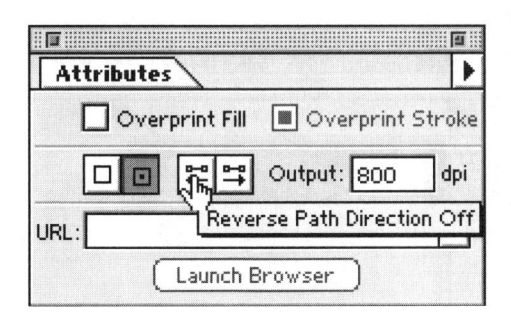

Figure 12.22 The transparency of compound objects is controlled by two buttons in the Attributes palette that reverse the relative path directions.

Cropmarks in General

Cropmarks define the trimmed edge of your artwork. They are necessary when printing color separations, and the Separation Setup dialog (see Chapter 17) can be used to create them. You can also add them directly to your artwork using the Cropmarks submenu commands.

NOTE: There can be only one set of cropmarks per document. However, you can use the Trim Marks filter (see Chapter 14) to create multiple sets of trim marks.

To Set Cropmarks

1. Draw a rectangle around your artwork exactly the size of the final trimmed print size. Leave the rectangle selected.
2. Choose **Object: Cropmarks: Make**. The rectangle is replaced by cropmarks set to the corners of the rectangle. There can be only one set of cropmarks in a document, and they cannot be selected or edited in any way (see Figure 12.23).

NOTE: If the Single Full Page option is selected in the Document Setup dialog (see Chapter 17), executing the **Object: Cropmarks: Make** command when there is no active selection creates crop marks at the page boundaries.

Figure 12.23 The cropmarks in this screen shot were created by converting a rectangle using the Objects: Cropmarks: Make command.

To Release Cropmarks

Choose **Object: Cropmarks: Release**. The cropmarks are replaced by the original rectangle, which can be edited or deleted as you wish.

NOTE You can replace cropmarks by creating a new rectangle and executing the **Object: Cropmarks: Make** command. This deletes the old cropmarks and creates new ones set to the boundaries of the new rectangle.

The Graphs Command in General

The last submenu in the Object menu, Graphs, is used to set and modify the properties of graph objects. There are five commands in the submenu: Type, Data, Design, Column, and Marker. Each of these commands opens a dialog, and each is explained in detail in Chapter 8.

LESSON 12

Mixing Business and Pleasure

It's impossible to show all of the commands of the **Edit** and **Object** menus in a single lesson, but many are so basic that they will show up in other lessons. In this lesson we'll use a few **Pathfinder** commands, because these are so important—they are easy to use and powerful, yet easily confused with one another.

Start by opening the file BUSINESS.AI from the LESSON12 folder on the CD. This contains the beginnings of my business card. The type is set in Poetica, which has an entire font of ampersands, and ITC Garamond Condensed. The letterforms have been converted to objects using the **Type: Create Outlines** command discussed in Chapter 13. This makes the type look a little ragged and bloated on screen, but it prints well at higher resolutions, 300 dpi and above.

1. Hold down the **Option/Alt** key and click in the Layers palette on the top layer, name/address. This selects all the type outlines on the layer.

284 CHAPTER 12

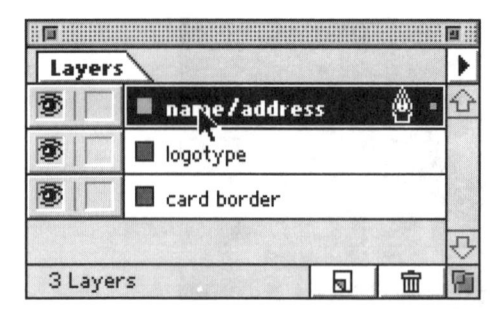

*Figure 12.24 Click on a layer name while holding down the **Option/Alt** key to select all visible objects in the layer.*

2. Choose **Object: Hide Selection** (**Command/Ctrl-u**). This will keep all the name-and-address type out of the way while we deal with other issues.

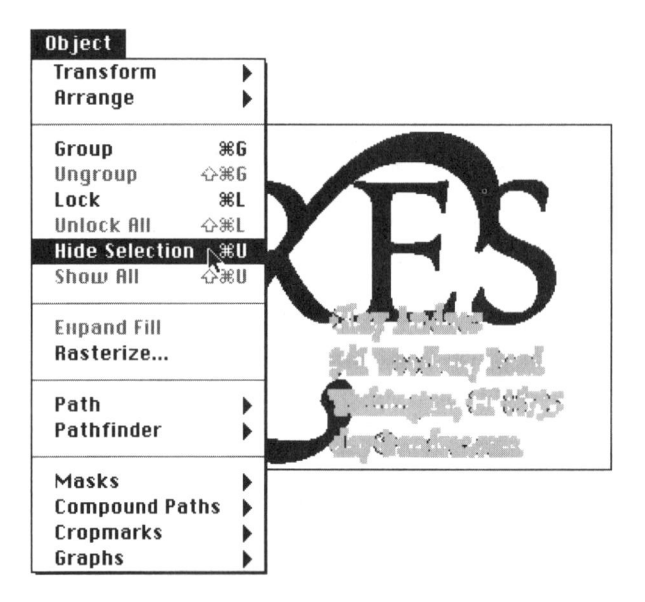

Figure 12.25 Choose the Hide Selection command to make the name-and-address text invisible and unchangeable while we work on other objects.

3. Choose the **Selection** tool (v) and click anywhere on the ampersand to select it, then move the cursor to the Swatches palette and click on the red spot swatch, second from the right on the second row. Now we have a nice red ampersand.

Edit and Object Commands 285

Figure 12.26 Pick a red spot color out of the Swatches palette.

4. Click on the *R*, then hold down the **Shift** key and click on the *E* and *S* so that the three letters are selected. Then move the cursor back to the Swatches palette and click on the aqua spot swatch, the first swatch on the second row.

Figure 12.27 Pick the aqua spot color to fill the three selected letters.

5. Hold down the **Shift** key and click on the ampersand so that all the letters are selected. Then choose **Object: Pathfinder: Divide**. The areas where the ampersand overlaps the other letters are divided into new objects.

We're going to try to make it appear as though the tail of the ampersand is woven through the other letters.

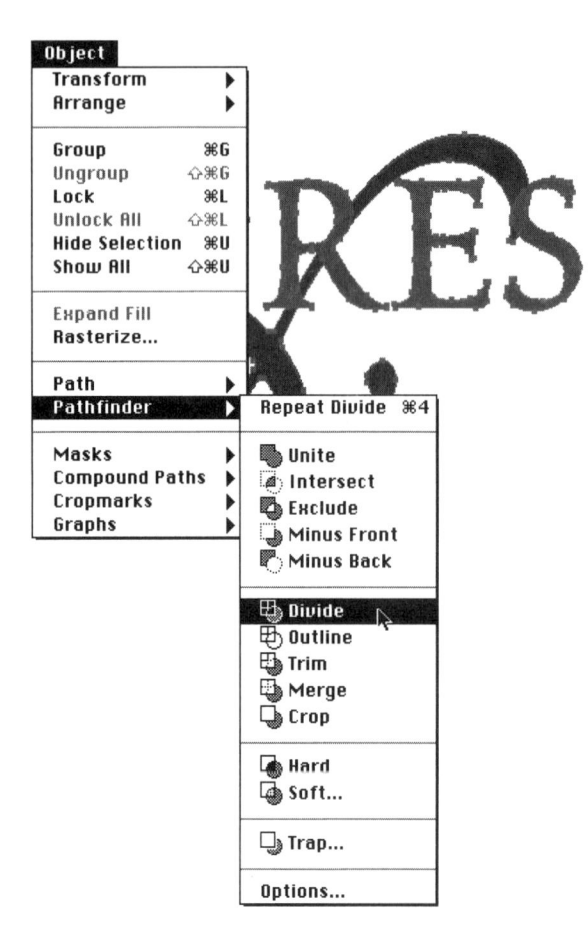

Figure 12.28 *With all the letterforms selected, choose **Object: Pathfinder: Divide** to create new objects at all the overlapping areas.*

6. Choose **Edit: Deselect All** (**Shift-Command/Ctrl-a**), then click the bowl and stem area of the *R* where the ampersand passes behind it. Everything is selected because the Divide command grouped all the objects. **Deselect All** again. Then choose the Group Selection tool (a), and click again on the *R*. This selects the area of overlap so that we can make it look as if the tail of the ampersand passes over the *R* at this point.

Figure 12.29 *An enlarged view showing the group selection of the new object created by the Divide command at the overlap of the R and the ampersand.*

7. Fill the selection red either by clicking on the red swatch in the palette again or by using the Eyedropper tool (i) and clicking on the red of the ampersand. Choose **Deselect All** again, and you can see that by making the overlap red instead of aqua, it appears that the ampersand starts underneath the other letters, passes over, and then finishes under the *S* (Figure 12.30).

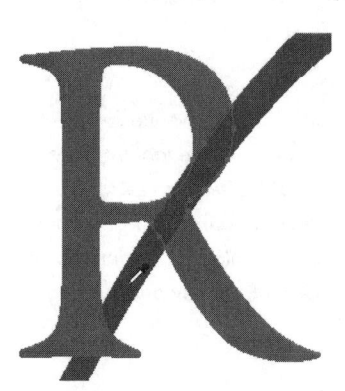

Figure 12.30 *Use the Eyedropper tool to sample the red from the ampersand to use as the fill for the selected overlap object. You can see how the swash of the ampersand appears at first to go under the R and then over it.*

8. Choose the **Selection** tool (v) and click on one of the letters to select the entire group of letterforms. Then choose **Object: Lock** (**Command/Ctrl-1**) so that the letters stay put while we work on the background (Figure 12.31).

288 CHAPTER 12

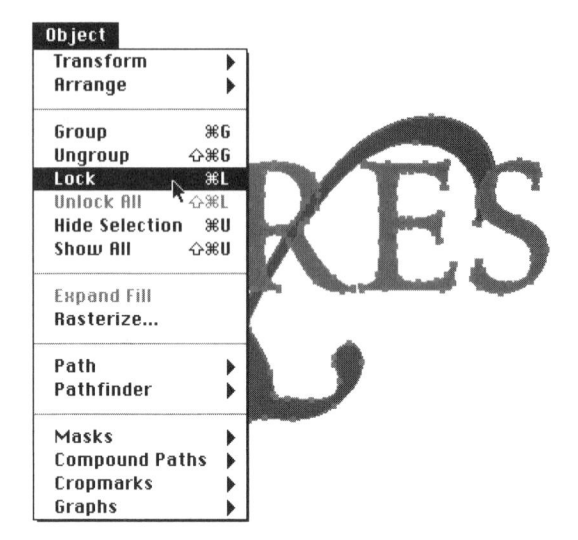

Figure 12.31 Use the **Object: Lock** command to lock the letterforms into place so that they cannot be moved while we're working on other objects around them.

9. Click on the rectangle that represents the border of the card to select it. Then choose the Scale tool (s), hold down the **Option/Alt** key, and click on the lower right corner of the rectangle to set the source point and open the Scale dialog.

Figure 12.32 Move the source point for the Scale tool from the center of the selected rectangle to the bottom right corner and open the Scale dialog by holding down the **Option/Alt** key and clicking.

10. Enter a Uniform scale of **50%** and click the Copy button to make a new half-size rectangle (Figure 12.33).

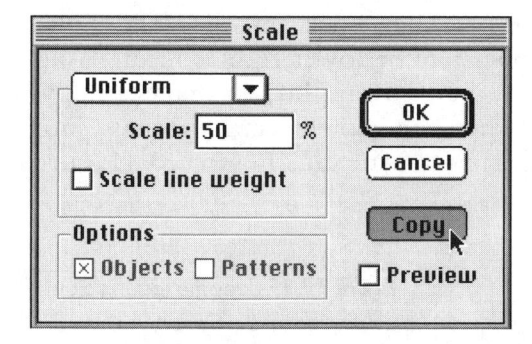

Figure 12.33 *Click on the Copy button after setting the scaling factor to make a half-size copy of the original rectangle.*

11. Click on the last swatch in the second row of the Swatches palette to set the fill to violet. Then click on the Stroke button (x) in the Toolbar and set the stroke to none by clicking on the None button (/). See Figure 12.34.

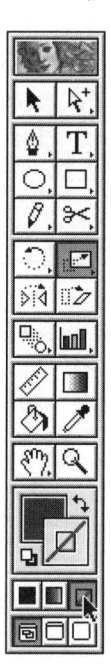

Figure 12.34 *After setting the fill to violet, click on the Stroke button and then the None button to eliminate the stroke.*

290   CHAPTER 12

12. Choose the **Selection** tool (v), then click and drag the violet rectangle by either the upper-left or lower-right corner. Hold down the **Option/Alt** key while dragging to make a copy. Release the mouse button when the copied rectangle snaps into place in the upper left corner of the business card (Figure 12.35).

*Figure 12.35 Copy the rectangle by holding down the **Option/Alt** key. The copy snaps into place at the corner, as indicated by the two hollow arrowheads, of the original rectangle.*

13. Click on the black-stroked rectangle that represents the border of the business card and choose **Object: Cropmarks: Make**. This replaces the visible border with printer's cropmarks (Figure 12.36).

Figure 12.36 After selecting the original black-stroked border rectangle, the Object: Cropmark: Make command produces these cropmarks.

14. Choose **Unlock All** (**Shift-Command/Ctrl-l**) to unlock the letterforms, then **Select All** (**Command/Ctrl-a**). Everything is selected except the cropmarks, which are locked until explicitly released.

Edit and Object Commands

Figure 12.37 You must select at least two or more overlapping objects before using the Pathfinder commands. Here, everything has been selected using the Edit: Select All command.

15. Choose **Object: Pathfinder: Hard**. The perimeter of the violet rectangles creates additional divides in the letterforms and mixes new darker fill colors for the overlapping objects. This makes it appear that the rectangles are above the letterforms and their color is translucent. Notice that the spot colors are all converted to CMYK equivalents when mixed this way.

Figure 12.38 After the Pathfinder: Hard command has been executed, the color of the letterforms is mixed with that of the rectangles to produce darker hues.

16. Choose **Edit: Show All** (**Shift-Command/Ctrl-u**) to bring back the hidden address information.

*Figure 12.39 I hope you haven't forgotten that my name and address, hidden since step 2, need to be brought back using the **Edit: Show All** command, which leaves the letterforms selected.*

17. Set the fill to white using any method you prefer. The easiest for me is to click on the white swatch in the **Swatches** palette. Choose **Edit: Deselect All** (**Shift-Command/Ctrl-a**), and we're done.

Figure 12.40 The finished business card with name and address in white letters and the logo blended as part of the background.

Thank you for helping to make this business card. Save a copy if you wish and give it to all your friends and associates. There's a finished version of the file saved as PLEASURE.AI in the LESSON12 folder on the CD.

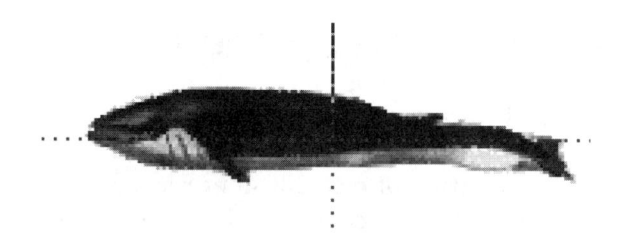

13 Type Commands and Palettes

In this chapter...

- Type menu and palettes in general
- Some type vocabulary
- Simple character formatting commands
- Total character control—Character palette
- Indents, spacing, and hyphenation—Paragraph palette
- Multiple Masters on the fly—MM Design palette
- Tabs on call—Tab Ruler
- What to make of a text block—link, wrap, and fit
- Word processing commands
- A few words about CJK text
- Lesson 13: Moby Typography

Type Menu and Palettes in General

Illustrator's capability with type is one of its crown jewels. I feel safe in stating categorically that there is no better program for typesetting anything from a line to a page of text. Illustrator lets you fit type horizontally and vertically. You can also space type by letter, word, or line. You can run type along or around any shape or fit it within an object. Multiple master faces can be edited in place to create custom instances exactly where you need them. You can even convert text to outlines and edit the letterforms to create your own custom letter designs.

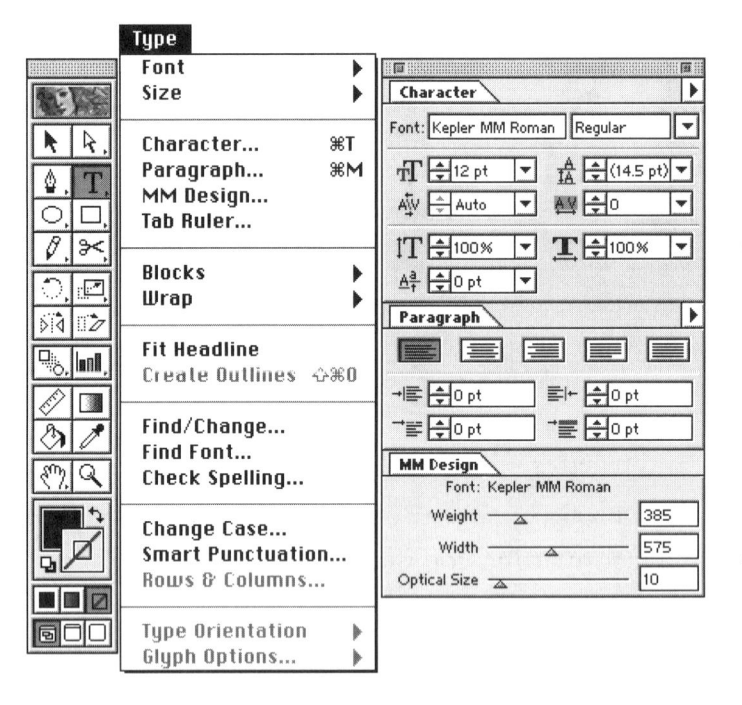

Figure 13.1 In Illustrator, text control is everywhere: the Type tool (t) and its variations in the Toolbox (discussed in Chapter 3), a long list of commands in the Type menu, and three type palettes: Character, Paragraph, and MM Design.

Illustrator also includes a modicum of word processing control, including commands to find text or fonts, check spelling, change case, and substitute so-called "smart" punctuation. There is also expanded international control for working with Chinese, Japanese, and Korean character sets.

Entering text into a drawing is a function of the Type tool, discussed in Chapter 3. The Type tool is used to create the special type objects that contain text. Text editing, changing characters and words, and inserting or deleting text is also discussed in Chapter 3. The Type menu, its commands and palettes, provides some additional word processing control, but primarily typesetting control: the multiple variables of sizing and spacing.

In fact, duplicating the extremely fine control available to typesetters who set type by hand turns out to be a rather complex endeavor. Even though the advent of scalable font technology provided type variations beyond the wildest dreams of typesetters who depended on type foundries to cast every font variation in lead, it has taken most of a decade for Illustrator to provide the level of typographic control that the most demanding designers need.

In addition to all the type commands, Illustrator 7's Type menu has incorporated the Character, Paragraph, and MM Design palettes. These palettes have received a substantial facelift so that they fit Adobe's product-wide palette format. These palettes aren't functionally different from those discussed in the chapters of Section III. The palette windows behave the same way, can be regrouped with other palettes or docked in any combination, but they do not have Show/Hide commands in the Window menu.

To show any of the three type palettes, choose the corresponding command in the Type menu. In their default setting, choosing one palette opens a palette window with all three type palettes in the group. If you move one of the palettes out of the group, choosing its menu command again closes this palette. It's a bit different from what you might expect, but I suspect that product research has shown that typography and illustration are separate activities, and this is Adobe's way of keeping the functions distinct within Illustrator.

All information in the type palettes is updated to reflect the settings of the current selection. If a selection contains type with different specifications, the field is blank. When a default setting is used, for instance the default line spacing, the specification is shown in parentheses.

If you set any of the type specifications when no selection is active, the settings will apply to the next type object you create. Illustrator's default type specification is 12-pt Helvetica. You can change this for a specific drawing by entering a new specification before entering any type. You must save a new startup document to change the default for all new documents (see Chapter 16).

NOTE To apply a value change in any of the type palettes' fields to the active selection, use the **Return/Enter** key or use the **Tab** key to apply the value and move to the next option in the palette.

Some Type Vocabulary

The vocabulary of type specification has its origins in the printing business and the use of lead type. Without going into the historical significance of each term, here is a brief description of the type vocabulary employed by Illustrator and used by most computer programs to specify type.

Point—A unit of measure equal to approximately $1/72$ of an inch. This is the default unit for measuring type in Illustrator, but it can be changed in the Units and Undo Preferences dialog (see Chapter 19).
Leading—The measure between lines of type measured from baseline to baseline. It refers to the amount of lead printers inserted to change the spacing between lines. The default measure is in points.
Kerning—Refers to intercharacter spacing, the distance between any two character pairs, and is measured in $1/1000$ of an *em space*. Em space is a relative measure equal to the current font size specification. It used to refer to the width of the *m* but now is equal to the type size in points. So 100 kerning units for a 10-point font is equal to $100/1000$ of 10 points, or $1/10 \times 10$ points, or 1 point of width.
Tracking—Similar to kerning and is used to change the intercharacter spacing for three or more characters simultaneously.
Baseline—An imaginary line that all characters sit on. It's like the lines on lined notebook paper. You can see the baseline for a simple type object by clicking on it with any selection tool. You can change a character's position relative to the baseline using the **Baseline Shift** option in the Character palette.

Simple Character Formatting Commands

The first two commands in the Type menu are Font and Size. Both duplicate capabilities in the Character palette but provide quick access to these most commonly used commands when you may not need to open the palette. Both use pop-up submenus to present the fonts available and default sizes. The Fonts submenu cascades so that typeface families are listed alphabetically and any predefined styles show up in a pop-up submenu.

The Size submenu gives you a choice of 15 commonly used type sizes from 6 to 72 points. Choosing **Other** from the top of the submenu opens the Character palette with the Font Size field active.

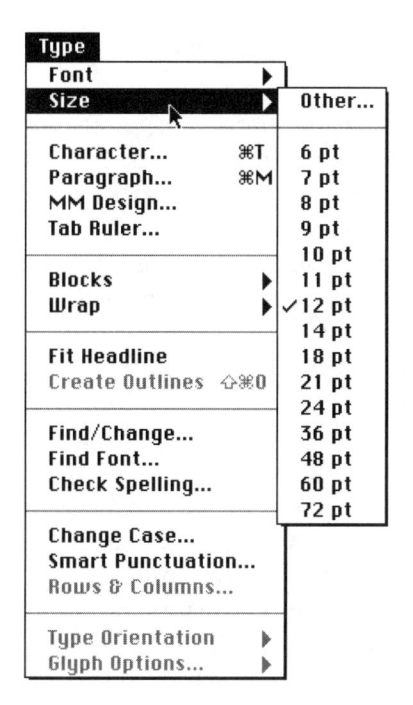

Figure 13.2 The Type: Size submenu lets you choose among 15 preset type sizes. Choosing Other from the top of the list opens the Character palette so that you can specify any type size.

NOTE As described in Chapter 3, type characteristics can be edited by selecting either the text itself or the type object. In the latter case, all text within the object will be updated.

To Set Font and Size Using Menu Commands

1. Select the character(s) to be edited. (Use the Type tool to select text or any of the selection tools to select an entire type object.)
2. In the Type menu, choose the **Font** submenu and slide the cursor to select a typeface. For typeface families, another submenu will pop up. Continue to hold down the mouse button and slide the cursor to select a particular face from the family of fonts.

    Or, in the Type menu, choose the **Size** submenu and slide the cursor to select one of the preset type sizes. Choose **Other** to open the Character palette and set the size from there.
3. Release the mouse button, and the selected type is updated.

TOTAL CHARACTER CONTROL—CHARACTER PALETTE

The Character palette allows you to choose fonts and font size, set letter and line spacing, adjust kerning, and scale type horizontally and vertically. The palette also includes controls for setting international type characteristics.

As mentioned before, the palette has been redesigned to fit with other palettes. So instead of the field labels of older Illustrator versions, all fields are identified by small icons. The icons are well-designed and distinct, but it may take a little while to get used to them.

When you first open the Character palette, by choosing **Type: Character** (**Command/Ctrl-t**), it opens in its smallest version. This includes font fields at the top and four size and spacing fields. Choosing **Show Options** from the palette drop-down menu expands the palette to include three additional fields for scaling and baseline shift. Choosing **Show Multinational** from the palette drop-down menu expands the palette to include all options, including language specification options (as shown in Figure 13.3). We won't be discussing the multinational options in this book. The Illustrator manual covers these completely.

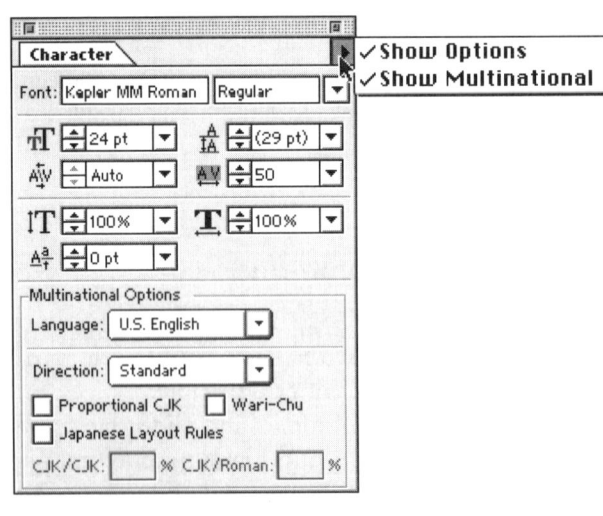

Figure 13.3 The Character palette fully expanded with all options, including multinational options, revealed.

By default, all type measurements are in points. You can change the default using the Units and Undo Preferences dialog (see Chapter 19), or you can enter any units into the measurements fields and it will be converted to the default. There are also several keyboard shortcuts that let you adjust fields by a set number of units. These defaults can be changed using the Keyboard Increments Preferences dialog (see Chapter 19).

Setting Fonts from the Character Palette

The Font specification is at the top of the Character palette and is divided into two fields. The left field shows the current typeface family, and the right, the specific font or style within the family, which in most cases will be a style such as bold or italic. The arrow to the right of the fields opens the Font drop-down menu. You can choose fonts from this menu just as you would from the Type: Font submenu described earlier, or you can type a font name directly into the fields. As you type, Illustrator will *autofill* the field using the first type name in alphabetical order that matches what you've typed.

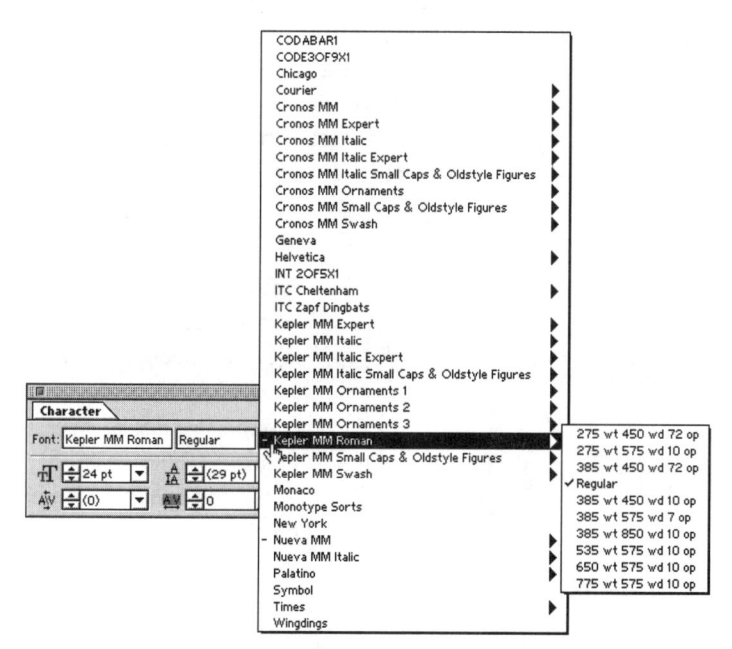

Figure 13.4 Every option in the character palette has a drop-down menu. Here, the character option drop-down menu lists all the fonts available on my system. Because the font I'm choosing is a multiple master family, an additional menu cascades off the first for further selection.

Setting Character Options

The seven options fields all work the same way. They are identified by an icon to the left. Up and down buttons let you increment and decrement the field by clicking. The largest area of each option displays the current setting and lets you type in a new setting, whereas the arrow to the right of each field lets you drop down a menu of predefined selections.

Font Size—Set the font size from .1 to 1296 points in increments of hundredths of points (see Figure 13.5). You can enter a size in any units supported by Illustrator, and it will be converted to the closest hundredth of a point.

- Click on the increment and decrement arrows to change the size by whole points, or hold down the **Shift** key and click to change by evenly divisible units of 4 points.
- Open the size drop-down menu and select one of the standard point sizes from the list or **Other**. Other is grayed out unless a nonstandard size is in use. In that case, the other size can be selected. Only one Other size is saved in the size drop-down menu.
- Use **Shift-Command/Ctrl->** and **Shift-Command/Ctrl-<** to increment and decrement the size to the next standard point size.

12 point type

24 point type

36 point type

Figure 13.5 The same font in three sizes. These happen to be commonly used size specifications, but Illustrator can specify fonts in any size from .1 to 1296 points in increments of hundredths of points.

Leading—Leading is the amount of space between lines of type measured between baselines (see Figure 13.6). The leading field works exactly the same way as the Font Size field, with the addition of the Auto-Leading option. Because this option is on by default, you never have to specify leading. Illustrator will calculate it for you as 120% of the type size. So a 10-point font size automatically has 12 points of leading. Auto-Leading amounts are indicated with parentheses. If you set a leading value, you can switch back to Auto-Leading by choosing **Auto** from the Leading drop-down menu.

Type Commands and Palettes

| These terms though formidable avoid much laborious periphrasis. | These terms though formidable avoid much laborious periphrasis. | These terms though formidable avoid much laborious periphrasis. |

Figure 13.6 The same text in the same font (Kepler) and size (18 point), but with different leading, 15, 21.5 (the auto-leading default), and 28 point.

NOTE To apply leading, you must select at least a single character of text. Also, when different leading specifications are set for a single line of text, the larger setting is used.

Kerning—Kerning, intercharacter spacing, is applied just like Leading, including an Auto option. (See Figure 13.7.) But in this case Auto values are not calculated. Instead, the Auto option uses the kerning values that are a part of all high-quality digital typefaces. These are referred to as kerning pairs, and they vary according to the typeface. Remember that kerning is a relative measure and changes as font size changes. Illustrator 7 displays auto-kerned values in parentheses.

- Hold down the **Shift** key while clicking on the increment and decrement arrows to change the value by multiples of 10.
- Press **Option/Alt-Left Arrow** or **Option/Alt-Right Arrow** to adjust kerning smaller or larger by 20/1000 of an em space, the default value set in the Units and Undo Preferences dialog (see Chapter 19). (The cursor must be between two characters with none selected.)
- Press **Option/Alt-Command/Ctrl-k** to open the Character palette with the focus on the Kerning option.

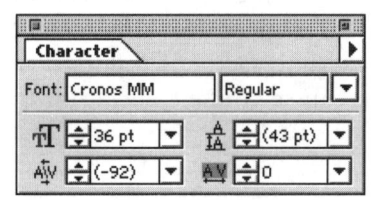

Figure 13.7 Illustrator 7 displays the built-in kerning values of type 1 fonts. The kerning value between the capital T and lowercase o is -92 thousandths of an em. The parenthesis around the kerning value shown in the Character palette indicate that this is the auto-kerning value.

302   CHAPTER 13

> **NOTE:** You can select text and use a kern value of 0 to turn off the Auto option.

Tracking—Tracking values are similar to kerning values (see Figure 13.8) except that there is no Auto option and you must select at least three characters to apply tracking.

- Press **Option/Alt-Left Arrow** or **Option/Alt-Right Arrow** to adjust tracking smaller or larger by multiples of 20.
- Press **Option/Alt-Command/Ctrl-Left Arrow** or **Option/Alt-Command/Ctrl-Right Arrow** to adjust tracking smaller or larger by 100/1000 of an em space, five times the default value set in the Keyboard Increments dialog (see Chapter 19).
- Press **Shift-Command/Ctrl-q** to reset the tracking to 0. This will also open the Character palette with the focus on the Tracking option.

A big book, a great evil.
A big book, a great evil.
A big book, a great evil.

Figure 13.8 The same sentence with three different tracking values applied, -50, 0, and +50 ems.

Vertical Scale and **Horizontal Scale**—Scaling is measured from 1% to 10,000% as a ratio of letter height to width. (See Figure 13.9.) Vertical and horizontal scaling work exactly the same way. Select text, type in a number in the scale field, click to increment or decrement, or choose a value from the drop-down menu to compress or expand type in either direction. If type has been scaled using any of the transform tools or commands, the scaling factor is reflected in the values in the Character palette. You can set these values to 0 to undo the effects of a transformation.

Type Commands and Palettes 303

Attenuated

Normal

Elongated

Figure 13.9 Text set in Palatino with 200% vertical scaling, no scaling, and 200% horizontal scaling applied.

Baseline Shift—There are many situations when letters need to be raised or lowered in relation to the baseline of text, including the creation of superscripts, subscripts, and drop caps. (See Figure 13.10.) Adjusting the baseline setting is also useful for positioning text on a path. For instance, if you set text on a circle, the text will be positioned outside the circle. But by applying a negative baseline shift, the text can be moved inside the circle.

- Use the Baseline Shift field as you would any of the character options fields.
- Hold down the **Shift** key while clicking on the increment and decrement arrows to change the value by multiples of 2 points.
- Press **Shift-Option/Alt-Up Arrow** or **Shift-Option/Alt-Down Arrow** to adjust the baseline shift smaller or larger by increments of 2 points, the default value set in the Units and Undo Preferences dialog (see Chapter 19).

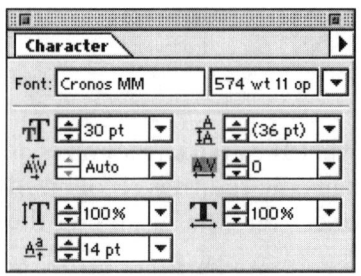

Figure 13.10 Where would the universe be without the superscript. Here, the 2 has been elevated 14 points above the baseline to make it an exponent.

$e=mc^2$

INDENTS, SPACING, AND HYPHENATION— PARAGRAPH PALETTE

Text formatting in Illustrator goes well beyond the recognition of individual characters and lines. It's great to be able to manipulate fonts, sizes, and placement to make text attractive or even showy, but it's also necessary to make text readable. This requires the recognition of the paragraph as an inherent unit. Illustrator's Paragraph palette lets you set the alignment, indents, and spacing of paragraphs, as well as word and letter spacing within paragraphs. You can also set hyphenation and punctuation options.

The Paragraph palette has two size settings. The default, smaller, size has buttons to set alignment and fields to set indents and paragraph spacing. By choosing **Show Options** from the palette pop-up menu, the palette expands to include word and letter spacing fields and four options fields, as shown in Figure 13.11.

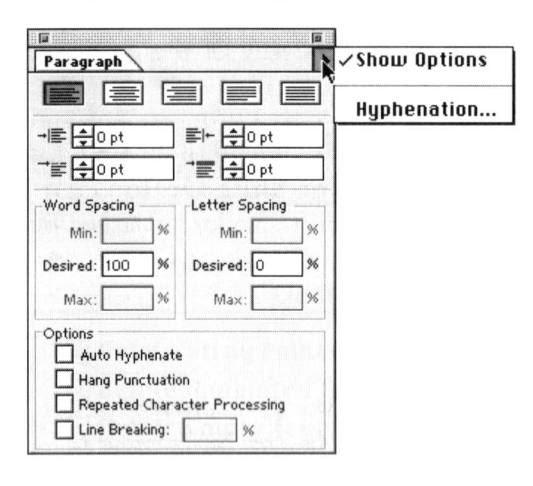

Figure 13.11 The fully expanded Paragraph palette.

To use the Paragraph palette, it helps to know what Illustrator recognizes as a paragraph. With most word processing programs the return is recognized as the end of a paragraph, with the next character you type beginning the next paragraph.

Illustrator always follows this rule when you are formatting paragraphs within a text block. But if the text is a freeform object or attached to a path, it doesn't. In these cases, Illustrator treats all text, regardless of carriage returns, as a single paragraph. This is not a limitation, just something to know, because it affects alignment, indentation, and spacing, which are described later in this chapter.

Type Commands and Palettes 305

> **NOTE:** As with the Character palette, changing settings in the Paragraph palette when no text is selected applies to the next text object you enter. When text is selected, changes are applied as soon as you press the **Return/Enter** or **Tab** key.

To Use the Paragraph Palette

1. Select text or a text object. (If no text object is selected, changed settings will apply to the next text object created.)
2. Open the Paragraph palette (**Type: Paragraph**) or press **Command/Ctrl-m**, or try **Option/Alt-Command/Ctrl-o**, which opens the Paragraph palette with the focus on the Desired Word Spacing field.

These two steps apply to all the following instructions for using the Paragraph palette's features.

To Set Paragraph Alignment

1. Select text and open the Paragraph palette as already described.
2. Click on one of the five buttons across the top of the Paragraph palette to get the results shown in Figure 13.12.

When a type design is good, it is not because each individual letter of the alphabet is perfect in form but because there is a feeling of unbroken harmony and rhythm that runs through the whole design, each letter to every other and to all.	When a type design is good, it is not because each individual letter of the alphabet is perfect in form but because there is a feeling of unbroken harmony and rhythm that runs through the whole design, each letter to every other and to all.	When a type design is good, it is not because each individual letter of the alphabet is perfect in form but because there is a feeling of unbroken harmony and rhythm that runs through the whole design, each letter to every other and to all.
When a type design is good, it is not because each individual letter of the alphabet is perfect in form but because there is a feeling of unbroken harmony and rhythm that runs through the whole design, each letter to every other and to all.	When a type design is good, it is not because each individual letter of the alphabet is perfect in form but because there is a feeling of unbroken harmony and rhythm that runs through the whole design, each letter to every other and to all.	

Figure 13.12 The five paragraph alignments include, across the top, Left Align, Center Align, and Right Align, and across the bottom, Justify Full Lines and Justify All Lines. (This quotation is from Frederic Goudy.)

The button icons indicate the effective paragraph alignment.

> **Align Left** (**Shift-Command/Ctrl-l**)—Aligns all lines of text in the paragraph to the left of the text object. This option leaves the right side of text lines in a text block unaligned.
>
> **Align Center** (**Shift-Command/Ctrl-c**)—Aligns all lines of text in the paragraph so that they are centered with respect to the text object. This option leaves both the left and right sides of lines in a text block unaligned.
>
> **Align Right** (**Shift-Command/Ctrl-r**)—Aligns all lines of text in the paragraph to the right of the text object. This option leaves the left side of text lines in a text block unaligned.
>
> **Justify Full Lines** (**Shift-Command/Ctrl-j**)—Affects only text in text blocks so that all full lines of text in the paragraph are aligned on both the left and right sides of the block. This is done by adjusting word spacing to pad out the text to fill the entire line length. The final line of the paragraph is aligned left and not padded.
>
> **Justify All Lines** (**Shift-Command/Ctrl-f**)—The same as Justify Full Lines, but justifies the final line in the paragraph as well. This sometimes results in an oddly spaced line and must be used with care.

To Set Paragraph Indents and Spacing

1. Select text and open the Paragraph palette as described earlier. There are four indent and spacing fields under the alignment buttons. They all work the same way.
2. Either type a specification into one of the indent or spacing fields or click on the increment or decrement arrows to change the specification by ±1 point. Hold down the **Shift** key while clicking on the arrows to change the specification by divisible units of ±10 points. The specification range is ±1296 points.

   > **Left Indent**—Sets the distance from the left edge of the text object to the leftmost text character(s) in the paragraph.
   >
   > **Right Indent**—Sets the distance from the right edge of the text object to the rightmost text character(s) in the paragraph.
   >
   > **First Line Left Indent**—Affects only paragraphs in text blocks to set the distance from the left edge of the text object to the leftmost text character(s) in the first line of the paragraph. The effect of the

Left Indent and the First Line Indent are additive.

Space Before Paragraph—Affects only paragraphs in text blocks to set the distance from the baseline of the first line of text in a paragraph to the baseline of the last line of text in the previous paragraph.

> **NOTE**
> It is possible to specify left and right indents in text blocks that leave you with less space than the total line length. This will cause the text to "disappear." Reset the indent specifications to rescue the text.

To Set Word and Line Spacing

1. Select text and open the Paragraph palette as described earlier. If the palette isn't expanded, choose **Show Options** from the palette pop-up menu. Also, using the **Option/Alt-Command/Ctrl-o** keyboard shortcut automatically expands the palette and sets the focus to Desired Word Spacing.
2. Specify the Min, Desired, and Max amount of Word Spacing and/or Letter Spacing as a percent of the space width, with 100% representing the default spacing.

Although both Word Spacing and Letter Spacing can be applied to any text object, they are most useful when applied to text containers. In fact, Letter Spacing can be applied more easily in many cases using tracking (see earlier discussion). Also, the Min and Max fields are available only when justified text has been selected. Curiously, if no text is selected, but the last selected text was justified, the Min and Max fields remain available.

Desired Word Spacing—Adjusts the width of spaces between words.
Desired Letter Spacing—Adjusts the space between all letters in the selected paragraph.
Min and Max Word Spacing and Letter Spacing—When spacing is applied to justified text, the word spacing is variable. The Min and Max specifications limit the width of spaces that can be used. Illustrator will also adjust letter spacing within words to achieve justification. The Letter Spacing Min and Max specifications limit can be used to limit the extent of letter spacing to a more desirable range.

To Set Paragraph Options

1. Select text and open the Paragraph palette as described earlier. If the palette isn't expanded, choose **Show Options** from the palette pop-up menu.
2. Click in the appropriate check box to turn on an option. All four options are deselected by default:

   Auto Hyphenate—Turns on Illustrator's built-in hyphenation capability, which is described later in this chapter.
   Hang Punctuation—Works only when a text container is selected. When selected, periods, commas, single and double quotation marks, apostrophes, hyphens, em dashes, en dashes, colons, and semicolons will be placed outside the margins of the container.
   Repeated Character Processing—Affects only CJK (Chinese, Japanese, Korean) text by substituting the special repeated character mark when a character is repeated in a line of text.
   Line Breaking—Affects only CJK text and is set in percent.

To Use Auto Hyphenation

1. Select text or not and open the Paragraph palette as described earlier. If the palette isn't expanded, choose **Show Options** from the palette pop-up menu.
2. Click on the **Auto Hyphenation** option check box to turn on hyphenation. Illustrator will hyphenate text in text containers according to its built-in rules and defaults. You can also specify hyphenation for specific words using the Hyphenation Options Preferences dialog (see Chapter 19).
3. Choose **Hyphenation** from the Paragraph palette pop-up menu to open the Hyphenation Options dialog (as shown in Figure 13.13). There are three options:

Figure 13.13 The Hyphenation Options dialog is used to change hyphenation settings but does not turn hyphenation on or off.

Hyphenate # letters from beginning—Sets the number of letters at the beginning of a word that must be left before Illustrator will hyphenate the word. The default is 2, which means that there will never be a single letter left hyphenated at the end of a line.

Hyphenate # letters from end—Sets the number of letters at the end of a word that must be left before Illustrator will hyphenate the word. The default is 2, which means that there will never be a single letter left dangling at the beginning of a new line after a hyphenation.

Limit consecutive hyphens to #—Limits the number of consecutive lines that can end in a hyphenated word. The default is 3.

4. Click **OK** to set the new hyphenation option values.

> **NOTE**
> You can manually hyphenate words using discretionary hyphens so that text will reflow unimpeded if it's edited. Press **Shift-Command/Ctrl-hyphen** to enter a discretionary hyphen as you type. The word will divide correctly if it is at the end of a line; it will be displayed without any hyphen if a break is not forced.

Multiple Masters on the Fly—MM Design Palette

We've gotten used to having scalable type where any typeface can be resized to any size. Adobe Type 1 and TrueType fonts include built-in hinting algorithms so that type can be resized without losing legibility. Multiple Master typefaces have additional design variations built in. Known as *design axes*, these vary by typeface, but might include weight, width, serif, optical size, and other characteristics.

Multiple Master typefaces come with a "design" utility that lets you change the parameters to create a customized type. By saving the custom setting, you can use this type version with other programs. Illustrator lets you skip this step by using the MM Design palette (as shown in Figure 13.14). You can actually change the Multiple Master parameters for text that is already in place without saving the custom settings. This makes designing with these versatile typefaces much easier.

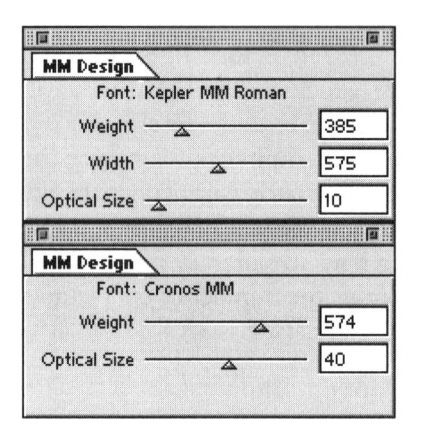

Figure 13.14 Two views of the MM Design palette. On top, with a Kepler selection active showing a three axis design, and on the bottom, with a Cronos selection active showing a two axis design. Moving the sliders interactively updates the selection and adds the font instance to the Character palette's font drop-down menu.

To Use the MM Design Palette

1. Make sure the MM Design palette is open (choose **Type: MM Design** if it isn't).
2. Select the text or text object you want to modify. The selected characters within the selection must all belong to a single multiple master type family. The MM Design palette will display all the axes for the Multiple Master font selected and the current settings. If more than one value for an axis has been selected, the value is left blank but is still editable.
3. Adjust the axis sliders. The text is updated as you make adjustments so that you can work interactively. This also obviates the need for any extra steps to apply the new design. Any new design you use is added to the list of available fonts in the Character palette Font drop-down menu so that you can reuse the design elsewhere in the artwork.

TABS ON CALL—TAB RULER

Illustrator facilitates the assignment of tabs to text through the Tab Ruler. Although you will sometimes see this referred to as a palette, it doesn't behave like Illustrator's other palettes, so I don't call it one.

The Tab Ruler is opened by choosing **Type: Tab Ruler**, which places the ruler either at the top of the drawing window or just above the selected text object. If the selected text is vertical, the Tab Ruler is displayed in a vertical orientation. You can create or modify left/top, center, right/bottom, or decimal tabs. (See Figure 13.15.)

The Tab Ruler has the helpful property of opening with the left edge of the ruler aligned to the left border of the selected type object (or the top edge for vertical type). This makes it easy to align tabs visually. Even though there can be only one Tab Ruler open, it can be used with any text object by dragging or by clicking on the realign button on the upper-right corner of the ruler.

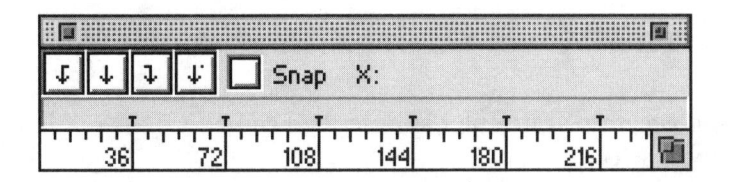

Figure 13.15 Illustrator's Tab Ruler is a special instance of a floating palette. It attaches itself to the active text selection or can be moved around the screen, but like all palettes, it applies either to the current selection or all future text objects if there is no active selection.

To Set Tabs

1. Select a text object. Tab settings apply to all the text within a text object.
2. Choose **Type: Tab Ruler**. The Tab Ruler opens with its left/top edge aligned to the left/top edge of the text object.
3. Click or drag and drop anywhere along the measured edge of the ruler. This sets a left tab. As you drag or click, an alignment guide follows the cursor across the text as visual feedback, and a readout of the exact position appears in the top of the Tab Ruler. After the tab is set, a tab icon appears in position along the ruler's measured edge.

4. Click on one of the Tab buttons to change the tab type.

   Left Tab—Aligns text to the left of the tab mark. This is the default.
   Center Tab—Aligns text so that it is centered to the tab mark.
   Right Tab—Aligns text to the right of the tab mark.
   Decimal Tab—Aligns text so that numerical text can be aligned with a decimal point at the tab mark.

5. Click on the **Snap** box to turn it on, or hold down the **Command/Ctrl** key to toggle Snap on so that tabs align to ruler units when set. You can also extend the Tab Ruler by dragging on the Extend Tab Ruler button in the lower-right corner.
6. Click in the text and enter tab characters as desired.
7. Choose **Type: Tab Ruler** again to dismiss the Tab Ruler, or click the close box in the upper-left corner.

To Modify Tab Settings

1. Select text and open the Tab Ruler as described earlier.
2. Click on a tab to select it.
3. There are a number of possible modifications:

   - Drag tabs to reposition them.
   - Click on one of the tab buttons to change the tab type.
   - Hold down the **Option** key and click on a tab to change its type. Multiple clicks will cycle through the four tab types.
   - Drag a tab off the ruler to delete it.
   - Hold down the **Shift** key while dragging to move multiple tabs together or delete multiple tabs. Note that this will move all tabs only if you drag on the left-hand tab; if you drag on any other tab, it moves only the selected tab and the tabs to its right.
   - Hold down the **Command/Ctrl** key while dragging to toggle the Snap command while adjusting tab position.

   Any tab characters in the selected text object are repositioned as you modify tabs.
4. Choose **Type: Tab Ruler** again to dismiss the Tab Ruler.

To Move or Re-align the Tab Ruler

- With the Tab Ruler open, move the mouse over the drag bar across the top of the ruler, click, and drag anywhere in the document.
- Click on the **realign** button in the upper-right corner of the drag bar. This will snap the ruler to the active text object. (Nothing happens if you haven't moved the ruler or text object.) This button has no other purpose and is very useful when you select another text object and want to move the Tab Ruler directly to it.

WHAT TO MAKE OF A TEXT BLOCK—LINK, WRAP, AND FIT

Text blocks, or containers, are useful in many ways. They can be used like a mini word processor imbedded in Illustrator artwork. Many of the paragraph options already discussed serve solely for the purpose of making text in blocks more attractive and readable. You can create columns of text or use text blocks simply to create text borders within your artwork.

Illustrator's text blocks can also be used the way you would use frames in PageMaker or other page layout programs. You can flow text into a block, link blocks, and even run text around objects. Adjusting the shape of a text block reflows the text to match.

The creation of simple text blocks was discussed in Chapter 3. Here we will look at the way text within blocks is handled.

To Enter Text into a Block

1. Create a text block as discussed in Chapter 3. (First draw the block using any of the drawing tools and then click on it with the Type tool, Area Type tool, or Vertical Area Type tool to turn the object into a text block.)
2. There are three ways to put type into a text block:

   - Type text directly into the selected block from the keyboard.
   - Copy text from another application to the Clipboard and use **Edit: Paste** to copy it into the selected text block.
   - Use **File: Place** to open a file and place the contents into the selected text block (see Chapter 16).

The text in a text block always remains editable, and you can use any of these methods to add text. When the text exceeds the boundaries of the block, a small square with a plus sign (+) is attached to the box to indicate that there is overflow text. You can edit and delete text, expand the size of the text block as you would any object, or link the block to another, and the overflow text will spill over the link into the new block.

To Link/Unlink Text Blocks and Reflow Text

1. Create two or more text blocks as described earlier and in Chapter 3 (see Figure 13.16). (The order in which you fill the blocks with text is unimportant to the linking procedure. You can link before or after adding text or change the links at any time.)

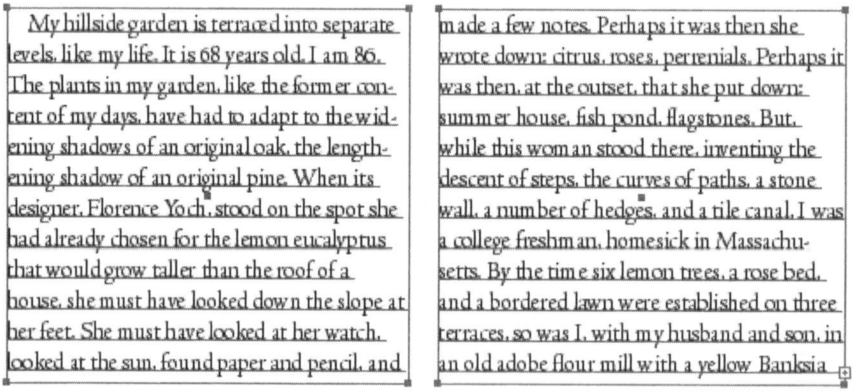

Figure 13.16 *Two text blocks with text flowing from one to the next after executing the Type: Blocks: Link command. The small square with a plus sign at the bottom right of the second text block indicates that there is overflow text. The quotation shown here is by Harriet Doerr.*

2. Select the blocks to be linked/unlinked using any selection method.
3. Choose **Type: Blocks: Link** to link the text blocks. Any type you enter (or have entered) will flow from the backmost object in the stacking order and finish with the topmost object. Linked blocks are grouped and, if necessary, moved to the same layer as the topmost text object.

- Choose **Type: Blocks: Unlink** to remove any links between selected text blocks. Text is not reflowed when unlinking blocks this way. Instead, the text in each object remains as it was, but retains no relation to the formerly linked text.

There are a few procedures to be aware of when using linked text blocks:

- Changing the stacking order of linked text blocks using the commands in the **Object: Arrange** submenu (see Chapter 12), changes the linking order and reflows the text accordingly.
- Deleting a linked text block deletes the object and the text. To reflow text when deleting the object, you must unlink the blocks and copy the text back to a previously linked block or to a new object. Then you can delete the object, and the text is preserved.
- You can flow overflow text into a linked block in a single step by copying the text block:

1. Choose **View: Artwork**. (This isn't necessary, but it's easier to see what you're doing if you do.)
2. Choose the **Direct Selection** tool (a).
3. Hold down the **Option/Alt** key, click on the side (not the baseline) of the text block, and drag to position the copy. You can also hold down the **Shift** key to constrain the drag to multiples of 45°, which is useful if you want neatly aligned columns.
4. Release the mouse button and then the **Option/Alt** key. The object is copied and linked, and the overflow text flows across the link into the new block. You can use **Object: Transform: Transform Again** (**Command/Ctrl-d**) to continue creating copies.

To Flow Text Around Objects

1. Select one or more text blocks and one or more graphic objects.
2. Choose **Type: Wrap: Make**. The graphic object and text block(s) become a group with the graphic forcing all text to flow around it, as shown in Figure 13.17.

My hillside garden is terraced into separate levels, like my life. It is 68 years old. I am 86. The plants in my garden, like the former content of my days, have had to adapt to the widening shadows of an original oak, the lengthening shadow of an original pine. When its designer, Florence Yoch, stood on the spot she had already chosen for the lemon eucalyptus that would grow taller than the roof of a

Figure 13.17 Two objects, one text block and one graphic, when grouped using the Type: Wrap: Make command create a border of text around the graphic.

- Choose **Type: Wrap: Release** to release a wrapping group.

There are several restrictions when creating wraps:

- The graphic object must be above the text block in the stacking order. If it is not, use any of various methods to change the stacking order (the commands of the Object: Arrange submenu or the Paste in Front/Paste in Back commands).
- You must create a graphic boundary around bitmapped objects to flow text around them. Use any of the drawing tools to create the boundary. If the boundary has any paint attributes, it must be above the text with the bitmapped object above the boundary in the stacking order.
- You can use an unpainted graphic boundary to define a wrapping distance around a graphic object.
- To wrap text around a nonrectangular Photoshop image, save the image with a clipping path before placing it in Illustrator. The clipping path serves as a graphic boundary.

To Fit Headlines

1. Click on the text with the Type tool (t). The text must be within a text block.
2. Choose **Type: Fit Headline**. Illustrator stretches the type so that it fills the width of the text block exactly. (With vertical type, it's stretched to fill the height of the text block.)

- With most type, Illustrator calculates the amount of additional space required between each letter of the headline to fill out the line. This supplies the correct tracking value.
- With Multiple Master type, Illustrator adjusts the weight and tracking value to spread the headline to fill the space.
- Illustrator assumes that the headline to be fitted includes all text within the current paragraph. If the paragraph is longer than one line, choosing **Fit Headline** will compress the text to fit.
- After a headline is fitted, it can still be edited and the tracking and weight settings can be changed.

When Type Is Not Type—Create Outlines

One of the great advances made in Illustrator several versions ago was the ability to read the outline font file for the type being used and convert the type into drawn outlines. This gives Illustrator the best of both worlds: the ability to work with type in a drawing and edit it as type, as well as the ability to convert type to an outline so that the letterforms can be manipulated as objects.

Some of the things you can't do with type, like fill with a gradient or create a mask, become possible when you use the Create Outlines command. The procedure is simple, but the ramifications are profound. After you have converted type to outlines, it's no longer editable using the Type tool. If the words change, you have to retype the text, reconvert, and reproduce any other steps you may have used to manipulate the outlines.

It's sometimes useful to save a copy of text you are converting. The copy can be kept on a locked and hidden layer so that it doesn't obscure your work but remains available in case you need to go back.

When type becomes outlines, it ceases to have any identity as type. You work on it not with the Type tool but as you would any other graphic object, by adjusting anchor points (see Figure 13.18).

Figure 13.18 The text on the left is editable text that can be altered from the keyboard or modified using any of Illustrator's text tools. After it is converted to outlines, as on the right, the letterform ceases to be text and becomes editable outlines no longer affected by any of the text tools.

To Convert Type to Outlines

1. Select type using the Type tool (t) or select entire type objects using any of the selection tools.
2. Choose **Type: Create Outlines**. The type is converted to objects and is left selected. You cannot convert outlines back into type except by using the Undo command.

To Turn Rectangles into Rows and Columns

1. Select one or more objects using the Selection tool (v). These may be text blocks or any object. If the object is not rectangular, Illustrator uses the object's rectangular bounding box when converting to rows and columns.

NOTE You can use the Rows and Columns command to create grids or simply to divide rectangles into even parts. The rows and columns are graphic objects and needn't be used as text containers.

2. Choose **Type: Rows and Columns** to open the Rows and Columns dialog (as shown in Figure 13.19). It's helpful to click on the **Preview** check box so that you can see the progress of the dialog as you make changes.

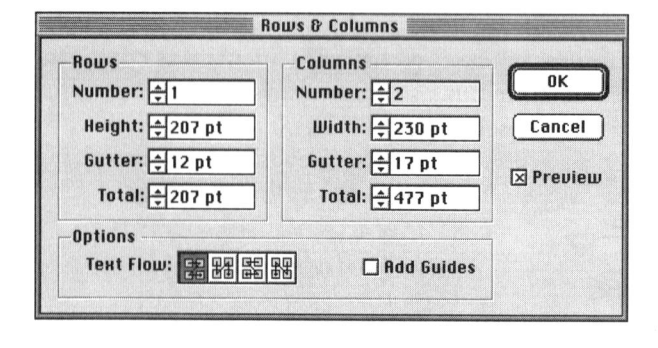

Figure 13.19 The Rows and Columns dialog lets you turn objects into rows, columns, or a matrix of cells. (The results are always rectangular even if the selected objects aren't.)

3. Specify the number and size of the rows and columns. The top portion of the dialog is divided into two nearly identical sections; one for

Rows and one for Columns. Each division has four specification fields: Number, Height/Width, Gutter, and Total. You can either type a number into the field or click on the increment or decrement arrow to change the specification by 1 unit. Hold down the **Shift** key while clicking to increment or decrement to even units of 10.

> **Number**—Specify the number of rows or columns. There can be between 1 and 1000 rows and/or columns.
> **Height/Width**—Specify the height for row cells and the width for column cells.
> **Gutter**—Specify the amount of space between row cells and column cells.
> **Total**—Specify either the total height for all rows or the total width for all columns, or specify all other fields and let Illustrator calculate these values automatically. If you specify the total, Illustrator will adjust the other dimensions (but not the number of divisions) as necessary.

4. Specify the order of the text by clicking on one of the four Text Flow buttons. The button icons indicate the order for flowing text:

   - left-to-right top-to-bottom
   - top-to-bottom left-to-right
   - right-to-left top-to-bottom
   - top-to-bottom right-to-left

5. Click the **Add Guides** check box to have Illustrator add path guides to the drawing.
6. Click **OK** to complete the Rows and Columns command, or click **Cancel** to leave the selected objects unchanged.

WORD PROCESSING COMMANDS

Over the years, Illustrator has added more and more features that are more typical of a word processing program than a drawing program. These are welcome tools because they allow artists and designers to enter much more text directly into Illustrator without the need to spell check or do global replacements in another program and then place the results back in Illustrator.

Five dialogs are associated with word processing—they are text- rather than type-oriented, and each is accessed from the Type menu: Find/Change, Find Font, Check Spelling, Change Case, and Smart Punctuation.

To Find/Change Text

1. Choose **Type: Find/Change** to open the Find/Change dialog (as shown in Figure 13.20).

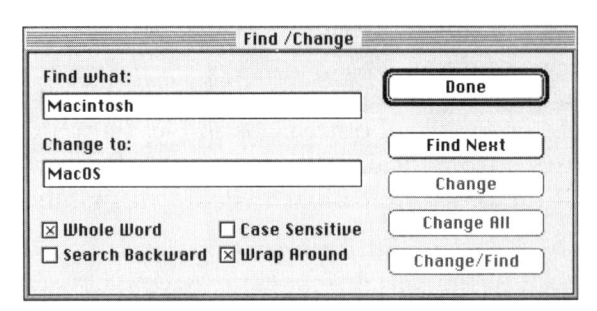

Figure 13.20 Illustrator's Find/Change dialog is similar to those found in any word processor. You have to find the first instance of a text string before the Change, Change All, and Change/Find buttons become operable.

2. Enter text into the Find What field and optionally into the Change To field.
3. Use one of the four options check boxes to constrain or broaden the search. Only Wrap Around is checked by default:

   Whole Word—Check this box to constrain the search to whole words that match the find field.
   Search Backward—Check this box to have Illustrator look through text objects in reverse order from the insertion point. The search order is determined by the stacking order of objects.
   Case Sensitive—Check this box to have Illustrator match the exact case of the text in the Find what and Change to fields when searching and replacing.
   Wrap Around—Uncheck this box to have Illustrator stop searching when it gets to the end of the document. When checked, the search will continue from the beginning and finish back at the selection point.

4. Click the **Find Next** button to find the next instance of the find string without replacing it. Once found, three more button choices become available.

Change—Changes the found string to the change string without searching onward.
Change All—Changes every instance of the found string to the change string.
Change/Find—Changes the found string with the change string and then finds the next instance of the find string.

5. Click the **Done** button to dismiss the dialog.

To Find/Change Fonts

1. Choose **Type: Find Font** to open the Find Font dialog (as shown in Figure 3.21). Illustrator creates a list of all the fonts in use in your document, including the name, type, style, color, and kerning. Each variation creates a new instance in the font list.

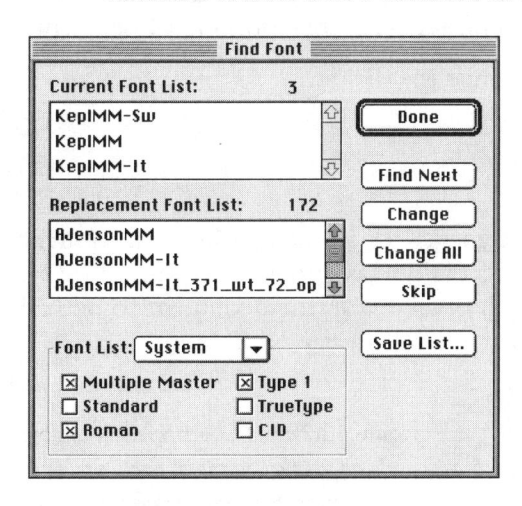

Figure 13.21 The Find Font dialog does not accept input. Instead, you select fonts from the current and replacement lists. Once specified, changes are made the way you would ordinarily make them using any Find/Change dialog.

2. Set the Font List options at the bottom of the dialog as needed. These include the Font List drop-down menu that lets you choose either Document, which limits the replacement font list to those in the document, or System, which expands the replacement list to include all fonts currently installed in your system. You can limit the listing of fonts by type by unchecking individual type boxes. These are: Multiple Master, Standard, Roman, Type 1, TrueType, and CID.

322 **CHAPTER 13**

> **NOTE:** Multiple Master typefaces are a kind of Type 1 typeface, so both boxes must be checked to list Multiple Master faces, and unless you're using a non-Roman typeface, this box must also be checked.

3. Click on a font instance from Current Font List.
4. Click on a font instance from Replacement Font List if desired.
5. Choose one of five buttons:

   Find Next—Searches for the next instance of the chosen current font and selects it.
   Change—Replaces the found selection with the replacement font.
   Change All—Finds and replaces all instances of the chosen current font with the chosen replacement font.
   Skip—Goes to the next name in the Current Font List and finds the next instance of it.
   Save List—Is used to save the Current Font List as a text document. This can be used as a press check when printing a document.

6. Click the **Done** button to dismiss the dialog.

To Check Spelling

1. Choose **Type: Check Spelling** to check all the text in the document and open the Check Spelling dialog (as shown in Figure 13.22). Illustrator does a global search of all text in the document to find all the words it doesn't recognize in its dictionaries.

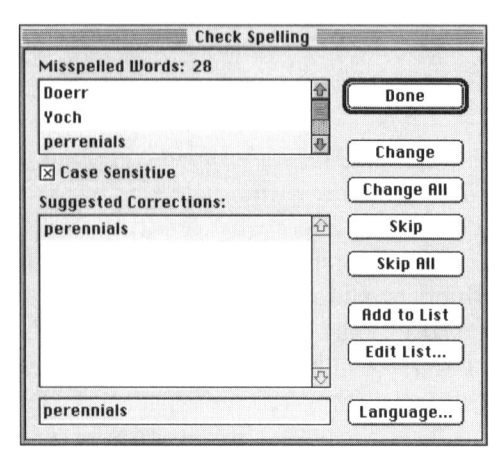

Figure 13.22 The Check Spelling dialog finds all suspect words at once, and you can correct them without leaving the dialog.

The dialog lists all suspect words on top with suggestions for correcting the selected word underneath. At the bottom, the currently selected suspect word is displayed in an editable field. You can either replace it with one of Illustrator's suggestions or type in the correction manually.

2. Click on a word in the Misspelled Words list to correct it. The first word is highlighted by default.
3. Click on a replacement spelling from the Suggested Corrections list. Checking the Case Sensitive box includes capitalization corrections in the list. Illustrator's best-guess correction is highlighted at the top of the list by default.
4. If none of the suggestions is correct, edit the replacement word directly in the text field at the bottom of the dialog.
5. Click on one of the six buttons:

   Change—Replaces the misspelled word.
   Change All—Replaces all instances of the misspelled word.
   Skip—Skips the suspect word without changing it.
   Skip All—Skips all instances of the suspect word and removes it from the Misspelled Words list. The word will be found again the next time you check spelling.
   Add to List—Adds the suspect word to your dictionary, removes it from the misspelled list, and will not add it the next time you check spelling. You can add multiple words to your dictionary simultaneously by Shift-clicking or Command/Ctrl clicking to select a range of words in the misspelled list.
   Edit List—Opens the Edit List dialog, which lists all words in your dictionary. You can Add, Change, or Remove words by selecting them from the list, editing them in the text field at the bottom of the dialog, and clicking on the appropriate button. Click Done to dismiss the dialog and update the dictionary.
   Language—Lets you change the dictionary to spell check in different languages. Illustrator dictionaries are usually in the Plug-ins folder, but you can move them anywhere and specify the location with this command.

6. When all words have been corrected or skipped, Illustrator tells you how many corrections have been made. Click the **Done** button to dismiss the dialog.

To Change Text Case

1. Make a selection using the Type tool (t). The Change Case command has no effect if no type is selected.
2. Choose **Type: Change Case** to open the Change Case dialog (as shown in Figure 13.23).

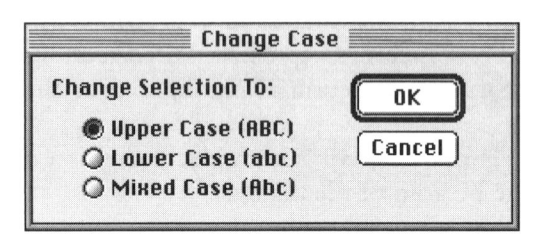

Figure 13.23 The Change Case dialog, sweet and simple.

3. Click on one of three radio buttons:

    Upper Case (ABC)—Capitalizes the entire selection.
    Lower Case (abc)—Makes the entire selection lowercase.
    Mixed Case (Abc)—Makes the first letter of selected words uppercase and all other letters lowercase.

4. Click **OK** to execute the command.

To Use "Smart Punctuation"

1. Select text or not, as desired.
2. Choose **Type: Smart Punctuation** to open the Smart Punctuation dialog (as shown at Figure 13.24).

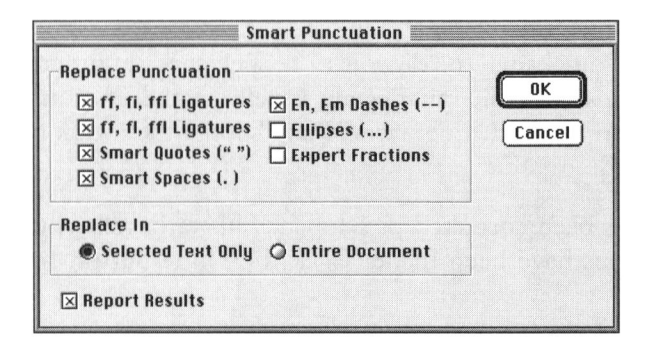

Figure 13.24 The Smart Punctuation dialog. This is a misnomer, because it's not all about punctuation. Typographer's or Printer's Substitutions would be more accurate names.

3. Select from the seven categories of punctuation that Illustrator will search out and replace:

   ff, fi, ffi Ligatures—Replaces these two or three letter combinations with one character ligatures.
   ff, fl, ffl Ligatures—Replaces these two or three letter combinations with one character ligatures.
   Smart Quotes (" ")—Replaces straight double quotes with curly double quotes.
   Smart Quotes (' ')—Replaces straight single quotes with curly single quotes.
   Smart Space (.)—Replaces double spaces after a period with a single space.
   En, Em Dashes (- —)—Replaces double dashes with en or em dashes as appropriate.
   Ellipsis (…)—Replaces three periods with the ellipsis character.
   Expert Fractions—Replaces two numbers with a slash character between them with single character fractions when available.

> **NOTE** Not all typefaces have ligatures or expert fractions, so Illustrator will not make any substitutions in these cases.

4. Choose either the **Selected Text Only** or **Entire Document** radio button to limit substitution or check everything.
5. Check the **Report Results** box to have Illustrator count the number of each kind of substitution and report the results in an alert box when done.
6. Click **OK** to execute the command or **Cancel** to leave the document unchanged.

A Few Words About CJK Text

Illustrator 7 supports certain Chinese, Japanese, and Korean alphabets, known collectively as CJK text. These alphabets are displayed vertically, and this accounts for Illustrator's new vertical text tools. (In previous versions the so-called "j" version of Illustrator supported vertical text.)

To use CJK fonts, you must first install specific extensions to your system. Then you can specify these fonts just like any Latin fonts. The subject of CJK fonts is well covered in the Illustrator manual, and so we won't go into the details here. However, two commands (one in Windows) show up at the bottom of the Type menu; you might want to know about them.

The Glyph Options command is available only in the MacOS. This command lets you use alternative glyphs supplied with some Japanese fonts.

To Change the Orientation of Type

1. Use any selection tool or the Type tool (t) to select a text object or text.
2. Choose either **Type: Type Orientation: Vertical** or **Type: Type Orientation: Horizontal** to change the orientation. This command was added specifically for CJK fonts, but it works with all fonts.

Moby Typography

For this lesson we will go whaling. I realize that this is not politically correct, so my solution is to go to sea with Herman Melville. Open the file WHALE.AI from the LESSON13 folder on the CD. This file has a bitmapped image of a whale grouped with a graphic outline, which we will use to make a text wrap. The two dotted lines are centerline guides, which are used for alignment only. The image is from PhotoDisc's on-line library, **www. photodisc.com**.

This lesson also uses one of the fonts that Adobe supplies free with Illustrator 7, ITC Cheltenham. You need to register the Type On Call disk that comes with Illustrator 7 to use this font. You'll also need to install Cheltenham in your system before proceeding. If for some reason, you don't have or can't get the correct font, Times is a suitable substitute.

1. Choose the **Text** tool (t) and click about 2 inches down from the top of the page on the vertical guideline. We'll style the type and paragraph before entering any text (see Figure 13.25).

328 CHAPTER 13

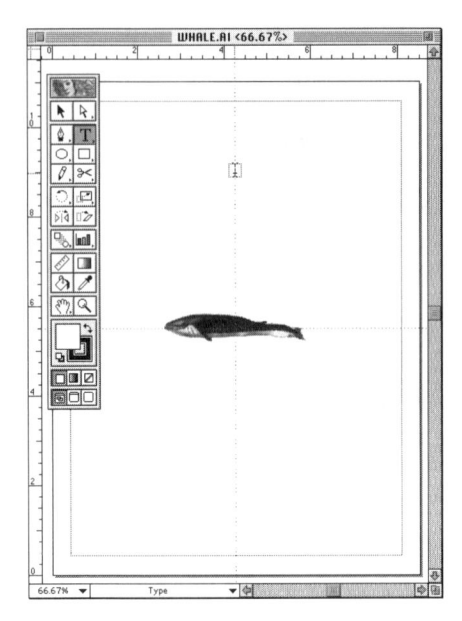

*Figure 13.25 The starting point, a blank page, save for whale and guidelines. To place the first line of text, click with the **Type** tool.*

2. Choose **Type: Character** (**Command/Ctrl-t**) to open the Character palette group. Hold down the Font Menu pop-up arrow and choose **ITC Cheltenham** and then choose the style **Book** before releasing the mouse button (see Figure 13.26).

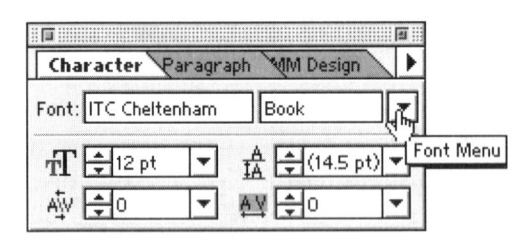

Figure 13.26 By changing the font to Cheltenham Book before entering any text, we can set the default font for the entire document.

3. Hold down the **Font Size** pop-up arrow and choose **48 pt** from the menu. Illustrator supplies the default leading of 57.5 pt (see Figure 13.27).

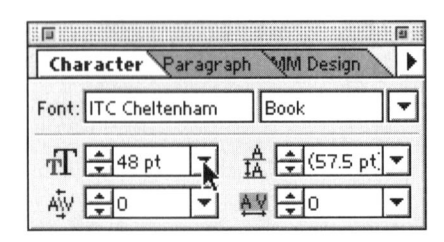

Figure 13.27 Choosing a font size of 48 pt also changes the leading to 57.5 pt. The parentheses around the leading value indicate that it is being supplied by the auto leading setting.

4. Click on the **Paragraph** tab in the Character: Paragraph: MM Design palette window, and then click on the **Align Center** button (see Figure 13.28).

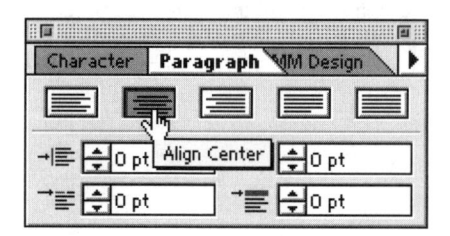

Figure 13.28 Click on the **Align Center** button in the Paragraph palette to center the text.

5. Type in the text **Moby Dick; or the Whale** and finish by pressing the **Return** key to start a new line. Then type the text **Herman Melville**. (See Figure 13.29.) All the text will be 48 pt Cheltenham with 59.5 pts of leading between the two centered lines.

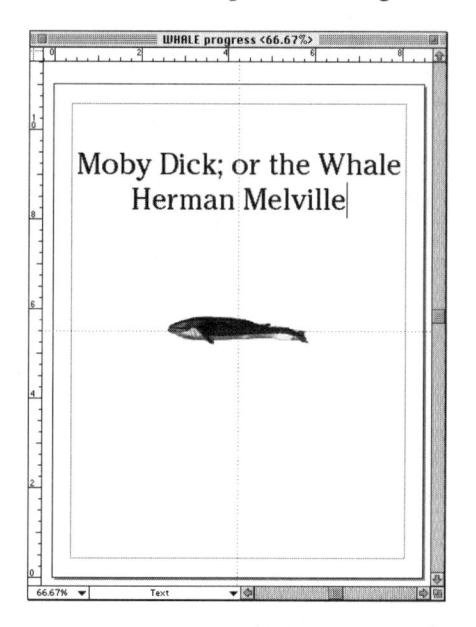

Figure 13.29 The centered and formatted text typed in above the image of the whale.

6. I don't like having the author's name typeset the same as the title. So drag the Type tool over the second line of text to select it. Choose **Type: Font: ITC Cheltenham: Book Italic** and then **Type: Size: 24 pt**. (See Figure 13.30.) This is the alternative to using the Character palette, and you can probably see that it is much less convenient.

330 CHAPTER 13

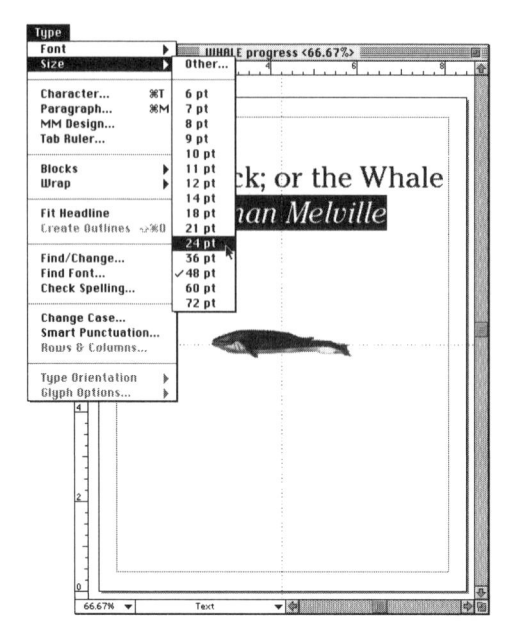

Figure 13.30 Change the selected text size to 24 pt using the menu. You can see in the background that the text has already been changed to italic.

7. The previous font size change also changed the leading so that the two lines are now too close. Click on the **Character** tab in the Character: Paragraph: MM Design palette window, and then change the leading from Auto to 72 pt by holding down the Leading pop-up menu arrow and choosing from the list (as shown in Figure 13.31).

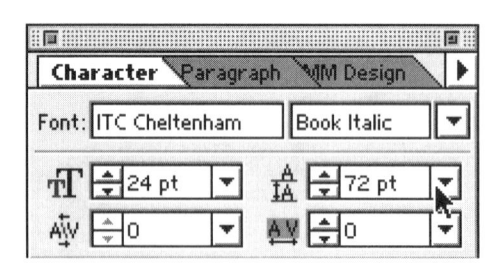

Figure 13.31 Change the leading to 72 pt in the Character palette.

8. Now use the Text tool and drag to select all the text in the first line. We'll compress this line a bit by setting the tracking. We could use the palettes, but the shortcut is quicker. Hold down the **Option/Alt** key and press the **Left Arrow** key once to set the tracking to -20/1000 of an em. (See Figure 13.32.) We could also apply kerning to some of the letter pairs, tightening up the *M* and *o*, but we'll leave that for another day.

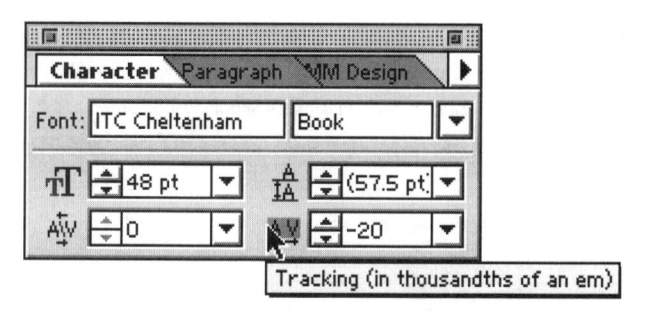

Figure 13.32 *Even though we used the keyboard shortcut to change the tracking, you can see the results in the Character palette.*

9. Choose the **Centered Rectangle** tool (m) and click on the vertical centerline about 4 inches from the bottom of the drawing. In the Rectangle dialog, specify a Width of 6 in and a Height of 5 in; then click **OK**. If the paint attributes are at their defaults, this will create a white rectangle with a black border that covers the image of the whale (as shown in Figure 13.33).

Figure 13.33 *A white rectangle obliterates the whale image.*

10. Choose the **Area Type** tool (t) and click on the edge of the rectangle to turn it into a text block. It immediately turns transparent, losing all paint attributes, and the flashing I-beam cursor appears at the top to indicate that the block is ready to receive type (see Figure 13.34).

332   CHAPTER 13

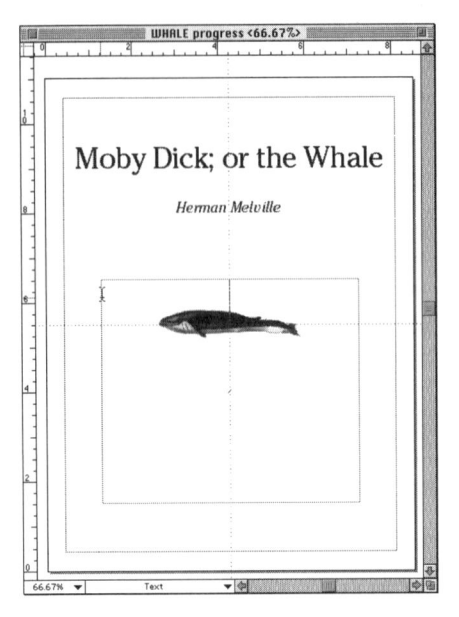

Figure 13.34 What was an opaque rectangle becomes transparent when turned into a text block by clicking on it with the Area Type tool.

11. Choose **File: Place** and select the file MOBY.TXT from the LESSON13 folder on the CD. Illustrator opens the file and places the text in the text block. Instead of the Cheltenham setting we used before, the file uses the default system font, Courier. (See Figure 13.35.)

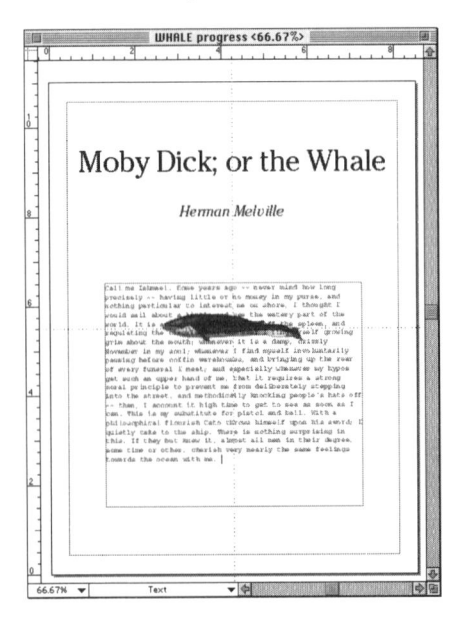

Figure 13.35 Place a text file in a text block to fill as much of the block as necessary without regard for any objects, like the whale image, beneath.

Type Commands and Palettes 333

12. Choose **Edit: Select All** (**Command/Ctrl-a**) to select all the text in the block. In the Character palette, choose **ITC Cheltenham** and **Book** again, as we did in Step 2, and set the type Size to 14 pt. The leading reverted to the Auto setting when the text was placed, which is now calculated at 17 pt. (See Figure 13.36.)

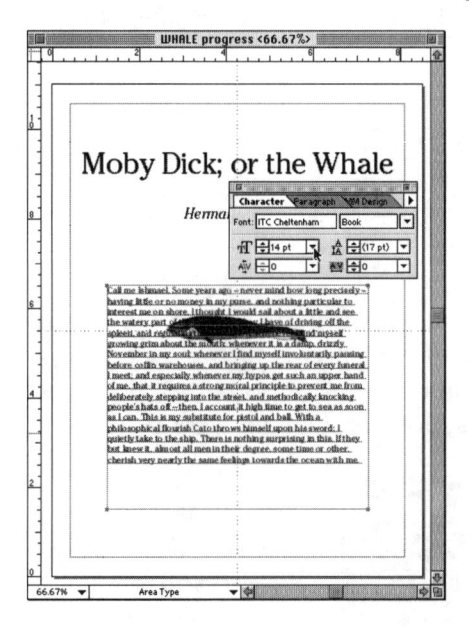

Figure 13.36 Change the character setting for the type to make the text more attractive, but it doesn't solve all our typesetting problems.

13. We should run some basic checks on this text, so choose **Type: Check Spelling**. Illustrator lists three misspelled words (see Figure 13.37). Two are proper nouns. Click the **Skip** button to skip them. The remaining word *hypos* has a list of suggested alternates. This one sent me to a large dictionary to discover that Melville was referring to hypochondria, an archaic use. Skip this one too, click the **Done** button, and Illustrator tells us that there are no more misspelled words.

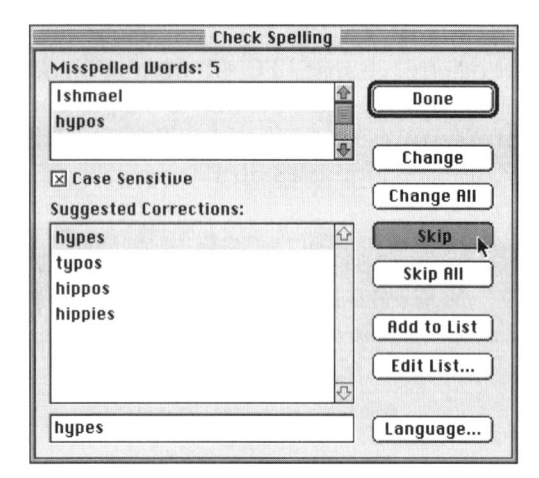

Figure 13.37 When you highlight a word in the Misspelled Words list of the Check Spelling dialog, Illustrator presents a list of possible alternative spellings for you to choose from.

14. Choose **Type: Smart Punctuation**, click on the **Entire Document** radio button, and leave the rest of the choices in the dialog set at their defaults. Click **OK**. (See Figure 13.38.) Illustrator reports that 4 ligatures, 1 quote, and 3 dashes, dots, or fractions were corrected.

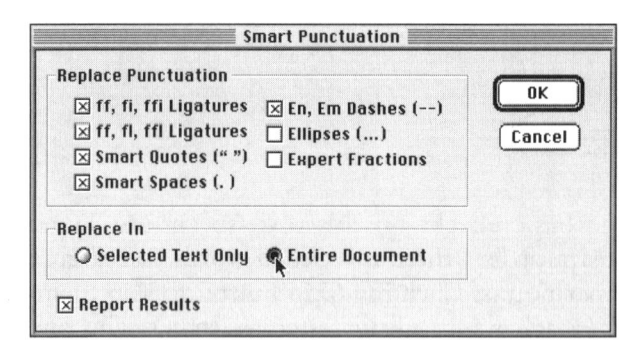

Figure 13.38 The Smart Punctuation dialog with its default settings and the Entire Document radio button selected.

15. Choose the **Select** tool (v) and click on the text block. Then choose **Type: Rows and Columns** and set the number of Columns to **2** and the Column Gutter to 14 pt (as shown in Figure 13.39). If you check in the Preview box, you can watch the changes in the drawing as you enter them in the dialog.

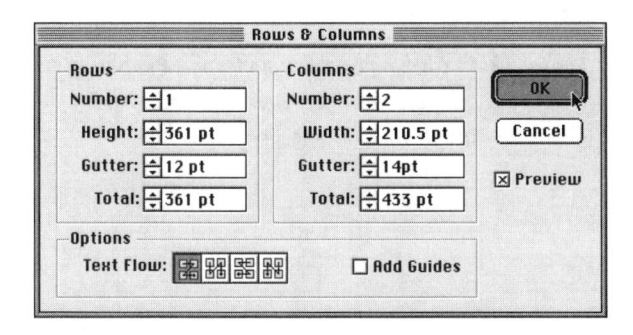

Figure 13.39 Turning a text block into two linked columns using the Rows and Columns dialog.

16. Choose the **Text** tool (t) and select the first sentence (**Call me Ishmael.**) by dragging over it. Is his name really Ishmael, or does he just want us to call him this? Since this is the first important literary question of this massive work, let's call attention to it by setting the Font Size to 24 pt in the Character palette (as shown in Figure 13.40).

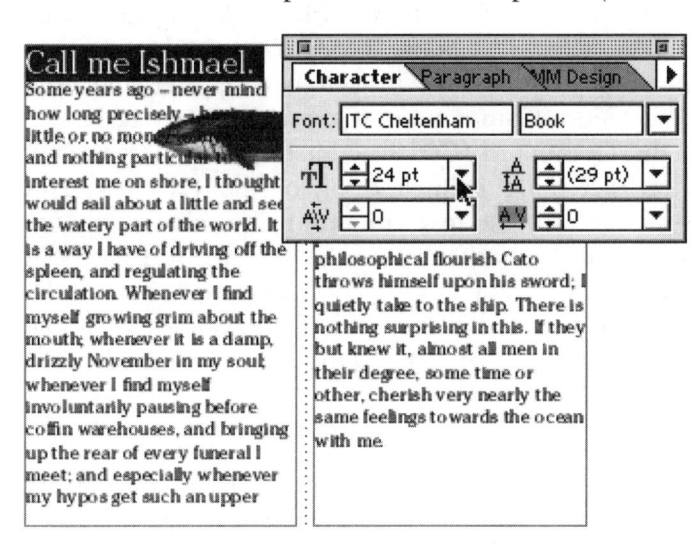

Figure 13.40 Enlarge the first sentence to 24-pt type so that it fills the entire first line.

17. Click on the **Paragraph** tab in the Character: Paragraph: MM Design palette. Choose **Show Options** from the Paragraph palette pop-up menu and click on the **Auto Hyphenate** box, and Illustrator immediately hyphenates the entire paragraph. (See Figure 13.41.)

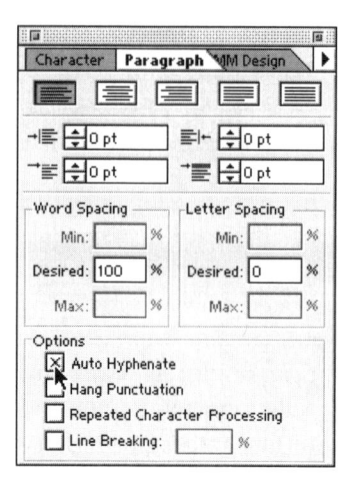

Figure 13.41 *Clicking on the Auto Hyphenate box in the Paragraph palette immediately hyphenates the entire paragraph with the selection cursor.*

18. Hold down the **Command/Ctrl** key to toggle to the Selection tool and move it over a portion of the text blocks, including the whale image, so that all are selected. Choose **Type: Wrap: Make**. Nothing appears to happen. This is because the image to be wrapped is under the text. Choose **Edit: Undo** (**Command/Ctrl-z**), and we'll try again.

    Hold down the **Command/Ctrl** key. First click away from any objects to deselect everything; then click only on the text block. This selects both blocks because the text link groups the blocks. Choose **Object: Arrange: Send to Back**. You can see that the text has been moved under the whale. Now you can choose both the text and the image of the whale as described in the previous paragraph and choose **Type: Wrap: Make**. The text flows around the outline of the whale (as shown in Figure 13.42).

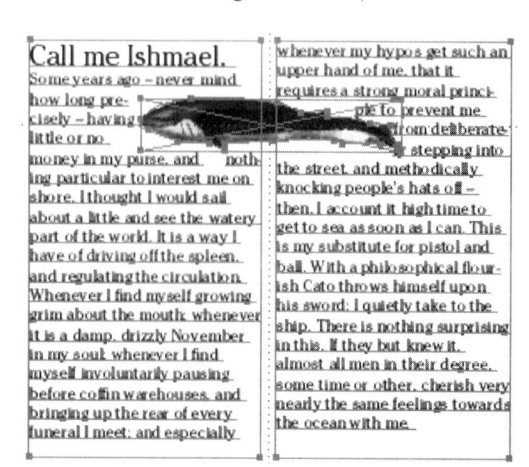

Figure 13.42 *Group text and whale using Type: Wrap: Make to let the words wrap around the outline of the image so that nothing is obscured.*

19. Set the leading to 18 pt in the Leading field of the Character palette (Figure 13.43) and we're done. Choose **Edit: Deselect All** (**Shift-Command/Ctrl-a**). Everything looks pretty good except for that nasty orphaned word on the last line of the paragraph, but I'll let you try and figure out how to fix it.

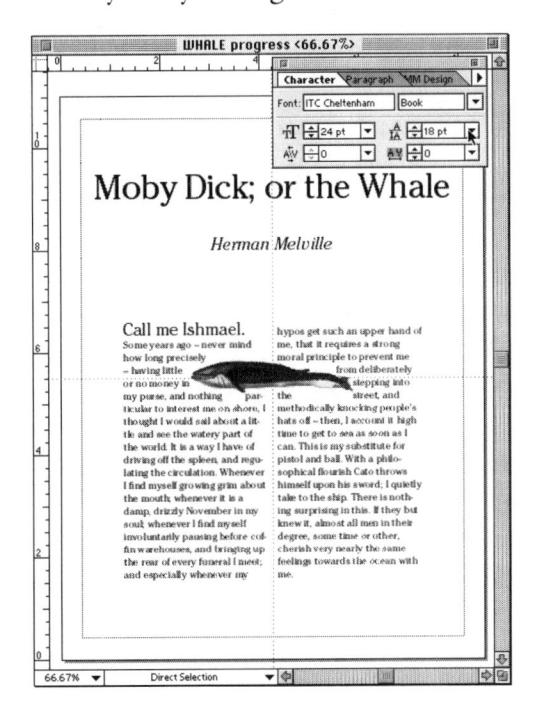

Figure 13.43 The finished page with the leading in the text blocks set to 18 points.

Save your work, if you wish. There's a finished version of this lesson saved as ISHMAEL.AI in the LESSON13 folder on the CD. You may notice that I changed the type size within the text blocks to 14.3 pt to get rid of the orphaned word.

14 Filter Menu and Submenus

In this chapter...

- Filters in general
- Color submenu commands
- Create submenu commands
- Distort filter submenu commands
- Ink Pen submenu commands
- Stylize submenu commands
- Lesson 14: A Few Good Filters

Filters in General

Filters allow you to choose objects and manipulate them through various commands and dialogs. Filters are supplied as plug-in modules and are loaded each time you launch Illustrator. The segregation of these tools into the Filter menu is slightly artificial. The fact is that there are plug-in tools in the Toolbox and plug-in commands in practically every menu. The ones that happened to end up in the Filter menu just had no other place to go.

I haven't felt it necessary to point out commands that were actually supplied as plug-ins, because Illustrator uses this feature so often. Even the basic palettes have become plug-ins. This makes a lot of sense from Adobe's point of view and is completely transparent to us as users. Filters look and are used exactly like any tool in Illustrator.

Adobe's plug-in architecture allows third-party developers to enhance Illustrator's capabilities through commercially available filters and sets, some of which are included on this book's CD. Also, because plug-ins are part of Adobe's product-wide API, filters can be shared between applications. Illustrator includes a complete set of Photoshop filters that can be applied to any bitmapped image you place or convert in Illustrator. This broadens the possibilities for filters well beyond the scope of this book.

In this chapter, we will discuss the vector-oriented filters that are included with Illustrator. The Filter menu includes five groups of about two dozen filters. The Photoshop, or bitmap-oriented filters, follow this first section in the menu. There is a thorough discussion of Photoshop filters included as Chapter 8 of the Illustrator *User Guide*.

The Filter menu has two commands at the top that you can use to reapply or reopen filters using shortcuts. These commands change to reflect the last-used filter and are not available until a filter has been used during the current drawing session.

> **Apply Last Filter (Command/Ctrl-e)**—Reapplies the last used filter to the current selection with the last used settings.
> **Last Filter (Option-Command/Ctrl-e)**—Reopens the last used filter so that you can change the settings before applying the filter to the current selection.

Filter Menu and Submenus 341

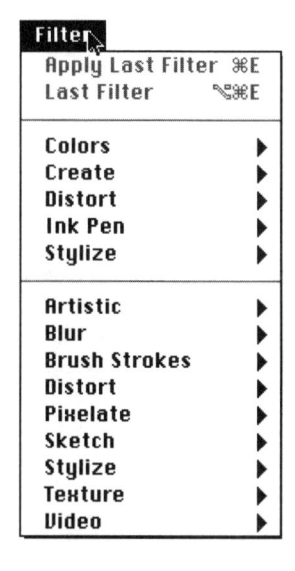

```
Filter
Apply Last Filter  ⌘E
Last Filter       ⌥⌘E

Colors      ▶
Create      ▶
Distort     ▶
Ink Pen     ▶
Stylize     ▶

Artistic       ▶
Blur           ▶
Brush Strokes  ▶
Distort        ▶
Pixelate       ▶
Sketch         ▶
Stylize        ▶
Texture        ▶
Video          ▶
```

Figure 14.1 The Filter menu is full of submenus of different filters.

COLOR SUBMENU COMMANDS

There are eleven commands/dialogs in the Filter: Color submenu (as shown in Figure 14.2), and they allow you to edit the color attributes of objects. This is a way to adjust colors individually or globally without the use of palettes. All these filters are object-oriented; in other words, you must first make a selection before executing the filter.

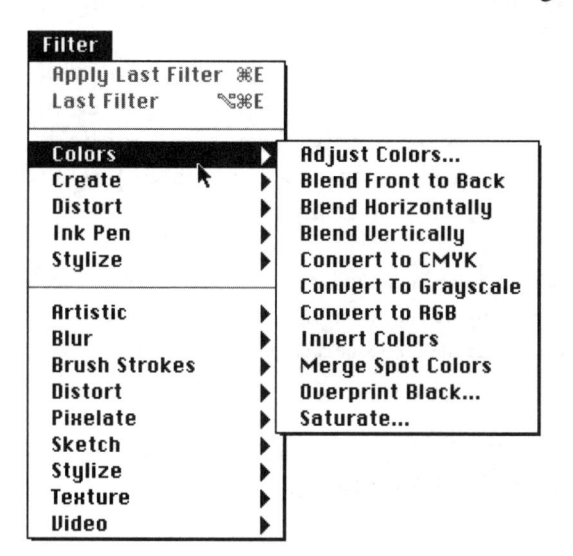

```
Filter
Apply Last Filter  ⌘E
Last Filter       ⌥⌘E

Colors      ▶   Adjust Colors...
Create      ▶   Blend Front to Back
Distort     ▶   Blend Horizontally
Ink Pen     ▶   Blend Vertically
Stylize     ▶   Convert to CMYK
                Convert To Grayscale
Artistic       ▶   Convert to RGB
Blur           ▶   Invert Colors
Brush Strokes  ▶   Merge Spot Colors
Distort        ▶   Overprint Black...
Pixelate       ▶   Saturate...
Sketch         ▶
Stylize        ▶
Texture        ▶
Video          ▶
```

Figure 14.2 The commands of the Filter: Colors submenu.

To Adjust Colors

1. Select an object or objects.
2. Choose **Filter: Colors: Adjust Colors** to open the Adjust Colors dialog (as shown in Figure 14.3).

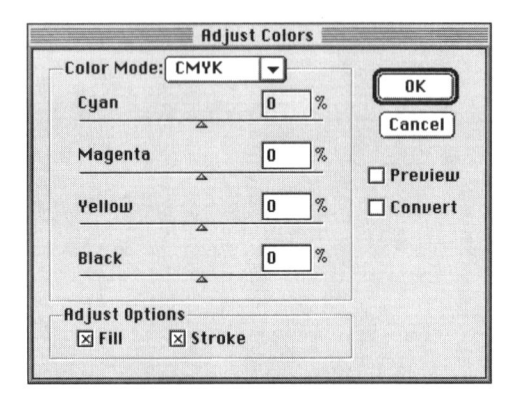

Figure 14.3 The Adjust Colors filter dialog.

3. Adjust the color sliders from -100% to +100%, or type a percentage into the field. 0% is the current color. All selected colors in the mode will be adjusted. Colors in other modes will not be affected.
4. Click on the **Adjust Options** check boxes to choose colors used for Fill, Stroke, or both.
5. Click on the **Preview** check box to see changes before closing the dialog.
6. Click on the **Convert** check box to allow the conversion of colors between CMYK, RGB, and grayscale modes. Custom spot colors cannot be converted. To convert, simply change the mode by choosing one from the Color Mode drop-down menu. Adjust one of the sliders, and the new color will also be in the new mode.

NOTE If the selection includes colors in more than one mode, the Convert check box is not available. This is because changing the slider display using the Color Mode drop-down menu allows you to edit the colors of each mode independently.

7. Click **OK** to set the adjustments and dismiss the dialog, or click **Cancel** to dismiss the dialog without changing any colors.

To Blend Filled Objects

1. Select three or more filled objects. The Blend filters have no effect on strokes or unfilled objects.
2. Choose one of the three Blend filters. These filters have no options:

    Filter: Blend Front to Back—Uses the stacking order of the selected objects to determine the blend sequence.
    Filter: Blend Horizontally—Uses the horizontal position of selected objects, leftmost to rightmost, to determine the blend sequence.
    Filter: Blend Vertically—Uses the vertical position of selected objects, topmost to bottommost, to determine the blend order.

Illustrator uses the first and last fill colors to calculate the correct number of equal gradations in between to replace the colors of the intermediate objects.

To Convert Color Modes

1. Select one or more objects.
2. Choose one of the three color mode filters, or use the Adjust Colors filter to convert modes and adjust colors simultaneously, as described earlier:

    Convert to CMYK—Converts custom, RGB, or grayscale colors to CMYK colors.
    Convert to Grayscale—Converts custom, RGB, or CMYK colors to a grayscale tint.
    Convert to RGB—Converts custom, CMYK, or grayscale colors to RGB.

> **NOTE** You cannot convert colors to custom colors using filters.

To Invert Colors

1. Select one or more objects.
2. Choose **Filter: Colors: Invert Colors**. Illustrator converts the selected colors, fills and strokes to their color negative.

To Add or Remove Black Overprint

1. Select the object(s) from which to add or remove black overprint.
2. Choose **Filter: Colors: Overprint Black** to open the Overprint Black dialog (as shown in Figure 14.4).

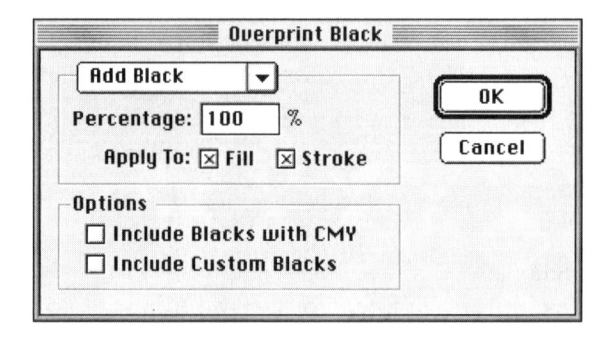

Figure 14.4 the Overprint Black dialog lets you add or remove black in percents. This affects only the plates for process color printing and not the artwork itself.

3. Choose **Add Black** or **Remove Black** from the drop-down menu. For example, enter **80%** to select only objects containing at least 80% black.
4. Set the Percentage of black required to apply overprinting. Objects equal to or greater than the specified percentage will have the add or remove applied.
5. Click the **Fill** and/or **Stroke** check boxes to set the paint attributes for application.
6. There are two Options check boxes:

    Include Blacks with CMY—Check this box to overprint paths that are also painted with cyan, magenta, and/or yellow, as long as black is contained at the specified percentage.
    Include Custom Blacks—Check this box to overprint custom colors, as long as black is contained at the specified percentage.

7. Click **OK** to add or remove the specified overprint, or click **Cancel** to dismiss the dialog without making any changes.

To Adjust Color Saturation

1. Select the objects whose color you wish to saturate or desaturate.
2. Choose **Filter: Colors: Saturate** to open the Saturate dialog (as shown in Figure 14.5).

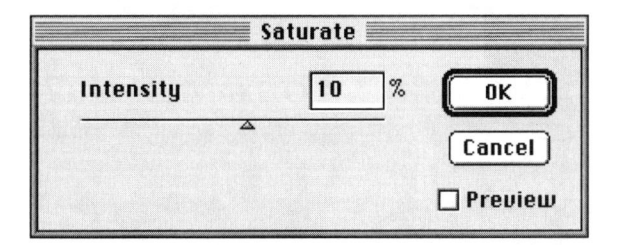

Figure 14.5 The Saturate dialog allows you to increase or decrease the color intensity of selected objects.

3. Adjust the Intensity slider by dragging, clicking, or typing in a percentage from -100% to +100%. The default is 10%. -100% always yields white. +100% yields 100% of each process or custom color tint in the selection. If the saturation of the process or custom color is already 100%, increasing the saturation makes no change.
4. Click the **Preview** check box to see the intensity changes before applying them.
5. Click **OK** to apply the changes, or click **Cancel** to dismiss the dialog without making any changes.

CREATE SUBMENU COMMANDS

There are three commands in the Create submenu (as shown in Figure 14.6) and each is used to turn existing objects into something different. Because you can't paint an object mask, the Fill and Stroke for Mask filter creates duplicate filled and stroked objects that make a mask look painted. The Object Mosaic dialog is more like a Photoshop filter in that it works with Illustrator bitmaps to create mosaic-like images. Trim Marks is similar to the Cropmarks command, except that you can have more than one set of trim marks.

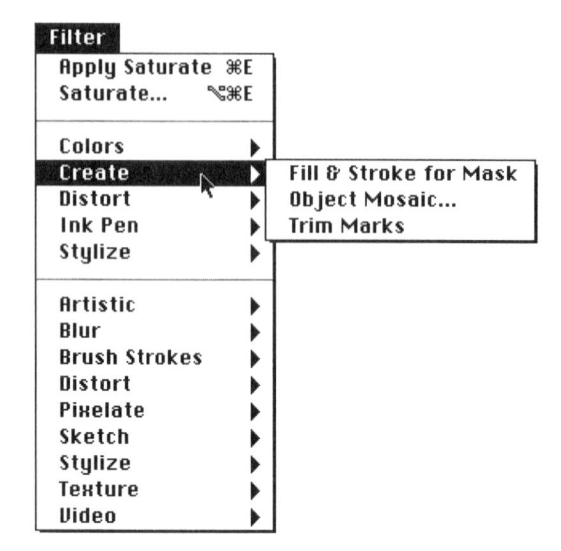

Figure 14.6 *The commands of the Filter: Create submenu.*

To Fill and Stroke Masks

1. Select the mask object you want to fill and/or stroke.
2. Choose **Filter: Create: Fill and Stroke for Mask**. Illustrator creates two objects exactly the same size as the mask; the stroked object is on top of the mask, and the filled object is behind the mask. The default stroke is CMYK black and the fill is CMYK 25% gray.
3. Use the Direct Selection tool (a) to select the filled object by clicking on the fill or the stroked object by clicking on the object edge. By selecting one or the other you can change the default paint attributes using any standard painting or color selection method.

To Turn Bitmaps into Mosaics

1. Select a bitmap object. (You must either convert an Illustrator object or place an imported bitmap file.)
2. Choose **Filter: Create: Object Mosaic** to open the Object Mosaic dialog (as shown in Figure 14.7).

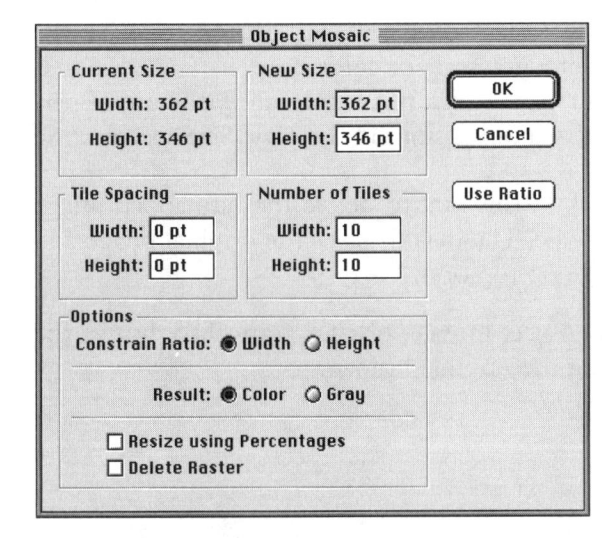

Figure 14.7 *The Object Mosaic dialog is used to specify the size and spacing of the mosaic effect that Illustrator can apply to bitmaps.*

3. The dialog is divided into four functional areas, each with Width and Height fields.

   Current Size—Shows the current Width and Height of the selected bitmap and cannot be edited.
   New Size—Shows the current Width and Height. Enter new specifications to change the size of the mosaic image. Use the Constrain Ratio option to maintain the aspect ratio of the image.
   Tile Spacing—Allows you to specify a spacing distance between the tiles being created. This leaves a gap between tiles. The default is 0, which leaves no gap.
   Number of Tiles—Allows you to specify the number of tiles used in the final mosaic. Specify both Width and Height, or specify one and use the Constrain Ratio option to let Illustrator calculate the other.

4. Choose from four options:

   Constrain Ratio—Choose either the **Width** or **Height** button; then click the **Use Ratio** button to constrain the specifications in the New Size and Number of Tiles fields. If you don't click the **Use Ratio** button, the size and/or number of tiles is not constrained.

Result—Choose either the **Color** or **Gray** button to make the resulting mosaic either a grayscale or color image.

Resize using Percentages—Click this box to allow the use of percentages instead of actual dimensions in the New Size specification fields.

Delete Raster—Click in this box to delete the bitmapped image after creating the mosaic. The default saves the original image and creates the new image on top of it.

5. Click **OK** to create the object mosaic, or click **Cancel** to dismiss the dialog without changing the original bitmap.

To Create Trim Marks

1. Select the object(s) around which you want trim marks.
2. Choose **Filter: Create: TrimMarks**. Illustrator creates stroked lines around the bounding area of the selected object(s). These are identical to crop marks in appearance, but differ in that they can be edited and are not recognized as special when printing or separating drawings.

> **NOTE**: Illustrator can only create a single set of crop marks (see Chapter 12). Crop marks have special significance when printing an image, and they cannot be deleted without using the **CropMarks: Revert** command. Trim marks are useful when there are repeated images on a page that will be cut from a single sheet of paper.

DISTORT FILTERS SUBMENU COMMANDS

The six distort filters allow you to pinch, punch, and pull at objects to create useful 3D effects or otherwise amusing distortions (see Figure 14.8). They are all controlled from dialogs.

Filter Menu and Submenus 349

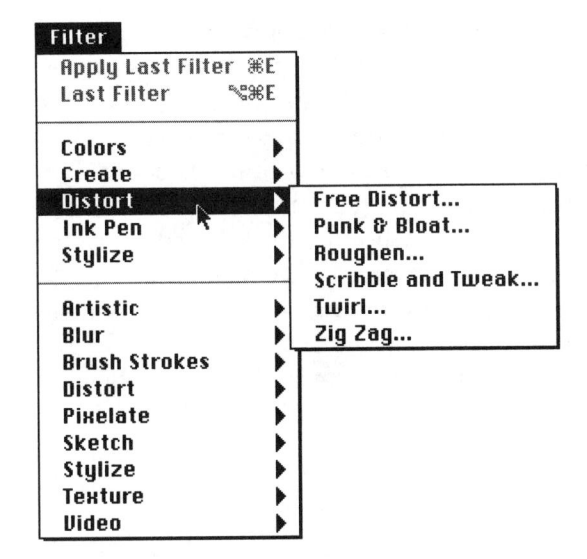

Figure 14.8 The commands of the Filter: Distort submenu.

To Distort Objects Freely

1. Select the object(s) you wish to distort.
2. Choose **Filter: Distort: Free Distort** to open the Free Distort dialog (as shown in Figure 14.9). Illustrator draws a rectangular bounding box around the entire selection and previews the artwork with handles at the corners of the box in the dialog.

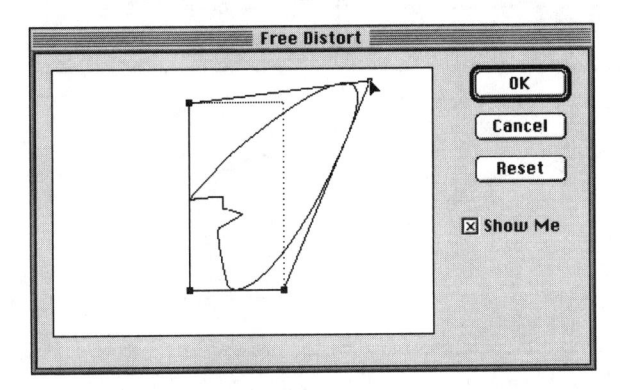

Figure 14.9 The Free Distort dialog is one of the few dialogs that has an editing field within it. Move the corners of the active selection's bounding box to distort the image.

3. Move the cursor over one of the corners of the preview rectangle and press down the mouse button. When the cursor becomes hollow (there may be a slight delay depending on the size of the selection and the speed of your computer), drag the corner in any direction.
4. Click the **Show Me** box to preview the distortions. You can continue dragging and redragging on corners until you achieve the effect you wish. When the Show Me box is not selected, only the bounding box is shown in the preview area of the dialog.
5. Click the **Reset** button to set the bounding box back to its unaltered state and continue distorting.
6. Click **OK** to apply the distortions and dismiss the dialog, or click **Cancel** to leave well enough alone.

To Punk or Bloat Objects

1. Select the object(s) to be distorted.
2. Choose **Filter: Distort: Punk and Bloat** to open the Punk and Bloat dialog (as shown in Figure 14.10). There is a single slider that goes from -200% (Punk) to +200% (Bloat). You can punk curved paths inward and bloat curved paths outward, each without moving anchor points.

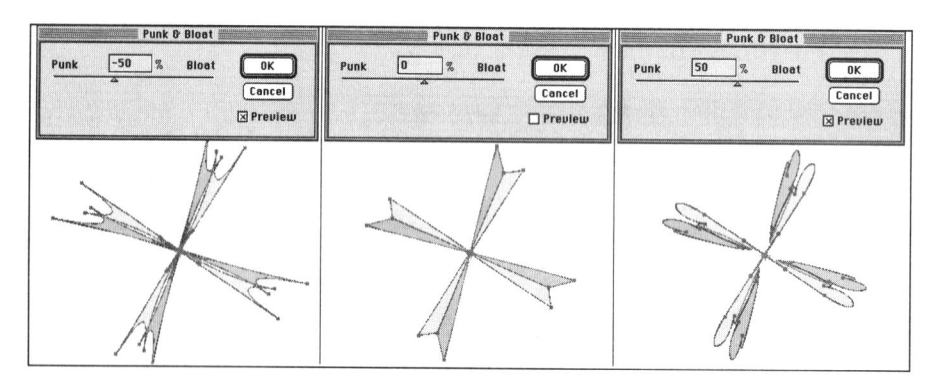

Figure 14.10 Punking and bloating are controlled from the same slider. The example on the left is punked -50%; no punk or bloat is applied in the middle; and on the right there is 50% bloating.

3. Drag the slider, click on the slider scale, or type a percentage specification into the field.

Filter Menu and Submenus 351

4. Click on the **Preview** box to preview effects in the drawing window.
5. Click **OK** to apply the distortions and dismiss the dialog, or click **Cancel** to stay on the straight and narrow.

To Roughen Objects

1. Select the object(s) to be distorted. The Roughen filter distorts the path of objects between anchor points and can roughen further by adding anchor points.
2. Choose **Filter: Distort: Roughen** to open the Roughen dialog (as shown in Figure 14.11). There are two option sliders and one radio button selection.

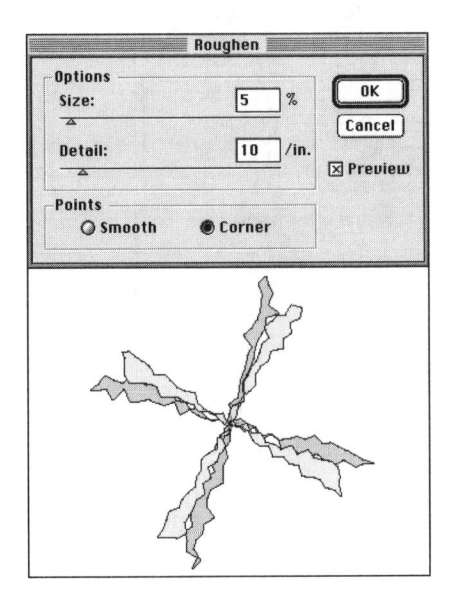

Figure 14.11 The Roughen dialog and its results.

3. Drag the sliders, click on the slider scales, or type a specification into the fields.

   Size—Set the amount of distortion from 0% to 100%. Size effects are randomized using the specification as a maximum distortion value.
   Detail—Detail is a measure of how many distorting anchor points are added per inch, from 0 to 100.

4. Choose either the **Smooth** or **Corner** radio button to set the roughened paths to be distorted about smooth or corner anchor points.
5. Click on the **Preview** box to preview the effects in the drawing window.
6. Click **OK** to apply the distortions and dismiss the dialog, or click **Cancel** to remain clean-shaven.

To Scribble and Tweak Objects

1. Select the object(s) to be distorted.
2. Choose **Filter: Distort: Scribble and Tweak** to open the Scribble and Tweak dialog (as shown in Figure 14.12).

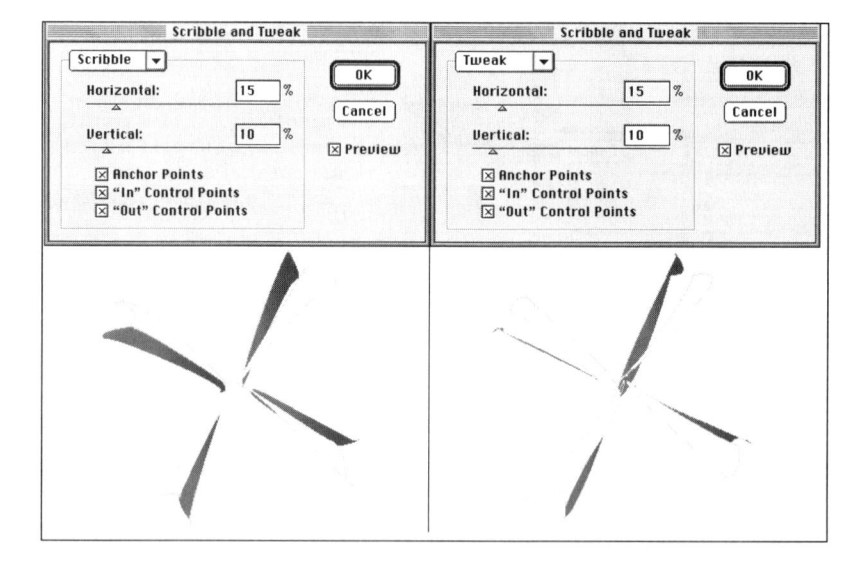

Figure 14.12 Scribble dialog and results on the left and Tweak on the right.

3. Use the drop-down menu to choose either **Scribble** or **Tweak**. The sliders and check boxes remain the same except that Scribble sliders are measured from 0% to 100%, while Tweak sliders range from 0 to 100 points.
4. Drag the sliders, click on the slider scales, or type a specification into the fields to set the amount of Horizontal or Vertical distortion.

Filter Menu and Submenus

5. Click on the **Preview** box to preview the effects in the drawing window.
6. Select the type of anchor points to use in creating distortions from the Anchor Points, "In" Control Points, and "Out" Control Points check boxes. The distinction of these is obscure to me and the effects so random that it almost doesn't matter. Try them and see what you like. You may select them in any combination, but one must always be selected.
7. Click **OK** to apply the distortions and dismiss the dialog, or click **Cancel** to stay out of trouble.

To Twirl Objects

1. Select the object(s) to be distorted.
2. Choose **Filter: Distort: Twirl** to open the Twirl dialog (as shown in Figure 14.13).
3. Set the amount of twirl from -3600° to +3600°. There is no preview option for this filter, but you can use the Twirl tool to achieve the same effects interactively (see Chapter 5).
4. Click **OK** to apply the distortions and dismiss the dialog, or click **Cancel** to stay out of the dance.

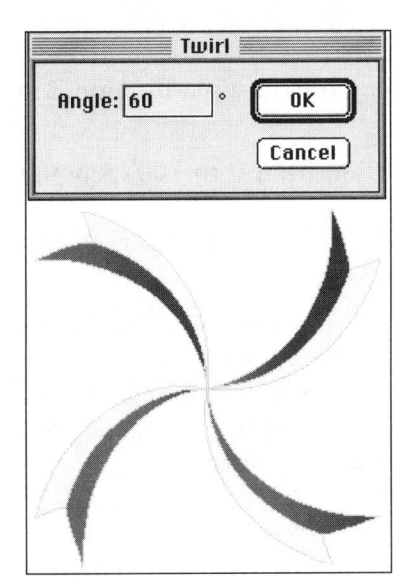

Figure 14.13 The Twirl dialog and results.

To Create Zig Zags

1. Select the object(s) to be distorted. The Zigzag filter is especially effective with open paths.
2. Choose **Filter: Distort: Zigzag** to open the Zigzag dialog (as shown in Figure 14.14). There are two option sliders and one radio button selection.

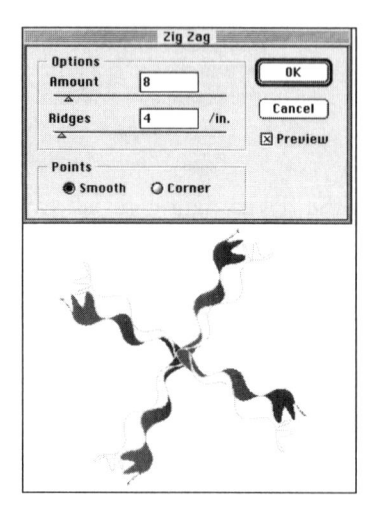

Figure 14.14 The Zigzag dialog and results.

3. Drag the sliders, click on the slider scales, or type a specification into the fields.

    Amount—Set the amount of distortion from 0 to 100. Amount sets the degree of zig and zag.
    Ridges—Ridges is a measure of how many distorting anchor points are added per inch, from 0 to 100.

4. Choose either the **Smooth** or **Corner** radio button to set the zig zags to be distorted about smooth or corner anchor points.
5. Click on the **Preview** box to preview the effects in the drawing window.
6. Click **OK** to apply the distortions and dismiss the dialog, or click **Cancel** if you're not prepared to take a sobriety test.

INK PEN SUBMENU COMMANDS

The ink pen filters are used to create regular patterned gradations such as cross-hatching or irregular textured fills such as wood grains. This is supposed to simulate the effects of drawing with an ink pen, thus the name. Ink pen effects are created by converting a selected object into a mask and then drawing strokes or shapes behind it.

> **NOTE** The process of creating ink pen effects can generate many small objects that require significant program memory. It is recommended that this effect be applied last or near the end of your work on any particular drawing.

There are two ink pen filters, Effects and Hatches. The former is used to design and apply the effect, whereas the latter is used to create or edit the hatch patterns used in the Ink Pen Effects dialog.

To Apply Ink Pen Effects

1. Select an object.
2. Choose **Filter: Ink Pen: Effects** to open the Ink Pen Effects dialog (as shown in Figure 14.15). This has got to be the most complicated dialog in all of Illustrator. Perhaps it is unfair to call it complicated, but with half a dozen drop-down menus and various other options, it is definitely capable of the most variation. All this variation makes the creation of effects a somewhat random exercise. Unless you use this filter often, it's likely that finding the effect you want will be a process of trial and error. On the other hand, so much variation does provide remarkable creative possibilities.

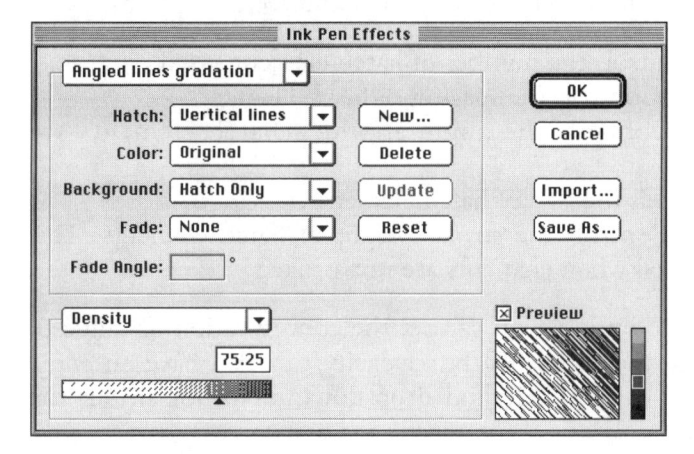

Figure 14.15 The Ink Pen Effects dialog is like a program within Illustrator. Unless you learn to use all the various options and can begin to guess the seemingly endless permutations, using it is more a matter of trial and error.

3. Click on the **Preview** button to see a representation of the effects as you edit them.
4. Choose an effect among the two dozen choices in the first drop-down menu. These are actually predefined options that recall the settings of all the drop-down menus and options in the dialog. Use one of these predefined settings, or customize the setting.

   Hatch—Choose one of the predefined hatch patterns. This is the actual pattern that is turned into the ink pen effect. There are seven predefined hatch patterns to choose from. Use the Hatches dialog, described later in this chapter, to edit or create new hatches for this list.
   Color—Choose **Original** to use the hatch's defined color or **Match Object** to use the fill color of the object being filled. Do not use Match Object for objects with patterned fills.
   Background—Choose **Retain Fill** to retain the original fill of the selected object or **Hatch Only** to delete the fill when the hatch is applied.
   Fade—There are four fade choices: **None** for no fade, **To White** fades to white, **To Black** fades to black, and **Use Gradient** uses the gradient fill of the object (if there is one) to define the direction and color of the fade. If one of the fades is chosen, specify a Fade Angle from -360° to +360°.

5. Choose one of the five pattern variable settings in the lower portion of the dialog. Each one can be set by choosing it from the drop-down menu and adjusting concentration and direction options.

   Density—Controls the number of hatch elements used.
   Dispersion—Controls the spacing of hatch elements.
   Rotation—Controls the angle at which hatch elements are applied.
   Scale—Controls the size of hatch elements.
   Thickness—Controls the stroke weight of hatch elements. This option is grayed when elements are not stroked.

   For each of these options you can set the concentration or range of the effect using the slider. All but Density can also have an angle specified. There is also a Method drop-down menu for all but the Density option.

None—Deselects the option.
Constant—Applies the effect evenly. No range is available with this option.
Linear—Varies the effect in a linearly increasing manner.
Reflect—Applies the effect from the center outward.
Symmetric—Varies the effect proportionately and evenly.
Random—Varies the effect irregularly.

6. Select one of the four buttons to modify or add to the predefined ink pen effects.

   New—Click the **New** button to save a new effect. Enter a name and click **OK**. The effect will be added to the list of effects in the drop-down menu.
   Delete—Click the **Delete** button to remove the current preset effect from the drop-down menu.
   Update—Click the **Update** button to update the settings of the chosen ink pen effect with the current settings.
   Reset—Click the **Reset** button to return all the settings to the stored presets for the currently chosen effect.

7. You can also save or import effects for use with other machines.

   Import—Click the **Import** button to open the standard File dialog. Find the predefined effects file and click **Open** to load the effect.
   Save As—Click the **Save As** button to open the standard File dialog. Name the effect and click **Save** to save it as a file. The effect can then be shared and imported on another machine or by another user.

8. Click **OK** to apply the effect or **Cancel** to dismiss the dialog without changing the drawing.

To Create a New Hatch Pattern

1. Draw the hatch pattern and leave it selected.
2. Choose **Filter: Ink Pen: Hatches** to open the Ink Pen Hatches dialog (as shown in Figure 14.16).

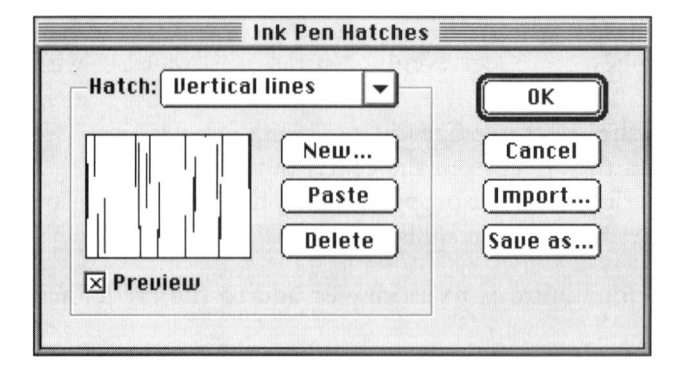

Figure 14.16 The Ink Pen Hatches dialog doesn't affect the drawing, but it is the place you create hatch patterns to apply using the Ink Pen Effects dialog.

3. Deselect the **Preview** check box only if your performance is so poor that you don't want to see a preview of the hatches.
4. Click the **New** button to open the New Hatch dialog. Name the hatch and click **OK**. Illustrator uses the selection in the drawing to create a new hatch pattern.
5. To save the hatch pattern for use with other drawings, click the **Save As** button to open the standard file dialog. Click **Save** to save the hatch as a file so that you can use the **Import** button to open the file and add the hatch pattern to another drawing.
6. Click **OK** to use the new hatch with the current drawing and dismiss the dialog. The new hatch will be listed in the Hatch drop-down menu of the Filter: Ink Pen: Effects dialog.

To Modify Hatch Patterns

1. Choose **Filter: Ink Pen: Hatches** to open the Ink Pen Hatches dialog.
2. Choose a pattern from the Hatch drop-down menu.
3. Click the **Paste** button to paste a copy of the hatch into the drawing. The pattern can be edited and used to create a new hatch as described earlier.
4. Click the **Delete** button to delete the hatch from the list.
5. Click **OK** or **Cancel** to dismiss the dialog.

STYLIZE SUBMENU COMMANDS

The Stylize submenu contains five dialog-based commands that amount to very useful shortcuts (see Figure 14.17). All of these filters affect the active selection and are grayed out and unavailable if there is no selection.

Filter Menu and Submenus

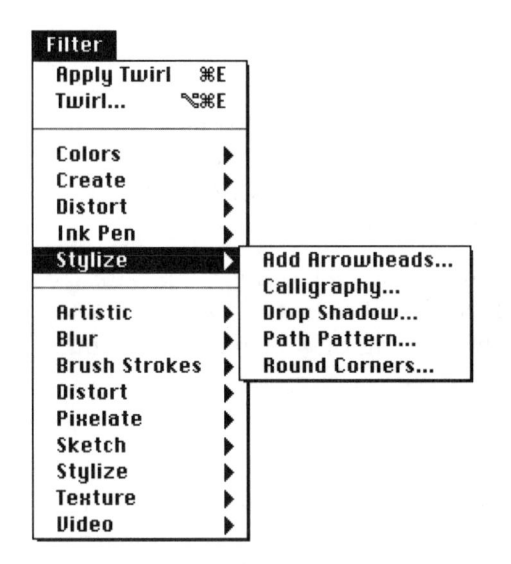

Figure 14.17 The commands of the Filter: Stylize submenu.

To Add Arrowheads to Paths

1. Select one or more open paths. The Add Arrowheads filter has no effect on closed paths.
2. Choose **Filter: Stylize: Add Arrowheads** to open the Add Arrowheads dialog (as shown in Figure 14.18).

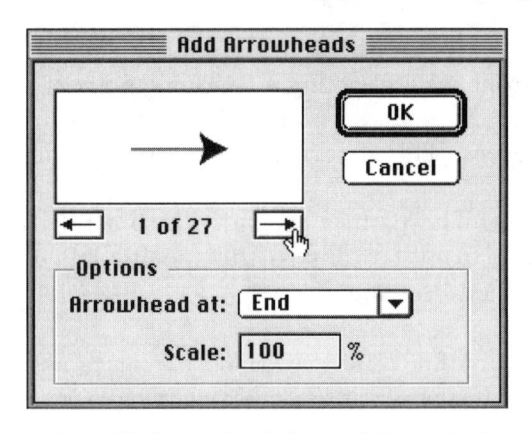

Figure 14.18 The Add Arrowhead dialog allows you to specify arrowhead styles by clicking through a list of 27 predefined designs.

3. Click on the left or right pointing arrows to browse through them. There are 27 predefined arrowhead and arrowtail shapes. There's no more convenient way to pick from the stack of designs, and there is no way to reorder it.

4. Select from the two options:

   Arrowhead at—Choose one of three locations from the drop-down menu: **Start**, **End**, or **Both Ends**. All paths have direction that is determined by the order of anchor points (see Chapter 3). **Scale**—The default scale is 100%, or you can scale the arrowheads relative to the stroke width, up to 1000%.

5. Click **OK** to apply arrowheads and dismiss the dialog. Illustrator creates the arrowheads as grouped editable objects. Use the Direct Select tool to edit arrowheads once drawn or ungroup them before editing.

To Create Calligraphic Strokes

1. Select one or more curved paths. The Calligraphy filter has no effect on straight paths.
2. Choose **Filter: Stylize: Calligraphy** to open the Calligraphy dialog (as shown in Figure 14.19).

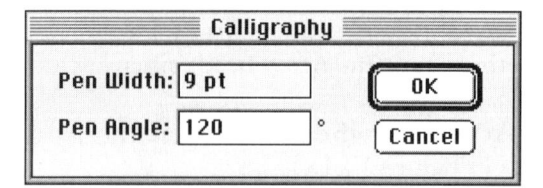

Figure 14.19 The Calligraphy dialog allows you to simulate the effect of a broad nibbed pen. The effect is noticeable only with curved strokes.

3. Specify a Pen Width. Any stroke weight setting is ignored and overriden by this field.
4. Specify a Pen Angle in degrees. This determines the calligraphic effect.
5. Click **OK** to apply the effect. The path is expanded into a filled object with a width varying from 1 point to the specified Pen Width, according to the specified Pen Angle.

NOTE

The Calligraphy filter is similar to the Brush Width option with a pressure sensitive pen (see Chapter 3). But the Brush tool varies width according to pen pressure rather than pen angle.

To Add Drop Shadows

1. Select one or more objects. The Drop Shadow filter affects any and all objects.
2. Choose **Filter: Stylize: Drop Shadow** to open the Drop Shadow dialog (as shown in Figure 14.20).

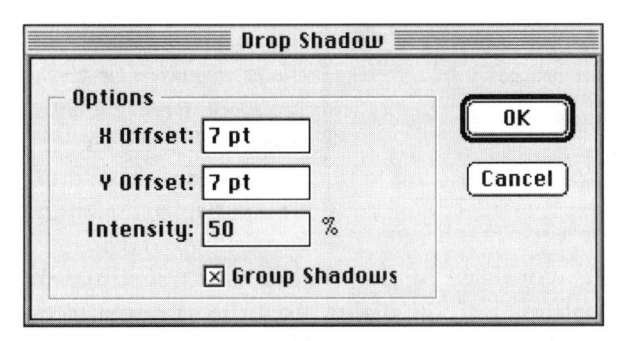

Figure 14.20 It's not that difficult to create drop shadows manually, but this dialog does simplify the process and can also group object and shadow together.

3. There are three options, one check box, and no preview:

   X Axis—Specify the offset distance in relation to the x-axis.
   Y Axis—Specify the offset distance in relation to the y-axis.
   Intensity—Specify a percentage intensity for the drop shadow fill. The default is 50%. 100% creates a black drop shadow, whereas 0% does not change the color from the selected object.
   Group Shadows—Deselect this check box to create drop shadows that are not grouped with the shadowed object.

4. Click **OK** to dismiss the dialog and create the drop shadow.

To Apply Path Patterns

1. Select the artwork you wish to apply the path pattern to.
2. Choose **Filter: Stylize: Path Pattern** to open the Path Pattern dialog (as shown in Figure 14.21). This dialog is one of the more complex filter dialogs, with options, lists, specifications, radio buttons, and check boxes, and there is no Preview button to see what you're doing.

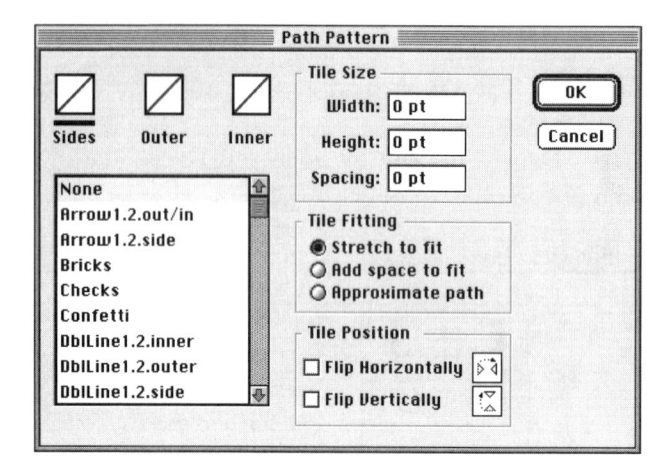

Figure 14.21 *The Path Pattern dialog lists all the predefined patterns that come with Illustrator and any that you add to the paths palette. There are many options when creating a path pattern, not the least of which is the ability to specify three different patterns for the sides, inner, and outer curves of the path being converted.*

Before I describe the workings of this dialog, it's necessary to explain what a path pattern is. This dialog uses the same patterns found in the Swatches palette (see Chapter 10) to trace the contours of paths and create chains of tiled patterns. Patterns are saved with the document, so if there's a pattern you want to load, open the document's library. There are over 200 additional path pattern designs on the Illustrator CD. Open these files using the **Window: Other Libraries** dialog to make their patterns available to the file you're working on (see Chapter 15).

You must select patterns, specify tile size and spacing, and set options to create a path pattern.

3. Click on one of the three buttons at the top left of the dialog:

    Sides—Applies the pattern to path sides.
    Outer—Applies the pattern to outer corners. All the corners of regular polygons are outer.
    Inner—Applies the pattern to inner corners. The inward facing corners of irregular polygons or paths are inner.

4. Select a pattern from the scrolling pattern list, which contains all the patterns in the current Swatches palette. You'll notice that there are multiple versions of some patterns as indicated by appended file names (*.side*, *.outer*, and *.inner*). This is Adobe's naming convention. It is a useful one to follow, but it does not limit the application of patterns in any way.

None, the first choice in the list, is the default pattern. You must repeat steps 3 and 4 to specify patterns for all three path buttons, sides, and corners.

5. Specify the Tile Size for the pattern. Each pattern has its own default tile size, which is the size of its bounding box. (Tile Size ignores any stroke weight you may have specified.) Changing the Height or Width scales the tile size proportionally. Scaling a side tile scales corner tiles as well. Specify Spacing to leave a measured distance between each tile.

> **NOTE**
> When applying a path pattern to a circle, you can create a solid patterned fill by scaling the tile size to the diameter of the circle. Anything less creates a donut, and anything more creates a mess.

6. Specify the method used to fit the patterns to the path by choosing one of three radio buttons:

   Stretch to fit—Stretches tiles to fit the path, which can result in distorted patterns; the distortion is not necessarily a bad thing.
   Add space to fit—Inserts an equal amount of blank space between each tile to fit the object. Use this option instead of the Spacing specification described in the previous step.
   Approximate path—Works with rectangular shapes to shift the pattern inward or outward from the path centerline so that the tiles fit exactly.

7. If you wish, click on the **Tile Position** check boxes to flip the pattern horizontally, vertically, or both.
8. Click **OK** to dismiss the dialog and apply the path pattern as specified.

To Round the Corners of Objects

1. Select the object or objects whose corners you want to round. This filter has no effect on smooth anchor points.
2. Choose **Filter: Stylize: Round Corners** to open the Round Corners dialog shown in Figure 14.22 .

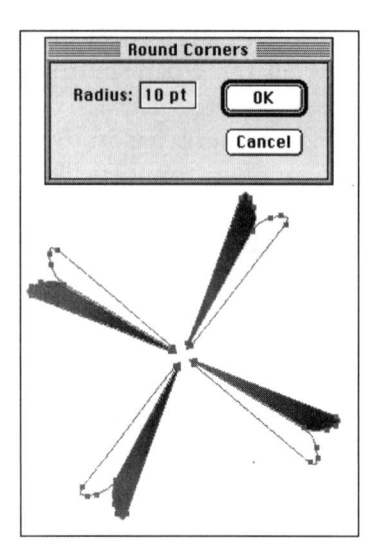

Figure 14.22 The Round Corners dialog and its result.

3. Specify a roundness Radius.
4. Click **OK** to dismiss the dialog and convert all path angles to rounded corners.

LESSON 14

A Few Good Filters

This lesson will exercise just a few of Illustrator's object-oriented filters. You'll see that the effects can range from subtle to striking. Start by opening the file TERSE.AI from the LESSON14 folder on the CD.

This file contains the characters of the word *terse* typeset using Adobe's Cronos Multiple Master typeface. It was created by sizing each letter individually from 800 points down to 400 points and then applying negative kerning between each letter pair so that the letters fall on top of each other. Each letter was filled with one of the standard custom colors from the Swatches palette, and then the letter group was converted to outlines using Type: Create Outlines. The final step was to use Object: Pathfinder: Soft with a blend percentage of 50% to divide the shapes and make the overlaps appear transparent. You can recreate these steps if you wish with any typeface and color choices.

1. Choose **Edit: Select All** (**Command/Ctrl-a**) to select everything before applying any filters. (See Figure 14.23.)

366 CHAPTER 14

Figure 14.23 The "TERSE" letterforms after being selected using Edit: Select All.

2. Choose **Filter: Colors: Adjust Colors**. The Adjust Colors dialog opens in CMYK mode, because the **Object: Pathfinder: Soft** command automatically converts custom colors to CMYK. (See Figure 14.24.)

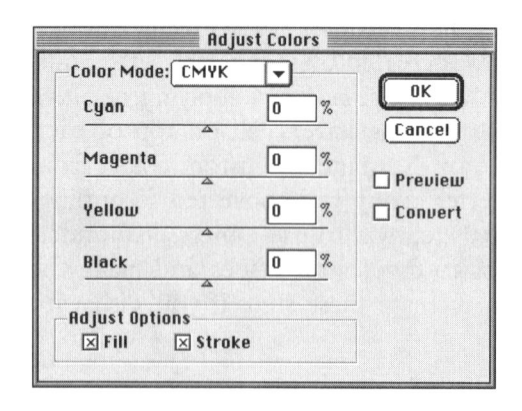

Figure 14.24 Even though the colors used in this drawing were custom colors, they were converted to CMYK equivalents when the Pathfinder: Soft command was used. As a result, the Adjust Colors dialog defaults to CMYK for this drawing.

3. Click the **Convert** check box and then select **RGB** from the Color Mode drop-down menu. I intend to use this graphic on the Web where RGB is the mode of choice. Click the **Preview** check box to see the effect as the sliders are adjusted. (See Figure 14.25.)

Filter Menu and Submenus 367

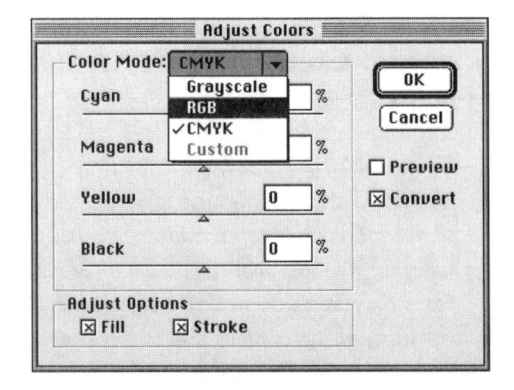

Figure 14.25 By checking the Convert box, the image can be converted to RGB using the Color Mode drop-down menu. Other modes are grayed out when the Convert box is left unchecked.

4. Adjust the Red and Blue sliders to -10% and the green to +10%, which has the effect of shifting the overall color toward green without too much darkening. (See Figure 14.26.) Click **OK** to dismiss the dialog and adjust the colors.

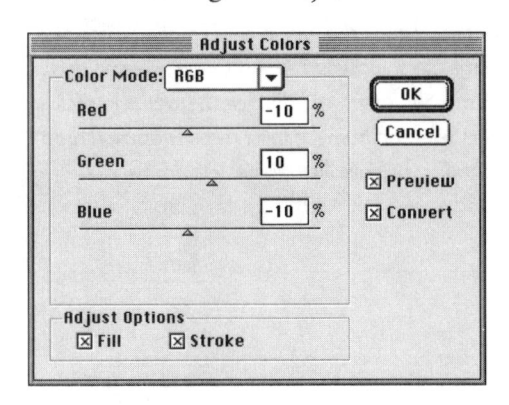

Figure 14.26 Adjust the sliders as indicated, and all the selected colors are adjusted accordingly. Check the Preview box to watch the image change as you move the sliders or type in the amounts.

5. Choose **Filter: Distort: Scribble and Tweak**. Choose **Tweak** from the drop-down menu and leave the default settings at 5% each. Check the **Preview** box to see the effect, and click **OK**. (See Figure 14.27.)

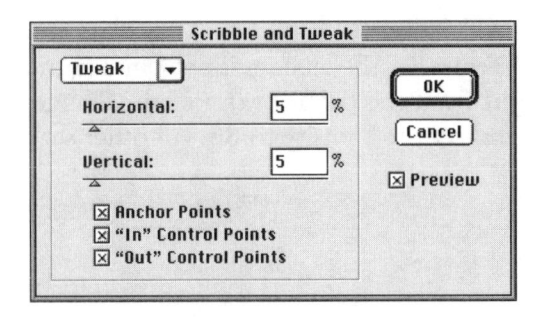

Figure 14.27 The default Tweak settings in the Scribble and Tweak dialog will produce sufficient distortion for the purposes of this lesson.

368 CHAPTER 14

6. Choose **Filter: Stylize: Drop Shadow**. Set the X and Y Offsets to 9 pt and the Intensity to 15%. Uncheck the **Group Shadows** box and click **OK** to create the drop shadow. (See Figure 14.28.)

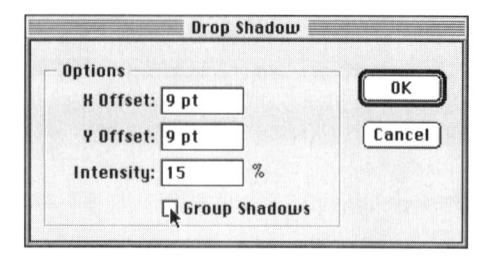

Figure 14.28 These settings in the Drop Shadow dialog will produce a simple and slightly darkened drop shadow of the letterforms. It's most important that the Group Shadows box be unchecked because we will be applying another filter to the letterforms but not to the shadow.

7. Choose **Edit: Select: Inverse** to select the original letters instead of the drop shadow. (See Figure 14.29.)

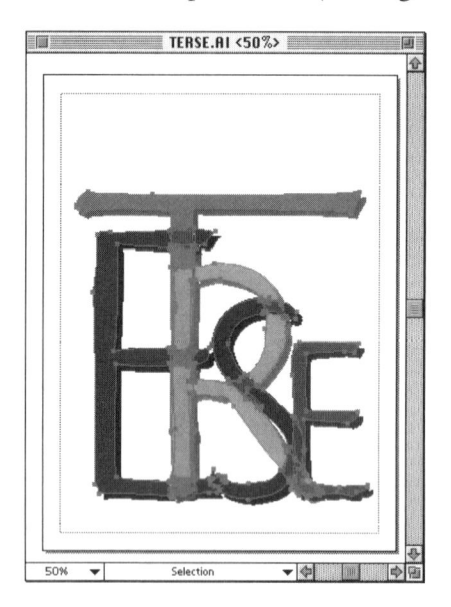

Figure 14.29 The image after creating using several filters, including Adjust Colors, Tweak, and Drop Shadow. Use **Edit: Select: Inverse** to switch the selection from the most recently applied drop shadow back to the original letterforms.

8. Choose **Filter: Ink Pen: Effects**. In the dialog shown in Figure 14.30, choose **Fiberglass light** from the drop-down menu. Change the Color to **Match Object** and set the Density to **85**. All other settings are fine where they are.

Filter Menu and Submenus

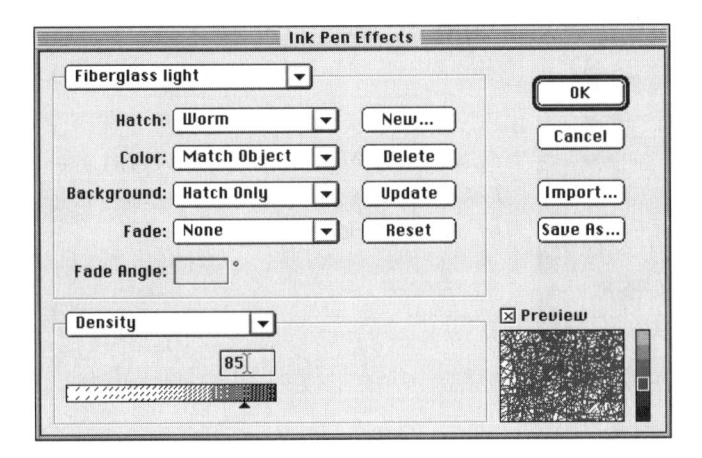

Figure 14.30 There are many fields to set in the Ink Pen Effects dialog, but most of them can be left at the defaults for the Fiberglass light effect we've chosen. Changing the Color to Match Object gives us a colored effect instead of the default black, and increasing the Density gives the effect more texture.

9. Click **OK** to apply the effect. It may take a few seconds for Illustrator to calculate this effect. When done, there is a mass of selected line segments, as shown in Figure 14.31.

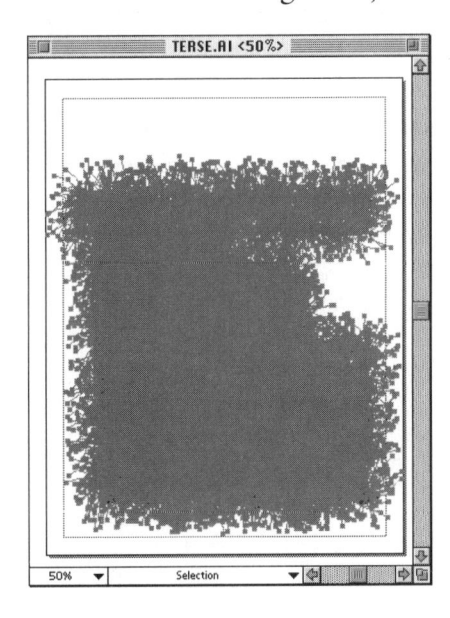

Figure 14.31 The hairy results of applying the Fiberglass light Pen Effect. The letterforms have been turned into a mask that will trim this mass of stroked paths.

370 CHAPTER 14

10. Choose **Edit: Deselect All** (**Shift-Command/Ctrl-a**) to see the effect. (See Figure 14.32.)

Figure 14.32 After everything has been deselected, you can see the effects of the Ink Pen filter on the letterforms.

11. Choose **Edit: Select: Masks** to select the original letterforms again, then choose **Filter: Create: Trim Marks** (as shown in Figure 14.33).

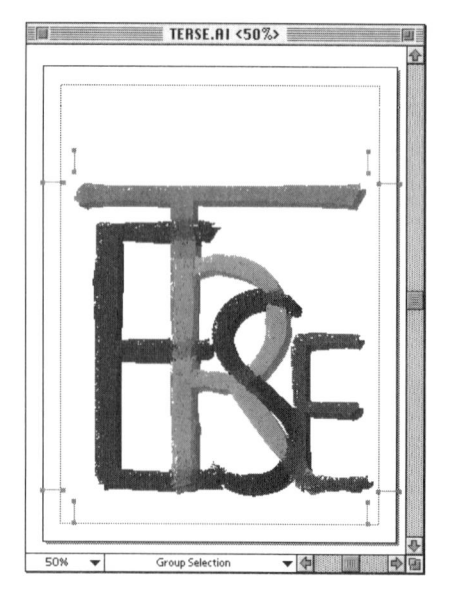

Figure 14.33 Trim marks can be used in this drawing instead of crop marks, because we will need to edit them; something that can't be done with crop marks.

There's a slight problem with the trim marks: they don't match the extent of the drop shadow. You can use the Group Selection or Direct Selection tool to select the bottom pair and right pair of trim marks and adjust them down and out slightly. You can use the arrow keys to adjust them more precisely. I'll leave this as an extracurricular activity because it isn't really part of this Filters chapter.

Save the file if you wish, or you can open a finished version of this file, which I saved as TERSE2.AI on the CD.

15 View and Window Menus

In this chapter...

- Views and windows in general
- Viewing mode—Preview and Artwork
- Viewing magnification—zooming
- Edges and tiles
- Rulers and guides
- Grid commands
- Creating and maintaining views
- Window commands

VIEWS AND WINDOWS IN GENERAL

Views and windows are closely related. The distinction is that Window menu commands affect the actual window on the screen, and View menu commands affect what is displayed within the windows.

The Window menu commands let you show and hide windows and open multiple windows for a single document. All drawing and most palette windows can all be controlled from the Window menu.

The View commands include display mode for drawings, preview or artwork, magnification control, rulers and guides. Guides can be used to align artwork. They behave like paths without attributes, but cannot be printed. There are special commands for creating and manipulating guides. Grids were a feature of the previous Windows version of Illustrator, but they are new to the MacOS with version 7.

None of the commands in either menu affects the printable portion of a drawing, and none are affected by selections.

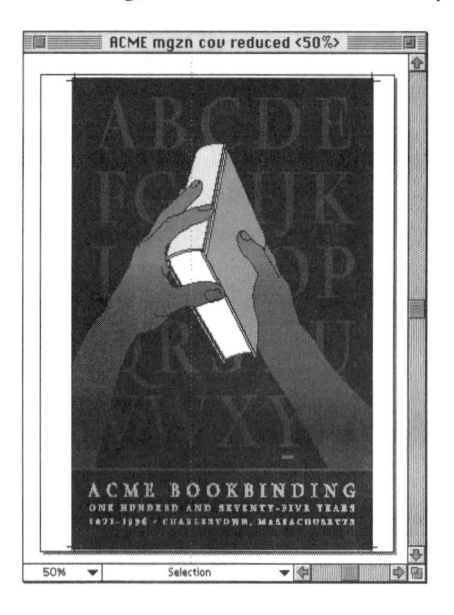

Figure 15.1 A window and a view. The window includes the scroll bars and title with the artwork displayed within. The view is a 50% reduction of the drawing in Preview mode. (The artwork used to illustrate this chapter is by digital artist Lance Hidy.)

VIEWING MODE—PREVIEW AND ARTWORK

In the earliest version of Illustrator, you could only edit artwork as a collection of vectors without attributes. If you wanted to see what your work looked like, you had to switch from Artwork to Preview mode, but then you couldn't edit. Computer processors just weren't powerful enough to support WYSIWYG editing.

Those days are long gone, but a few vestiges remain. While the default viewing mode is full Preview, it's still possible to switch back to Artwork mode and edit the object vectors without the clutter of paint attributes in the way. This can be very useful when editing complex drawings, blends, or masks, where it's difficult to distinguish object boundaries and make accurate selections (see Figure 15.2). It's also possible to change the mode for a selection within a drawing and mix modes simultaneously.

Figure 15.2 The same illustration pictured in Figure 15.1, but in Artwork mode. None of the object attributes, stroke or fill, are visible in this mode, only the anchor points and paths.

To Change Viewing Modes

Choose **View: Artwork** (**Command/Ctrl-y**) to view an entire drawing in Artwork mode (just vectors, no attributes). This command toggles to **View: Preview** when in Artwork mode. The keyboard shortcut also toggles between the two modes.

To Preview a Selection Only

1. Toggle to Artwork mode as described earlier.
2. Make a selection. You must select the vectors because area selection is not available in Artwork mode.

3. Choose **View: Preview Selection** (**Shift-Command/Ctrl-y**) to view just the selection in Preview mode (see Figure 15.3). Changing the selection also changes what is previewed. This command is off by default. When on, a check mark appears next to it in the View menu. The keyboard shortcut can be used to toggle the command on and off.

Figure 15.3 *You can choose to Preview a selection only using menu commands or tools in the Layers palette. The result is an illustration in mixed mode like the one shown here.*

VIEWING MAGNIFICATION—ZOOMING

Illustrator can display artwork at 17 different magnifications from 6.5% to 1600%, with 100% representing the actual print size of the drawing. The Zoom tool (see Chapter 7) can be used to adjust the drawing magnification, or you can use the commands in the View menu or the pop-up menu at the bottom of the active window. There are four Zoom commands, and each has a keyboard shortcut:

- **Zoom In** (**Command/Ctrl +**) increases the magnification by one step.
- **Zoom Out** (**Command/Ctrl -**) decreases the magnification by one step.
- **Fit In Window** (**Command/Ctrl-0**) magnifies or demagnifies the drawing so that the entire image can be displayed within the drawing window.
- **Actual Size** (**Command/Ctr-1**) displays the drawing at 100% magnification.

Figure 15.4 The same illustration at 300% magnification. We could magnify all the way up to 1600%, but this is large enough to see all the details for this drawing.

EDGES AND TILES

When you make a selection, Illustrator highlights the edges and anchor points. This can interfere with the way the image looks as you edit. **View: Hide Edges** (**Command/Ctrl-h**) hides this selection highlight so that you can edit without visual interference. The problem is that you have to remember what's selected, because there's no visual feedback. Hide Edges toggles between on and off. A small check mark appears next to the command when it is on.

Illustrator allows you to create multiple-page documents by tiling artwork (see Chapter 17). By default, Illustrator displays guides to indicate page tiles and printable borders for single-page documents. To turn off the tile and border guides, choose **View: Hide Page Tiling**. This commands toggles to Show Page Tiling.

RULERS AND GUIDES

By default, Illustrator's rulers are turned off. When turned on, ruler scales are displayed across the top and left of the drawing window. As you pan or zoom the drawing, the rulers adjust accordingly. Rulers are displayed in the default units as set in the Units and Undo Preferences dialog box (see Chapter 19). The default is picas.

Guides can be used to align objects within the drawing, but they are not printable. There are two kinds of guides: ruler guides, which are dragged from the rulers, and object guides, which are created using commands. Guides appear as gray dotted lines (which can be changed in the Guides and Grids Preferences dialog box) and are usually left locked in place. They can be unlocked and moved, modified, deleted, or converted into graphic objects.

> **NOTE** Functionally, once a guide is created, it makes no difference whether it was a ruler or object guide.

To Show Rulers

Choose **View: Show Rulers** (**Command/Ctrl-r**). Illustrator displays rulers across the top and left edges of the window. The zero point is at the bottom-left corner of the page border.

To Reset the Ruler Zero Point

1. Put the cursor in the upper corner of the ruler where there are no measurement markings.
2. Click and drag to the point in the drawing where you want the zero measurement to be. You can snap to an object if you wish.
3. Release the mouse button and the zero point is adjusted accordingly.

To Create Ruler Guides

1. If they aren't already visible, choose **View: Show Rulers** (**Command/Ctrl-r**).
2. Put the cursor inside the ruler.
3. To create a vertical guide, click and drag from the vertical ruler (see Figure 15.5). To create a horizontal guide, click and drag from the horizontal ruler.

> **NOTE** Hold down the **Option/Alt** key to toggle between a vertical or horizontal guide while dragging.

4. Release the mouse button and a guide is left behind.

Figure 15.5 This guide is being dragged from the vertical ruler at the left edge of the drawing window.

To Create Object Guides

1. Select the objects you want to convert to guides.
2. Choose **View: Make Guides** (**Command/Ctrl-5**). The selected paths are converted into guides.

To Manipulate Guides

There are four Guide commands in the View menu. The first two affect all guides, and the last two work only with selections:

- **Hide/Show**—Choose **View: Hide** (**Command/Ctrl-;**) to make all guides invisible. The command toggles to Show, which makes all guides visible again.
- **Lock**—Choose **View: Lock** (**Shift-Command/Ctrl-;**) to lock all guides, which is the default. A check mark is displayed next to the command when it is on. It toggles to off, which unlocks all guides and makes them selectable. Once selected, guides can be moved around using any of the selection tools.

> **NOTE:** It's possible to lock a single guide by unlocking all guides from the View menu, selecting the guides, and choosing **Object: Lock**. The **View: Lock** command no longer affects a guide locked from the Object menu, which can only be unlocked by choosing **Object: Unlock All**.

- **Make**—As described earlier, choose **View: Make** (**Command/Ctrl-5**) to convert a selection into a guide.
- **Release**—Choose **View: Revert** (**Shift-Command/Ctrl-5**) to turn a selected guide into an object. The object takes on the currently set paint attributes. Guides must first be unlocked and then selected for this command to be available.

> **NOTE:** Guides exist on layers. In other words, when you define a guide, it is created as the bottom object on the currently active layer. It's sometimes convenient to create a layer for guides and keep all guides locked on this layer. Doing so can simplify guide maintenance.

GRID COMMANDS

Illustrator 7 has implemented a very simple grid capability that can be used to turn on a grid of lines either under or on top of all drawing layers. The grid settings can be adjusted in the Guides and Grid Preference dialog (see Chapter 19). The View menu includes the only two grid commands:

- **Show/Hide Grid**—The default view hides the grid, which must be turned on by choosing **View: Show Grid** (**Command/Ctrl-"**) This command then toggles to Hide Grid, which can be chosen to turn the grid off again.
- **Snap to Grid**—Choose **View: Snap to Grid** (**Shift-Command/Ctrl-"**) to snap to the grid as you move or draw objects. A check mark appears next to the command when it is on. It toggles between on and off. The grid need not be visible to turn Snap to Grid on.

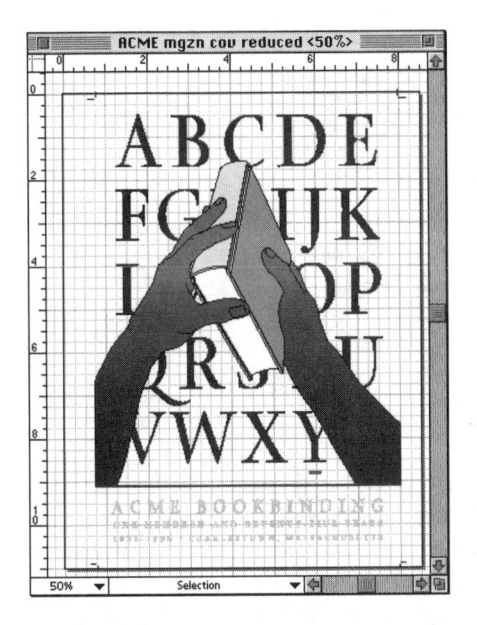

Figure 15.6 With the grid turned on, it's easy to align objects by dragging them to grid lines. The grid lines serve only as an alignment aid and are not part of the artwork. They do not print.

CREATING AND MAINTAINING VIEWS

It's possible to save preset views and recall them. This can be very useful when you are working on large complex drawings with many areas of detail that you'd like to focus on and return to. You can create as many views as needed for the document.

To Name a View

1. Set the view, which includes the zoom factor and position of the drawing within the window.
2. Choose **View: New View**.
3. Name the view and click **OK**.

The new view is saved with the document and is added to the bottom of the View menu, where it can be selected at any time. The views are listed in the order in which they were created and can be selected using **Shift-Option/Alt-Command/Ctrl-#**, in which # represents the view's position in the view stack. (Any views past 9 cannot be selected this way.)

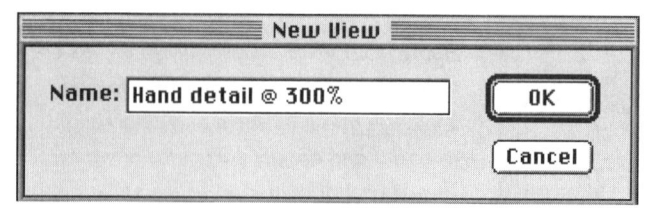

Figure 15.7 The New View dialog allows you to name and save specific views so that you can return to them for further editing or future changes.

To Edit Views

1. Choose **View: Edit Views** to open the Edit Views dialog, which lists all the views for the document (see Figure 15.8). You can change view names or delete views, but you can't reorder the list or change the shortcut keys.
2. Select a view by clicking on its name in the list. You can **Shift**-click to select a range of names or **Command/Ctrl**-click to make a discontinuous selection.
3. If you've selected a single view, you can edit the name in the edit box.
4. Click the **Delete** button to delete selected views.
5. Click **OK** when you're finished.

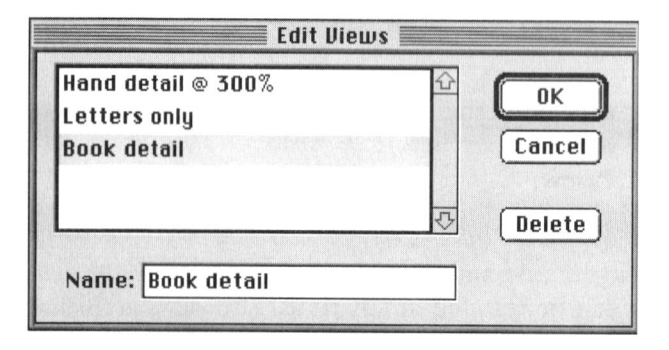

Figure 15.8 Although it's called the Edit Views dialog, you can't really edit views—only their names. You can also delete saved views using this dialog, which in no way affects the drawing itself.

WINDOW MENU COMMANDS

The Window menu is very simple. At the top is the New Window command, which we will discuss momentarily. At the bottom is a list of all open document windows. You can make a document window active by clicking on its name in the Window menu. In between are all the Show/Hide palette window commands.

When a palette window is displayed, the corresponding Window command changes to Hide and toggles to Show if the palette window is not visible.

To Open Multiple Windows for a Single Document

Choose **Window: New Window**. This opens a second window for the currently active document and adds a new listing to the bottom of the Window menu.

If you have opened multiple windows for a single document, one can be in Preview mode and the other in Artwork mode. You can also view different parts of large documents at the same time or view the document at two different magnifications simultaneously.

> **NOTE** Multiple views and multiple windows differ in that the first changes the view within a single window, while the second makes multiple views available simultaneously by displaying a single document in multiple windows.

This chapter has no lesson, but you are welcome to try out the various commands and techniques covered using some of the documents from previous lessons.

Section V

Illustrator Environment

In this section…

- Illustrator in its broader context
- Chapter 16: Files
- Chapter 17: Printing
- Chapter 18: Web and Multimedia
- Chapter 19: Performance, Preferences, and Help

ILLUSTRATOR IN ITS BROADER CONTEXT

To be good citizens of the computer world, applications must deal with file systems, printing issues, and the Web. Illustrator 7 has benefited from Adobe's broad product and platform approach, and it is able to read and write files in more formats than before. It is also less likely to cause perplexing printing problems, and it has some strong Web production capabilities.

We'll examine these real-world capabilities in the context of menu commands and design issues. There are a number of File menu commands, but there is only one Print command (although there are a couple of setup commands). And there's really no way to discuss Illustrator's Web and multimedia features in terms of commands. These are issue oriented.

This section, and the book, finishes with a look at performance issues and a summary of Illustrator's preference settings. Only Chapter 18, Web and Multimedia, includes a brief lesson. The other chapters await your personal experimentation.

16 Files and File Commands

In this chapter…

- Simple file commands
- Importing files and artwork
- Exporting to other formats
- Interactive import and export
- Document info

Simple File Commands

This is where we'll deal with the straightforward File menu commands. In the way it handles files, Illustrator is no different from other applications, though perhaps it has a few extra options.

To Open a New Blank Drawing Window

1. Launch Illustrator from its icon or name without opening a document. (When you launch the program by opening a previously saved Illustrator document, the document opens in Illustrator and not a new blank drawing window.)
2. Choose **File: New** (**Command/Ctrl-n**) to open a new blank drawing window at any time while Illustrator is running. Whenever you open a new blank drawing window, Illustrator uses the file named **Adobe Illustrator Startup** (Macintosh) or **Startup.ai** (Windows) in the **Plug-ins** folder as a template to determine the window size, position, and magnification, as well as the settings for the Swatches palette, Document Setup, Page Setup, and graph styles (see Chapter 19).

NOTE: You can change this default startup document by changing all the settings you want to have part of the default and then using **File: Save As** to overwrite the file **Adobe Illustrator Startup** (MacOS) or **Startup.ai** (Windows) in the Illustrator **Plug-ins** folder.

To Open an Existing Illustrator Document

You can open an Illustrator document from the MacOS or Windows desktops using any of several methods supported by your operating system. Read your operating system manual if you're not sure how to do this.

1. Choose **File: Open** (**Command/Ctrl-o**) to open the standard file dialog. Click on the file to open it from the list in the dialog. There are two options:

    Show Preview—Check this box to show a thumbnail preview of the highlighted file in the dialog. This option is not be available on Macs if the QuickTime extension is not loaded.

Files and File Commands 389

Show All Files—This is a check box in MacOS and a pop-up menu in Windows. By default, MacOS displays files of all the formats Illustrator recognizes (and there are many). Check the box to display all files, regardless of type. The Windows pop-up lets you choose a single file type or all file types for display in the dialog.

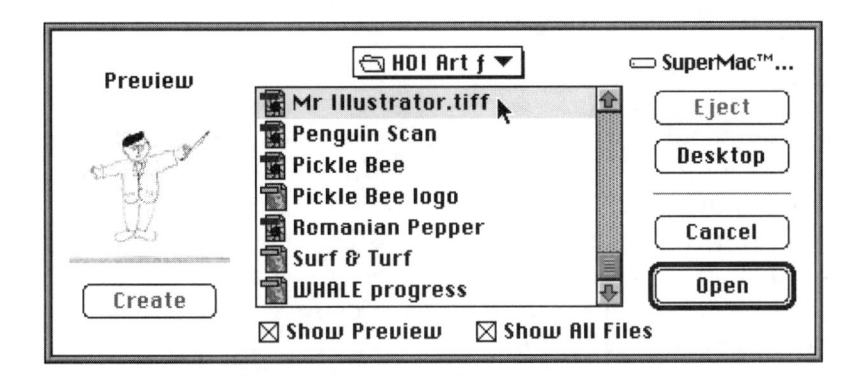

Figure 16.1 The Open dialog is highly operating system-specific in appearance, but the function is the same. The Show Preview and Show All Files check boxes let you change the display within the dialog.

NOTE
The current list of all file types supported by Illustrator is included in the program Read Me file in the Illustrator folder.

2. Click the **Open** button to load the file into Illustrator.

To Close an Open File Window

There are two ways to close an open file window:

- Choose **File: Close** (**Command/Ctrl-w**) or
- Click on the Close box in the corner of the window's title bar.

In either case, Illustrator closes the active window. If you have multiple open windows for a single document, the document will still be open. If you have made changes to the file since last saving it, an alert box asks if you want to save changes, close without saving changes, or cancel and leave the window open.

NOTE: Hold down the **Option/Alt** key while choosing **File: Close** to close all open windows with a single click.

To Save Illustrator Drawings

There are three save commands:

- Save (**Command/Ctrl-s**)—Saves the current drawing using the same name, location, and file type. There is no dialog. This command is not available for drawings that have not yet been saved to disk.
- Save As (**Shift-Command/Ctrl-s**)—Brings up the Save dialog, which allows you to name the file, choose the location for the file, and pick a file format (PDF, Illustrator, or EPS) from the Format drop-down menu (see Figure 16.2).
- Save a Copy (**Option/Alt-Command/Ctrl-s**)—Similar to the Save As command, except that it appends the word *copy* to the file name (although you can change this name to anything you like), and the original file version remains active.

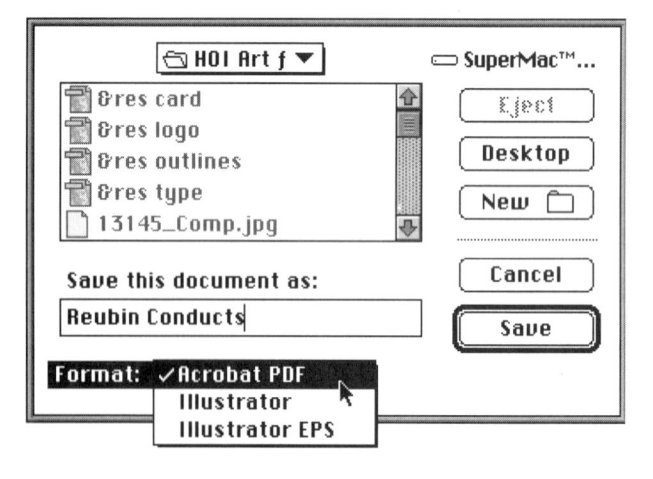

Figure 16.2 The Save dialog lets you select one of three "native formats" for your artwork. For other formats, you need to use the **File: Export** command.

To Discard Changes without Saving—Revert

Choose **File: Revert**. Any changes made to the document are discarded and the last saved version is restored.

To Place Files into Open Documents

1. Choose **File: Place** to open the standard File dialog.
2. Locate and select a file to be placed from the list. The Place File dialog (shown in Figure 16.3) is identical to the Open File dialog, with one additional choice:
   Link—This check box controls one of the important new features of Illustrator 7. When unchecked, Illustrator will embed the placed file, which can make the file size very large. When it is checked, a link between the placed document and the current drawing is created, which saves space.
3. Click **Place** to open the file and place it into the current drawing window.

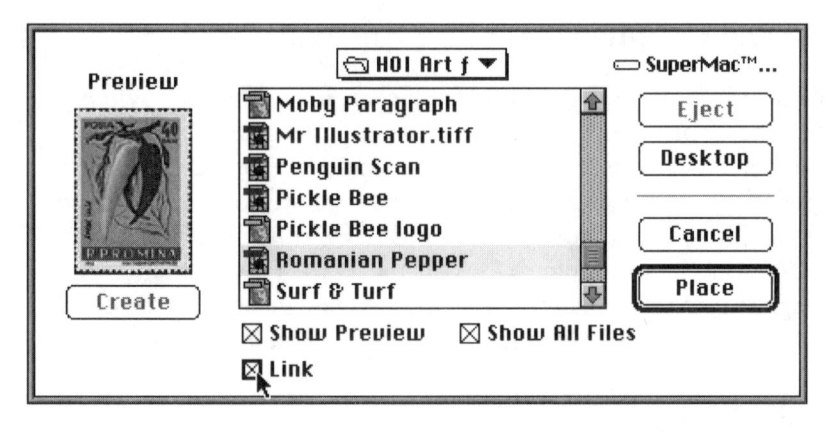

Figure 16.3 The Place dialog is pretty much like any open dialog, but with the addition of a Link check box that lets you link (checked) or embed (unchecked) images with artwork.

IMPORTING FILES AND ARTWORK

Illustrator doesn't use the term *importing*. There is no import command per se. Instead, you can *open* files directly from various formats (as described earlier), you can *place* artwork or text inside an already open Illustrator drawing, or you can *paste* data from the Clipboard.

Illustrator 7 has a file linking capability so you don't need to embed all placed images. This has the advantage of keeping Illustrator file sizes smaller, and the original placed file can be edited and will be updated automatically the next time the file is opened in Illustrator. This feature is very convenient.

About Placing Text

You can import text using the Place command. If there is no active selection, Illustrator creates a text container in the middle of the drawing when it places the text. If you click with the Text tool (t) before placing text, text is placed as *point text* that converts word wraps into carriage returns.

Most text styles are retained if the imported text is in one of Illustrator's supported file formats. (The file won't even show up in the dialog if it is not a supported file format, or it will be imported as a graphic file if you check the **Show All** check box in the Place File dialog.)

About Placing Graphics

Illustrator 7 can be used to open or place files in many formats. When you place a file instead of opening it, it becomes a part of the currently open drawing. Vector artwork is converted to Illustrator paths, and raster artwork is opened or placed as bitmaps. You can use any of the bitmap-oriented filters or Illustrator's transform commands with bitmap images.

If you deselect the **Link** check box in the Place File dialog to embed an EPS image, the discrete elements of the image can be edited individually in Illustrator. Linked EPS images are treated as single objects.

About Linked Files

When you link a placed file instead of embedding it, Illustrator reads the source file every time you open the destination file. This has the advantage of allowing you to edit the source file without relinking or updating the destination. However, if you move the file, the link is lost and must be updated.

You can change a linked file into an embedded file when you choose **Save As** for a drawing with linked elements. In the Illustrator Format dialog, click on the **Include Placed Files** option check box. Click **OK** and the link will be dropped and the file embedded.

Exporting to Other Formats

Illustrator has both a group of Save commands and an Export command. The Save commands allow you to save in Illustrator's native formats, PDF, Illustrator, and EPS. To save in any of Illustrator's other supported formats, you must use the Export command.

To Export Drawings in Non-Native Illustrator Formats

1. Choose **File: Export** to open the Export File dialog. This dialog is similar to all other file dialogs, with the addition of a Format drop-down menu.
2. Choose one of more than a dozen export formats from the Format (MacOS) or Save as Type (Windows) drop-down menu.
3. Name the file and choose a location, then click **Save** to export the file. Illustrator can save files for export to many different programs by converting artwork to variously formatted bitmaps and even several text formats.

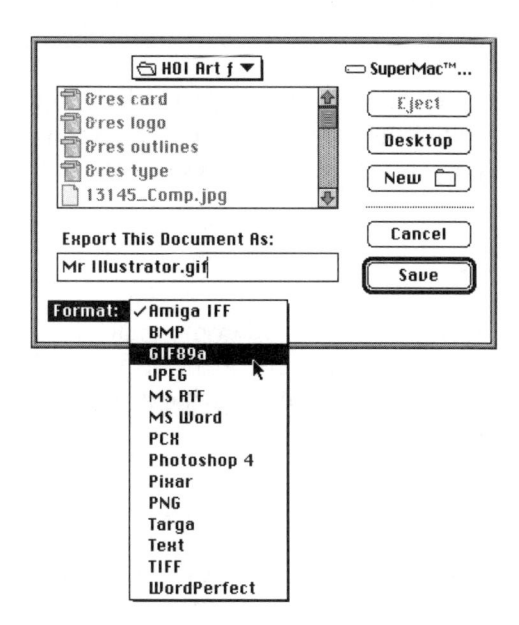

Figure 16.4 Another typical-looking Save dialog, this one has a substantial drop-down list of formats, because it is the Export dialog.

I don't think Illustrator needs both Save and Export commands, but it's hard to change old habits. The various available formats are described in the Illustrator *User Guide*. However, the Export command is one of Illustrator's main links to the World Wide Web. We will discuss Web-specific formats in Chapter 18.

> **NOTE** When exporting files to other formats, it's usually a good idea to save the file in one of Illustrator's native formats, PDF, Illustrator, or EPS, as well.

A Few Words about EPS Files

While some earlier Illustrator file formats received wide support from other applications, such is not the case with current formats. Adobe's application family may understand the various native formats, but to import Illustrator artwork into most other applications, it's best to use the Illustrator EPS format. Illustrator documents saved this way remain Illustrator documents, but they can require considerably more disk space.

EPS (Encapsulated PostScript) format retains a faithful representation of the image, complete with color and color-mode information. All desktop publishing and many other applications can place EPS images, and the images will print correctly. EPS images include a special preview, PICT for MacOS and TIFF for Windows. Not all applications can use the preview image, but the image will print correctly, even if the preview does not display.

INTERACTIVE IMPORT AND EXPORT

It's possible to move data between drawing windows and even applications without stopping to use the file system. The Clipboard in both MacOS' and Windows' implementation of so-called drag and drop make it possible to move data around almost instantaneously.

The Clipboard

Both MacOS and Windows include a data buffer known as the Clipboard. Whenever you use the Cut or Copy commands in an application, the data is copied to this system buffer. The Clear command deletes the selection without copying it to the Clipboard. (The **Delete/Backspace** key also acts as a Clear command.) To access this data, use the Paste command to copy the Clipboard data into your application.

This capability works within applications as well as across applications. You can Cut or Copy text from a word processor, switch to Illustrator, click in a drawing with the Text tool, and paste the text from Clipboard to artwork. The clipboard will retain a certain amount of text formatting, as well. You can use the same technique (minus the Text tool) to copy an image or path from Photoshop to Illustrator.

Drag and Drop

Drag-and-drop capability has been a part of the MacOS since System 7, and it is also built into Windows95. It allows you to use the mouse to drag a selection out of one application and drop it into an open window of another application. This is the fastest and most interactive way to copy data between open applications.

While the Clipboard has almost universal support, some applications still do not support drag and drop. All Adobe applications are drag-and-drop capable.

The only trick to drag-and-drop copying is to be sure that both the source and destination windows are visible on your computer screen.

To Drag out of Illustrator and Drop Elsewhere

1. Make sure that both the Illustrator document and destination windows are open. The Illustrator drawing window must be the active window.
2. Choose any selection tool.
3. Click on an object or selection and drag from the Illustrator window to the destination window.
4. Release the mouse button and the selection is copied. The Illustrator window remains active.

To Drag into Illustrator from other Applications

1. Make sure that both the Illustrator document and source window are open. The source document must be the active window.
2. Use any tool to make a selection within the source application. For instance, if you are dragging out of Photoshop, you need to use one of its selection tools.

3. Drag the selection from the source document to the open Illustrator document (see Figure 16.5).
4. Release the mouse button. Hold down the **Shift** key before releasing the mouse button to center the copied object in the Illustrator window. (The **Shift** centering shortcut works in all Adobe applications.)

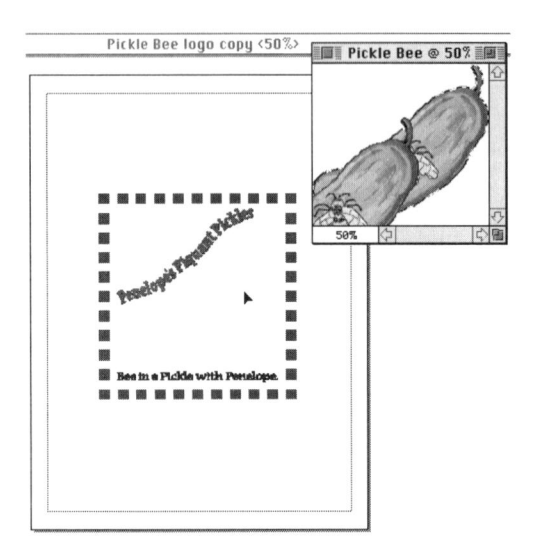

Figure 16.5 Dragging a selection in Photoshop into an Illustrator image in the background. Releasing the mouse button copies the selection and leaves the source window active.

DOCUMENT/OBJECT INFO WINDOW

Illustrator keeps track of all the details of the drawing and each object within it. You can view this information or print it out using the **File: Document Info** and **File: Selection Info** commands. Document Info lists general document information, including dimensions, number and type of objects, fonts, colors, and the status of various document-related options. If there is an active selection in the drawing, the Document Info command is replaced by the Selection Info command. The same information is available, but it is specific to the selection. This information can be saved as a file, which is especially useful for sending drawings to a service bureau or for press checks.

To View and Save Document/Selection Info

1. Deselect everything for Document Info, or make a selection for Selection Info.
2. Choose **File: Document/Selection Info** to open the Info dialog.

3. This dialog includes a drop-down menu and a scrolling window that lists the information (see Figure 16.6). Use the drop-down menu choices to view different information. The choices are Document (Document Info only), Objects, Spot Colors, Patterns, Gradients, Fonts, Linked Images, Embedded Images, and Font Details.
4. Choose **Save** to write out all the document/object information as a text file.
5. Click **Done** to dismiss the dialog.

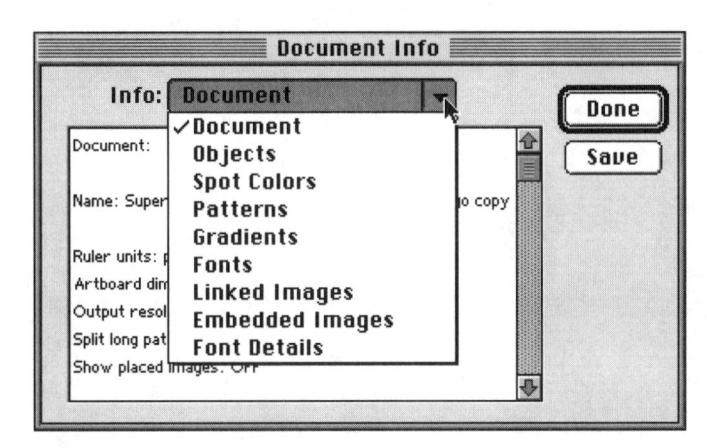

Figure 16.6 The list of info choices from the drop-down menu within the Document Info dialog. The list is the same, minus the Document choice, if there is an active selection in the artwork.

17 Printing

In this chapter...

- Printing terminology
- Print preparation
- Print command
- Color separations
- Improving print performance

PRINTING TERMINOLOGY

It would be nice if printing were a simple matter of choosing the Print command and having exactly what you see on the screen come out of the printer. That doesn't happen for a number of reasons, but fundamentally it's because toner, ink, and pigments are not capable of accurately reproducing the visible spectrum of light.

With the limitations of electronic and mechanical reproduction in mind, here are some printing matters to consider when creating artwork.

> **NOTE** Often, you will create artwork that is not meant to be printed because the delivery medium is the computer screen. The information in this chapter does not apply to such work. Graphics for the Web and other multimedia applications are discussed in Chapter 18.

- **Resolution**—Printer resolution is measured two ways. Desktop printer resolution is measured in dots per inch (dpi). The resolution of standard laser printers is 300 dpi, which is sufficient for office correspondence but shows noticeable "stair stepping" when used for graphics. Imagesetters, most often used for producing high-quality film for offset reproduction, typically have a resolution of 2,540 dpi. When reproducing shaded graphics instead of line art, resolution is measured in lines per inch (lpi). This refers to the screen frequency used to produce halftones, discussed later in the chapter.
- **Proofing**—The imperfections of printers are a given, so it's necessary to proof graphic work before sending it to a commercial print shop. Many problems can be caught just by proofing work on an office printer. Even color work can be proofed this way, although it helps to have a color printer of some kind. You won't be able to check the accuracy of colors at the office, but you'll get a reasonable approximation of the finished product.
- **Separations**—Color printing is particularly problematic. You can use a desktop inkjet printer to achieve acceptable results for business graphics. But if you need accurate, "realistic" color you usually need color separations. Most printing presses use the four process-color inks—cyan, magenta, yellow, and black (CMYK)—to produce high-quality color fidelity. This requires four printing plates, one for each

ink color. The image is "separated" to produce the four color plates, which are then overlaid to create a "full color" printout.
- **Overprint**—When inks are printed on top of each other, they produce a transparent blended effect. This is sometimes desirable, but it is not the way Illustrator shows images on screen, where drawing one fill on top of another "knocks out" the background. You can specifically set colors to be overprinted, or you can achieve a similar effect by using the Pathfinder commands.
- **Trapping**—The color separation process is capable of reproducing color very accurately, but if the individual plates do not line up exactly, there can be white gaps or noticeable overprinted borders where colors should abut. The process of adjusting for this inevitable printing problem is called *trapping*, and it provides a way to set overlaps and compensate for misalignment.
- **Halftones**—While there are ways to print true photographic quality images, most printers use dots of ink to produce the illusion of continuous tones. Varying the size and density of dots on the printed page causes the eye to see smooth color gradations. In its simplest form, a grayscale halftone can be produced using only black ink. Shades of gray are the result of varying dot density. In four-color process printing, mixing the densities of four colors of dots produces a reasonable approximation of the visible spectrum.
- **Screen Frequency**—The quality of halftone reproduction is dependent on dot density or screen frequency. The halftone screen is measured in lines per inch (lpi). For newspaper graphics, where printing speed is more important than quality, 85 lpi is the standard. For most color magazines, which demand good quality, but not extreme accuracy, 133 lpi is the standard. Screen frequencies of 150 lpi and above are used when highest quality is demanded, while frequencies as low as 65 lpi are commonly used for advertising circulars.

PRINT PREPARATION

At any time while you are working with a document, you can change the document settings that determine its basic printing characteristics. This is important, because it allows you to change the page size, output resolution, and the way Illustrator prints multiple-page documents.

To Set up Documents for Printing

1. Choose **File: Document Setup (Shift-Command/Ctrl-p)** to open the Document Setup dialog shown in Figure 17.1. This dialog shows the current settings for the active document and can be changed at any time. The settings are saved with the document.

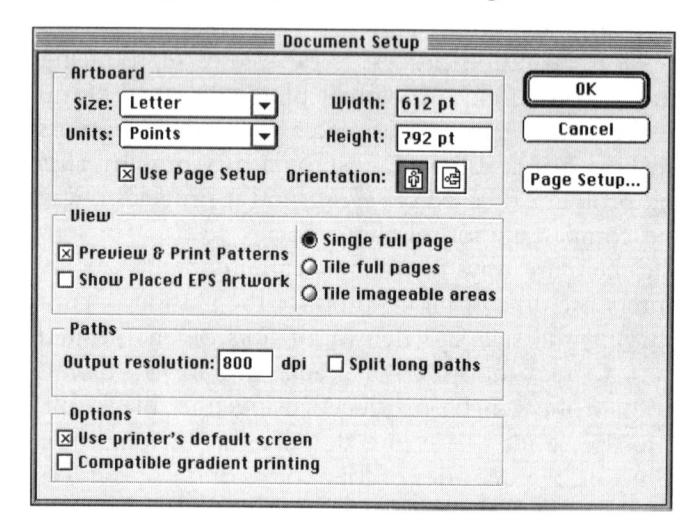

Figure 17.1 The File: Document Setup dialog box includes many options that affect the way your artwork will be displayed and printed.

2. Set the Artboard options. The Artboard defines the printable region of the drawing. The U.S. default size is 8.5" × 11", but it can be set to any size up to Illustrator's maximum work area of 120" × 120".

   Size—Choose one of the standard paper sizes from the Size drop-down menu, or choose **Custom** and specify a Width and Height for the Artboard.
   Units—Choose one of Illustrator's supported dimensional units from the Units drop-down menu. The default is points. This does not affect the size of the Artboard but determines the units used in displaying rulers and in the various palettes and dialogs used with the document.
   Width and Height—The dimensions of the Artboard are shown in the chosen units. These fields can be edited to create a custom Artboard size.
   Use Page/Print Setup—Check this box to use the MacOS Page Setup dialog, or Windows Print Setup dialog to determine the

Printing 403

Artboard size and orientation. You can click the **Page/Print Setup** button to open the dialog and change the settings.
Orientation—Click either the vertical or horizontal button to set the page orientation. Vertical is the default.

3. Set the View options. There are two check boxes and a set of three radio buttons.

    Preview and Print Patterns—Patterns can require large amounts of RAM and processing power when displayed or printed. You can turn off patterns by deselecting this box. This can be useful when proofing some artwork, but you have to remember to reselect the option for final printing.
    Show Placed EPS Artwork—Placed EPS artwork can make large processing demands when previewed on screen, which can make it difficult to edit other work. Deselect this box to turn off EPS preview and show only a bounding box for the placed image.
    Tiling—There are three radio buttons that let you set the way Illustrator views and prints multiple-page images. The default is Single full page, which limits artwork to a single printable page. Illustrator tiles artwork if you choose either of the other two radio buttons. Choose **Tile full pages** to use the Artboard dimensions as the tile size. Choose **Tile imageable area** to use the chosen printer's imageable area (Artboard dimensions minus the unprintable border dimension). This will change if you change printers.

4. Set the Paths options. This includes a specification field and check box.

    Output resolution—PostScript uses the output resolution setting to calculate curves. A higher resolution produces more accurate curves, but it requires additional processing that can cause PostScript errors on some output devices. The Illustrator User Guide recommends an optimum setting of 800 dpi and implies that you only need to change this setting if printing is slow or impossible.
    Split long paths—Check this box to have Illustrator turn long path segments into two or more shorter segments. This does not affect the way the drawing looks, but it can avoid PostScript errors when printing.

5. Two additional check box options can be set:

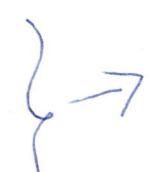

Use Printer's default screen—It's possible to make an EPSF Riders file to create a custom printing screen. This esoteric capability is described in detail on page 308 of the User Guide. Leave this box checked to use the default screen of the printer you are using.
Compatible gradient printing—Leave this box unchecked unless you are printing to a PostScript Level I imagesetter that has trouble printing gradients and your file contains gradients.

6. Click **OK** to save the settings for the current document.

PRINT COMMAND

Printing Illustrator documents, as well as any other documents, is handled by your operating system. When you choose **File: Print** (**Command/Ctrl-p**), the dialog that opens (see Figure 17.2) is operating system–specific. If you don't know how to use this dialog, read the users manual that came with your computer.

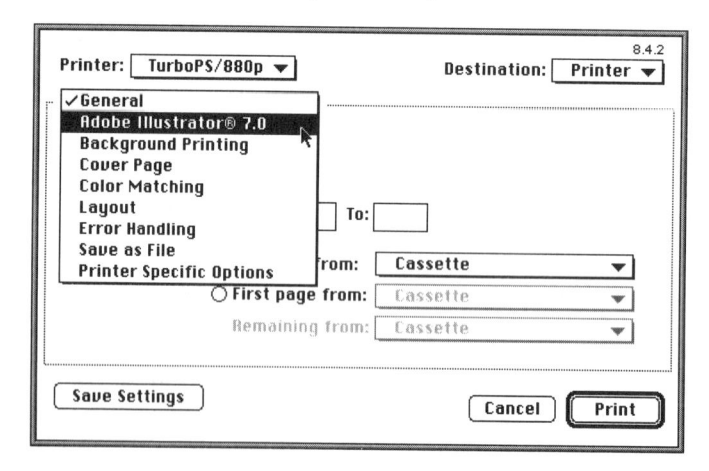

Figure 17.2 *The Print dialog is highly operating system–specific. This one for MacOS 7.6.1 includes a drop-down menu with an Illustrator-specific option.*

We'll discuss some Illustrator-specific options here, but they aren't always in the same place in the Print dialog. Usually you'll find all options in the Print dialog. Newer MacOS printer drivers have numerous additional options, and you must choose Illustrator from the drop-down box at the top of the dialog to bring up the three drop-down menus:

Output—Choose **Composite** to print all colors together or **Separate** to make color separations directly from Illustrator. The default is Composite.

PostScript—Choose **Level 1** or **Level 2**, depending on your PostScript output device. The default is Level 2, which will work in most cases, even if you don't have a PostScript Level 2 printer.

Data—Choose **Binary** (the default) or **ASCII**. This refers to the encoding used to send data to the printer. ASCII creates larger files that take longer to download, but this option can be used to avoid some PostScript errors with certain printers.

There are also two Illustrator-specific check boxes and a button (see Figure 17.3):

Selection Only—Click on this box to print the current selection rather than the entire document. The default is unchecked.

Force Fonts to Download—Check this box to download all fonts for the document. The default is unchecked, which won't download fonts that are resident in the printer.

Separation Setup—Click this button as a shortcut to the Separations dialog. You can also open the dialog directly from the File menu, as discussed below.

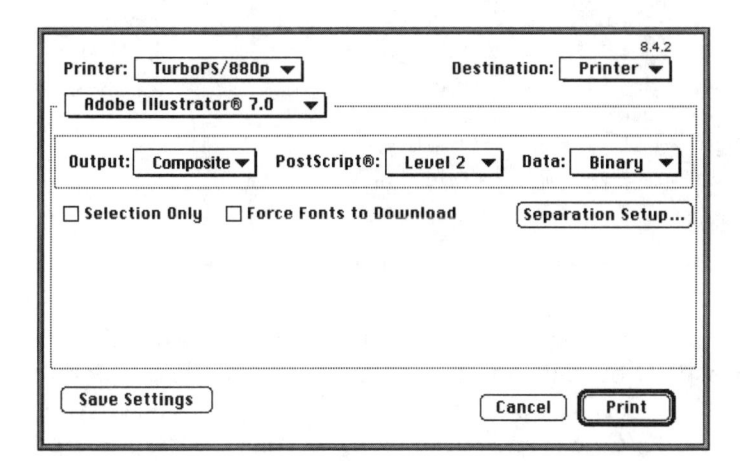

Figure 17.3 The Illustrator-specific print dialog options for MacOS 7.6.1 includes a shortcut button that takes you directly to the Separation Setup dialog.

COLOR SEPARATIONS

The Illustrator *User Guide* contains an excellent chapter on producing color output that includes a discussion of color calibration and color separations. Rather than restate this information, I recommend that you read the manual. We'll deal with the Color Separation dialog specifically.

TO PRINT COLOR SEPARATIONS

1. Choose **File: Separation Setup** (**Option/Alt-Command/Ctrl-p**) to open the Separations dialog. You can also open this dialog by clicking on the Separation Setup button in the Print dialog.

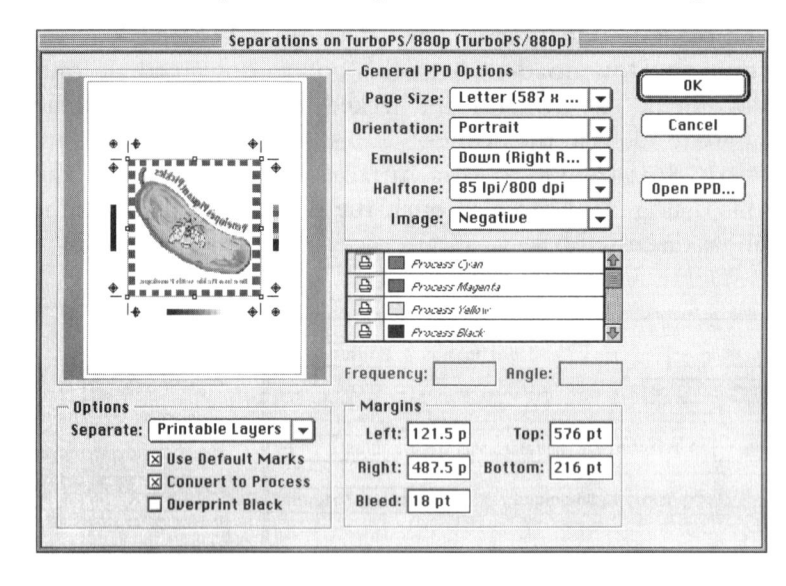

Figure 17.4 The Separation Setup dialog will vary somewhat depending on the PPD you choose.

2. If you haven't chosen one before, or if the setting has changed, click on the **Open PPD** button. This brings up a standard file dialog that lets you select the correct PostScript Printer Description file for your printer. Click **OK/Open**, and the options for that printer are used to fill the Separations dialog.
3. A preview of the composite view of the image is displayed along with numerous options.

- You can choose to separate printable layers, visible layers, or all layers.
- You can select Default Marks, Convert to Process colors, or Overprint Black ink.
- The General PPD Options let you set the page size, page orientation, emulsion side, halftone screen frequency, and image reversal, all from drop-down menus.
- By highlighting colors in the scrolling list, you can specify the Frequency and Angle for each.
- You can also specify custom margins and add a bleed to the separations.

4. Click **OK** to update the settings for the file.
5. Choose **File: Print** (**Command/Ctrl-p**) to open the Print dialog. From the Output drop-down menu, choose Separate.
6. Click **OK/Print** to print the separations as specified.

IMPROVING PRINT PERFORMANCE

If you know what kinds of things are likely to cause printing problems, you can improve the performance of your printer and streamline your workflow. Obviously, the more complex your drawing, the longer it will take to print. You can judge some aspects of complexity using the **File: Document/Selection Info** dialog (see Chapter 16).

Many masks or compound objects can cause printing problems. Try to eliminate these using Illustrator's Pathfinder tools where possible.

Select **Edit: Select: Stray Points** (see Chapter 12) to delete any obviously unnecessary anchor points.

To assure smooth gradients and proper resolutions, use the tables on pages 302 and 303 of the Illustrator *User Guide* to calculate line screens and gradient steps and lengths.

Use the **Split Long Paths** option in the Document Setup dialog, described earlier, to decrease object complexity, which can cause PostScript errors in low memory situations.

If you need to, decrease the output resolution of the document or individual objects as described earlier using the Document Setup dialog and as described in Chapter 10 using the Attributes palette.

As a general rule, you should try to eliminate extra anchor points. Careful use of anchor points to draw curved segments is the surest way to improve not only printing but program efficiency.

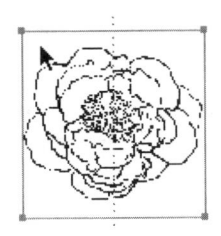

18 The Web and Multimedia

In this chapter...

- The screen as an output device
- Working with screen resolution
- Color: palettes, swatches, and modes
- File formats: GIF, JPEG, and PNG
- URLs and browsers
- Lesson 18: Brief Imagemap Lesson

The Screen As an Output Device

This chapter is more of an advice column than a compendium of Illustrator tools and commands. It brings together information from several other chapters and adds a multimedia and Web flavor to it.

What makes multimedia and Web graphics different from other Illustrator artwork is that the destination is the same as the source: created on the screen for distribution on other computer screens. This has the advantage of being a WYSIWYG environment, which we tend to forget. We get used to forgiving the jagged or rough appearance of on-screen graphics because we know that they will look fine when printed. There is no such forgiveness when producing multimedia or Web graphics.

Producing graphics for screen distribution takes some getting used to. We have to relearn how to look at our work. There are also some basic limitations and a few Illustrator-specific commands to know about.

Working With Screen Resolution

Not all the work you do in Illustrator will be printed. Illustrator is an excellent resource for multimedia developers, especially Web designers, where the final output is on the computer screen. Designing for screen viewing has significant limitations in terms of resolution, size, and color. The Web has additional limitations of bandwidth and font usage. In the best of all possible worlds, every computer will have a 21-inch, 24-bit color monitor and a direct T1 link to the Internet. Reality is somewhat different.

There are multimedia presentations that aren't distributed widely, and with these you can control the display environment. But in most cases your graphics need to be designed for the least common denominator: a monitor resolution of 640 × 480 or 832 × 624 ppi and 8-bit color.

Choose a Custom page size in the File: Document Setup dialog and set the Height and Width (see Chapter 17). (See Figure 18.1.) I don't mean to suggest that you must use these sizes, but be aware that these are the two common, maximum page sizes for most users. Multimedia presentations may be chopped off if they exceed these sizes, but Web users can always scroll to view larger graphics or pages.

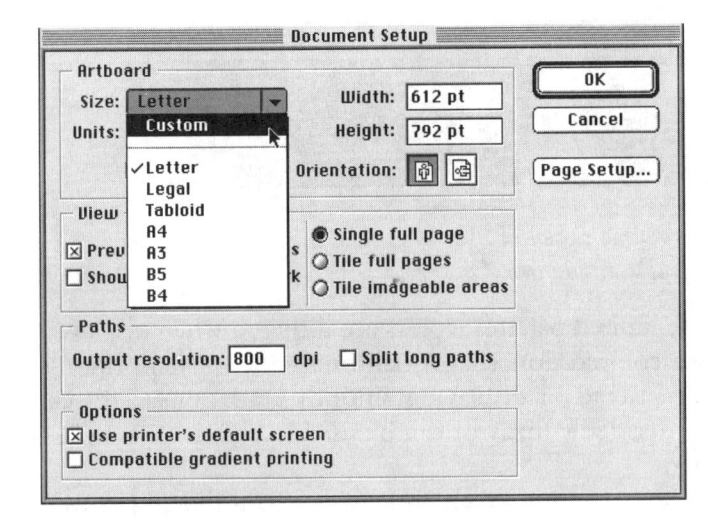

Figure 18.1 When designing for the screen instead of paper, choose **Custom** from the File: Document Setup dialog and specify the Height and Width of the screen size.

Screen density is also a limiting factor because monitors are usually set at 72 or 75 dpi as opposed to most printers, which are 300 dpi and higher. Don't expect to do highly detailed drawing or use small point sizes of type. They'll just get lost in the blur.

COLOR: PALETTES, SWATCHES, AND MODES

You can make your designs using glorious 24-bit color, but just as average screen sizes tend to be smallish, average color depth doesn't go beyond 8-bits or 256 color choices. Illustrator includes built-in 256 color system palettes for both MacOS and Windows. There is also a combined Web palette of 216 platform-independent colors. (It's fewer than 256 because not all MacOS and Windows system colors are the same.)

To use custom color palettes, choose **Window: Swatch Libraries** and choose either **System (MacOS)**, **System (Windows)**, or **Web** (see Chapter 10). This loads a custom swatches palette that you can use like the standard Swatches palette to assign system or Web-safe colors (as shown in Figure 18.2).

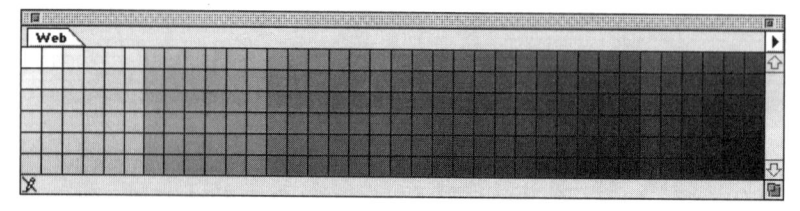

Figure 18.2 *The Web Swatches palette of 216 "Web-safe" colors is one of several Swatch Libraries that ships with Illustrator 7.*

If you stray from these limited palettes, colors are dithered when displayed. Dithering intersperses colored dots (like a halftone screen when printing) to approximate color instead of displaying smooth gradations. This can make graphics appear decidedly fuzzy or can be used to positive effect. It is more likely the former.

When creating color images for screen presentation, you should use RGB colors. Illustrator 7 added RGB capability specifically for Web-bound graphics. This is because CMYK is strictly a printer-based technology that relates to the four colors of ink used to print process color separations (see Chapter 17).

Monitors are RGB devices with three electron guns projecting the image onto phosphors or three colors of diodes on a flat-panel display. RGB actually produces a larger color gamut than the CMYK process, but when you're limited to a palette of 216 colors, this hardly matters.

To switch to RGB color, choose the **RGB** command from the Color palette pop-up menu before you start drawing (see Chapter 10). To convert CMYK colors to RGB, choose **Filter: Color: Adjust Colors**, click the **Convert** button, and choose **RGB** from the Color Mode drop-down menu (see Chapter 14).

FILE FORMATS: GIF, JPEG, AND PNG

Illustrator is not a multimedia program. Any graphic that you create in Illustrator needs to be saved as a file and then imported into the multimedia application you're using to assemble your presentation. Multimedia applications support many file formats, and it's a question of using whichever is most convenient for you.

The Web is different. You may be using an HTML editor or layout program to position graphics, or you may be coding HTML and inserting links without the need ever to import a graphic. In either case, you will be uploading your artwork to a Web server where it is available for all to load and see. The limiting factor is that the browsers in common use, most notably Netscape Navigator and Internet Explorer, can view only two graphic file formats: GIF and JPEG. The PNG format is being developed to replace GIF but isn't yet supported by many browsers.

About GIF Files

GIF (Graphic Interchange Format), also known as CompuServe GIF or, in its most recent incarnation, as GIF89a, is actually a proprietary format that has been made publicly available. (This may change, but it could take a while.) GIF, pronounced with either a soft or hard g, is the most widely supported graphic format on the Web, the one that has been around longest.

GIF provides some image compression and one level of transparency. It is strictly an 8-bit format. If your image contains more than 256 colors, an *indexed* color palette is created with the 256 most frequently occurring colors in the image. (See Figure 18.3.)

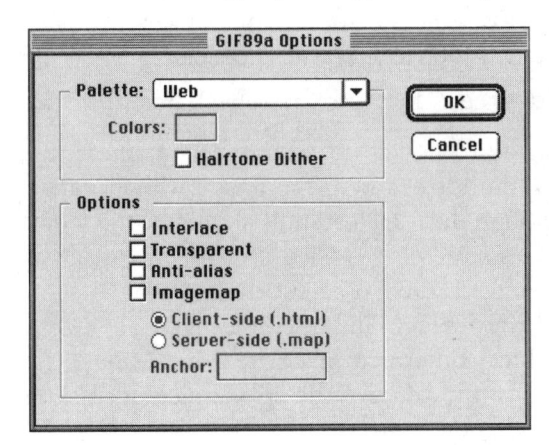

Figure 18.3 The GIF89a Options dialog lets you select a color palette and specify several Web-specific options.

To Save Files as GIF

1. Choose **File: Export** to open the File Export dialog.
2. Choose **GIF89a** from the Format drop-down menu. Name the file and click **Save** to open the GIF89a Options dialog.
3. Choose a Palette type from the drop-down menu. There are six palettes, one specification, and one check box:

    Exact—Uses only the colors in the image for the palette and can only be used if there are already fewer than 256 colors.
    System (Macintosh) and System (Windows)—Use the system palettes for these platforms.

Web—Uses the 216 colors common to MacOS and Windows system palettes.

Adaptive—Samples the colors in the image to create a representative palette of the image colors.

Custom—Allows you to save custom palettes as files (see Chapter 10) and loaded by selecting this palette type.

Colors—Specifies the number of colors contained in the image when the Exact or Adaptive palettes are chosen. You can use the default amount or reduce the number of colors by changing the specification. Fewer colors can reduce file size significantly without reducing image quality. This is highly variable, and you'll need to experiment to find the fewest number of colors acceptable for a given image.

Halftone Dither—Uses dithered dots to approximate colors when this box is checked. Dithering can make colors look muddy and images look fuzzy, but it can be useful for some continuous-tone images like photographs. It's best not to dither Web images when possible.

4. Choose image options as desired. There are four check box options:

    Interlace—Causes an image to download to browsers in successive passes when checked. When not checked, the image will appear to load more slowly, even though the total load time should be the same.

    Transparent—Saves images with all non-filled areas of the image as transparent. This allows you to create transparent effects on Web pages.

    Anti-alias—Anti-aliases the image. This is not usually a concern with vector-based graphics, but once saved in GIF format, the image is a bitmap. Anti-aliasing can give the appearance of smooth edges to curves and angled lines.

    Imagemap—Saves the image as a clickable imagemap. This is only useful if you have first defined "hot spots" and linked URLs to the image (described later in this chapter). Choose either the **Client-side** or **Server-side** radio buttons. Client-side imagemaps are more efficient but are not supported by all browsers. (Navigator and Explorer do support client-side imagemaps.) Server-side imagemaps require the use of CGI scripting on the server side but are supported by most browsers. When you save a client-side imagemap, two files are created, the image itself and the map or *anchor*. You can change the anchor name, but it's useful to use the default name so that the two files can be paired easily.

5. Click **OK** to save the GIF file.

About JPEG Files

JPEG (Joint Photographic Experts Group) format was developed to provide maximum compression without color loss. Compression is adjustable from slight to great, but because JPEG is a *lossy* technology, the greater the compression, the greater the loss in image detail.

JPEG works well for photographic or other continuous-tone images. Files can be much smaller than GIF files, which means that they will download much faster. The amount of image loss is adjustable; however, because the Web is a low-resolution medium, most images can be compressed quite small before the image loss is noticeable.

JPEG is not supported by all browsers, but Navigator and Explorer do support it. I wouldn't use JPEG with an Illustrator image unless it contained a placed bitmap image. In this case, JPEG is the format of choice.

To Save Files as JPEG

1. Choose **File: Export** to open the File Export dialog.
2. Choose **JPEG** from the Format drop-down menu. Name the file and click **Save** to open the Resolution Options dialog.
3. Choose one of the resolution radio buttons: **Screen** (72 dpi), **Medium** (133 dpi), **High** (300 dpi), or **Other** (see Figure 18.4). For Web-bound images, 72 dpi is all you need and is the default.

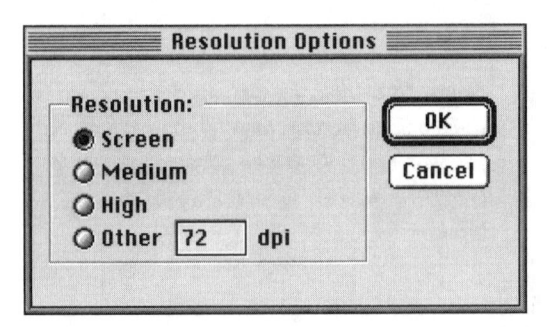

Figure 18.4 The JPEG Options dialog lets you specify the image resolution. For Web work, this will usually be 72 dpi.

4. Click **OK** and the Image Quality/Compression alert pops up. There is a single slider that can be dragged between Fair Image Quality/Excellent Compression and Excellent Image Quality/Fair Compression. (See Figure 18.5.) The default is toward the Excellent Compression side, which should work well for most images. If you need an image to load

faster, try compressing it more. In most cases, the image quality, although fair, is likely to be good enough for Web viewing.
5. Click the **Save** button to save the JPEG file.

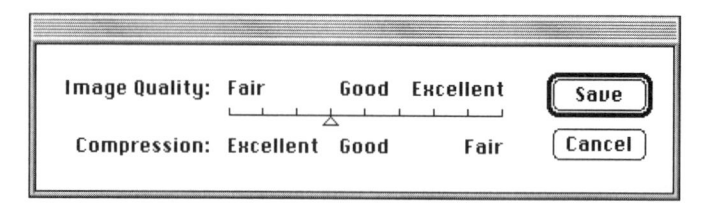

Figure 18.5 JPEG provides variable compression ratios, which are set from this alert box. Greater compression yields poorer image quality, but for the Web, this is often not noticeable.

About PNG Files

PNG (Progressive Network Graphics) has been developed to replace GIF. It has superior compression, color retention, and transparency options to GIF and does not require image loss like JPEG. It has everything going for it except support. Future browsers are supposed to include PNG support, but they don't as of this writing. (See Figure 18.6.)

Illustrator includes the PNG format as one of the Export formats, but you won't be able to use this format until the big browsers throw their full support behind it.

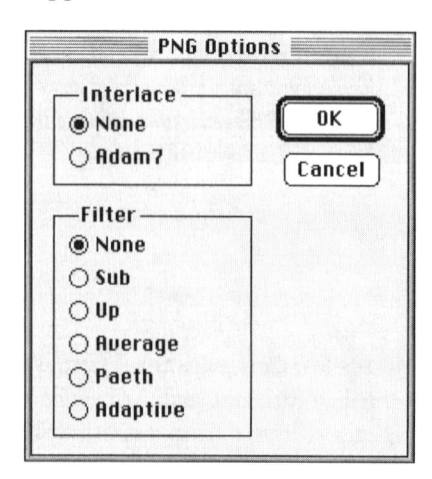

Figure 18.6 The PNG Options dialog provides some unique features for Web-bound files, but you won't be able to take advantage of these until PNG receives support from the major browsers.

URLs and Browsers

Creating imagemaps within Illustrator requires the ability to link images to URLs—the Universal Resource Locators that serve as the addresses for all Web pages. This capability makes Illustrator perhaps the finest tool for creating imagemaps, which is no mean feat.

Imagemaps allow you to create images with "hot spots" that when clicked on, open a linked page. Using imagemaps to link pages is such a powerful Web device that it has become almost ubiquitous.

Illustrator uses new features in the Attributes palette (see Chapter 10) and the newly added GIF89a format in the Export command (discussed earlier in this chapter) to create imagemaps.

To Create an Imagemap

1. Either select the object that will contain the link or create an object.
2. Open the Attributes palette shown in Figure 18.7 by clicking on its tab or choosing **Window: Show Attributes**.

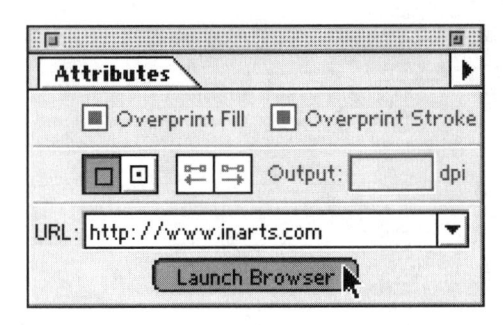

Figure 18.7 The new Attributes palette provides several Web-specific tools that make it possible to create imagemaps and even a button to launch your browser to check the imagemap links.

3. Click in the URL field and type in the full or relative name for the link. Full links will begin with **HTTP://**, whereas relative links assume that the beginning part of the URL is the same as the page it is being called from.

   Illustrator saves any URLs that you enter with the drawing, and you can select previously entered URLs from the drop-down box next to the URL field.
4. Press the **Return/Enter** or **Tab** key to associate the link with the object.

5. If you wish, click on the **Browser** button. This will open your browser (or ask you to locate the browser so it can be opened) so that you can check your links. You can use this to copy URLs from the browser to the Attributes palette.
6. Choose **File: Export** and select **GIF89a** from the Format drop-down menu. Fill out the options as already described, being sure to check the **Imagemap** check box.
7. Click **OK** to save the imagemap. At this point, the imagemap can be included in your HTML document or loaded directly to your Web server.

LESSON 18

Brief Imagemap Lesson

Half a book ago, at the end of Lesson 9, I promised that we would return to the Chinese Tree Peonies for some Web work. Now is the time. Open the file PEONY.AI from the LESSON18 folder on the CD. (There are no Lesson 15–17 folders.) I've changed this file slightly since you last saw it to add some type. I used the Hiroshige typeface, which was inspired by the eponymous Japanese watercolorist, despite the fact that these peonies are Chinese. Let's hope it doesn't cause an international incident.

1. Choose the **Group Selection** tool (a). We need to use this tool to select the individual icons, because they're still grouped from Lesson 9. (See Figure 18.8.)

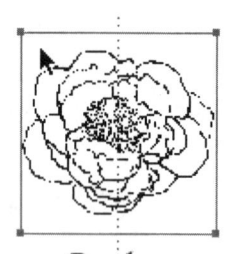

Figure 18.8 *We can't use the Selection tool (v) to select individual icons because they are grouped. Clicking on one selects all three, as shown here.*

Enslaved by Peonies   Garden Craft   About Tree Peonies

2. Either **Shift-Click** on the first icon and its caption (Enslaved by Peonies) or drag a selection marquee to select both. (See Figure 18.9.)

Figure 18.9 *Use the Group Selection tool (a) to drag a selection marquee over the first icon and its caption to select both.*

3. Open the Attributes palette either by clicking on its palette tab (as shown in Figure 18.10) or by choosing **Window: Show Attributes**.

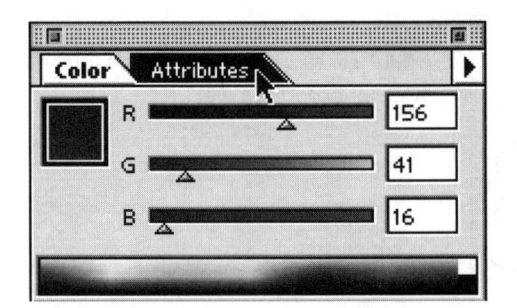

Figure 18.10 Clicking on the Attributes tab in the Color/Attributes palette window to activate the Attributes palette.

4. In the URL field, type **http://www.treepeony.com/enslave.html** (as shown in Figure 18.11); then press the **Return/Enter** or **Tab** key. This is an absolute URL specification.

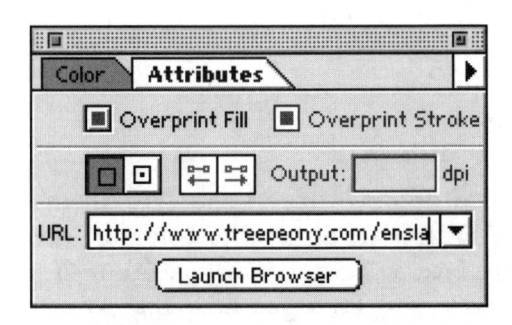

Figure 18.11 Typing an absolute address into the URL specification field.

5. Select the second icon and its caption (Gardening Craft) as you did the icon and caption in Step 2.
6. With the Attributes palette still open, click in the **URL** field and enter **/craft.html**. This is a relative URL specification. It has the immediate advantage of being shorter to type, but, more importantly, if we ever wanted to move the entire site, the relative address would remain the same.
7. Repeat Steps 5 and 6 for the third icon and caption pair and then enter the URL **/about.html**.
8. Choose **File: Export** and then choose **GIF89a** from the Format drop-down menu. Choose a location to save the file on your hard disk, enter the name peony.gif, and click **Save** to open the GIF89a Options dialog (as shown in Figure 18.12).

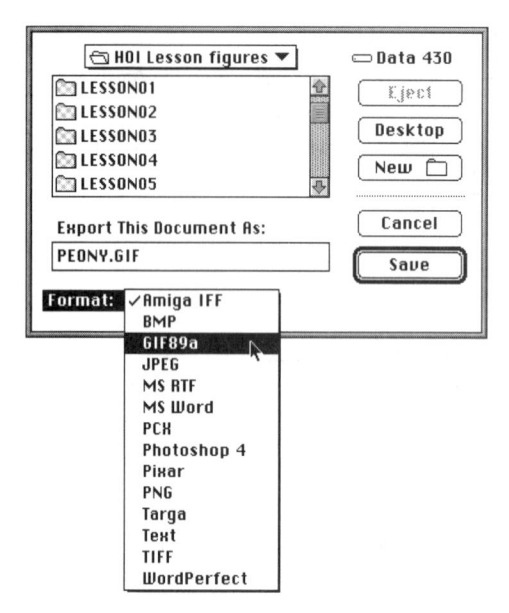

Figure 18.12 Choose the GIF89a format from the Export File dialog.

9. Choose **Web** from the Palette drop-down menu and click all the drop-down boxes: **Halftone Dither** to dither the colors of the placed peony photograph, **Interlace** to have the image load in successive passes rather than one slow pass, **Transparent** so that we can put this image on a red background (more efficiently done as an HTML background than in Illustrator), **Anti-alias** so that the type and line drawings render more smoothly on screen, and **Imagemap** so that this image will be a clickable imagemap. Click the **Client-side** radio button and leave the Anchor name at the default choice. Click **OK**. (See Figure 18.13.)

NOTE If we were being fanatical about compressing images as small as possible, we would have pared the palette down for the peony photograph in Photoshop before placing it in Illustrator. We might manage as few as 32 colors. Then we could limit the palette in Illustrator to 32 colors, since the only other color is black, and turn off dithering.

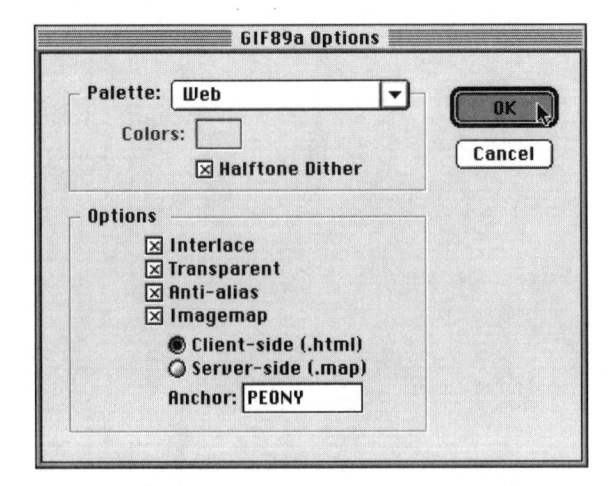

Figure 18.13 *The GIF89a Options dialog with all options selected, including the Imagemap check box that will turn this graphic into a clickable imagemap when loaded onto a Web server with its map file.*

If you get the message **Insufficient memory was available to complete the operation**, click **OK** to the Alert (what choice do you have?) and repeat Steps 8 and 9, deselecting the **Anti-alias** check box. Click **OK** again, and the file and imagemap are saved. You can also increase Illustrator's memory allocation (see Chapter 19). It turns out that anti-aliasing the lattices is a very memory-intensive operation.

You'll notice that two files were created, **peony.gif** and **peony.html**. The first is the image itself, and the second is the imagemap, which is a text file in HTML format. Both must be uploaded to your server for the imagemap links to function. Saving this file also embeds the placed images and converts the peony photograph to RGB.

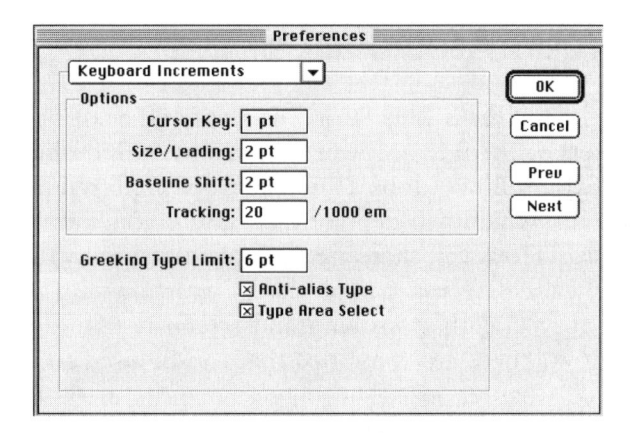

19 Performance, Preferences, and Help

In this chapter...

- A Few words about performance
- Setting preferences
- Color settings
- Help system

A Few Words About Performance

The fact of the matter is Illustrator 7 is a very efficient performer on most systems. Users with older, slower systems may find themselves bogged down, but if you follow Adobe's guidelines for preferred platforms (not the minimal system, which will definitely be slow), you should find Illustrator very responsive. However, there are a couple of issues to keep in mind.

Obviously, the size and complexity of your drawing will affect performance. You may find that scrolling and screen redraw slow down or that printing is slow. There are some tips that can be used to improve printing efficiency (see Chapter 17). The biggest culprits in on-screen unresponsiveness are bitmaps and patterns. You can turn off the display of both of these using the File: Document Setup dialog (also in Chapter 17) to get a slight performance improvement. (See Figure 19.1.)

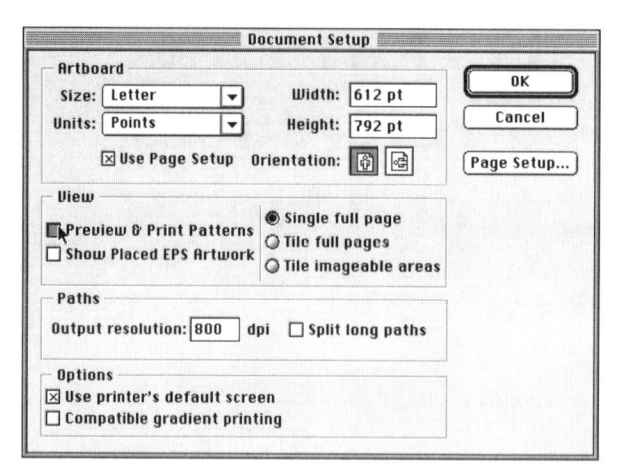

Figure 19.1 Use the View option check boxes in the Document Setup dialog to turn off the display of patterns and/or EPS artwork. This will improve on-screen performance when you find Illustrator's responsiveness lagging.

Illustrator 7's ability to work with bitmap images raises the same kind of issues that Photoshop users face because bitmap images tend to be bigger, and can be much bigger, than vector images. When you place or open a bitmap image that exceeds Illustrator's memory allocation, instead of closing or bombing, Illustrator grabs disk space. Even though Adobe's implementation of "virtual memory" works well, it is necessarily slower than real RAM. If you're not doing much with bitmap images in Illustrator, you can skip this section. Otherwise, read on.

The performance of virtual memory is affected by the amount of RAM allocated to Illustrator, as well as the speed and efficiency of the scratch disk. (Scratch disk options are set using the Plug-ins and Scratch Disk preferences discussed later in this chapter.) The more RAM you have, the less often Illustrator will use its scratch disk. In Windows, Illustrator will grab a percentage of available RAM, so that installing more RAM will increase Illustrator's allotment automatically. MacOS RAM is not allocated dynamically, so you have to increase Illustrator's RAM allocation using the File: Get Info dialog in the Finder. (If you don't know how to do this, read your operating system manual or the Illustrator *User Guide*.)

Not only should you use your fastest hard disk as the assigned scratch disk, but you must also have plenty of free defragmented space available. Use a utility such as Norton Utilities or Defrag to keep your disk space defragmented and operating at peak efficiency.

SETTING PREFERENCES

Illustrator includes a single preferences dialog with six modes, all available from the File: Preferences submenu shown in Figure 19.2, that allow you to customize various Illustrator options to suit your work habits. We've referred to these dialogs throughout the book, and now we will look at the details of each.

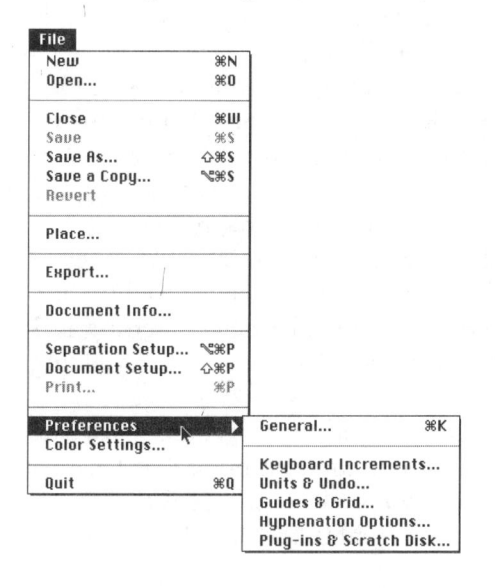

Figure 19.2 The File: Preferences submenu is slightly different from others in Illustrator in that the six dialogs are actually all part of the same modal dialog, so the Command/Ctrl-K keyboard shortcut can access all preferences.

Preferences in General

You can open the Preferences dialog to any of its six options windows using the File: Preferences submenu or use the keyboard shortcut,

Command/Ctrl-k, to open the Preferences dialog with the General options. After it is open, you can switch to any of the options windows using either the drop-down menu to select a particular window or the **Prev** and/or **Next** buttons to page through the windows in order.

Change any of the options in any of the windows. The Preferences dialog stays open until you click the **OK** button to apply the new settings or the **Cancel** button to close without making any changes.

General Preferences Options

There are four Tool Behavior settings:

> **Constrain Angle**—When you hold down the **Shift** key when moving, copying, or performing certain transforms, the operation is limited to increments of 45°. This setting does not change the 45° setting, but instead changes the axes on which this setting is based. In other words, Illustrator assumes that the x- and y-axes are at 0° and 90° and constrains actions relative to these. Enter a number between -360° and +360° to change the position of the default x- and y-axes. This only affects drawing behavior when using the **Shift** key.
>
> **Corner Radius**—When you draw a rectangle using the Rounded Rectangle tool (m), the size of the rounded corners is determined by this setting. The default is 12 pt, and the range of values is 0 pt to 1296 pt. You can override the corner radius preference using the options dialog of either Rectangle tool (m) (see Chapter 3).
>
> **Curve Fitting Tolerance**—This setting determines the level of detail used to draw curved paths created with the Pencil tool (y) and Autotrace tool (b) (see Chapters 3 and 8). The default setting is 2 pixels, and the range is 0–10 pixels, with larger numbers yielding simpler, less detailed paths.
>
> **Auto Trace Gap**—When calculating a path created with the Autotrace tool (b), Illustrator looks for continuous pixels (see Chapter 8). You can have it skip over one or two pixels when calculating continuity by changing the Auto Trace Gap from 0, the default, to 1 or 2.

There are ten Options check boxes:

> **Snap to Point**—Snap affects the behavior of all selection and image creation tools. When you drag to within 2 pixels of an anchor point,

as indicated by a hollow arrowhead cursor, the operation will snap exactly to the point. This makes it much easier to align objects and is on by default. Deselect this check box to turn snap off.

Transform Pattern Tiles—Off by default, pattern fills are not affected by the transform tools or commands. When checked, patterns are transformed along with objects.

Use Precise Cursors—Most tools use iconic cursors so that you can see at a glance which tool you are using. These icons can get in the way of detailed drawing and can be turned off by clicking on this check box. Cross hairs are used for all tools as precise cursors. This can be toggled by engaging the **Caps Lock** key.

Paste Remembers Layers—Even though the stacking order of objects is maintained when cut, copied, and pasted, all layer information is lost. Click on this check box to have Illustrator remember and paste objects back to their original layers. If the layer has been deleted or the name changed, Illustrator creates a new layer when pasting.

AI 6.0 Tool Shortcuts—Many tool shortcuts have been changed in Illustrator 7 for consistency across Adobe's product line. If Illustrator is the only Adobe product you use, you can check this box to continue your fond use of the old shortcuts.

Area Select—On by default, this feature allows you to select objects by clicking anywhere inside their fill. This can be a burden rather than an aid when you have many overlapping objects. When this option is clicked off, objects can be selected only by clicking on paths or anchor points, as in Artwork mode.

Scale Line Weight—By default, operations that change the scale of objects do not affect the line weights used to stroke paths. Click on this option to have weights scale with objects. You can also scale line weights using the Scale tool dialog (see Chapter 5).

Show Tool Tips—When you let your cursor linger over any of Illustrator's floating palettes for 2 seconds, a tool tip pops up identifying the tool, option, or field. Deselect this box to turn off the tool tips.

Japanese Cropmarks—Standard Japanese cropmarks are different from Illustrator's standard. Check this box to switch to the Japanese style.

Disable Warnings—When you create CMYK colors that are out of gamut (see Chapter 10), Illustrator displays a warning exclamation point in the affected palettes. When this option is unchecked, no warning is displayed.

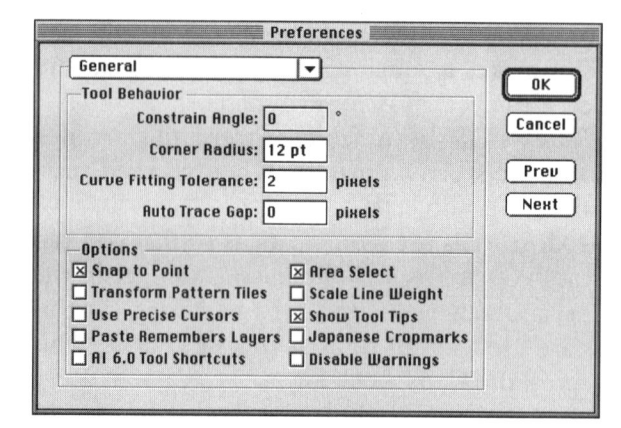

Figure 19.3 *The General Preferences dialog includes four settings to control Tool Behavior, along with ten Options check boxes.*

Keyboard Increments Preferences Options

There are four options in the Preferences dialog, and all involve amounts. These keyboard shortcuts are always on.

>**Cursor Key**—Sets the distance a selected object will move when using the keyboard arrow keys. The default is 1 pt and the range is 0–1296 pt.
>
>**Size/Leading**—Sets the change increment for leading when using **Option/Alt-Up Arrow** or **Down Arrow** with a selected text object. The default is 2 pt and the range is .1–1296 pt.
>
>**Baseline Shift**—Sets the change increment for baseline shift when using the Shift-Option/Alt-Up or Down arrow keys with a selected text object. The default is 2 pt and the range is .1–1296 pt.
>
>**Tracking**—Sets the change increment for tracking and kerning when using **Option/Alt-Left Arrow** or **Right Arrow** with a selected text object. The default is 20 thousandths of an em, and the range is -1,000 to +10,000 thousandths of an em.
>
>**Greeking Type Limit**—When text goes below a certain display size, it becomes essentially unreadable. Rather than have Illustrator try to render type at small sizes, you can set the size at which type will be *greeked* or displayed as gray bars representative of type. The default is 6 pt and the range is 1–1296 pt.

Anti-alias Type—On by default, this option anti-aliases on-screen type. It affects the display only and not the way the file prints.

Type Area Select—Like the Area Select option in the General Preferences dialog, this option allows you to click on any letter to select text objects. When this check box is deselected, you have to click on the text baseline, path or bounding box directly in order to select.

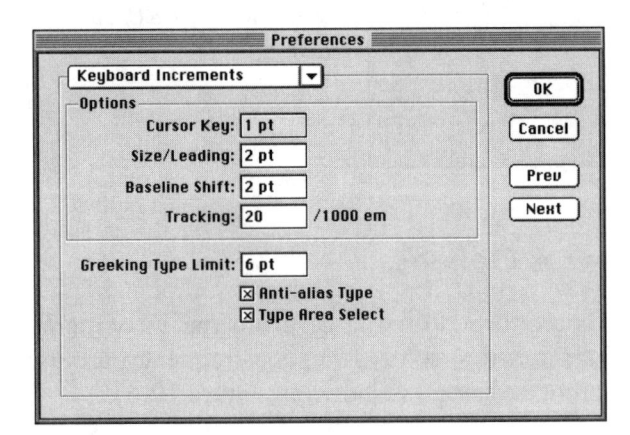

Figure 19.4 All keyboard increment options are set in the Keyboard Increments Preferences dialog.

Units & Undo Preferences Options

Illustrator supports measurements in points, picas, inches, millimeters, and centimeters. The settings in this dialog (shown in Figure 19.5) affect the default units, but you can mix and match units in dialogs and palettes as convenient. Illustrator will convert them to the default units as necessary.

General—Set the default measurement units for all dialogs and palettes.

Type—Set the default measurement for all type-related fields. It's possible to use different units for type and everything else.

Illustrator keeps an Undo stack (see Chapter 12) so that you can restore backward several steps. You can set the number of undo steps.

Min. Undo Levels—The default number of undo steps Illustrator retains is five; the range is 0 to 200 steps.

432 CHAPTER 19

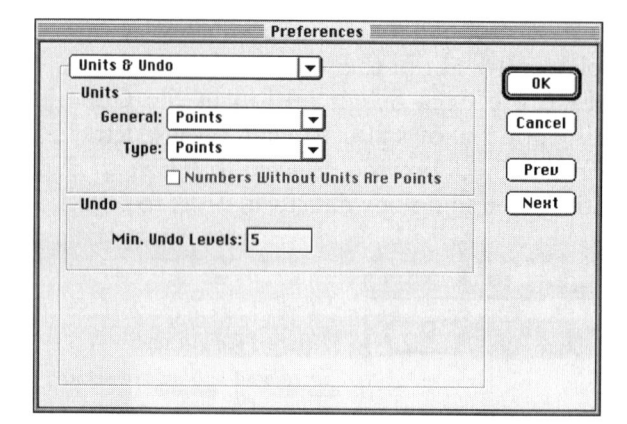

Figure 19.5 The Units and Undo Preferences dialog includes choices to set Illustrator's default measurement units and the number of steps saved by the Undo buffer.

Guides & Grid Preferences Options

Even though guides and grids are turned on and off from the View menu (see Chapter 15), all their characteristics, color, style, and frequency, are set in the Guides and Grids Preferences dialog (as shown in Figure 19.6).

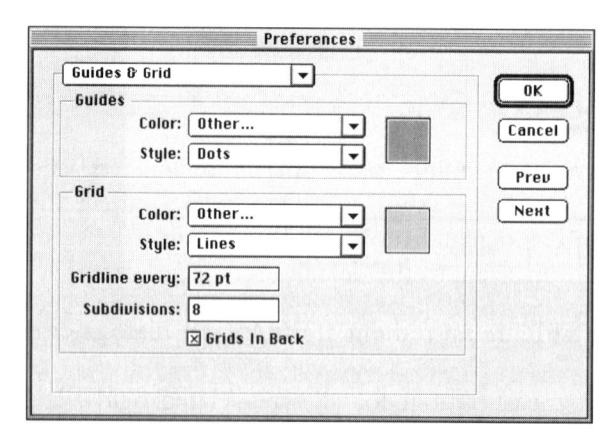

Figure 19.6 Guides and grids are turned on and off from the View menu, but they are designed in the Guides and Grid Preferences dialog.

These Guides settings affect both ruler and object guides, which, as mentioned before, are functionally identical.

> **Color**—Choose one of eight preset colors from the drop-down menu or **Other** to open the System palette from which you can

choose any color. You can also double-click on the preview color square to open the System palette and change the Color setting. The default is a pale blue.
Style—Choose either **Dots** or **Lines** from the Style drop-down menu. **Dots** is the default.

There can be only one grid in Illustrator (see Chapter 15), and these settings determine its characteristics. Color and Style are identical to the Guides options. There are also two specifications and a check box.

Color—Choose one of eight preset color from the drop-down menu or **Other** to open the System palette, from which you can choose any color. You can also double-click on the preview color square to open the System palette and change the Color setting. The default is a light gray.
Style—Choose either **Dots** or **Lines** from the Style drop-down menu. **Lines** is the default.
Gridline every—Set the specification for the frequency of major gridline markers. 72 pt is the default, and the range is .01–1000 pt.
Subdivisions—Specify the number of minor divisions between each major gridline. The default is 8, and the range is 1–1000.
Grids In Back—This box is checked by default, which sets the gridlines behind all objects. Uncheck this box to show gridlines on top of all objects in the drawing.

Hyphenation Options Preferences

The Hyphenation Options Preferences dialog is used to choose a hyphenation language. Choose one of twelve from the Default Language drop-down menu, and maintain a list of hyphenation Exceptions. Hyphenation is turned on and off using the **Auto Hyphenate** option in the Paragraphs palette (see Chapter 13).

> **NOTE**
> You can change the hyphenation rules for a single document by using the Languages drop-down menu in the Character palette (see Chapter 13).

To Add or Delete Hyphenation Exceptions

1. Choose **File: Preferences: Hyphenation Options**. (See Figure 19.7.)
2. In the New Entry field, type the word for which you want to specify a hyphenation exception. Enter hyphens where the word can be correctly hyphenated, or if you enter no hyphens, Illustrator will never hyphenate the word.
3. Click the **Add** button to add the word to the Exceptions list.
4. To delete a word from the list, highlight it in the Exceptions list and click the **Delete** button.

> **NOTE:** You can also enter hyphens in any word in a text object by using **Shift-Command/Ctrl-Hyphen**, the discretionary hyphen character, between syllables of any word.

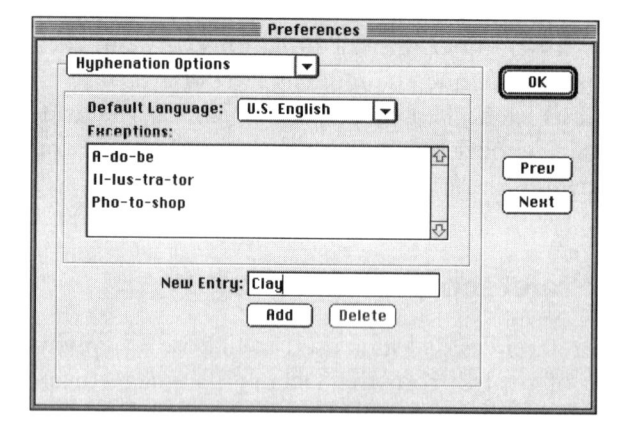

Figure 19.7 It may seem like an odd place for it, but Illustrator maintains its hyphenations exceptions list through the Hyphenation Options Preferences dialog.

Plug-ins & Scratch Disk Preferences

The purpose of the Plug-ins and Scratch Disk Preferences dialog is to let you change or reassign the location of Illustrator's plug-ins folder and the disk used when Illustrator requires additional space for virtual memory. (Virtual memory is discussed earlier in this chapter.)

To Reassign Illustrator's Plug-ins Folder

1. Choose **File: Preferences: Plug-ins and Scratch Disk**.
2. Click on the **Choose** button in the Plug-ins & Scratch Disk Preferences dialog.
3. Select the custom folder location in the file dialog and click **OK**. The default location is inside your Illustrator folder, but this option allows you to use any name and location for the Plug-ins folder.

NOTE: If you have several Adobe applications, they can share the same plug-ins folder. This will save you from having duplicate plug-ins because some plug-ins, particularly Photoshop's, can be shared.

To Reassign Scratch Disks

1. Choose **File: Preferences: Plug-ins & Scratch Disk**.
2. From the Primary and Secondary Scratch Disk drop-down menus, choose any of your hard disks or **Startup**. Startup uses your System drive (most likely the C: drive in Windows). You should choose your fastest drive to be the Primary drive, and you should make sure that you leave plenty of empty defragmented space on it.

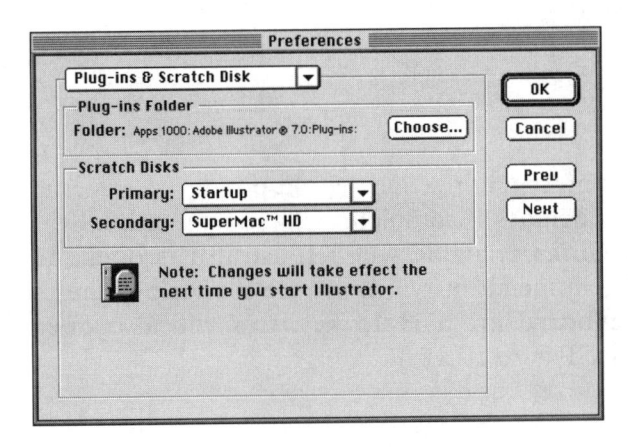

Figure 19.8 Just like Photoshop, Illustrator keeps a plug-ins folder and scratch disk space. Both can be reassigned using the Plug-ins and Scratch Disk Preferences dialog.

Color Settings

The File: Color Settings dialog varies widely depending on your operating system and color management software. Adobe assumes that you will be using ColorSync in MacOS and Kodak's ICC-compliant color-management engine in Windows and describes their use in the Chapter 16 of the Illustrator *User Guide*. This is a good chapter to read if you intend to produce high-quality color output.

I'll refer you to this chapter rather than discuss the various options here because of the Color Settings dialog that gives a brief description of each option when selected. (See Figure 19.9.) You should at least read pages 315–317 to calibrate your monitor as a first step toward achieving predictable color results.

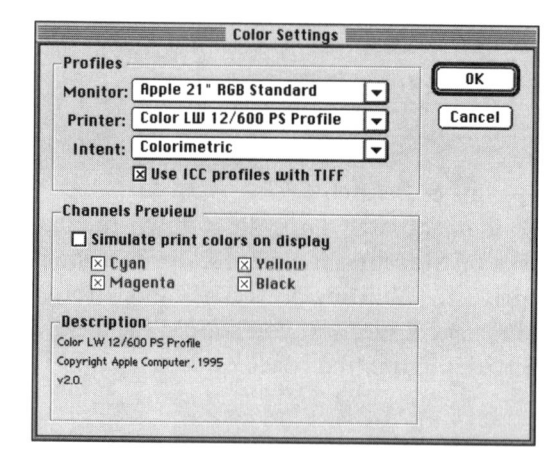

Figure 19.9 The Color Settings dialog is highly platform-specific. This is the MacOS version.

Help System

We discussed Illustrator's context-sensitive menus and pop-up messages in Chapter 2. Illustrator also includes a complete help system with all the information of the *User Guide* available when Illustrator is open. In MacOS, use the Balloon Help menu; in Windows, use the Help menu to turn help on. If your keyboard has a **Help** key, this will also open Illustrator's help system. (See Figure 19.10.)

Performance, Preferences and Help 437

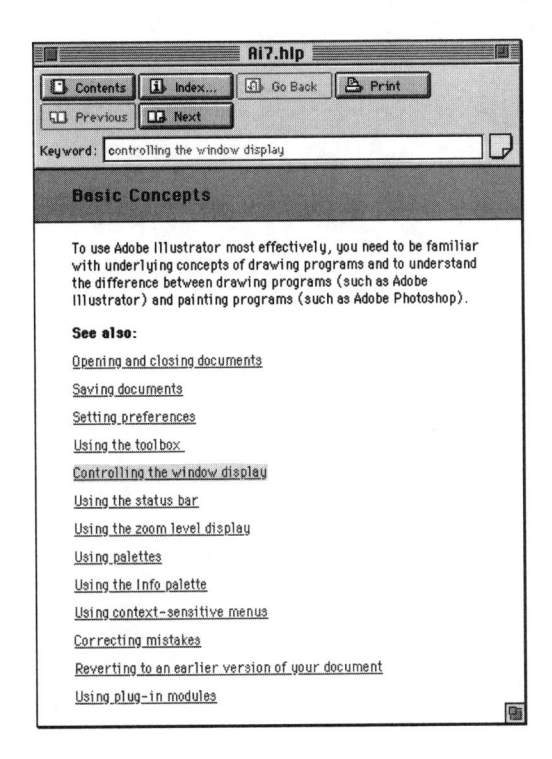

Figure 19.10 Illustrator's basic help system. Type in a keyword, and Illustrator opens the appropriate help page.

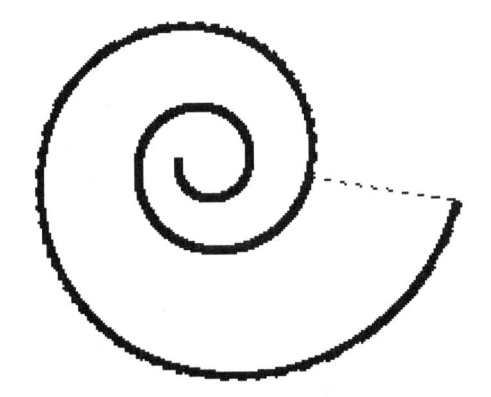

Index

A

additive color spectrum, 200
Adobe Illustrator, 4
    background, 2
        graphs in, 142, 143
            entering data in, 143
            graph object creation, 143
    help in, 4-7
    launching, 8, 9
    new features in, 15
        document window, 16
        floating window, 17, 18
        menus, 19, 20
        palette windows, 17
        scratch window, 17
        Toolbox window, 18, 19
    PostScript and, 2
    vocabulary used in, 4, 5, 8-14
Align palette, 186
        aligning objects, 190
        distributing objects, 190
        one-click adjustments, 189, 190
aligning objects, 190

anchor point, 5, 10
    adding and deleting, 48, 49
    converting, 49, 50
    selecting, 68
API (application programming interface), 16
Apply Last Filter command, 340, 341
Arrange submenu, Object menu, 264
    commands listed, 265
arrowheads, adding to paths, 359, 360
attributes, paint. *See* paint attributes
Attributes palette, 218
    features summarization, 219
    pop-up menu commands, 219, 220
Auto Hyphenation, using, 308, 309
Auto Trace tool, tracing with, 140, 141
    bitmap shapes, converting to Illustrator paths, 141
    pain and peppers lesson, 162
        anchor points, setting, 165
        curves, handling, 166
        filling and stroking, 164, 165
        opening file, 162
        paper, selecting, 169
        rotating anchor points, 167
        selecting Auto Trace tool, 163

439

INDEX

tints, setting, 166, 167, 168
toggling selection cursor, 167, 168
Zoom tool, selecting, 163, 164

B

baseline, 296
    shift, 303
bitmap
    shapes, converting to Illustrator paths, 141
        turning into mosaics, 346-348
        vs. vectors, 3, 4
black overprint, adding or removing, 344, 345
Blend tool, shaping and shading with blending two shapes, 139
    limitations of, 138, 139
        pain and peppers lesson, 162
        anchor points, setting, 165
        curves, handling, 166
        filling and stroking, 165, 166
        opening file, 162
        paper, selecting, 169
        rotating anchor points, 167
        selecting Auto Trace tool, 163
        tints, setting, 166, 167, 168
        toggling selection cursor, 167, 168
        Zoom tool, selecting, 163, 164
blended color, 210. *See also* Gradient palette
blends, 150. *See also* Blend tool
browsers and URLs, 417, 418
    imagemaps, creating, 417, 418
        lesson in, 419-423
Brush Tool, 41

C

calligraphic strokes, creating, 360
Cap attributes, setting in Stroke palette , 214, 215
category
    axis options, setting, 156
    labels, entering, 148, 149
cell, graph
    properties, changing, 151
    editing range of, 146, 148
Clear command, 258, 259
Character palette, 295, 298
    character options, 299
      baseline shift, 303
      font size, 300
      kerning, 301, 302
        leading, 300, 301
        scaling, 302, 303
        tracking, 302
    default settings, 298
    fonts, setting, 299
    fully expanded, 298
CJK (Chinese, Japanese, Korean), text, 325
    type orientation, changing, 326
Clipboard, 394, 395
closing open file windows, 389, 390
CMYK (Cyan Magenta Yellow Black)
Color palette and, 202, 203
    color reproduction, 200, 201
color. *See also* color reproduction
    adjusting, 342
    buttons, using, 102, 103
    Color palette, 200
    color models, changing, 204
      CYMK and, 202
      Fill and Stroke, 202
      RGB and, 202
      storing color, 216, 218
      swatch libraries, 216-218

INDEX 441

Gradient palette, 200, 211-213
inverting, 344
modes, converting, 343
printing, 406, 407
    color usage and, 411, 412
preferences, setting, 440
quilting and coloring lesson, 221-234
  anchor points, snapping, 224
  dragging and copying diamond, 223
  dragging color range to New Swatch button, 222
  fill, changing in copied diamond, 223
  gradient editor, using, 229, 230
  multiple diamond copies, creating, 228
  Reflect tool, using, 227
  rows of diamonds, creating, 224, 225
  process color equivalents, obtaining, 231
  selecting color from Swatches palette, 221, 222
  Selection tool, choosing, 222, 223
  saturation, adjusting, 345
  separations, 406
  Swatches palette, 200, 205-210
  drawback of, 216
  transformation of different, 87
color models, changing, 204
  CYMK and, 202
  Fill and Stroke, 202
    editing, 203, 204
  RGB and, 202
  storing color, 216, 218
  swatch libraries, 216-218
Color palette, 200. *See also* color reproduction
color reproduction, 200

color models supported by Illustrator
  CYMK, 201
  grayscale, 201
  HSB, 201
  RGB, 201
  problems in, 200
  WYSIWYG, 200
Color submenu commands, 341
  adjusting colors using, 342
  black overprint, adding or removing, 344, 345
  blending filled objects, 343
  color modes, converting, 343
  color saturation, adjusting, 345
  inverting colors, 344
columns, transposing in worksheet, 155, 156
Compound Paths command, 279
  creating, 279, 280
  releasing, 280
  transparency, adjusting, 280, 281
Copy command, 258, 259
copying data, graphs, 151
copying paths, objects, or groups, 70, 71
corners, rounding object, 363, 364
Create submenu commands, 345, 346
  bitmaps, turning into mosaics, 346-348
  masks, filling and stroking, 346
  trim marks, creating, 348
Cropmarks command, 281
  releasing, 282
  setting, 281, 282
curves, 43
  creating
    angled curved path segments, 44, 45
    smooth curved path segments, 43, 44
    mixing straight and curved path segments, 45

custom graph design, 156, 157
    applying, 159-161
    creating, 157, 158
    managing, 158, 159
Cut command, 258, 259

D

dashed lines, creating in Stroke palette, 216
data, entering into graphs, 144, 145
data values, reverting in graphs, 151
demagnifying with Zoom tool, 123, 124
direct selection, 66, 67
discarding changes without saving, 390
Distort Filters submenu commands, 348, 349
    distorting objects freely, 349, 350
    punk and bloat objects, 350, 351
    roughen objects, 351, 352
    scribble and tweak objects, 352, 353
    twirl objects, 353
    zigzags, creating, 354
distributing objects, 190
docking palette, 140, 141
document/object info window, 396
        save document/selection info, 396, 397
        viewing document/selection info, 396
document window, 16
drag
        into Illustrator from other applications, 395, 396
        out of Illustrator to other applications, 395
drag-and-drop, 395
drop shadows, 361

E

edges, 377

edit commands, 258. *See also* Object commands
    Clear, 258, 259
    Copy, 258, 259
    Cut, 258, 259
    Paste, 258, 259
        patterns, defining new, 259, 260
    Redo, 258
        Selection commands, 260, 261
        Macintosh, 261
    Undo, 258
ellipse
    centered, creating, 37, 38
        creating, 36, 37
        dimensions, specifying, 38
        rounded edges, creating, 38
        squares and circles, creating, 38, 41
EPS (Encapsulated PostScript) files, 394
exact transformations, specifying, 84-87
Expand Fill command, 266
    gradient, expanding into object, 267
    pattern, expanding into object, 267
exporting files to other formats, 393
    EPS files, 394
    non-native Illustrator formats, 393, ,394
Eyedropper tool, 104, 105
    pasting attributes on to objects, 105
    sampling or applying selective attributes, 106
    sampling using, 105
    toggling with Paintbucket tool, 106

F

File commands, 388
    closing open file windows, 389, 390
    discarding changes without saving 390
    document/object info window, 396

INDEX 443

save document/selection info, 396, 397
viewing document/selection info, 396
exporting files to other formats, 393
   EPS files, 394
   non-native Illustrator formats, 393, 394
files, placing into open documents, 391
importing files and artwork, 391, 392
   placing text, 392
   placing graphics, 392
interactive import and export, 394
   Clipboard, 394, 395
   drag-and-drop, 395
   drag into Illustrator from other applications, 395, 396
   drag out of Illustrator to other applications, 395
linked files, 392
opening
   existing Illustrator document, 388, 389
   new black drawing window, 388
revert, 390
saving Illustrator drawings, 390
file formats, 412, 413
   GIF files, 413-415
   JPEG files, 415, 416
   PNG files, 416
fill, 5, 14
Fill button, 100
   color buttons, using, 102, 103
   editing color attributes using, 101
   default settings, returning to, 101
   gradient buttons, using, 102, 103
   setting to none, 102
Filter menu, 340
   Apply Last Filter command, 340, 341
   Color submenu commands, 341

adjusting colors using, 342
black overprint, adding or removing, 344, 345
blending filled objects, 343
color modes, converting, 343
color saturation, adjusting, 345
inverting colors, 344
Create submenu commands, 345, 346
   bitmaps, turning into mosaics, 346-348
   masks, filling and stroking, 346
   trim marks, creating, 348
Distort Filters submenu commands, 348, 349
   distorting objects freely, 349, 350
   punk and bloat objects, 350, 351
   roughen objects, 351, 352
   scribble and tweak objects, 352, 353
   twirl objects, 353
   zigzags, creating, 354
ink pen effects, applying, 355-357
Ink Pen submenu commands, 354, 355
   hatch patterns, creating new, 357, 358
   hatch patterns, modifying, 358
Last Filter command, 340, 341
lesson in using, 367-371
Stylize submenu commands, 358, 359
   arrowheads, adding to paths, 359, 360
   calligraphic strokes, creating, 360
   corners, rounding object, 363, 364
   drop shadows, adding, 361
   path patterns, applying, 361-363

filters, overview, 340. *See also* Filter menu
floating window, 17, 18
font size, 300
    size, settings, 304
    find/change, 321, 322
formatting commands, 296, 297
    character size, setting, 297
    font, setting, 297
Freehand tool, 41
Full Screen Mode, 125, 126, 127
    with menu bar, 125, 126

G

general preferences options, 432-434
GIF (Graphic Interchange Format) files, 413
    saving files as GIFs, 413-415
gradient extensions, 103
    defining, 103
gradient fill, applying to object, 103, 104
Gradient palette, 200
    defining gradients, 211, 211
    detailed, 210
    editing gradients, 212, 213
    shrinking, 213
Gradient tool, 103. *See also* gradient extensions
gradients, 144
graphics, 3
    pixels, 3
    vector vs. bitmap, 3, 4
Graphs command, 282
graphs, handling with Graph tool
    category axis options, setting, 156
    category labels, entering, 148, 149
    cell properties, changing, 151
    columns, transposing in worksheet, 149, 150
    copying data, 145

custom graph design, 156, 157
    applying, 159-161
    creating, 157, 158
    managing, 158, 159
data, entering into, 144, 145
data values, reverting, 151
editing range of cells, 146, 148
graph object, creating, 143, 144
graph options, setting, 152-154
Graph Type dialog, 152
    opening, 172
graph types, listed, 142
graphs in Illustrator, 142, 143
    entering data in, 143
    graph object creation, 143
importing data, 146
integrating graph design, 173
    Column Design dialog, opening, 176, 177
    Graph Design dialog box, opening, 175
    none, fill and stroke attributes, applying, 174
    renaming design, 176
    selecting object, 174
    single object, creating, 169
lesson, 169
    activating window, 171
    centering graph on page, 173
    default values, adjusting, 170, 171
    elements, selecting, 172
    global worksheet style, setting, 170
    Graph Type dialog box, opening, 172
    opening Column Graph tool, 169, 170
pasting data, 145
rows, transposing in worksheet, 149, 150
value axis options, setting, 155

INDEX

value labels, entering, 148, 149
worksheet cell, editing, 147
X and Y values, switching for scatter graphs, 15
grid commands, 380, 381
grid preferences options, 436, 437
group selection, 66, 67
groups
    copying, 70, 71
    deleting, 71
    moving, 69, 70
guides, 377, 378
    manipulating, 379, 380
    object guides, creating, 379
    preferences options, 436, 437
    ruler guides, creating, 378, 379

H

halftones, 401
Hand tool, 120
    panning with, 120, 121, 122
hatch patterns
    creating new, 357, 358
    modifying, 358
Help, 5
    Context-sensitive menus, 6
    Pop-up help, 6, 7
    system, 440, 441
hidden tools, selecting, 33, 34
hiding Toolbox, 32, 33
highlighted path, 23
hyphenation preferences options, 437
    adding or deleting hyphenation exceptions, 438

I

Illustrator. *See* Adobe Illustrator
imagemaps, creating, 417, 418
    lesson in, 419-423
importing

data, graphs, 152
    files and artwork, 391, 392
    placing text, 392
    placing graphics, 392
indents, setting paragraph, 306
Info palette, 186, 187
ink pen effects, applying, 355-357
Ink Pen submenu commands, 354, 355
    hatch patterns, creating new, 357, 358
    hatch patterns, modifying, 358
interactive adjustment, 187, 188
interactive import and export, 394
    Clipboard, 394, 395
    drag-and-drop, 395
    drag into Illustrator from other applications, 395, 396
    drag out of Illustrator to other applications, 395
inverting colors, 344

J

Join attributes, setting Stroke palette, 214, 215
JPEG (Joint Photographic Experts Group) files, 415
    saving files as JPEGs, 413-415

K

kerning, 296, 301, 302
keyboard increments preferences options, 434, 435

L

Last Filter command, 340, 341
layers, detailed, 236. *See also* Layers palette
    creating, 237-241

deleting, 241
duplicating, 240
hiding layers, 244, 245
layer information, 244
locking, 246
    objects and layers, 241, 242
    moving objects among, 242, 243
    pasting multilayer selections, 243
    selecting all objects in layer, 243
merging, 246
rearranging layers, 240, 241
showing layers, 244, 245
toggling layers to Artwork view, 245, 246
unlocking, 246
viewing options, 244
Layers palette, 236. *See also* layers
    anatomy of, 236, 237
    creating layers, 237-241
    default state, 237
    deleting layers, 241
    duplicating layers, 240
    lesson in using, 247
        creating new layer, 247
        dragging objects between layers, 248, 249
        dragging objects into place, 249
        item selection, 248
        locking layers, 249
        masks, handling, 252, 253
        moving objects to new layer, 250, 251
    pop-up menu, 246
    rearranging layers, 242, 243
leading, 296, 300, 301
line spacing, setting, 306, 307
lines, 4
linked files, 392

M

Macintosh selection commands, 261
magnification, 376, 377
    Zoom tool, 122, 123
manipulation, 69. *See also* selection
    copying paths, objects, or groups, 70, 71
    deleting paths, objects, or groups, 71
    moving paths, objects, or groups, 69, 70
mapping views lesson, 129
    opening, 129
    page guides, dragging, 130
    panning, 132, 133
    paths, changing anchor points, 134, 135
    screen mode, changing, 130
    zooming, 131, 132
    toggling tools, 133
Mask command, 276
    adding objects to mask group, 279
    turning objects into masks, 277, 278
    turning off masks, 278
masks, filling and stroking, 346
Measure tool, 107
    measuring between two points, 107
menus, 19, 20
MM Design palette, 309
    using, 310
monitors, web and multimedia, 412
morphing, 144
mosaics, turning bitmaps into, 346-348
moving paths, objects, or groups, 69, 70
multimedia, 409
    color usage and, 411, 412
    file formats, 412, 413
        GIF files, 413-415
        JPEG files, 415, 416
        PNG files, 416
    screen as output device, 410
    screen resolution, 410, 411
    URLs and browsers, 417, 418

INDEX

imagemap lesson, 419-423
imagemaps, creating, 417, 418

O

object creation, 35, 36
    editing paths, 48
        anchor point, adding and deleting, 48, 49
        converting anchor points, 49, 50
        dividing paths, 51
        making one path two, 51
        Pen cursors, listed, 50
    ellipse or rectangle
        centered, creating, 37, 38
        creating, 36, 37
        dimensions, specifying, 38
        rounded edges, creating, 38
        squares and circles, creating, 38, 41
    paths, creating, 41
        closed paths, drawing,
        curved path segments, 43-45
        ending paths, 46, 47
        freehand paths, drawing, 45, 46
        mixing straight and curved path segments, 45
        Paintbrush options, setting, 47, 48
        straight path segments, 41, 42
    regular shapes, 36
    speciality shapes, 39
        drawing by dragging, 39
        specifying shape options, 39, 40
    Type tool, 51, 52
        editing typo, 53
        entering type, 52, 53
        type selection, 54
Object menu, 261, 262
    Arrange submenu, 264
    commands listed, 26
Compound Paths command, 279
    creating, 279, 280
    releasing, 280
    transparency, adjusting, 280, 281
Cropmarks command, 281
    releasing, 282
    setting, 281, 282
Expand Fill command, 266
    gradient, expanding into object, 267
    pattern, expanding into object, 267
Graphs command, 282
grouping objects, 265, 266
hiding objects, 266
lesson in using, 283-292
locking objects, 266
Mask command, 276
    adding objects to mask group, 279
    turning objects into masks, 277, 278
    turning off masks, 278
Path submenu, 268
    anchor points, adding along path, 273
    averaging two anchor points, 270
    cleaning up a drawing, 272
    join two end points, 269, 270
    offsetting a path, 271, 272
    outlining a path, 270, 271
    slicing on object with another, 272, 273
Pathfinder submenu, 268, 269
    using commands in, 273-276
Rasterize command, 266
    converting objects to, 267, 268
show all objects, 266, 267

448　INDEX

Transform submenu, 262
  transforming object separately in a group, 263, 264
  ungrouping objects, 265, 266
  unlocking objects, 266
objects, 22
  blending filled, 343
  copying, 70, 71
  deleting, 71
  distorting freely, 349, 350
  grouping, 265, 266
  hiding, 266
  layers and, 241, 242
    moving objects among, 242, 243
    pasting multilayer selections, 243
    selecting all objects in layer, 243
  locking, 266
  moving, 69, 70
    punk and bloat, 350, 351
    roughen, 351, 352
    scribble and tweak, 352, 353
  show all objects, 266, 267
    ungrouping objects, 265, 266
    unlocking objects, 266
open paths, 5, 11
opening
  existing Illustrator document, 388, 389
  new black drawing window, 388
outlines, 317
  converting type to, 318

P

page guides, moving, 128
Page tool, 127
  page guides, moving using, 128
paint attributes, 100
  Eyedropper tool, 104, 105
    pasting attributes on to objects, 105
    sampling or applying selective attributes, 106
    sampling using, 105
    toggling with Paintbucket tool, 106
  gradient extensions, 103
    defining, 103
    gradient fill, applying to object, 103, 104
  Measure tool, 107
    measuring between two points, 107
  Paintbucket tools, 104, 105
    pasting attributes on to objects, 105
    sampling or applying selective attributes, 106
    toggling with Eyedropper tool, 106
  Penguin Patchwork lesson, 108-117
  Stroke and Fill buttons, 100
    color buttons, using, 102, 103
    editing color attributes using, 101
    default settings, returning to, 101
    gradient buttons, using, 102, 103
    setting to none, 102
    swapping colors, 101, 102
Paintbrush tool, 41
  options, setting, 47
  style options, 48
  width options, 47, 48
Paintbucket tools, 104, 105
  pasting attributes on to objects, 105
  sampling or applying selective attributes, 106
  toggling with Eyedropper tool, 106
Palette menu, opening, 181
panning, 120
paragraph options, 308

INDEX 449

size settings, 304
spacing, setting, 306, 307
using, 304, 305
word spacing, setting, 307
Paragraph palette, 304
    Auto Hyphenation, using, 308, 309
    indents, setting, 306
    line spacing, setting, 307
    paragraph alignment, setting, 305, 306
Paste command, 258, 259
pasting
    attributes on to objects, 105
    data, graphs, 145
path, 4
    alphabet paths lesson
        part 1, 55-58
        part 2, 58-63
    arrowheads, adding to, 359, 360
        bitmaps, converting shapes to, 145
    closed paths, drawing,
    copying, 70, 71
    creating, 41
    curved path segments, 43-45
    deleting, 71
    editing paths, 48
        anchor point, adding and deleting, 48, 49
        converting anchor points, 49, 50
        dividing paths, 51
        making one path two, 51
    ending paths, 46, 47
    freehand paths, drawing, 45, 46
    mixing straight and curved path segments, 45
    moving, 69, 70
    Paintbrush options, setting, 47, 48
    patterns, applying, 361-363
Path submenu, 268
    anchor points, adding along path, 273
    averaging two anchor points, 270
    cleaning up a drawing, 272
    join two end points, 269, 270
    offsetting a path, 271, 272
    outlining a path, 270, 271
    slicing on object with another, 272, 273
Path tool, 41
Pathfinder submenu, 268, 269
    using commands in, 273-276
patterns, defining new, 259, 260
Pen tool, 41
    alphabet paths lesson
        part 1, 55-58
        part 2, 58-63
Pencil tool, 41
Penguin Patchwork lesson, 108-117
Penguin Selection lesson, 73-79. *See also* selection
performance, Illustrator, 430, 431
plug-ins and scratch disk preferences, 438
    re-assigning plug-ins folder, 439
    re-assigning scratch disks, 439
PNG (Progressive Network Graphics) files, 416
point, 296
polygons, creating, 39
position. *See* shape and position
PostScript, described, 2
preferences, setting, 431, 432
    color settings preferences, 440
    general preferences options, 432-434
    guides and grid preferences options, 436, 437
    hyphenation preferences options, 437
        adding or deleting hyphenation exceptions, 438
    keyboard increments preferences options, 434, 435
    plug-ins and scratch disk preferences, 438

450 INDEX

    re-assigning plug-ins folder, 439
    re-assigning scratch disks, 439
    units and undo preferences options, 435, 436
Print command, 404, 405
print performance, improving, 407, 408
printing, 399
    color separations, 406
        printing, 406, 407
        PostScript and, 2
    preparations for, 401, 402
        setting document for printing, 402-404
    Print command, 404, 405
    print performance, improving, 407, 408
    terminology used in, 400, 401
proofing, 400
punk and bloat objects, 350, 351

R

Rasterize command, 266
    show all objects, 266, 267
rectangles
    centered, creating, 37, 38
        creating, 36, 37
        dimensions, specifying, 38
        rounded edges, creating, 38
        squares and circles, creating, 38, 41
Redo command, 258
Reflect, transformation tool, 82, 83
regular shapes, 36
repositioning Toolbox, 32
Reshape, transformation tool, 8
    objects, transforming interactively, 83, 84
        selection, 88, 89
resizing
    palette, 140
        Toolbox, 32

resolution, screen, 400
revert, 390
RGB (Red Green Blue)
    Color palette and, 202, 203
    color reproduction and, 200
    web and multimedia, 412
Rotate, transformation tool, 8 82, 83
roughen objects, 351, 352
rounding object corners, 363, 364
rows, transposing in worksheet, 155, 156
rulers and guides, 377, 378
    manipulating guides, 379, 380
    object guides, creating, 379
    resetting ruler zero point, 380
    ruler guides, creating, 378, 379
    showing rulers, 378

S

saving Illustrator drawings, 390
Scale, transformation tool, 82, 83
scaling, 302, 303
scatter graphs, switching X and Y graph values for, 15
scratch disk preferences, 438
    re-assigning scratch disks, 439
scratch window, 17
screen
    as output device, 410
    frequency, 401
    real estate, 3
    resolution, 410, 411
Screen Modes, 125
    changing, 125-127
scribble and tweak objects, 352, 353
selection, 66. *See also* manipulation
    direct, 66, 67
    general, 66, 67
    group, 66, 67
    making selection with selection tool, 67

INDEX

penguin selection lesson, 73-79
selecting
    anchor points, 68
    objects within group, 68, 69
    single segments, 68
    text selection, 71, 72
Selection commands, 260, 261
Selection tool, 66. *See also* selection
separations, printing, 400, 401
shading. *See* shaping and shading
shape and position, 186
    Align palette, 186
        aligning objects, 190
        distributing objects, 190
        one-click adjustments, 189, 190
    Info palette, 186, 187
    Transform palette, 186
        interactive adjustment, 187, 188
        selecting, editing using, 188, 189
        uses for, 188
shaping and shading with Blend tool
    blending two shapes, 139
    limitations of, 138, 139
Shear, transformation tool, 82, 83
showing Toolbox, 32, 33
smart punctuation, 324, 325
speciality shapes, 39
    displaying, 40
    drawing by dragging, 39
    specifying shape options, 39
        polygon options, 40
        spiral options, 40
        star options, 40
spelling, checking, 322, 323
spirals, creating, 39
Standard Screen Mode, 125
stars, creating, 39
static feed back, 186
straight path segments, 41, 42
stroke, 5

Stroke button, 100
    color buttons, using, 102, 103
    editing color attributes using, 101
    default settings, returning to, 101
    gradient buttons, using, 102, 103
    setting to none, 102
Stroke palette, 200
    Cap attributes, setting, 214, 215
    dashed lines, creating, 216
    detailed, 213
    Join attributes, setting, 214, 215
    stroke weight, setting, 214
    viewing options, 213
stroke weight, setting, 214
Stylize submenu commands, 358, 359
    arrowheads, adding to paths, 359, 360
    calligraphic strokes, creating, 360
    corners, rounding object, 363, 364
    drop shadows, adding, 361
    path patterns, applying, 361-363
Swatch library
    opening, 218
    storing color, 216-217
Swatches palette, 200
    color gradient, adding to, 207, 208
    deleting swatches, 208, 209
    detailed, 205
    drawback of, 216
    expanding, 205
    new display mode options in, 205, 206
    pattern, adding to, 207, 208
    pop-up menu, using, 209, 210
    replacing swatches, 209,
    using swatches, 206, 207
subtractive color spectrum, 200

T

Tab ruler, 211
    modifying settings, 312

moving, 313
re-aligning, 313
setting tabs, 311, 312
tabs. *See* tab ruler
text. *See also* Type tool
    case, changing, 324
    find/change, 320, 321
    selection, 71, 72
text blocks, 313
    entering text into, 313, 314
    fitting headlines, 316, 317
    flowing text around objects, 315
    linking, 314, 315
    reflowing text, 314, 315
    unlinking, 314, 315
texture, 5
tiling, 376
toggling between Paintbucket and Eyedropper tool, 106
Toolbox, 32
    hidden tools, selecting, 33, 34
    hiding, 32, 33
    options, selecting, 34
    repositioning, 32
    resizing, 32
    selecting tools, 33
        hidden tools, 33, 34
    showing, 32, 33
    window, 18, 19
tools, menu-based, 255
tracing with Auto Trace tool, 146, 147
    bitmap shapes, converting to Illustrator paths, 147
tracking, 296, 302
Transform palette, 186
    interactive adjustment, 187, 188
    lesson in using, 191, 192
        aligning group center points, 197
        applying transformation, 193
        centering composition, 198
        copying object, 192, 193
        distributing objects, 197
        insertion point, placing, 195
        keeping lines together, 194
        placing images on each other, 194
        reference point, changing, 192
        selecting images, 195, 196
        selecting, editing using, 188, 189
    uses for, 188
Transform submenu, Object menu, 262
transforming object separately in a group, 263, 264
transformation tools, 82
    color transformation, 87
    exact transformations, specifying, 84-87
    lesson, 90-98
    Reflect, 82, 83
    Rotate, 82, 83
    Scale, 82, 83
    Shear, 82, 83
    Reshape
        selection, 88, 89
        transforming objects interactively, 83, 84
    Twirl
        selection interactively, 87, 88
        specifying twirl, 88
trapping, 401
trim marks, creating, 348
twirl objects, 353
Twirl, transformation tool, 8
    selection interactively, 87, 88
    specifying twirl, 88
Type menu, 294. *See also* Type tool
    Character palette, 295, 298
        character options, 299
        default settings, 298
        fonts, setting, 299
        fully expanded, 298
    CJK text, 325
        type orientation, changing, 326
    formatting commands, 296, 297

INDEX

character size, setting, 297
font, setting, 297
lesson in using, 327-338
MM Design palette, 309, 310
    using, 310
outlines, 317
    converting type to, 318
overview, 294, 295
  paragraph options, 308
    size settings, 304
    spacing, setting, 306, 307
    using, 304, 305
    word spacing, setting, 307
  Paragraph palette, 304
    Auto Hyphenation, using, 308, 309
    indents, setting, 306
    line spacing, setting, 307
    paragraph alignment, setting, 305, 306
  Tab ruler, 211
    modifying settings, 312
    moving, 313
    re-aligning, 313
    setting tabs, 311, 312
  text blocks, 313
    entering text into, 313, 314
    fitting headlines, 316, 317
    flowing text around objects, 315,
    linking, 314, 315
    reflowing text, 314, 315
    unlinking, 314, 315
  vocabulary used in, 296
  word processing commands, 319, 320
    find/change fonts, 321, 322
    find/change text, 320, 321
    smart punctuation, 324, 325
    spelling, checking, 322, 323
    text case, changing, 324
Type tool, 51, 52. *See also* Type menu

editing typo, 53
entering type, 52, 53
text selection, 71, 72
type selection, 54

U

Undo command, 258
units and undo preferences options, 435, 436
URLs (Universal Resource Locator)
  and browsers, 417, 418
  imagemaps, creating, 417, 418
  lesson in, 419-423

V

value axis options, setting in graphs, 155
value labels, entering in graphs, 148, 149
vector
  described, 4
  vs. bitmap, 4, 5
View menu commands
  edges, 379
  grid commands, 382, 383
  guides, 379, 380
    manipulating, 381, 382
    object guides, creating, 381
    ruler guides, creating, 380, 381
  overview, 376
  magnification, 378, 379
    rulers and guides, 379, 380
    manipulating guides, 381, 382
    object guides, creating, 381
    resetting ruler zero point, 380
    ruler guides, creating, 380, 381

454 INDEX

showing rulers, 378
tiling, 377
viewing mode, 374, 375
    changing, 375
    previewing selections only, 375, 376
    views, creating and maintaining, 381
    editing, 382
    naming views, 381, 382
    zooming, 376, 377
View tools, 120, 121
    Hand tool, 120
        panning with, 120, 121, 122
    mapping views lesson, 129
        opening, 129
        page guides, dragging, 130
        panning, 132, 133
        paths, changing anchor points, 134, 135
        screen mode, changing, 130
        zooming, 131, 132
        toggling tools, 133
    Page tool, 127
        page guides, moving using, 128
    Screen Modes, 125
        changing, 125-127
    Zoom tool, 121
        changing zoom factor, 120
        magnification, changing with pop-up menu, 124
        zooming in, 122, 123
        zooming out, 123, 124
views, creating and maintaining, 381
    editing, 382
    naming views, 381, 382

W

web, 409
    color usage and, 411, 412

file formats, 412, 413
    GIF files, 413-415
    JPEG files, 415, 416
    PNG files, 416
screen as output device, 410
screen resolution, 410, 411
URLs and browsers, 417, 418
    imagemaps, creating, 417, 418
    imagemap lesson, 419-423
What You See Is What You Get, (WYSIWYG), 200
    screen as output device, 410
Window menu commands, 375, 383
    opening multiple windows for single document, 383
word processing commands, 319-325
word spacing, setting, 307
worksheet cell, editing graphs, 153
WYSIWYG (What You See Is What You Get), 200
    screen as output device, 410

X

X and Y graph values, switching for scatter graphs, 15

Z

zigzags, creating, 354
Zoom tool, 121
    changing zoom factor, 120
    magnification, changing with pop-up menu, 124
    zooming in, 122, 123
    zooming out, 123, 124
zooming, 376, 377

ABOUT THE CD-ROM

The *Hands-On Illustrator 7* CD-ROM contains sample images and demo software.

FULL-COLOR IMAGES FROM THE BOOK

All the images used in the Lesson section of the book are located in the Hands-On Lessons folder on the CD. The images are saved in TIFF, PSD, EPS, and AI (Illustrator) formats and can be accessed by Macintosh and Windows 95 users. Copy these files onto your hard drive and use them to practice what you learn.

DEMONSTRATION SOFTWARE

The CD contains a slew of demo software from Extensis, Hot Door, Inc., Alien Skin, and others. For installation instructions, see the *ReadMe* files that accompany each program.